American Bibliography

A Preliminary Checklist

for

1819

Items 46913-50192

Compiled by

Ralph R. Shaw

and

Richard H. Shoemaker

The Scarecrow Press, Inc.

New York   1963

A

A., Z.
Presbyterian ordination doubtful...1819. MWA.
46913

Abbott, Abiel
Sermons to Mariners. Boston, Samuel T. Armstrong, 1819. 275 p. MBeHi. 46914

Account of the massacre of the family of Gerald Watson by J. Jackson, the father-in-law of Watson. Boston, 1819. 24 p. MH. 46915

An account of the murder of Richard Jennings... Newburgh, N.Y., Pr. by Benjamin F. Lewis & Co., 1819. MWA. 46916

An account of the trial and execution of Rose Butler who was executed in New York, July 9, 1819 for attempting to burn a dwelling house. New York, 1819. 8 p. DLC. 46917

Accounts of happy deaths of two young Christians. Boston, Nathaniel Willis, 1819. 22 p. MWA. 46918

Adam, Alexander, 1741-1809
Roman antiquities: or, An account of the manners and customs of the Romans...Rev., cor., and illustrated with notes and additions, by P. Wilson... New-York, Pr. by William A. Mercein, for Kirk & Mercein, W.B. Gilley...1819. 565 p. CtW; DLC; MWA; NRSB; NcD; OCl; TxAbM. 46919

Adams, Daniel
Geography; or a description of the world. In three

parts... Ed. 4.   Boston, Lincoln & Edmands, 1819.
335 p.   Ct; CtY; CtHT-W; MWA; NNA; NNC; PLFM.
46920

-- The scholar's arithmetic; or Federal accountant...
Stereotype ed., rev. and cor. with additions.   Keene,
N. H., Pr. by John Prentiss, 1819. 224 p.   DLC; MH;
MStou; MWA; MWbor; TxU-T; WBeloHi.   46921

-- The understanding reader... Ed. 9, improved... Boston and Portland, Isaiah Thomas, Jr., 1819. 228 p.
CtSoP; ICP; MB; MSaE; MTemNHi; MWA; MWHi; NN; Nh.
46922

Adams, John, pres. U. S., 1735-1826
   Novanglus, and Massachusettensis; or, Political
essays, published in the years 1774 and 1775, on the
principal points of controversy, between Great Britain
and her colonies... Boston, Hews & Goss, 1819. 312 p.
C; CLU; CSfCW; CSmH; CSt; CU; Ct; CtHT-W; CtSoP;
CtY; DLC; ICU; IaU; LNT; M; MA; MB; MBAt; MBBC;
MBC; MC; MDeeP; MHi; MNF; MSaE; MW; MWA;
MWiW; MdBP; MdHi; MeB; MeBat; MiD-B; MiU-C;
MnHi; MnM; MnU; MoSHi; NBuG; NN; NNHuC; NNUT;
NRHi; NcWfC; NjP; NjR; OClWHi; OFH; PHi; PPA;
PPL; RNHi; RNR; RP; RPB; ViU; WBeloC; WHi; WaU.
46923

[Adams, John, 1760?-1829]
   The life of Alexander Smith, captain of the island
of Pitcairn; one of the mutineers on board His Majes-
ty's ship Bounty; commanded by Lieut. Wm. Bligh.
Written by Smith himself, on the above island, and
bringing the accounts from Pitcairn, down to the year
1815.   Boston, Pr. by S. T. Goss, 1819. 240 p. DLC;
NN.   46924

Addison, Joseph
   Cato; a tragedy, in five acts... Ed. 3.   New York,
David Longworth, 1819. 59 p. MMal; MWA; MCanHi.
46925

An address delivered to the children of a Sunday
School in Boston, on the last Sabbath in December,
1818.   [Boston] Boston Sabbath society for the moral
and religious instruction of the poor, Pr. by U.
Crocker, 1819. 12 p. DLC.   46926

Address 5

Address of a committee from the counties of Cumberland, Lincoln and Kennebec, to the people of Maine on
separation. [1819] Broadside. Noyes 838   46927

An address to the Christian public, in two parts. 1st.
A correct view of the transactions of an ecclesiastical
council, convened at Deerfield, Aug. 11, 1807, for the
purpose of ordaining Samuel Willard, over the church
and people in said town. Also, 2d. A correct view of
sundry facts and circumstances relative to the doings of
another ecclesiastical council which met in Greenfield,
Nov. 2, 1813, for the purpose of ordaining Gamaliel S.
Olds. Greenfield [Mass.] Pr. by Ansel Phelps, 1819.
20 p. MH.   46928

An address to the citizens of the United States, on the
subject of ardent spirits. No. 8. New York, Pr. by
Clayton and Kingsland, 1819. 12 p. MNBedf.   46929

An address to the Freeholders of Mecklenburg County.
Richmond, Va., Pr. by Shepherd & Pollard, 1819. 30 p.
ViRut.   46930

Address to the Republican electors of the Southern District, by the General Committee friendly to the general
government and state administration. Unanimously
adopted at a meeting held at Connolly's Long Room in
the City of New York, March 25, 1819. New York,
Pr. by E. Conrad, 1819. 16 p. NBu.   46931

An address to the spectator of the awful execution, in
Boston, February 18, 1819. Boston, Pr. by U.
Crocker, 1819. 11 p. DLC; ICN; MH-AH; MWA. 46932

An address to the spectator of the awful execution of
the pirates in Boston, February 18, 1819. [1819]
MWA.   46933

Addresse an die Einwohner von Dauphin County. Harrisburg, Pa., 1819. 11 p. Seidensticker p. 207. 46934

Addresses to the people of Maine. Addresses by John
Holmes, Nathan Goold, John Davis, W.P. Preble.

[1819] 8 p. Noyes 839.   46935

An affectionate address of a son to his father, on the
doctrine of Universalism... New York, pub. by the author [1819] 20 p. MWA.   46936

An affectionate address to young Christians. New
York [N. Y. Religious Tract Society] 1819. 8 p. CtY.
                                                 46937
Affection's gift to a beloved Godchild. From the London ed., by H. M. Boston, Pr. by Wells & Lilly,
1819. 148 p. MMeT.   46938

[Agg, John]
    The ocean harp: a poem; in two cantos: with some
smaller pieces; and a monody on the death of John
Syng Dorsey, M. D. ... Philadelphia, Pr. by J. Maxwell, for M. Thomas, 1819. 182 p. CSmH; DLC;
MSaE; MWA; NNNAM.   46939

[Agnew, Eleanor C.]
    Geraldine; a tale of conscience, by E. C. A. Phila-
delphia, Eugene Cummiskey, 1819. 3 v. MdBS. 46940

Agricultural almanac, for 1820. Philadelphia, Solomon W. Conrad, [1819] MWA; NjR.   46941

The agricultural and economical almanack, for 1820.
New Haven, Sidney's press, for John Babcock & son,
[1819]   CSmH; Ct; CtHi; MNF; MWA.   46942

Agricultural Society of Jefferson Co., N. Y.
    Proceedings of the second cattle show and fair...
September, 1819. Watertown, N. Y., Pr. by Seth Al-
den Abbey, for the Society, [1819] 33 p. CSmH; MWA;
N; NHi; NN.   46943

Agricultural Society of North-Carolina
    Constitution of the Agricultural society of North-
Carolina, established at Raleigh, in Dec. 1818...
Raleigh, N. C., Pr. by J. Gales, 1819. 13 p. NN;
NcU.   46944

[Aikin, John]
The farm-yard journal. For the amusement and instruction of children. Cooperstown [N. Y.] H. & E. Phinney, 1819. 30 p. CSmH.   46945

[--] -- ... Also The history of the marten... New-Haven, Sidney's press, for J. Babcock & son, 1819. 30 p. CtHi; MH.   46946

Akenside, Mark
The pleasures of imagination... New York, Pr. by J. Gray & Co., for R. & W. A. Bartow, and W. A. Bartow, Richmond [Va.] 1819. 144 p. CSt; Ct; MWA; MdBD; NLC; PHC; RPB; ViU.   46947

Alabama (State)
An act passed at the first session of the General Assembly of the state of Alabama, to incorporate the city of Mobile. [Huntsville, Ala. ? 1819?] 8 p. MBAt.
46948
-- Acts of the legislature... 1819. Ct.   46949

-- The constitution of the state of Alabama. Adopted Aug. 2, 1819. Huntsville, Pr. by John Boardman [1819] 26 p. DLC; MiU-L; NN; OCLaw; PPPrHi.
46950
Alabama (Territory)
Journal of the Convention of the Alabama Territory, begun July 5, 1819. Huntsville, Pr. by John Boardman, 1819. 40 p. Ar-U; MH-L; Mi-L; OCLaw; PPPrHi; PU-L.   46951

Alabama Courier. Claiborne, Ala., Tucker & Turner, Mar. 19, 1819, 1st issue. MWA (Weekly newspaper)
46952
Albany, N. Y.
Fourth of July, 1819. Arrangements adopted by the Committees of the Corporation (of Albany) and Military Association. [Albany, 1819] 1 p. NN. 46953

-- Report of the Finance committee... The Committee to whom was referred the annual account of the Chamberlain, report... [Albany, Pr. by Websters and Skinners, Dec. 1819]   4 p. N.   46954

Albany Academy
      The statutes of the...academy passed December
5th, 1816, and revised, September 14th, 1819. Albany,
Pr. by Websters and Skinners, 1819. 21 p. M; NAL;
NN.   46955

Albany Bible Society
      Anniversary report...February, 1819. Albany,
Pr. by G.J. Loomis & Co., 1819. 39 p. NN.   46956

Albany county, N. Y.
      At a meeting of the inhabitants of the city and
county of Albany, held at the Capitol in the city of Albany, on Tuesday the 21st of December, 1819, in pursuance of public notice, to express their opinions upon
the subject of extending slavery into the territories of
the United States westward of the river Mississippi --
the Hon. John Tayler was called to the chair, and Teu-
nis Van Vechten, Esq. appointed secretary. 1. Resolved...[Albany, N. Y., 1819] Broadside. NHi. 46957

Albany county agricultural society.
      Constitution and by-laws...Albany, N. Y., 1819.
24 p.   MB.   46958

Alden, Abner
      Introduction to reading and speaking. Ed. 5. Bos-
ton, Thomas & Andrews, 1819. 2 v. CtHT-W; MH;
MTaHi; MWA.   46959

-- -- Ed. 8. Boston, Thomas & Andrews, 1819. 2 v.MWA.
                                                        46960

Alden, Cyrus
      An abridgment of law, with practical forms, in two
parts.   Part I.   An abridgment of Blackstone's Com-
mentaries--Massachusetts statute laws, and Massachusetts term reports.   Part II.   The justices' guide--The
conveyancer's guide--The sheriff's guide--The execu-
tor's, and guardian's guide--The town officer's guide--
The petitioner and complainant's guide--and the juror's
guide...Boston, Pr. by Hews & Goss, 1819. 763 p.

MB; MBAt; MBS; MH-L; MMeT; MNBedf; MWCL; NcD;
NjR; OC; WaU.   46961

Alden, Ebenezer
   An address, delivered in Hanover, N. H. before the
Dartmouth Medical Society, on their first anniversary,
Dec. 28th, 1819.   Boston, Pr. by James Loring [1819]
16 p.   DLC; MBAt; MBM; MWA; NNNAM; OC.   46962

Alexander, Caleb, 1755-1828
   A grammatical system of the English language...
Rutland, Vt., Fay & Burt, 1819. 96 p.   CSmH; DLC;
MH; MWA; OClWHi; Vt; VtHi.   46963

Allen, Joseph
   A discourse, delivered at Northborough, December
8th, 1818.   At the interment of Winslow Brigham, Jun.
Worcester, Mass., Pr. by Manning & Trumbull, 1819.
14 p.   ICMe; MWA; MWHi; MiD-B; NN.   46964

Allen, Paul, 1775-1826
   A history of the American revolution... Baltimore,
Pr. by Thomas Murphy, for John Hopkins, 1819. 2 v.
CtB; DLC; DeGE; MWA; MdBL; MdFr; NjR; RPB.
                                                46965
[Allen, Silas] 1762-1840
   A letter to Prof. Stuart, in answer to his letter to
Rev. William E. Channing... Boston, S. T. Goss, 1819.
22 p.   CBPac; CtY; M; MH; MSaE; MWiW; NNUT; RPB;
VtU.   46966

Allen, Wilkes
   An address, delivered before the Western society
of Middlesex husbandmen... Concord, Mass., Pr. by
Caleb Cushing, 1819. 19 p. MBAt; MBHo; MWA; NN.
                                                46967
[Allen, William]
   Thoughts on the importance of religion... Philadel-
phia, Pr. [by J. R. A. Skerrett] for Benjamin & Thomas
Kite... 1819.   MWA.   46968

Allen's New-England almanack, for the year of our
Lord 1820... Hartford, Peter B. Gleason, 1819. 124 p.

Ct; CtHi; MWA; MiD-B; NCH.   46969

American. New York, Charles King, Mar. 3, 1819.
1st issue. Semi-weekly and daily newspaper. DLC;
NHi.   46970

American Academy of the Fine Arts
    Fifth exhibition, May, 1819. New York [1819?]
NHi.   46971

American antiquarian society, Worcester, Mass.
    Address to the members of the American anti-
quarian society; together with the laws and regulations
of the institution, and a list of donations to the Society
since the last publication. Worcester, Mass., Pr. by
William Manning, 1819. 38 p. DLC; MBNEH; MWA;
MdBJ; MeHi; MiD-B; NN; NjP; OClWHi; RNHS; RPB;
WHi.   46972

American Bible Society
    Circular...recommending to its auxiliary societies
the more general adoption of the practice of selling the
Holy Scriptures at cost or at reduced prices...[New
York? 1819?] Broadside. NN.   46973

-- Memorial of the board of managers of the American
Bible Society...New York, Pr. by Daniel Fanshaw,
1819. 16 p. MWA; NNMr; NjR; WHi.   46974

-- Third report of the American Bible Society, presented May 13, 1819...New York, Pr. by D. Fanshaw,
for the Society at their depository, 1819. 176 p. DLC;
GDC; MdHi; MeB; MeBat; NHi.   46975

American Board Commissioners for Foreign Missions
    Instructions to Levi Parsons and Pliny Fisk, mis-
sionaries designated for Palestine. Delivered in Boston, Oct. 31, 1819. 12 p. MH-AH; OClWHi.   46976

-- Instructions from the prudential committee...to the
Rev. Hiram Bingham and the Rev. Asa Thurston (and
others)...members of the mission to the Sandwich Islands. Boston, Pr. by U. Crocker, for Samuel T.

Armstrong, 1819. xvi p. NjPT.   46977

-- Instructions from the Prudential Committee to the
Rev. Levi Parsons and the Rev. Pliny Fisk, mission-
aries designated for Palestine. Boston, 1819. 12 p.
MB.   46978

-- Mission to the Sandwich Islands...[Boston, Pr. by
U. Crocker, 1819] MWA.   46979

-- Report of the American board of commissioners for
foreign missions; compiled from documents laid before
the Board at the tenth annual meeting which was held at
Boston [Mass.] Sept. 15, 16, & 17, 1819...Boston, Pr.
by Uriel Crocker, for Samuel T. Armstrong, 1819.
88 p.   CSt; MWiW; MeB; MiKC; N; OC.   46980

American colonization society.
    The second annual report of the American society
for colonizing the free people of colour in the United
States...Ed. 2.   Washington, D.C., Pr. by Davis and
Force, 1819. 153 p. CtHT; MA; MDHi; MWA; MeB;
NHi.   46981

-- Address of the Board of managers of the American
colonization society to the public. [Washington, D.C.,
1819] 10 p. DLC.   46982

American convention for promoting the abolition of
slavery, and improving the condition of the African
race.
    An address to the free people of color and de-
scendants of the African race, in the United States...
Philadelphia, Pr. by Hall & Atkinson, for the Convention, 1819. 6 p. DLC.   46983

-- Constitution...Philadelphia, Pr. by Hall & Atkinson,
1819.   MWA.   46984

-- Minutes...fifth of October, and the tenth of November, 1819. Philadelphia, Pr. by William Fry, 1819.
65 p. MWA; NNG; NjP.   46985

American Education Society.   Northwestern Branch.
Constitution of the Northwestern Branch of the
American Society for Educating Pious Youth for the
Gospel Ministry.   Middlebury, Vt., Pr. by Francis
Burnap, 1819. 9 p. VtMiS; WHi.   46986

American Farmer.   Baltimore, John S. Skinner, Apr.
2, 1819, 1st issue. Weekly. CSmH; MWA; MdBD;
MdHi.   46987

American gardener's calendar, adapted to the climates
and seasons of the United States.   Philadelphia, 1819.
618 p. (Montgomery Cooper cat. 179, Dec. 1937, no.
57)   46988

American ladies pocket book, 1820.   Philadelphia, A.
Small [1819] MWA; RPB.   46989

The American lady's preceptor... Ed. 7, compiled by
the editor of Tooke's Pantheon revised.   Baltimore,
Edward J. Coale, 1819.   MWA.   46990

American Philosophical Society
Transactions of the historical and literary commit-
tee of the American Philosophical Society, held at
Philadelphia, for promoting useful knowledge. Vol. I.
Philadelphia, Abraham Small, 1819. 464 p. CSmH;
CtHT-W; CLSM; MBGCT; MeBat; FSa; NcWfC.   46991

American School for the deaf.
Third report of the directors of the Connecticut
Asylum for the education and instruction of deaf and
dumb persons, exhibited to the asylum, May 15, 1819.
Hartford, Pr. by Hudson and Co., 1819. 15 p. CSmH;
CtHC; CtHT; CtY; DLC; KHi; M; MB; MdFred; MoS;
MWiW; NAuT; NN; WHi.   46992

American society for educating pious youth for the gos-
pel ministry.
Fourth report... Andover, Mass., Pr. by Flagg &
Gould, 1819. 55 p. DLC; GDC; ICU; MWA; MWiW;
MeBat; NjPT; NjR; OClW.   46993

American Unitarian Association
    Tracts.   Deutsche serie. No. 2. Boston, 1819.
WHi.   46994

Amerikanischer Stadt- und Land-Calender. Auf das
Jahr 1820. Zum 4ten mal herausgegeben. Baltimore,
Pr. by Schäffer u. Maund, 1819. DLC; MWA. 46995

Americanischer Stadt und Land Calender for 1820.
Philadelphia, Conrad Zentler [1819] MWA.   46996

Analysis of the authorities of dangers. New York, Pr.
by William Hooker, 1819. 76 p. MMeT; MdAN. 46997

Anderson, Isaac Parsons, 1798-1818
    Memoirs of Isaac P. Anderson, A.B. who died at
Beverly, Mass., Dec. 16, 1818, in the twenty-first
year of his age. Boston, Pr. by U. Crocker, for
Samuel T. Armstrong, 1819. 143 p. CtY; IEG; MWA;
MBeHi; MeB.   46998

Andover Theological Seminary
    Catalogue of the library belonging to the theologi-
cal institution in Andover. Andover, Mass., Pr. by
Flagg and Gould, 1819. 161 p. DLC; MA; PPAmP;
PPPrHi; RPat.   46999

-- Catalogue of the professors and students of the
Theological Seminary, Andover, Mass. January, 1819.
[Andover, Mass.] Pr. by Flagg & Gould, 1819. Broad-
side. MHi.   47000

Andrewes, Lancelot, bp.
    The devotions of Bishop Andrews... Charleston,
S.C., Pr. by A.E. Miller, for E. Thayer, 1819. 132 p.
MWA; MdBD; ScU.   47001

Andrews, Ethan Allen
    Remarks on the present state of agricultural sci-
ence, and the general means of improving the art of
husbandry in the county of Hartford, read before the
Hartford County Agricultural Society at their annual
meeting, February, 1819. Hartford, G. Goodwin &

14   Andrews

Sons, 1819. 24 p. Ct; CtHC; CtHi; CtSoP; CtY; MBAt;
MWA; NHi; WUA.   47002

Andrews, John
    Elements of logick...Ed. 4. Philadelphia, Abra-
ham Small, 1819. 152 p. GDC; MWA; NcGw; OMC.
                                                 47003
Annapolis, Md. (City)
    By-laws of the corporation of the city of Annapolis.
Annapolis, Pr. by J. Green, 1819. 59 p. (J.W. Garrett Library)   47004

Anne Walsh; a narrative; founded on fact. To which is
added, an address to the Friends of religion, and to all
who are interested in the benevolent purpose of holding
societies for religious worship. Philadelphia, Religious
tract society of Philadelphia, William Bradford, agent,
1819. 12 p. CSt; MWA.   47005

The annual messenger or farmer's almanack, calculated for the New England states on a new and improved plan, for the year of our Lord 1820...Boston,
Sylvester T. Goss [1819] DLC; MMal; MWA.   47006

Annual visiter[!] and citizens and farmer's almanac for
1820. Calculated by Joshua Sharp. Wilmington, Del.,
J. Wilson [1819] 36 p. DLC; MWA; PHi.   47007

An appeal to the government and Congress of the U-
nited States, against the depredations committed by A-
merican privateers, on the commerce of nations at
peace with us. By an American citizen...New York,
Pr. for the booksellers, 1819. 100 p. DLC; MdHi;
ScU.   47008

Appleton, George W.
    Minister's hope, etc. Sermon, ordination of Geo.
W. Appleton. Boston, 1819. 24 p.   47009

Appleton, Jesse
    A sermon, delivered at Portland, Nov. 19, 1818,
at the formation of the Maine Branch of the American
Society for Educating Pious Youth for the Gospel Soci-

ety.   Hallowell, Me., Pr. by E. Goodale, 1819. 28 p.
CSt; MWA; MeB; MeLewB; Nh-Hi; NjPT.   47010

Ardenond, Mr.
     A new and interesting mechanical exhibition, Con-
cert Hall, Boston, June 3, 4, 1819. Broadside. MHi.
                                                  47011
Arkansas Gazette.   Arkansas Post, Woodruff & Briggs,
Nov. 20, 1819, 1st issue.   Weekly newspaper. DLC.
                                                  47012
[Armstrong, John] 1758-1843
     A treatise on agriculture; comprising a concise
history of its origin and progress.   The present condition of the art, abroad and at home, and the theory
and practice of husbandry, which have arisen out of the
present state of philosophical attainments in Europe.
By a practical farmer.   Albany, Pr. by J. Buel, 1819.
168 p.   MB; MH.   47013

Arrowsmith, Aaron
     New and elegant atlas... by Arrowsmith and Lewis
... Boston, Thomas & Andrews, 1819. 63 p. NjP.
                                                  47014
Associate Reformed Church of North America
     Extracts from the minutes of the proceedings of
the Sixteenth General Synod, of the Associate Reformed
Church in North America.   Held at Philadelphia, on
Wednesday, the 19th Mar. 1819.   Philadelphia, Pr. by
Jacob Frick & Co., 1819. 55 p.   MWA; NcMHi; PLT.
                                                  47015
Associate Reformed Presbyterian church of Baltimore.
     The Baltimore collection of sacred musick selected
and compiled under the direction of a committee of the
Associate Reformed Presbyterian church of Baltimore.
Baltimore, Pr. by Thomas Murphy, for Cushing and
Jewett, 1819. 95 p. ICN; NjPT.   47016

Association for the Relief of Respectable Aged Indigent
Females.
     The sixth annual report... New-York, Pr. by J. C.
Totten, 1819.   10 p. NN; NNG.   47017

An astronomical diary or almanack for the year of our

Lord and Saviour 1820 by Thomas Spoffard.   Exeter,
N. H. ,   Pr. by J. Williams, for Nath'l Boardman,
[1819] [36] p. MPeHi; MWA.   47018

An astronomical diary or almanack for 1820...by Joel
Sanford. New Haven, Flagg & Gray [1819] [24] p.
CtHi; NjR.   47019

-- by Joel Sanford.   Norwalk, Conn. , Nichols & Price,
[1819] [24] p. MWA.   47020

Asylum company.
     Catalogue of the lands and stock of the Asylum
company... Philadelphia, Pr. by William Fry, 1819.
MWA.   47021

Atall, Peter
     The hermit in America on a visit to Philadelphia:
containing some account of the human leeches, belles,
beaux, coquettes, dandies, cotillion parties... of that
famous city and the poets and painters of America;
ed. 2, with cor. and additions. Philadelphia, M.
Thomas, 1819. 246 p. NjR.   47022

Atherton, Theophilus
     Account of the fearful state of Francis Spira.
Poughkeepsie, N. Y. , 1819. MWA.   47023

Atmore, Charles
     Serious advice from a father to his children...
Philadelphia, J. H. Cunningham... 1819. MWA. 47024

The attributes of God... New Haven, Sidney's press,
for J. Babcock & son, 1819. 30 p. CtHi; MWA. 47025

Eine Auselene Sammlung geistlicher Lieder. Lancaster, Pa. , J. Ehrenfried [1819?]   BrMus. Cat. Sup.
6. Henry: 647.   47026

[Austin, Benjamin]
     In consequence of some remarks on the layman,
he offers the following arguments in addition to the
former observations on the doctrine of the Trinity.

[Boston, 1819?] 8 p. MH-AH. 47027

[--] A letter to Rev. Mr. Channing in favor of the doctrine of the Trinity and in opposition to the sentiments contained in his Baltimore sermon. [Boston, 1819?] 8 p. MH-AH. 47028

[--] Observations on the pernicious practice of the law. As published occasionally in the Independent chronicle, in the year 1786, and republished at the request of a number of respectable citizens. With an address never before published. Corrected and amended. By Honestus [pseud.] ...Boston, Pr. by True & Weston, 1819. 60 p. DLC; MBAt; MH; MMeT; MWA; NIC-L; RPL. 47029

Auxiliary Baptist Mission Society of Kentucky
Proceedings of the board of managers for the Auxiliary Baptist Mission Society of Kentucky, from June 27, 1816 to May 31, 1819. And of the society inclusive Georgtown [sic] Ky., Pr. by J.S. Lyle [1819] 19 p. ICU; NRAB. 47030

Auxiliary Bible society in the county of Bristol, Mass.
Report of the committee...September 15, 1819. Taunton, Mass., Pr. by A. Danforth, 1819. MWA. 47031

Auxiliary Bible Society of Boston
The fifth report of the Auxiliary Bible Society of Boston...Boston, J. Noble, 1819. 26 p. BrMus. Cat. 7. Boston: 63. 47032

Auxiliary education society of the young men of Boston.
Constitution...Boston, Pr. by Parmenter and Norton, 1819. 7 p. MB; MWA. 47033

Auxiliary Bible Society of Montgomery Co., N.Y.
Second report of the Auxiliary Bible Society of Montgomery County...Johnstown [N.Y.] printed for the Society by Asa Child, Feb., 1819. CSmH. 47034

Auxiliary New-York Bible and Common Prayer-Book Society.
The third annual report of the managers of the Aux-

iliary New-York Bible and Common Prayer Book Society.   New York, Pr. by William A. Mercein, 1819.
19 p.   DLC; InID; MBD; MWA.   47035

B

Babbit, James
    The substance of a sermon, delivered at Dana,
[Mass.] August, 1815, in commemoration of the un-
timely death of William and Alonzo Babbit, two eldest
sons of the Rev. James Babbit: who were instantaneous-
ly killed by an explosion, which took place in the U-
nited States laboratory, at Albany, N.Y. Dec. 13, 1815
...Hudson, N.Y., Pr. by Ashbel Stoddard, 1819. 32 p.
CSmH; CSt; MPiB; MWA; NBuG; RPB.   47036

Babington, Thomas
    A practical view of Christian education in its earli-
est stages...3d Amer. from the 3d London ed. Boston,
Cummings and Hilliard, 1819. 188 p.   CtW; DLC; ICT;
IEG; ICP; MB; MBC; MBrZ; MFiHi; MH; MS; MWA;
MdBLC; MdW; MiD; MiU; MnM; NGH; NN; NjP; NjPT;
NjR; OO; PLT; PPM; ScCC; ScNC; TNDL.   47037

Bache, Franklin
    A system of chemistry for the use of students of
medicine...Philadelphia, Pr. by William Fry, for the
author, 1819.   624 p.   NWM; NcD.   47038

[Bacon, Nathaniel]
    An account of the fearful state of Francis Spira...
Poughkeepsie, N.Y., Pr. by P. Potter, 1819.   MWA.
                                                47039
Bailey's Rittenhouse almanac for 1820.   Calculated by
Joshua Sharp.   Philadelphia, Thomas Desilver [1819]
MWA.   47040

[Bainbridge, Joseph] d. 1824
    To the officers of the navy and marine corps.
[New York? 1819?]   14 p. DLC.   47041

[--] To the public.   [New York? 1819?]   16 p. CSmH.
                                                47042

Baines, Edward
     History of the wars of the French revolution...
Philadelphia, M. Carey & son, 1819. DeWI; MB;
MWA.   47043

Baker, Mrs. Caroline (Horwood)
     The brother and sister;...written by Miss Hor-
wood. Philadelphia, William Charles, 1819. 15 p.
NNC.   47044

-- Little Emma and her father; or, The effects of
pride...Written by Miss Horwood. Philadelphia, Wm.
Charles, 1819. 15 p. NNC.   47045

Baker, John Martin
     A view of the commerce of the Mediterranean;
with reflections arising from personal experience...
Washington, D.C., Pr. by Davis and Force, 1819.
117 p. DLC; MB; MH; MWA; OClWHi; WvU.   47046

Baldwin, Briscoe Gerard
     Preamble and resolutions offered by Mr. Baldwin
to the House on the Missouri Question. Richmond,
Va., Pr. by T. Ritchie, 1819. 4 p. Vi.   47047

Baldwin, Lewis
     A candid development of facts, tending to exhibit
the real grounds of differences exhibiting between the
first Baptist Church of Philadelphia and the Philadelphia Association and between the Baptist Board of Foreign Missions and their late vice-presidents: in letters
to Henry Holcombe, D.D., William Rogers, D.D., of
Philadelphia, and the Rev. Daniel Dodge, formerly of
Wilmington, Delaware...Philadelphia, Pr. by Anderson
and Meehan, 1819. 92 p. DLC; PCC; PPL; PPPrHi.
                                              47048

Baldwin, Thomas, 1753-1825
     Christian baptism...Ed. 3. Boston, Lincoln and
Edmands, 1819. 36 p. MWA; NjPT.   47049

-- The danger of living without the fear of God. A
discourse on robbery, piracy, and murder. In which
duelling and suicide are particularly considered: de-

livered in Boston, February 21, 1819.   The Lord's
day following the execution of the pirates.   Boston,
James Loring, [1819] 24 p.   CSt; MB; MH-AH; MSaE;
MSaP; MWA; NjPT.					47050

Baldwin, William, 1779-1819
	An account of two species of Cyperus and of Kyl-
lingia... New York, 1819. PPL-R.			47051

[Balfour, Alexander] 1767-1829
	Campbell, or The Scottish probationer, a novel.
London, pr. 1819; New-York, Repr. by W. A. Mercein
for Kirk and Mercein... 1819. 2 v.   CtY; MH; MWA;
NjP; ViAl.						47052

Ballou, Hosea, 1771-1852
	The child's scriptural catechism... Ed. 2. Boston,
Henry Bowen, 1819. 36 p. DLC; MWA.		47053

-- No. 13.   Lecture sermon, delivered at the second
Universalist meeting in Boston, January 17, 1819.
[Boston] pub. semi-monthly by Henry Bowen [1819]
DLC.							47054

-- No. 14. Lecture sermon, delivered at the second
Universalist meeting, in Boston, January 17, 1819.
[Boston] Pub. semi-monthly by Henry Bowen [1819]
CtHT-W; DLC.						47055

-- Lecture sermon, delivered at the Second Universalist Meeting in Boston, February 14, 1819.   Boston,
Henry Bowen [1819] 226-240 p. MMeT-Hi.		47056

-- No. 16. Lecture sermon delivered in Boston, February 28, 1819.   Boston, 1819.   (Caption-title (Sermons, vol. 45, no. 3) Published semi-monthly by Hen-
ry Bowen.) MSaE.					47057

-- No. 21. Lecture sermon, delivered in Boston, May
9, 1819. [Boston, 1819] (321-336 of his lecture ser-
mons.) MH.						47058

-- A lecture sermon, delivered in the Second Univer-

salist meeting house, in Boston, on the evening of the
first Sabbath in December, 1819.   Boston, H. Bowen,
1819.   16 p.   CtHT-W; DLC; MB; MMeT; MWA; NN.
47059
-- A lecture sermon, delivered in the Second Universalist meeting house, in Boston, on the evening of the
third Sabbath in December, 1819...Boston, Henry
Bowen, 1819.   16 p.   MB; MMeT; MPiB; MWA.   47060

-- A sermon, delivered at the Second Universalist
meeting house, in Boston...Boston, H. Bowen, 1819.
16 p.   CtHT-W; DLC; MMeT; MPiB; MWA; VtU.   47061

-- A sermon, delivered in the Second Universalist
meeting house, in Boston, on the morning of the third
Sabbath in November, 1819...Boston, Henry Bowen,
1819.   12 p.   MB; MMeT-Hi; MWA; Nh-Hi.   47062

Ballou, Silas
    Poem on occasion of death of William and Alonzo
Babbit, delivered August 1815.   Hudson, N.Y., 1819.
32 p.   PHi.   47063

Baltimore (City)
    Ordinances of the corporation of the City of Balti-
more; passed at the extra session in September 1818,
and at the January session, 1819, to which is annexed
a list of the officers of the corporation.   Baltimore,
Pr. by William Warner, 1819.   48 p.   MdBB; MdHi;
MHi.   47064

Baltimore almanac; or, Timepiece for 1820...by John
Sharp.   Baltimore, Pr. by William Warner [1819]
[32] p.   DLC; MWA; MdHi.   47065

The Baltimore collection of sacred musick...Baltimore,
Pr. by Thomas Murphy, for Cushing and Jewett...1819.
95 p.   ICN; MWA; NjPT.   47066

The Baltimore directory.   Corrected up to June, 1819.
Compiled by Samuel Jackson.   Baltimore, Pr. by Richard J. Matchett, 1819.   MdHi.   47067

Bancroft, Aaron
    A discourse on conversion. Worcester, Mass.,
Pr. by William Manning, 1819. 40 p. DLC; MAnP.
                                                    47068
-- The doctrine of immortality. A Christmas sermon
delivered in Worcester, 1818...Worcester, Mass., Pr.
by William Manning, 1819. 23 p. CSt; ICMe; M;
MBAt; MDeeP; MHi; MWA; NNUT; NjPT.   47069

-- A sermon, delivered at the installation of the Rev.
Luther Willson to the pastoral care of the Church in
Petersham, June 23, 1819...Worcester, Mass., Pr.
by William Manning, 1819. 28 p. MB; MH; MTemNHi;
MWA; NN; NjPT.   47070

Bank for savings, New York.
    Charter and by-laws...New York, Pr. by J. Sey-
mour, 1819. 12 p. MWA; NHi.   47071

Bank of the state of South Carolina
    Report...Oct. 1, 1819. [Charleston, S.C.] Pr. by
A.E. Miller [1819] MWA.   47072

-- Report. To the Honorable the Senate and House of
Representatives of the state of South-Carolina. [1819?]
76 p. Caption title. No title-page or cover title.
CSmH; MH; NNS.   47073

Banks, Henry, fl. 1781-1826
    A series of essays, published in the Commentator
during the session, 1818-1819 relating to the bank of
the United States, the bank of Kentucky - the independent banks &c. under the signature, a Virginian republished in the pamphlet form at the request of many;
these essays were from the pen of Henry Banks, as a
voluntary proof of his regard for the prosperity of Kentucky. Frankfort, Ky., Pr. by Moses O. Bledsoe,
1819. 64 p. OC.   47074

Banks, W.H.
    Observations in the medical arrangements for the
relief of the sick poor...By W.H. Banks. Newport, E.
Taylor [1819] 19 p. IEN-M.   47075

Baptist almanac, for the Middle States for 1820. Calculated by Wm. Collom. Philadelphia, Anderson and
Meehan [1819] MWA.   47076

Baptist Auxiliary Education Society, Boston
    The constitution of the Baptist auxiliary education
society of the young men of Boston. Boston, Pr. by
True & Weston, 1819. 12 p. NjR.   47077

Baptist Board of Foreign Missions
    The fifth annual report of the Baptist Board of
Foreign Missions for the United States. Philadelphia,
Pr. by Anderson and Meehan, for the Board, 1819.
47 p. MH-AH.   47078

Baptists. Alabama. Bigbee Association.
    Minutes of the Bigby[!] Baptist Association, con-
vened at Ulconsh Meeting House, Clarke County, Alabama...Sept. 1819. 8 p. NRAB.   47079

-- -- Cahawba Association.
    Minutes of the Cahawba Baptist Association...Oc-
tober, 1819...[Tuscaloosa, Ala., Thomas M. Davenport, 1819] 8 p. NRAB.   47080

-- Connecticut. Hartford Association.
    Minutes of the Hartford Baptist Association, held
at Amenia [N.Y.] the sixth and seventh of October,
1819. Middletown, Conn., Pr. by Clark & Lyman,
1819. 15 p. Ct; CBB; NRAB.   47081

-- -- New London Association.
    Minutes of the New-London Baptist Association,
held at Montville, County of New-London, State of Connecticut, on the 19th and 20th of October, 1819. 8 p.
CBB; NRAB.   47082

-- Delaware. Delaware Association.
    Minutes...June 5, 6, and 7, 1819. [1819] 8 p.
MWA; NRAB.   47083

-- Illinois. Illinois Association.
    Minutes of the Illinois Baptist Association held at

the Looking-Glass Prairie Meeting-House, St. Clair
County, Illinois, October 8th, 9th and 10th, 1819.
Edwardsville, Ill., Pr. by Hooper Warren, 1819. 8 p.
ISBHi.   47084

-- Indiana. Blue River Association.
    Minutes of the Blue River Association, held at
Union meeting-house, Washington county, state of Indiana.   (Commencing the 2d Saturday in September,
1819) [Salem, Ind., Pr. by E. & M. Patrick, 1819]
4 p. InFrlC; NRAB; TxDaHi.   47085

-- -- Laughery Association.
    Minutes of the Laughery Association of Baptists,
begun and held in the town of Hartford, on Saturday,
the 18th September, 1819.   4 p. InFrlC.   47086

-- -- Silver Creek Association
    Minutes of the Silver-Creek Association, held at
Mount Pleasant meeting house, commencing 4th Satur-
day in August, 1819.   [Madison, Ind., Pr. by Lodge
& Arion, 1819] 4 p. InFrlC.   47087

-- -- Whitewater Association.
    Minutes of the White Water Baptist Association,
held at Lick Creek meeting house, Fayette county, Indiana, on the 13th, 14th, and 15th of August, 1819. [4] p.
NRAB; TxDaHi.   47088

-- Kentucky. Bracken Association.
    Minutes of the Bracken Association of Baptists,
held at the Long-Branch Meeting-House, in Nicholas
County, on the first Saturday in September, 1819; and
continued by adjournment until the Monday following.
Washington, Ky., Pr. by Rannels and Collins [1819]
11 p. KyLoS.   47089

-- -- Cumberland River Association.
    Minutes of the Cumberland River Association of
Baptists.   Held at Flat Lick Meeting House Pulaski
County [Ky.] the first Saturday in September, and con-
tinued by adjournment, till Monday the 6th, 1819.
[Richmond, Ky., Joseph Turner, 1819] 4 p.

KyLoS.   47090

-- -- Elkhorn Association.
    Minutes of the Elkhorn Baptist Association, held
at Big Spring meeting house, Woodford County, Aug.
1819.   8 p.   KyLoS; NRAB.   47091

-- -- Licking Association.
    Minutes of the Licking Association of Baptists,
held at Bryan's the 2d Saturday in September, 1819.
3 p.   KyLoS; OClWHi.   47092

-- -- Long Run Association.
    Minutes of the Long-Run Association of Baptists,
convened at Long-Run meeting-house, Jefferson County,
the first Friday and Saturday in September, 1819.
[Shelbyville, Ky., Pr. by J.D. Grant & Co., 1819]
4 p.   KyLoS; NRAB.   47093

-- -- North District Association.
    Minutes of the North District Association of Bap-
tists, held at Spencer Meetinghouse, in Montgomery
County, and state of Kentucky; the fourth Saturday in
July, in the year of our Lord eighteen hundred and
nineteen, and the two following days...Winchester, Ky.,
Pr. by Dillard & Hukill, at the office of the "Kentucky
Advertiser," 1819.   7 p.   KyLoS.   47094

-- -- Russell's Creek Association.
    Minutes of the Russell's Creek Association of Bap-
tists, held at Union Meeting House, in Adair County,
Kentucky, on Friday and Saturday the 17th and 18th of
September, 1819.   8 p.   (Henry S. Robinson's Pri.
Library, Campbellsville, Ky.)   47095

-- -- Salem Association.
    Minutes, of the Salem Association of Baptists,
held at Nolin Meeting House, in Hardin County, on the
4th Friday and Saturday in September, 1819, being the
24th and 25th of said month.   [Bardstown, Marquis
Barnett, 1819]   4 p.   47096

-- Maine.   Bowdoinham Association.
   Minutes of the Bowdoinham Association, holden at
the Baptist meeting-house in Bloomfield [Me.] September 22 & 23, 1819.   Together with their circular and
corresponding letters.   Hallowell, Me., Pr. by S.K.
Gilman, 1819.   8 p.   MH-AH; MWA; NHi; NRAB.47097

-- -- Cumberland Association.
   Minutes of the Cumberland Baptist Association;
held at the Baptist meeting house in Paris, Sept. 29-
30, 1819.   Portland, Me., Pr. by A. Shirley, 1819.
12 p.   MeHi; NRAB.   47098

-- -- Eastern Association.
   Minutes of the Eastern Maine Association, held at
Steuben, October 6th and 7th, 1819.   Eastport, Me.,
Pr. by Benjamin Folsom, 1819.   8 p.   NRAB.   47099

-- -- Lincoln Association.
   Minutes of the Lincoln Association, held at the
first Baptist Church in Thomaston, September 15 and
16, 1819.   Hallowell, Me., Pr. by S.K. Gilman,
1819.   8 p.   MWA; NRAB.   47100

-- -- York Association.
   Minutes of the York Baptist Association, held at
the Baptist meeting-house, in Cornish [Me.] June 9th
and 10th, 1819.   Kennebunk, Me., Pr. by J.K. Remich, 1819.   8 p.   MWA; MeBa; NRAB.   47101

-- Maryland.   Baltimore Association.
   Minutes of the Baltimore Baptist Association, held
by appointment, at Alexandria, District of Columbia,
May 13th, 14th, and 15th, 1819.   Alexandria, Va., Pr.
by Samuel H. Davis, 1819.   14 p.   MWA; NRAB. 47102

-- Massachusetts.   Boston Association.
   Minutes of the Boston Baptist Association held at
the Baptist Meeting House in Beverly, Sept. 15th and
16th, 1819.   Boston, Pr. by Lincoln & Edmands,
[1819]   16 p.   CBB; DLC; MH-AH; MWA; MiD-B; NRAB.
                                                     47103

-- -- Sturbridge Association.
Minutes of the Sturbridge Baptist Association, held
at Monson, Hampden Co. [Mass.] August 25 and 26,
1819. Worcester, Mass., Pr. by William Manning
[1819] [8] p. MWA; NRAB. 47104

-- -- Warren Association.
Minutes of the Warren Association, held at the
Meeting-House of the Third Baptist Church in Middle-
borough, September 7 & 8, 1819. Boston, Pr. by
James Loring [1819] 14 p. MH-AH. 47105

-- -- Westfield Association.
Minutes of the Westfield Baptist Association, held
in the Baptist meeting-house, in Middlefield, Mass.,
Wednesday, Sept. 1st, 1819. Pr. by E. Terry [1819]
8 p. NRAB. 47106

-- -- Worcester Association.
Minutes of the Worcester Baptist Association, held
at the Baptist Meeting-House, in Shrewsbury [Mass.]
Oct. 27, 1819. Worcester, Mass., Pr. by Manning &
Trumbull, 1819. 11 p. MWA; NRAB. 47107

-- Mississippi. Mississippi Association.
A summary of church discipline... Natchez [Miss.]
Pr. by Marschalk & Evans, 1819. 23+ p. NN. 47108

-- New Hampshire. Dover Association.
Circular letter of the Dover Baptist Association,
to the churches composing their body. On the subject
of close communion. Written by Elder Jacob Grigg.
Exeter, N.H., Josiah Richardson, 1819. 16 p. MWA.
47109
-- -- Meredith Association.
Minutes of the Meredith Baptist Association, holden
at Conway, New Hampshire, Sept. 8th & 9th, 1819.
With their circular and corresponding letters.
Concord, N.H., Pr. by Hill and More, 1819. 8 p.
NRAB. 47110

-- -- Salisbury Association.
Minutes of the Salisbury Association, held with the

Central Baptist Church in Bow, October 13th and 14th,
1819. Concord, N.H., Pr. by Hill and Moore, 1819.
8 p. DLC; NRAB. 47111

-- -- Woodstock Association.
Circular letter from the ministers and messengers
of the...association, to the churches whom they represent. Exeter, N.H., J. Richardson, 1819. 12 p.
MBC. 47112

-- New York. Black River Baptist Association.
Minutes...June 10 and 11, 1819...Sacket's Harbor,
Pr. by George Camp, 1819. 12 p. NRAB; NRCR;
OClWHi. 47113

-- -- Franklin Association.
Minutes of the Franklin Baptist Association, held
at the Baptist Meeting House in New-Lisbon County of
Otsego, on Wednesday & Thursday, June 16th and 17th,
1819. Together with their circular and corresponding
letter. Cooperstown, N.Y., Pr. by H. & E. Phinney,
1819. 12 p. NRAB. 47114

-- -- Holland Purchase Association.
Minutes...June 9th and 10th, 1819...Buffalo, N.Y.,
Pr. by David M. Day, 1819. 7 p. MWA; NHC. 47115

-- -- Hudson River Association.
Minutes of the Hudson River Baptist Association,
held in the Baptist Meeting-House, at Mount-Pleasant,
Westchester County [N.Y.] on the 4th and 5th of August,
1819. Hudson, N.Y., Pr. by Ashbel Stoddard, 1819.
12 p. MWA; NRAB. 47116

-- -- Madison Association.
Minutes of the Madison Baptist Association, held
at Sherburne, the 8th and 9th of September, 1819. Together with their circular and corresponding letters.
[Cazenovia, N.Y.] Pr. by John B. Johnson & Son,
1819. 12 p. NRAB. 47117

-- -- New York Association.
Minutes of the New-York Baptist Association, held

in the Meeting House of the First Baptist Church,
New-York, May 26 and 27, 1819. New-York, Pr. by
Charles N. Baldwin, 1819. 15 p. NRAB.   47118

-- -- Ontario Association.
Minutes of the Ontario Baptist Association, held at
Avon, September 22d and 23d, 1819: together with their
circular and corresponding letter. [1819] 8 p. NRAB.
                                                47119

-- -- Otsego Association.
Minutes of the Otsego Baptist Association, convened in the meeting-house, in Western, county of
Oneida, state of New-York, on the 1st and 2d of September, 1819. Utica, N. Y., Pr. by William Williams,
1819. 8 p. MWA; NRAB; OClWHi.   47120

-- -- St. Lawrence Baptist Association.
Minutes... Potsdam, N. Y., F. C. Powell, 1819.
NRAB.   47121

-- -- Warwick Association.
Minutes of the Warwick Baptist Association, held
in the Baptist Meeting House at Clinton Town, (Dutchess County) June 9th and 10th, 1819. [1819] 8 p.
NRAB.   47122

-- North Carolina. Flat River Association.
Minutes of the Flat River Association, held at
Camp Creek meeting-house, on the Saturday before
third Lord's day in October, 1819. [1819?] 11 p.
NRAB.   47123

-- Ohio. Beaver Association.
Minutes, of the Beaver Baptist association, held by
appointment at Newlisbon, Columbiana County, Ohio,
August 19, 20, 21, and 22, 1819. Newlisbon, Pr. at
the office of the "Ohio Patriot," 1819. 12 p. CSmH;
OClWHi.   47124

-- -- Columbus Association.
Minutes of the Columbus Baptist association begun
and held at Troy Baptist meeting house, Delaware
County (Ohio) Sept. 4th, 5th and 6th, 1819. Delaware,

Ohio, Pr. at the Delaware gazette office, 1819. 8 p.
OClWHi.   47125

-- -- East Fork of the Little Miami Association.
     Minutes of the East Fork of the Little Miami Bap-
tist association, held at Round Bottom, Hamilton County, Ohio, on the 4th, 5th, and 6th of September, 1819.
Cincinnati, O., Pr. by Looker, Reynolds & Co., [1819]
8 p. NRAB.   47126

-- -- Grand River Association.
     Minutes... holden at Madison, Geauga County,
Ohio, Sept. 8 and 9, 1819. Newlisbon, Pr. by Wm.
D. Lepper, 1819. 4 p. NRAB.   47127

-- -- Miami Association.
     The minutes of the Miami Baptist association,
held at the Baptist meeting house, Springfield Town-
ship, Hamilton County, Ohio on the 11th, 12th and
13th September, 1819. Dayton, O., Pr. by R. J. S.
Skinner, 1819. 7 p. OClWHi.   47128

-- -- Salem Association.
     Minutes of a convention of Baptist churches, by
their delegates, held by appointment at the dwelling
house of Elder Peter Aleshire, Salem, Meigs County,
Ohio, on the 22d of October, 1819, and the three following days. [Gallipolis, O., Pr. by J. Cushing,
1819] 8 p. NRAB.   47129

-- -- Scioto Association.
     Minutes of the Scioto Baptist association, held by
appointment, at Union meeting house, Salt-Creek,
Pickaway County, Ohio, September 25, 1819... Chillicothe Pr. at the office of the Scioto gazette, by Bailhache and Scott, 1819. 8 p. OClWHi.   47130

-- Pennsylvania. Abington Association.
     Minutes of the Abington Baptist Association, held
at Mount-Pleasant, Wayne county, the first and second
days of September, 1819. Wilkesbarre, Pa., Pr. by
Samuel Maffet, 1819. 11 p. NRAB; PScrHi.   47131

-- Pennsylvania.   Philadelphia Association.
    Corresponding letter.   The Philadelphia Baptist
Association, to their sister associations with whom
they correspond and to the Friends of Truth throughout our Union.   October, 1819.   Philadelphia, Pr. by
McCarty and Davis, 1819.   8 p.   MWA; NRAB.   47132

-- -- -- Minutes of the Philadelphia Baptist Association.   Convened in the Meeting House of the Third
Baptist Church of Philadelphia, October 5, 6, and 7,
1819.   [Philadelphia? 1819?]   MWA; NRAB.   47133

-- -- Susquehanna Association.
    Minutes of the Susquehanna Baptist Association,
held by appointment, at Huntington, Luzerne County,
Pa., the 8th, 9th, 10th and 11th days of September,
1819.   Wilkesbarre, Pa., Pr. by Samuel Maffet, 1819.
12 p.   NRAB.   47134

-- Rhode Island.   Warren Association
    Minutes of the Warren Association, held at the
Meeting-House of the Third Baptist Church in Middle-
borough, Sept. 7 and 8, 1819.   Boston, Pr. by James
Loring, [1819?]   15 p.   MWA; NRAB.   47135

-- South Carolina.   Charleston Association.
    Minutes of the Charleston Baptist Association, con-
vened at Mechanicville, on Saturday, the 6th November, 1819.   [Pr. by T. B. Stephens, 1819]   16 p.
NRAB.   47136

-- Tennessee.   Concord Association.
    Minutes...July 31, 1819...[Nashville, Tenn., Pr.
by Tunstall & Norvell, 1819]   8 p.   MWA.   47137

-- Vermont.   Barre Association.
    Minutes of the Barre Association, holden at Bethel,
Vt. Sept. 15 and 16, 1819.   With their circular and
corresponding letter.   Montpelier, Vt., Pr. by E. P.
Walton, Oct., 1819.   8 p.   NRAB.   47138

-- -- Leyden Association.
    Minutes of the Leyden Baptist Association, holden

at Wendell, Mass. October 13 and 14, 1819. Together
with their circular and corresponding letters. Greenfield, Mass., Pr. by Denio & Phelps, 1819. 12 p.
MWA; NRAB.   47139

-- -- Shaftsbury Association.
    Minutes of the Shaftsbury Baptist Association, held
at the Baptist meeting house in Pittstown, June 2d -
3d, 1819. Ballston-Spa, N. Y., [Pr. by U. F. Doubleday, 1819] 8 p. NRAB.   47140

-- -- Vermont Association.
    Minutes... Oct. 7 and 8, 1818... Rutland, Vt., Pr.
by Fay & Burt, [1819] MWA.   47141

-- -- -- Minutes of the Vermont Baptist Association,
held in the meeting-house in Hinesburgh, October 6 and
7, 1819. With the circular and corresponding letter.
Rutland, Vt., Pr. by Fay and Burt, 1819. 11 p. MH-
AH; NRAB.   47142

-- -- Woodstock Association.
    Circular letter... Exeter, N. H., Josiah Richardson,
1819. MWA.   47143

-- -- -- Minutes... Sept. 29 and 30, 1819. Windsor,
Vt., Pr. by W. Spooner [1819] 12 p. MH-AH; MWA;
NRAB; VtHi.   47144

-- Virginia
    Proceedings of the sixth annual meeting of the
Richmond Baptists Foreign and Domestic Mission Society held in Richmond, April, 1819... Richmond, Pr.
by W. W. Gray, from the Franklin Press, 1819.
NRAB.   47145

-- -- Accomac Association.
    Minutes of the Accomac Baptist Association, held
at Hungar's meeting-house, Northampton County, August 14th, 15th and 16th, 1819. Norfolk, Pr. by
Shields, Charlton & Co., Beacon office, 1819. NRAB.
                                                   47146

-- -- Appomattox Association.

Minutes of the Appomattox Association, holden at Union Hill meeting-house, Campbell County, May 1st, 2nd and 3rd, 1819. Lynchburg, Va., Pr. by Joseph Boyce, 1819. 12 p. NRAB.   47147

-- -- Dover Association.

Minutes of the Dover Baptists Association, held in the City of Richmond, Henrico County, Virginia, October 9th, 10th, 11th, 1819. Richmond, Pr. by Ritchie, Trueheart & Co., 1819. 15 p. DLC; NRAB; ViRU.
47148

-- -- Goshen Association.

Minutes of the Baptist Association, in the district of Goshen: held at Waller's meeting-house, Spottsylvania County, Virginia: beginning on the first Saturday in October, 1819. Fredericksburg, Pr. by Wm. F. Gray, 1819. 22 p. NRAB; ViRU.   47149

-- -- Ketocton Association.

Minutes of the Ketocton Baptist Association, held by appointment, at Zion meeting-house, Frederick County, Va. Aug. 12th, 13th, 14th and 15th, 1819. Winchester, Va., Pr. by John Heiskell, 1819. 8 p. ViRU.   47150

-- -- Middle District Association.

Minutes of the Baptists Middle District Association holden at Tomahawk meeting house, Chesterfield County, the last Saturday in August, 1819. Richmond, Va., Pr. by Shepherd and Pollard [1819] 8 p. NRAB. 47151

-- -- Portsmouth Association

Minutes of the Virginia Portsmouth Baptist Association, held at Racoon Swamp meeting-house, Sussex County, May 8th, 9th, and 10th, 1819. Norfolk, Pr. by Shields, Charlton & Co., 1819. 11 p. NRAB. 47152

-- -- Shiloh Association.

Minutes of the Shiloh Baptist Association, held at ...F. T. meeting-house, Culpeper county, Virginia, September 3rd & 4th, 1819. Fredericksburg, Va., Pr. by Wm. F. Gray, 1819. 12 p. NRAB; ViRU; ViU. 47153

-- -- Strawberry Association.
Minutes of the Baptist Associations, in the Straw-
berry district, held at Buffaloe Church, Rockbridge
County, Va. beginning Saturday before the first Sab-
bath in October, 1818, and at Leatherwood Church,
Henry County, Va., beginning Saturday before the last
Sabbath in May, 1819. Lynchburg, Va., Pr. by Jo-
seph Boyce, 1819. 16 p. NRAB.   47154

-- -- Union Association.
Minutes of the Union Baptist Association, held at
Pricketts Creek, Monongalia County, Virginia, Aug.
27th, 28th, and 29th, 1819. Clarksburg, Va., Pr. by
Gideon Butler, 1819. 7 p. NRAB.   47155

Barbauld, Anna Letitia (Aikin), 1743-1825
Hymns in prose, for children... New-Haven, Pr.
for J. Babcock and Son, Sidney's press, 1819. 36 p.
CtHi; CtY.   47156

-- Hymns in prose, for children. New York, B. T.
Swan, 1819. MSaE.   47157

-- Hymns in prose for the use of children... Boston,
Timothy Swan, 1819. 32 p. MSaE; NN; RPB.   47158

-- -- New York, Samuel Wood & sons, 1819. 43 p.
MBedf-Hi.   47159

-- Mrs. Barbauld's lessons... New-York, D. Smith,
1819. 108 p. ICP.   47160

-- A summer's walk to view the beauties of nature.
Extracted from Mrs. Barbauld's Hymns in prose.
Boston, Pr. by Nathaniel Willis, 1819. 14 p. MHolliHi;
MWA.   47161

Bard, Samuel, 1742-1821
A compendium of the theory and practice of mid-
wifery... Ed. 5, enl. New York, Collins and Co.,
1819. 419 p. DLC; MBM; MWA; NClsM; NNNAM.
                                            47162
-- A discourse on medical education, delivered at the

medical commencement of the College of physicians
and surgeons of the University of the state of New-
York, on the sixth of April, 1819... New-York, Pr. by
C.S. Van Winkle, 1819. 28 p. DLC; MWA; MeB;
NNNAM.   47163

[Barker, Henry Aston] 1774-1856
    Explanation of the view of the interior of the city
of Paris, now exhibiting in the large circle at the cir-
cus, George-street, Baltimore. Baltimore, J. Robinson, 1819. 12 p. CtY; NKings.   47164

Barker, Jacob, 1779-1871
    Jacob Barker to the public. [New York? 1819]
49 p. MH-BA; MWA.   47165

-- A letter from Jacob Barker to his friend at Bristol,
Pennsylvania, in relation to the late conspiracy to de-
stroy the Exchange bank... New-York, 1819. CtY;
OCHP.   47166

Barnaby, James
    A discourse, addressed to the Baptist church in
Harwich... February, 1819... New Bedford, Mass., Pr.
by Benjamin Lindsey, 1819. 47 p. MWA; NjPT. 47167

[Barrell, George]
    Letters from Asia... New York, Pr. by Elliott &
Bellamy, for A. T. Goodrich & Co., 1819. MWA.
                                                   47168

Barrett, John
    A grammar of the English language... Ed. 2, enl.,
and more correct than the former... Boston, Lincoln &
Edmands, 1819. 214 p. MWA; NNC; NRHi; TxU-T.
                                                   47169

Bartlett, John
    God, not the author of sin... Salem, Mass., Pr. by
John D. Cushing, 1819. 28 p. MMbHi; MNe; MWA;
NjR.   47170

-- -- Ed. 2. Salem, Mass., Pr. by John D. Cushing,
1819. 23 p. MH-AH; MWA; MeHi.   47171

Barton, William Paul Crillon, 1786-1856
    Syllabus of the lectures delivered on vegetable ma-
teria medica, and botany, in the University of Pennsylvania... Pr. by J. R. A. Skerrett, for the use of the
classes, 1819. 12 p. DLC; PPAmP; PPL; PU. 47172

The basket-woman, and the orphans... New Haven, Sid-
ney's press, for J. Babcock & son [and   S. & W. R.
Babcock, Charleston, S. C.] 1819. 35 p. CtHi; MWA;
NN.   47173

Baton-Rouge Gazette. Baton-Rouge, La., Morison &
Devalcourt, Feb., 1819, 1st issue. Weekly newspaper.
MWA.   47174

The battle of Waterloo; or, a faithful and interesting
history of the unparalleled events connected therewith;
from the period of Bonaparte's escape from Elba, to
his arrival at St. Helena... New York, J. Evans, 1819.
562 p. DLC; MWA; NN; PU.   47175

Baxter, Richard
    A call to the unconverted... Middletown, Conn.,
Clark & Lyman, 1819. MWA.   47176

-- The saint's everlasting rest... Northampton, Mass.,
Pr. by J. Metcalf, for Simeon Butler, 1819. 383 p.
LNH; MDeeP; MLow; MWA.   47177

[Beach, Samuel Bellamy] 1780-1866
    Considerations against continuing the great canal
west of the Seneca: addressed to the members-elect of
the Legislature of the state of New York. By Peter
Ploughshare... Utica [N. Y.] William Williams, 1819.
29 p. DLC; M; MWA; NCH; NCanHi; NN; NNS. 47178

Bean, James
    Family worship; a course of morning and evening
prayers for every day in the month, ... 1st Amer.,
from 12th London ed. Philadelphia, S. Potter & Co.,
1819. MWA; NjPT.   47179

Beattie, James
   The minstrel; or, The progress of genius. Hartford, Pr. by Lincon and Stone, for Samuel G. Goodrich, 1819. 70 p. CtHi; RPB; WBeloC.   47180

Beauchamp, William
   Letters on the call and qualifications of a minis-
ter of the Gospel... Nashville, Tenn., E. Stevenson &
P.A. Owen, 1819. 132 p. IEG.   47181

Beazley, Samuel
   Is he jealous? An operetta in one act... New York,
the Longworths, 1819. 27 p. MdHi; NNC; WHi. 47182

Beccaria, Cesare Bonesana, marchese di.
   An essay on crimes and punishments... 2d Amer.
ed. Philadelphia, Philip N. Nicklin, 1819. 239 p.
CSmH; IaU-L; MWA; MWCL; NIC-L; OCLaw.   47183

Beecher, Lyman
   The design, rights, and duties of local churches.
A sermon delivered at the installation of the Rev.
Elias Cornelius as associate pastor of the Tabernacle
Church in Salem, July 21, 1819... Andover, Mass.,
Pr. by Flagg and Gould, for Henry Whipple, Salem,
1819. 54 p. DLC; ICN; MBNEH; MH-AH; MNe; MWA;
MWiW; NNG; PHi; PPPrHi; RPB.   47184

-- A sermon delivered at the funeral of Henry Obookiah... Elizabeth-Town, N.J., Pr. by J. & E. Sanderson, for Edson Hart, agent of the Foreign mission
school, 1819. MWA.   47185

-- -- New Haven, Pr. by S. Converse, for Nathan
Whiting, agent of the Foreign mission school, 1819.
40 p.   CO; CSf; CSt; CU; Ct; CtHi; CtY; MSaE; MWA;
NRAB; OClWHi; RP; ViU.   47186

Beers' almanac for 1820. Hartford, George Goodwin
and sons [1819] [24] p. CtHi; MWA.   47187

-- New Haven, A.H. Maltby & co., [1819] [24] p. CtY;
MWA; NBuG.   47188

Beer's calendar; or, Hosford's almanack for the year
of our Lord 1820... Albany, E. & E. Hosford [1819]
36 p. MB; MH; MWA; MiD-B; NHi; NN; NT.   47189

Beers' calender; or Loomis's almanack for... 1820, by
Andrew Beers... Albany, G. J. Loomis & Co. [1819]
36 p. NT.   47190

Bell, Samuel
    Communication from the governor covering the re-
port of the justices of the Superior court on the ques-
tion of granting new trials. Concord, 1819. MSaE.
                                            47191
[--] Message. Gentlemen of the Senate, and House of
Representatives. [1819?] 8 p. (Caption title, signed
Samuel Bell, Concord, June 7, 1819) IaHi.   47192

Belles-Lettres Repository, afterward New York Literary Journal and Belles-Lettres Repository. New York,
1819-21. Vols. 1-4. NBLiHi.   47193

Benedict, David
    A general history of the Baptist denomination in
America, and other parts of the world... Boston, Manning & Loring, 1819. 2 v. LNB; PScrHi.   47194

-- The Pawtucket collection of conference hymns... Ed.
3. Boston, Lincoln & Edmands, 1819. 124 p. MWA.
                                            47195
The benevolent old man of the rock... Montpelier, Vt.,
E. P. Walton, 1819. 30 p. MWA.   47196

Bennet, Benjamin
    Devout meditations... Norristown, Pa., James Win-
nard, 1819. MWA.   47197

Bennett, R. O. K.
    Origin, progress and achievements of Bible socie-
ties; being an address delivered before the Troy department of the Rensselaer county Bible society, at
their quarterly meeting. Troy, N. Y., Pr. by Parker
& Bliss, 1819. 28 p. MH-AH; NjPT.   47198

Bennett, Titus
New system of practical arithmetic, particularly
calculated for the use of schools in the United States
...Ed. 8. Philadelphia, Bennett & Walton, 1819. 204 p.
MWA; PU. 47199

Bennett & Walton's almanac for 1820. Calculated by
Joshua Sharp. Philadelphia, Bennett & Walton, [1819]
MWA. 47200

[Benson, Egbert] 1746-1833
Brief remarks on the "wife" of Washington Irving
...New-York, Pr. by Grattan and Banks, 1819. 16 p.
MBAt; MWA; NGeno; NN; NjP. 47201

-- Vindication of the captors of Major André. New
York, 1819. MBAt. 47202

Berington, Joseph
The history of the lives of Abeillard and Heloisa
...1079-1163, with genuine letters... Philadelphia,
Abraham Small, 1819. 408 p. MWA; NcRA; TSewU;
VtU; WU. 47203

Berkshire county, Mass.--Meeting of citizens, 1819.
Williams college...[1819] MWA. 47204

[Berquin, Arnaud]
The looking-glass for the mind... Philadelphia,
John Bioren, 1819. 271 p. DLC; MWA; NBuG; RPB.
47205

Bible
Biblia, das ist: die ganze Heilige Schrift Alten und
Neuen Testaments... Lancaster [Pa.] J. Bär, 1819.
2 pts. in 1. DLC; KNM; MWA; MiU-C; PPeSchw.
47206

-- Evangelius Nicodemi oder Historischer Bericht von
dem Leben Jesu Christi... Harrisburg, Pa., J.S. Wiestling, 1819. 98 p. MWA; P; PPLT; PPeSchw. 47207

-- Das Evangelium Nicodemus... Reading, Pa., Pr. by
C.A. Bruckman, 1819. 302 p. MWA; NjR. 47208

-- -- Reading, Pa., Pr. by C.A. Bruckman, for
Joseph Stocker & andere, 1819. MWA.   47209

-- The Holy Bible, containing the Old and New Testa-
ments translated out of the original tongues...Boston,
Pr. by W. Greenough, for Lincoln and Edmunds, 1819.
MWA; NN.   47210

-- -- ...Apocrypha...an index; an alphabetical table
...Brown's concordance...account of the lives and
martyrdom of the apostles and evangelists with plates.
J. Holbrook's stereotype copy.   Brattleborough [Vt.]
1819. MB; MDux; MPlyA; MWA.   47211

-- -- Stereotyped for the American Society, by D. &
G. Bruce, New-York.   Lexington, Ky., Pr. by William G. Hunt, for the Kentucky Auxiliary Bible Society,
1819. NN.   47212

-- -- New York, Stereotyped by E. & J. White, for
the American Bible Society, 1819. 1087 p. MRev;
MWA; NN.   47213

-- -- Stereotyped for the American Bible Society.
New York, Pr. by D. Fanshaw, for J. & G. Bruce,
1819. 837 p. MWA; NNS; VtMiS.   47214

-- -- New York, Collins & Co., 1819. 932 p. DLC;
MnU; MsNF; NNC.   47215

-- -- Philadelphia, M. Carey & Son, 1819. 1080 p.
MBeHi.   47216

-- -- Philadelphia, Pr. by W. Hill Woodward, for W.
W. Woodward, 1819. MWA.   47217

-- Das neue testament unsers Herrn und heilandes
Jesu Christi, nach der Deutschen uebersetzung D. Martin Luthers...Erste Auflage.   New Berlin, Pa., Salo-
mon Miller & Henrich Neibel, 1819. 540 p. DLC;
MWA; PReaAT.   47218

-- -- Achte Auflage. Germantown, Pa., Pr. by M.

Billmeyer, 1819. 537 p. MWA.   47219

-- The New Testament of our Lord and Saviour Jesus
Christ; translated out of the original Greek...1st
Amer. stereotype ed. Boston, Pr. by John H. A.
Frost, for West, Richardson & Lord, 1819. [312] p.
MBC; MWA.   47220

-- -- 1st Amer. stereotype ed. Boston, Pr. by John
H. A. Frost, for West, Richardson & Lord, 1819.
[312] p. MWA.   47221

-- -- ...And with the former translations diligently
compared and revised, (Holbrook's Stereotype ed.)
Stereotyped by B. & J. Collins, New-York. Brattleborough, Vt., John Holbrook [1819] [248] p. DLC;
PPL.   47222

-- -- Brattleborough, Vt., J. Holbrook, 1819. 335 p.
(2 varying copies, plates are different) MWA; Vt.47223

-- -- Stereotyped by B. & J. Collins, New-York.
Exeter, N. H., John I. Williams, 1819. [312] p. MWA.
                                                  47224
-- -- Hopkinton [N. H.] Isaac Long, Jun., 1819. 380 p.
MWA; Nh; Nh-Hi.   47225

-- -- Leicester, Pr. by Hori Brown, 1819. 336 p.
MWA.   47226

-- Stereotype ed.   The New Testament of our Lord
and Saviour Jesus Christ, translated out of the original Greek... New York, Stereotyped by B. & J. Collins,
for L. and F. Lockwood, 1819. 237 p. PReaHi. 47227

-- -- Stereotyped by D. & G. Bruce, for the American Bible Society. New-York, Pr. by D. Fanshaw,
1819. 311 p. DLC; MWA; NN; NjR.   47228

-- -- New York, American Bible Society, 1819. 215 p.
RPB.   47229

-- -- Stereotyped by B. & J. Collins. Philadelphia,

Isaac Peirce, 1819. 290 p. MWA.   47230

-- -- Philadelphia, Pr. by W. Hill Woodward, for W.
W. Woodward, 1819. 208 p. MoSU.   47231

-- -- 2d Amer. ed.   Utica, N. Y., William Williams,
1819.   333 p.   N; NUtHi.   47232

-- El Nuevo Testamente de nuestro Senor Jesu Cristo,
traducido de la biblia vulgata latina en espanol por el
Rllo. P. Felipe scio de S. Miguel, obispo electo de
Segovia. Reimpreso literal y diligentemente, conforme
a la seconda edicion hecha en Madrid, ano de 1797,
revista y corregida por su misneo traductor.   Nueva
York, edicion estereotypa, per Elihu White. a costa
de la sociedad Americana de la biblia.   Ano de 1819
375 p.   DLC; DGU; IAIS; MdBS; NN.   47233

-- Psalms carefully suited to the Christian worship in
the United States of America... Geneva, N. Y., James
Bogert, 1819.   587 p.   MWA.   47234

-- -- Philadelphia, Pr. by W. Hill Woodward, for W.
W. Woodward, 1819.   274 p.   MWA; NSyHi.   47235

-- Psalms of David.   Imitated in the language of the
New Testament, and applied to the Christian state and
worship.   Boston, 1819. 460 p.   MWA.   47336

-- -- Boston, Lincoln and Edmands, 1819. 585 p.
MFiHi; MWA.   47337

-- -- Boston, Pr. by U. Crocker, for Samuel T. Armstrong, 1819.   460 p.   MAnHi; MBNMHi; MWA; MWey;
MeB; MeBat; MiD-B; VtMiS.   47338

-- -- A new ed... by Timothy Dwight... Hartford, Geo.
Goodwin and sons, 1819.   473 p.   CtHT-W; CtHi; CtW;
MA; NN; NNUT; WBeloHi.   47339

-- The Psalms of David in metre... by the authority of
the general assembly, of the Kirk of Scotland, ... Philadelphia, 1819.   68 p.   (Mrs. Katie Buford, 300 Pine St.

Minden, La.   47340

-- Sainte Bible qui contient le vieux et le nouveau
Testament; revue sur les originaux par David Martin.
New York, Societe Biblique Americaine, 1819. WBeloC.
                                               47341
-- ...Selectae e veteri Testamento historiae ad usum
eorum qui Latinae linguae rudimentis imbuuntur. Nova
editio...Baltimore, A. Neal, 1819. 149 p. MiU; NN.
                                               47342
-- -- Baltimore, Pr. by J.D. Toy, for N.G. Max-
well, 1819. 149 p. MdBE; WyU.   47343

-- Testament und abschrift der zwölf patriarches, der
söhne Jacobs, wie ein jeder vor seinem ende seine
kinder gelehrt...Harrisburg, Pa., Pr. by J.S. Wiestling, 1819. 92 p. MWA; P; PPLT.   47344

-- The whole book of psalms, in metre; with hymns,
suited to the feasts and fasts of the church and other
occasions of public worship. New-York, W.B. Gilley,
1819. 224 p. MH; MWA.   47345

-- -- ...Stereotyped by D. & G. Bruce, New York.
New York, Henry I. Megarey, 1819. 274 p. MH;
MMeT; MWA; NNG; NNS; RPB.   47346

-- -- New York, Pr. by J. & J. Harper, 1819. 274 p.
MMeT.   47347

Bible atlas. New Haven, N. & S.S. Jocelyn, 1819.
[21] p. (Gray printed paper covers. CtHi; MWA. 47348

-- New Haven, N. & S.S. Jocelyn, 1819. [21] p. CtHi;
MWA. (Tan printed paper covers.)   47349

Bible Society of Massachusetts
    Report of the executive committee of the Bible So-
ciety of Massachusetts, prepared for the anniversary of
the society, June 3, 1819. Boston, Pr. by Sewell
Phelps, 1819. 16 p. MWA; MiD-B.   47350

Bible society of Philadelphia.
The eleventh report... Philadelphia, Pr. by William
Fry, 1819. MWA.   47351

Bible society of Rensselaer county, N. Y.
The fourth report... May 26, 1819. Troy, N. Y.,
Pr. by W. S. Parker, 1819. 16 p. MWA; NT.   47352

Bible society of Salem and vicinity.
The eighth report of the Bible society of Salem
and vicinity, June 9, 1819. Salem, Mass., 1819.
[3] p. MSaE.   47353

[Bickersteth, Edward]
Memoirs of Simeon Wilhelm, a native of the Susoo
country, West Africa; who died at the house of the
Church Missionary Society, London, Aug. 29, 1817;
aged 17 years: together with some accounts of the su-
perstitions of the inhabitants of West Africa. New
Haven, S. Converse, 1819. 108 p. CtHC; CtHi; CtY;
DLC; IAlS; ICN; MB; MBAt; MH; MS; MWiW; NN;
OClW; TNF; WHi.   47354

[Bigelow, William]
A letter to "a layman," in reply to his "Letter to
Rev. Mr. Channing." By Layman, junior. [Boston,
1819?] MH.   47355

Bigland, John, 1750-1832
Letters on French history, for the use of schools.
Baltimore, Pr. by Richard J. Matchett, for John J.
Harrod, 1819. 342 p. CSmH; DLC; MB; MWA; MdBP;
PU.   47356

Bingham, Caleb, 1757-1817
The American preceptor improved... sixty first
(1st improved) ed. Boston, Pr. by Parmenter & Balch,
for C. Bingham & Co., 1819. 228 p. MWA; MeU;
MtGr; OClWHi.   47357

-- Astronomical and geographical catechism. Ed. 15.
New-Haven, John Babcock & Son, 1819. CtHi; CtY;
MWA; MiGr.   47358

-- The child's companion, being an easy and concise reading and spelling book...Ed. 17, cor. and rev. Boston, Pr. by U. Crocker, for Caleb Bingham & Co., 1819. 84 p. DLC; MH; MWA; NNC. 47359

-- The Columbian orator. Philadelphia, Isaac Pierce, 1819. 303 p. MWA; NjR; PWaybu; RPB. 47360

-- Juvenile letters; being a correspondence between children from eight to fifteen years of age...1st western from 2d Boston ed. Cincinnati, O., Pr. by Mason and Palmer, for Cornelius Wing, 1819. 80 p. OC; OClWHi. 47361

Bingham, H.
Memoirs of Mrs. Sally Fornis who died at Beverly, Massachusetts...with remarks by H. Bingham. Andover, Mass., Pr. by Flagg & Gould, 1819. 89 p. MBev. 47362

Bioren's Pennsylvania pocket remembrancer for 1820. Philadelphia, John Bioren [1819] MWA. 47363

Bioren's town and country almanack for 1820. Calculated by William Collom. Philadelphia, John Bioren [1819] MWA; NjR. 47364

Birkbeck, Morris
Extracts from a supplementary letter from the Illinois, dated Jan. 31, 1819. Address to British emigrants arriving in the eastern ports, July 13, 1819. Reply to Wm. Cobbett, July 31, 1819. New York, 1819. 29 p. CtY; LNH. 47365

-- Notes on a journey in America, from the coast of Virginia to the Territory of Illinois. With proposals for the establishment of a colony of English...Ed. 2, rev. Philadelphia, M. Carey & sons [Doylestown, Asher Miner] 1819. 189 p. MSaE; P. 47366

Black, John, 1768-1849
Church fellowship. A sermon, preached at the opening of the Synod of the Reformed Presbyterian

church, Philadelphia, May 16, 1816... Pittsburgh [Pa.]
Pr. by E. Pentland, 1819. 109 p. CSmH; MB; MWA;
N; NN; NNUT; NcMHi; NjPT; OClWHi; PHi; PLT;
PPPrHi; PPiXT; TxDaM.   47367

The blackbird's nest; a tale... New York, Juvenile library, 1819. RPB.   47368

Blackstone, Henry
    Reports of cases argued in Courts of Common
Pleas and Exchequer Chamber, 1788-1796. 2d Amer.
ed. Philadelphia, Philip H. Nicklin, 1819. 2 vols.
MWA; MWiW; VtBrt.   47369

Blair, Hugh
    Abridgment of lectures on rhetoric. New York,
L. & F. Lockwood, 1819. MWA.   47370

-- -- Salem, Mass., Thomas Carey [1819?] 300 p.
MSaE.   47371

-- Lectures on rhetoric and Belles Lettres... 8th Amer.
from the last Edinburgh ed. New York, Pr. by Jas.
& John Harper, for Collins & Hannay, 1819. 500 p.
KyCovV; MWA; MdBG; RPB; TxBrdD.   47372

-- -- 8th Amer., from the last Edinburgh ed. New
York, Pr. by Jas. & John Harper, for W.B. Gilley,
1819. 500 p.   47373

-- -- 8th Amer., from the last Edinburgh ed. New
York, L. & T. Lockwood, 1819. 800 p.   47374

-- -- New York, Scott & Sanguin, 1819. NPV. 47375

Blair, Robert
    The grave, a poem... Portsmouth, N.H., Pr. by
S. Whidden, for William F. Laine, Hallowell, 1819.
30 p. MWA; MeLewB.   47376

[Blake, John L.]
    Questions adapted to Blair's rhetoric abridged by
an experienced teacher of youth, for the use of schools

and academies. Ed. 3. Salem, Mass., Pr. by Thomas C. Cushing, 1819. 36 p. MNF; MSaE; MeHi. 47377

Blakely Gazette. Blakely, N. C., Dismukes & Carney, 1819. Newspaper. Brigham, p. 758. 47378

Blanchard, Stephen
    Letter to Mr. Walter Harris, of Dunbarton, on his two discourses entitled Characteristics of false teachers. Concord, N. H., 1819. 20 p. Nh-Hi. 47379

Bland, Theodoric
    Report... on South America. Washington, D. C., 1819. MWA; PPL-R. 47380

Bledsoe, Jesse
    The speech of Jesse Bledsoe... on the resolutions proposed by him concerning banks. Delivered in the Senate of Kentucky, at the annual session of 1818. Lexington, Ky., Norvell, 1819. 45 p. CSmH; DLC; ICN; ICU; KyLoF; MBAt; NNC; PHi. 47381

Blunt, Edmund March
    Analysis of the authorities upon which the dangers have been inserted in Blunt's new chart of the Atlantic or Western ocean... New York, Pr. by J. Seymour, for William Hooker, 1819. 76 p. DeGE; MHi; MMeT; MSaE; MWA. 47382

Blunt, Joseph, 1792-1860
    An examination of the expediency and constituionality of prohibiting slavery in the state of Missouri... By Marcus [pseud.] New York, C. Wiley & co., 1819. 22 p. MH; RPB. 47383

Bolivar, Simon, 1783-1830
    An address of Bolivar at the Congress of Angostura, (Feb. 15, 1819). Reprint ordered by the government of the United States of Venezuela, to commemorate the Centennial of the opening of the Congress. Translated from the original Spanish by Francisco Javier Yanes. Washington, D. C., Byron S. Adams, 1819. 39 p. LNH. 47384

Bolles, Lucius
    A sermon, delivered in Newburyport...December
9, 1818, at the ordination of the Rev. Hosea Wheeler
...Newburyport, Mass., Pr. by W. & J. Gilman,
1819. 24 p. CSmH; MNe; MWA; NRAB.   47385

Bollmann, Erick, i.e. Justus Erich, 1769-1821
    A letter to Thomas Brand...on the practicability
and propriety of a resumption of specie payments...
Re-pub. from the London ed.   Philadelphia, M.
Thomas; New York, J. Haly and C. Thomas, 1819.
76 p. DLC; MWA.   47386

Bonnycastle, Sir Richard Henry, 1791-1848
    Spanish America; or, A descriptive, historical,
and geographical account of the dominions of Spain in
the Western hemisphere...Philadelphia, A. Small,
1819. 482 p.   CHi; DLC; MWA; MoSM; NjP; ScNC;
PU.   47387

Booth, Abraham
    The reign of Grace, from its rise to its consum-
mation...2d Amer. ed.   New-York, Pr. by D. & G.
Bruce, for John Tiebout, 1819. 306 p. NSchU. 47388

Boston (City)
    At a legal meeting of the inhabitants of the town
of Boston, held at Faneuil Hall, on Monday, the 31st
day of May, A.D. 1819.   The following report was
read, accepted, ordered to be printed, and distributed
for information of the inhabitants. Attest, Thomas
Clark, Town Clerk. [1819] 4 p. MBr.   47389

-- A memorial to the Congress of the United States,
on the subject of restraining the increase of slavery in
new states to be admitted into the Union.   Prepared in
pursuance of a vote of the inhabitants of Boston and
its vicinity, assembled at the State house, on the third
of December, A.D. 1819.   Boston, Pr. by Sewell
Phelps, 1819. 22 p. CtY; DLC; ICMe; IEN; M; MBC;
MFi; MH-BA; MNBedf; MWA; MdBLC; MdHi; MiD-B;
MsJS; NN; NNHuC; NcD; Nh-Hi; NjPT; OClWHi; OO;
PHi; RHi; RPB; TNF; ViHaI; WHi.   47390

-- Order of performance...43d anniversary of American independence. [Boston, 1819] MB.   47391

-- Rules, regulations and orders of the Board of Health of Boston, relative to the police of said town. [Boston] The Board, 1819. 16 p. DLC; MBr; MH-M.
47392

-- May, 1819. Seventh annual report of the Committee of finance of the town of Boston. [Boston, 1819] 15 p. CSt; DLC; MBB; MBr; MWA.   47393

Boston female society for missionary purposes.
A brief account of the origin and progress of the society. With extracts from the reports of the society, in May 1817 and 1818, and extracts from the reports of their missionaries James Davis and Dudley D. Rosseter. Boston, 1819. 24 p. MB.   47394

Boston Juvenile Education Society
The constitution of the Boston Juvenile Education Society, auxiliary to the Massachusetts Baptist Education Society. Instituted Jan. 1, 1819. Boston, Pr. by Lincoln & Edmands, 1819. 8 p. MiD-B.   47395

Boston Medical Association
Rules and regulations...Boston, Pr. by J.T. Buckingham, 1819. 8 p. MH-M; MWA; NNNAM. 47396

Boston, Mass. - Public Latin School
Catalogue [Boston] 1819-21.   MH.   47397

The Boston recorder. Boston, N. Willis, 1819-24. 56 vols. illus. NjP.   47398

Boston Society for the Moral and Religious Instruction of the Poor.
Third annual report of the Boston Society for the Moral and Religious Instruction of the Poor; presented at their anniversary, Nov. 8, 1819. Boston, Pr. by U. Crocker, 1819. 24 p. CSt; MB; MWA; NN. 47399

Boston weekly report. Boston, P. P. F. Degrand, May 1, 1819, 1st issue. Newspaper. MWA; NHi.   47400

A botanical catechism: containing introductory lessons
for students in botany. By a Lady. Northampton,
Mass., Pr. by T.W. Shepard and co., 1819. 34 p.
DLC; MH; MNF; MSaP; MWA.   47401

Botsford, Edmund
    The spiritual voyage, performed in the Ship Con-
vert...Philadelphia, Anderson and Meehan, 1819. 32 p.
MWA; OCHP; OClWHi.   47402

Boucherie, Anthony
    The art of making whiskey...also the art of con-
verting it into gin...translated from the French by C.
M. ...Lexington, Ky., Pr. by Worsley & Smith, 1819.
43 p. ICU; PPiU.   47403

[Boudinot, Elias]
    Memoirs of the life of the Rev. William Tennent.
Chambersburg, Pa., 1819. 36 p. ICN; NBLiHi. 47404

[--] -- Philadelphia, Pr. by D. Dickinson, for Emmor
Matlack, 1819. 36 p. MWA.   47405

-- -- Wilmington, Del., R. Porter, 1819. DLC; DeHi;
DeU; DeWI; MWA; PHi; PPM.   47406

Bourne, Hugh
    A general collection of hymns and spiritual songs,
for camp meetings, revivals, etc. Bingham, Me. ?
1819. IEG.   47407

[Bowditch, Nathaniel]
    Elements of the orbit of the comet of 1819. [1819]
MWA.   47408

-- Remarks on the comet of 1819. Salem, Mass.,
1819. 3 p. MB.   47409

Bowdoin College
    Catalogue of the officers and students of Bowdoin
College, Brunswick, October, 1819...Hallowell, Me.,
Pr. by E. Goodale [1819] Broadside. MH; MeB. 47410

-- Catalogus Senatus Academici, et eorum qui Munera
et Officia Gesserunt, Donati Sunt, in Collegio Bowdoin-
ensi, Brunsvici, In Republica Massachusettensi. ...
Hallowell, Me., Pr. by Ezekiel Goodale, 1819. 12 p.
MH; MHi; MeB; MeHi. 47411

-- Order of exercises for commencement, September
1, 1819. Hallowell, Me., Pr. by Ezekiel Goodale,
1819. 4 p. MWA; MeB; MeHi. 47412

Brackenridge, Henry Marie, 1786-1871
    Voyage to South America, performed by order of
the American government, in the years 1817 and 1818,
in the frigate Congress... Baltimore, Pr. by John D.
Toy, for the author, 1819. 2 v. C; CSmH; DLC; MB;
MH; MPiB; MdBD; PCC; PHi; PHatU; PPA; PPAmP;
PPL-R; PPPrHi; PU. 47413

Brackenridge, Hugh Henry, 1748-1816
    Modern chivalry: containing the adventures of a
captain and Teague O'Regan, his servant... Pittsburgh,
Pa., R. Patterson & Lambdin, 1819. 2 v. ICU; LNH;
MB; MBAt; MDeeP; MH; MWA; MnU; NBuG; MoWarbT;
NNF; NNHuC; NcAS; NjP; NN; OCHP; OCY; PHi; PPi;
PWW; NcWsS; TxDaM. 47414

[Bradford, Gamaliel]
    The Christian orator, or, A collection of speeches
delivered on public occasions before religious benevolent societies, by a Gentleman of Massachusetts. Ed.
3. Charlestown, Mass., S. Etheridge, 1819. 298 p.
M. 47415

Bradford's Tennessee almanac, for the year of our
Lord, 1820... Nashville, Tenn., Pr. by T. G. Bradford,
[1819] 32 p. T. 47416

Bradley, Joshua, 1773-1855
    Accounts of religious revivals in many parts of the
United States from 1815 to 1818... Albany, N.Y., Pr.
by G. J. Loomis & co., 1819. 300 p. CSmH; DLC;
ICN; ICT; MWA; NGlf; OC. 47417

Brady, John
A correspondence between Rev. Mr. Brady and Rev. Mr. Edelen, of St. Mary's County, Maryland; which was commenced, in consequence of a report in circulation that the latter had burned several Protestant Bibles... Washington City, Pr. by Davis & Force, 1819. 76 p. DLC.   47418

-- Faithful statement of the correspondence between the Rev. Mr. Brady, Rector of William and Mary, and St. Andrew parishes, St. Mary's County; and the Rev. Leonard Edelen, Pastor of the congregation at New-Town, of the same county. Washington City, Pr. by Davis & Force, 1819. 43 p. MBrigStJ; MdBS.   47419

Branch, William, jr.
Life, a poem in three books... Richmond, Va., Pr. by W. W. Gray, on the Franklin press, 1819.   CSmH; CtY; DLC; ICB; MH; MWA; NBuG; NcD; NcU; PHi; RPB; TNP; TxU; Vi; ViHi; ViU; ViW.   47420

Brantly, William Theophilus
The lenitive of sorrow. A sermon, delivered in the First Baptist Church, Beaufort [S. C.] 25th Oct. 1818, on the death of Mrs. Ann Brantly... Charleston, S. C., Pr. by A. E. Miller, 1819. 28 p. CSmH; MBC; PHi.   47421

Brantz, Lewis
Meteorological observations; made in the vicinity of Baltimore, during the year 1818. Baltimore, Pr. by William Gwynn, at the office of the Federal gazette, 1819. [56] p. MdHi.   47422

-- ... Survey of the river Patapsco and part of Chesapeake bay, instituted by the marine insurance companies of Baltimore and executed at their expense under the direction of Lewis Brantz... Baltimore, F. Lucas, 1819. Chart. MdBE.   47423

Brevard, Joseph
Reports of judicial decisions. Charleston, S. C., Pr. by J. Seymour, for John Mill, 1819. 480 p.

Me-LR.   47424

[Brewster, Francis E.]
    Roberts's second edition of The secret "customs,"
and revenue of the sheriff's office... Philadelphia,
Sylvester Roberts, 1819. MWA.   47425

[--]   The secret "customs," and revenue of the sheriff's
office. Philadelphia, Sylvester Roberts, 1819. MWA.
                                              47426
The Bridgewater collection of sacred music. Boston,
Richardson, Lord & Holbrook, 1819. 320 p. KU.   47427

A brief account of the horrid massacre of the Captain,
Mate, and supercargo of the Schooner Plattsburg, of Baltimore, on the high seas, in July, 1816. by a part of the
crew of said vessel... Ed. 3. Boston, 1819. (Goodspeed's
Amer. cat. no. 263, Boston, July 1936, no. 433)   47428

A brief account of the religious experience, sickness
and death, of the late pious Miss Mary N. Tooker;...
John C. Totten, 1819. 48 p. NNG.   47429

Brief of the title of the Maison Rouge grant of land.
With documents explanatory thereof. [Natchez? 1819]
14 p. Streeter collection.   47430

A brief review of the origin, progress, and administration of the Bank of the United States... By a friendly
monitor. [Philadelphia] 1819. 44 p. DLC; MWA. 47431

Bristol adult school society, Bristol, England.
    Lessons for the instruction of adults; or, An in-
troduction to the reading of the Sacred Scriptures...
Baltimore, Pr. by John D. Toy, for the Union male
Sunday school society of Baltimore, 1819. 60 p. DLC.
                                              47432
British Charitable Society, Boston, Mass.
    For the year 1819. Annual report of the British
Charitable Society, for the sick and distressed. Bos-
ton, Sewell Phelps, 1819. 28 p. ICMe; MWA.   47433

Bromwell, Jacob
   Jacob Bromwell's patent self feeding wheat fan...
Permission is hereby granted to use one of Jacob
Bromwell's patent wheat fans...[Baltimore, 1819] 2 p.
DLC.   47434

Brookville Enquirer. Brookville, Ind., John Scott and
Co., Feb. 5, 1819, 1st issue. Weekly newspaper.
DLC.   47435

[Brown, Alling]
   Candid appeal to the author (H. Croswell) of the
"Sober appeal to the Christian Public." New Haven,
1819. 12 p. CtY.   47436

[Brown, Bartholomew] 1772-1854
   Templi carmina. Songs of the temple... Ed. 7,
impr. and enl. Boston, Pr. by J.H.A. Frost, for
West, Richardson & Lord, 1819. MB; RPB.   47437

Brown, Clark
   Select sermons, on important subjects... George-
town, D.C., Pr. [by Wm. A. Rind & Co.] for Elijah
Weems, 1819. 304 p. DLC; MWA; MdBD; MdBP.
                                                       47438

Brown, Erastus
   The trial of Cain, the first murderer, in poetry,
by rule of court; in which a Predestinarian, a Univer-
salian, and an Armenian, argue as attornies at the
bar...Bridgeport, Conn., Stiles Nichols, 1819. 32 p.
CtHi; MWA; RPB.   47439

Brown, Frederick W.A.S.
   A valedictory poem; addressed to the inhabitants of
Rainsford's, George's, Gallop's, Light house, and
Deer islands, in Boston harbour...(Ed. 2) Boston, Pr.
by True & Weston, 1819. 52 p. CSt; DLC; MBAt;
MBCH; MBL; MH; MWA; NBuG; RPB.   47440

Brown, Isaac Van Arsdale, 1784-1861
   Memoirs of the Rev. Robert Finley, D.D., late
pastor of the Presbyterian congregation at Basking
Ridge, New-Jersey, and president of Franklin College,

located at Athens, in the state of Georgia...New-
Brunswick, N.J., Terhune & Letson, 1819. 370 p.
CSansS; CSmH; CtHC; DLC; GU-De; MWA; NjR.   47441

[Brown, J.]
A letter to the Rev. William E. Channing. [Bos-
ton, Pr. by James Loring, 1819] MWA.   47442

Brown, James
A grammatical treatise, being an exposition of the
difficulties found in the present system of English grammar...Albany, Pr. by Jeremiah Tryon, 1819. 40 p.
N.   47443

Brown, John, of Haddington
Address to the students of divinity, by John Brown.
Boston, 1819. 27 p. (Bound in: Porter, E. Young
preacher's manual) NjPT.   47444

Brown, John, 1722-1787
A compendious view of natural and revealed religion...1st Amer., from a late London ed.   Philadelphia, David Hogan, 1819. 576 p. KTW; MWA; NcWfC;
OO; ViRut.   47445

-- A concordance to the Holy scriptures...Philadel-
phia, Pr. by G. L. Austin, for Benjamin Johnson,
1819. MWA.   47446

Brown, Samuel
The equality of Christ with the Father; a sermon
preached at a camp-meeting...Cincinnati, O., Pr. by
Looker, Reynolds & co., 1819. 23 p. OClWHi.   47447

Brown, William
Some account of Abigail Brown, who died 22d of
8th month 1814, aged about 15 years...New York,
Samuel Wood & Sons, 1819. 16 p. MWA; PHC; RNHi.
                                               47448
Brunton, Mrs. Mary (Balfour)
Emmeline...New York, Pr. by Clayton & Kings-
land, for A.T. Goodrich and Co., 1819. MWA. 47449

-- -- New York, Pr. by Clayton & Kingsland, for W.
B. Gilley, 1819. CtY; MH; MWA.   47450

Bucklen, Isaac
    A discourse, delivered in Middlebury, Vt., before
Union lodge, No. 5...June 24, A.L. 5812...Middle-
bury, Vt., Pr. by J.W. Copeland, 1819. 26 p. MBFM;
MWA; NjPT; VtMiM; VtMiS.   47451

Bucks county, Pa.
    Minutes of the alms-house visitation; containing the
charges against the directors and steward of the institution.   As laid before the visitors appointed by the
Court, and the testimony of the several witnesses examined in the course of the investigation. Doylestown
[Pa.] Simeon Siegfried, 1819. 120 p. CSmH.   47452

Bucks County Messenger. Doylestown, Pa., Simeon
Sigfried, June 28, 1819, 1st issue. PDoBHi.   47453

[Buel, Jesse] 1778-1839
    A treatise on agriculture; comprising a concise
history of its origin and progress, the present condition of the art abroad and at home, and the theory and
practice of husbandry which have arisen out of the
present state of philosophical attainments in Europe, by
a practical farmer.   Albany, J. Buel [1819] 168 p.
NIC-A.   47454

[Buel, Samuel]
    The book, or fragments of modern chronicles...
Burlington, Vt., Samuel Buel, 1819. 158 p. MBAt;
MWA; Vt; VtU.   47455

Buffum, Gaskill
    The surrejoinder...Providence, 1819. MWA; RPB.
                    47456
Bull, William
    Music, adapted to language...Greenfield, Mass.,
Pr. by Denio & Phelps, for the author, 1819. 123 p.
MB; MDeeP; MWA.   47457

Bull-us, Hector, pseud.
The diverting history of John Bull and Brother
Jonathan. By Hector Bull-us. Ed. 3. Philadelphia,
Pr. by T.H. Palmer, for M. Carey & son, 1819.
144 p. MeU.   47458

[Bunyan, John]
The Christian pilgrim...Montpelier, Vt., E.P.
Walton, 1819. 141 p. MWA; MiU; VtHi; VtU.   47459

-- The pilgrim's progress...Exeter, N.H., Pr. by J.
J. Williams, 1819. 287 p. MLit; MWA.   47460

[--] The pilgrim's progress exhibited in a metamor-
phosis; or, a transformation of pictures for the entertainment and instruction of youth. Hartford, J.W.
Barber, 1819. MSaE; MWA; NPV.   47461

[--] -- Hartford, Loomis & Barnes, 1819. MB;
MLexHi; MSaE; MWA; NPV; RPB.   47462

-- -- Newark, N.J., Pr. by J. and E. Sanderson, for
Benjamin Olds, 1819. MWA.   47463

-- The water of life...Exeter, N.H., Josiah Richardson, 1819. MWA.   47464

Burbank, Gardner
Defense of Lieut. Col. Gardner Burbank before the
General Court Martial, whereof Maj. Gen. Nathaniel
Goodwin was President, held at Hathaway's Hall in
Worcester, on the 8th September, 1818, against charges
preferred against him by Col. Prentice Cushing and
others...Worcester, Mass., Pr. by William Manning,
1819. 44 p. CBPSR; CSt; CtY; MB; MHi; MWA; MWCL;
MWHi; WHi.   47465

Burbank, Caleb, 1761-1849
Defense of Maj. Gen. Caleb Burbank, and the argument of the complainants, before the general court-
martial, whereof Maj. Gen. Nathaniel Goodwin was
president, held at Worcester, on the 8th day of Sept.
1818, against charges preferred against him, by Col.

Prentice Cushing and others.   Worcester [Mass.] Pr.
by William Manning, Jan. 1819. 60 p. CBPSR; DLC;
MWA; MWCL; NHi; NN; Nh-Hi.   47466

Burder, George
     A collection of prayers... New Haven, A. H. Malt-
by, 1819. 90 p. Ct; CtHi; CtY; MWA; MeBaT; ViRUt.
                                              47467
-- The doctrine of the Trinity... [Exeter, N. H., Josiah
Richardson, 1819] MWA.   47468

Burges, G.
     Present spirit of the times.   Norwich, Conn.,
1819. NPV.   47469

Burnap, Jacob
     A discourse, delivered at Dunstable, N. H., Sept.
8, 1818, at the funeral of the Rev. Joseph Kidder...
Amherst, N. H., Pr. by Richard Boylston, 1819. 24 p.
MH; MSaE; MWA; MiD-B.   47470

-- A discourse, delivered at Merrimack, N. H. January 3, 1819... Amherst, N. H., Pr. by Richard Boylston, 1819. 16 p. DLC; ICT; MWA.   47471

[--] Funeral sermon: precious in the sight of the Lord
is the death of His saints. [Amherst, N. H., 1819]
22 p. MPiB.   47472

Burris, William
     The farmer's farrier book. Wilmington, O., Pr.
by Rice Gaddis, 1819. (Henderson's Bibliography of A-
merican sport.)   47473

Burtt, John, 1789-1866
     Horae poeticae; or, The transient murmurs of a
solitary lyre. Consisting of poems and songs, in English and Scotch. ... Bridgeton, N. J., Pr. by William
Schultz, 1819. 183 p. CSmH; DLC; NN; NcAS; PPL-R;
RPB.   47474

Burton, Judge
     Vindication of the measures of the President and

his commanding generals in the commencement and termination of the Seminole war. Washington, D. C., 1819. MSaE. 47475

No entry. 47476

Butcher, Edmund
The New Year's gift, or Moral tales, designed to instruct and improve the minds of youth. From the London ed. Boston, L. C. Bowles, 1819. MH. 47477

Butler, Frederick, 1766?-1843
A catechetical compend of general history, sacred and profane; from the creation of the world, to the year 1817... Ed. 4. Hartford, Cooke and Hale, 1819. 216 p. CSt; Ct; CtHi; CtHT; CtHT-W; DGU; DLC; FStPHi; ICU; MB; MBev-F; MDedHi; MDeeP; MH; MPiB; MWA; MiD-B; NAHi; NSyHi; NcWsHi; NjMD; OMC; PPPrHi; ScCMu. 47478

-- The farmer's manual... Hartford, Pr. by Clark & Lyman, for Samuel G. Goodrich, 1819. 224 p. CUAL; CtHi; DLC; MHi; MWA; NIC; NjR. 47479

-- Sketches of universal history, sacred and profane, from the creation of the world, to the year 1818, of the Christian era... Ed. 2, cor. by the author. Hartford, Pr. by Lincoln & Stone, for Cooke & Hale, 1819. 407 p. CSt; Ct; CtHi; CtSoP; CtW; MH; MWA; MdBLC; MiU; NjP; OC; RPB; VtCas; WGr. 47480

Butler, Joseph, bp. of Durham, 1692-1752
The analogy of religion, natural and revealed, to the constituion and course of nature... 3d Amer. ed. Hartford, Pr. by C. J. Newcomb, for Samuel G. Goodrich, 1819. 239 p. CtHi; CSmH; DLC; MWA; MWat; MeB; MsJMC; NN; ScCoB. 47481

Butrick, Daniel Sabin.
TSVLVKI SQCLVCLV. A Cherokee spelling book
...Knoxville, Tenn., Pr. by F.S. Heiskell & H.
Brown, 1819. 62 p. MWA. 47482

Buzz, Bumblery, pseud.
Ephemira; or, The history of the Cockney dandies.
Philadelphia, 1819. RPB. 47483

[Byron, George Gordon Noël Byron]
Don Juan... Philadelphia, Pr. by James Maxwell,
for M. Thomas and J. Haly and C. Thomas, New
York, 1819. 194 p. MWA; NFred; PHi. 47484

-- Mazeppa... Boston, Wells and Lilly, 1819. 61 p.
MB; MH; MWA. 47485

-- -- New York, Pr. by J. Maxwell, repub. M. Thomas, Philadelphia; and J. Haley & C. Thomas, 1819.
MWA. 47486

-- The vampyre... Albany, Pr. by E. and E. Hosford,
1819. MWA; NN. 47487

-- -- Philadelphia, Pr. by J. Maxwell, for M. Thomas,
1819. 46 p. MWA. 47488

C

Cady, Eunice
Poem in four parts... Newtown [Conn.] Pr. for the
publisher, 1819. 35 p. CtHi; RPB. 47489

Caesar, C. Julius
C. Julii Caesaris, quae extant, interpretatione et
notis illustravit Johanes Godvinus... Ed. 3. Philadelphia, M. Carey and son; Baltimore, F. Lucas, jun.,
1819. 410 p. KyDC; MH; MNBedf; NCH; OMC; ViU.
47490

Cahawba Press and Alabama Intelligencer. Cahawba,
Ala., William B. Allen, June 12, 1819, 1st issue.
Weekly newspaper. MWA. 47491

Cahill, Frank
The ocean harp; a poem, with some smaller pieces and a monody on the death of John S. Dorsey. Philadelphia, M. Thomas, 1819. 182 p. MiD. 47492

Caldwell, Charles
An inaugural address, on the advantages and facilities for establishing a Medical school in the Western states... Lexington, Ky., Thomas Smith, 1819. 28 p. CtY; DNLM; KyU; MB; MH; MiD-B; NNNAM; OC; PHi; PPC; PU. 47493

-- Memoirs of the life and campaigns of the Hon. Nathaniel Greene... Philadelphia, Pr. by J. Maxwell, for Robert Desilver, and Thomas Desilver, 1819. 452 p. GU; MWA; NWM; NcAS; NcWfC; PAtM; RPB. 47494

Callender, Charles
Catalogue of the Shakespeare circulation library. Boston, Charles Callender, 1819. MHi. 47495

Calvin, Jean
The institutes of the Christian religion... Preceded by a memoir of the life of Calvin, by John Mackenzie ... New York, Pr. by C.S. Van Winkle, for S. Huestis, 1819. 639 p. KyLoU; MWA; MMet-Hi; NNG; NbCrD; VtMiM. 47496

Cambridge synod, Cambridge, Mass., 1648.
A platform of church discipline... Boston, Pr. by True & Weston, for J. Weston [Reading, Mass.] 1819. 51 p. MBrZ; MWA. 47497

Campbell, Archibald, b. 1787
A voyage round the world, from 1806 to 1812; in which Japan, Kamschatka, the Aleutian Islands, and the Sandwich Islands were visited... 2d Amer. ed. New-York, Pr. by Broderick and Ritter, 1819. 219 p. CtY; DLC; MSaP; MWA. 47498

Campbell, John
Walks of usefulness, in London... Northampton, Mass., Pr. by J. Metcalf, for Simeon Butler, 1819.

108 p. MWA.   47499

[--] Worlds displayed... Boston, Lincoln & Edmands,
1819. MWA.   47500

[--] -- Philadelphia, Pr. by Lydia R. Bailey, 1819.
MWA.   47501

Campbell, Thomas
    An essay on English poetry. Boston, Wells and
Lilly, 1819. 231 p. DLC; LNDil; MB; MBAt; MBL;
MH; MHi; MWA; MeB; Nh; NjMD; OrPD; RNHi; RNR;
ScU; WU.   47502

[Campe, Joachim Heinrich] 1746-1818
    New Robinson Crusoe. Designed for youth... New
Haven, Sidney's press, for J. Babcock & son, 1819.
38 p. CtHi.   47503

A candid appeal to the author of the "Sober appeal to
the Christian public, "... New Haven, Pr. by Flagg &
Gould, 1819. 12 p. MBC; MWA.   47504

Canning, Richard
    Account of the gifts and legacies that have been
given and bequeathed to charitable uses in the town of
Ipswich... New ed. Ipswich, Dorkin, 1819. 300 p.
PU.   47505

Canton, O. House carpenters.
    The book of prices adopted by the house carpenters
of the town of Canton, April 10, 1819. Canton, O.,
Pr. by John Saxton, 1819. 8 p. OClWHi.   47506

Capen, Lemuel
    A farewell address, delivered at Sterling, on
Thursday, January 21, 1819... Worcester, Mass., Pr.
by William Manning, 1819. 20 p. CBPSR; CSt; ICMe;
MH; MHi; MSaE; MWA; MWHi; MiD-B.   47507

-- -- Ed. 2. Boston, Pr. by J. T. Buckingham, 1819.
24 p. DLC; ICMe; M; MBAt; MH; MSaE; MWA; MiD-B;
NCH; NjPT; OClWHi.   47508

Cardelli, Peter
[Announcement of Mr. Peter Cardelli, sculptor
from Rome of the sale of casts from his busts of
James Monroe, James Madison and Thomas Jefferson.]
Washington, D. C., Dec. 1819. 1 p. DLC.   47509

Carew, Thomas
Select poems; with a life of the author by Ezekiel
Sanford. Philadelphia, Mitchell, Ames & White, 1819.
34 p. (Bound with Davies, Sir J., Select poems)
MS.   47510

[Carey, Mathew] 1760-1839
Address of the Philadelphia Society for the Promotion of Domestic Industry, to the citizens of the United
States, no. II. [Philadelphia, 1819] 11 p. DeGE.
47511
[--] Addresses of the Philadelphia society for the promotion of national industry... Philadelphia, M. Carey
and son, 1819. 280 p. DeWI; MdHi; NjP.   47512

[--] -- Ed. 4. Philadelphia, M. Carey and son, 1819.
248 p. (Written by Mathew Carey, except no. XII and
XIII, which were by Dr. Samuel Jackson; and read before the society.) DeGE.   47513

[--] National interests and domestic manufactures. Address of the Philadelphia society for the promotion of
domestic industry, to the citizens of the United States.
Boston, Pr. by W.W. Clapp, 1819. 116 p. CSmH;
DLC; MH-BA; DeGE; WHi.   47514

-- Vindicae Hibernicae... Philadelphia, Pr. [by Lydia
R. Bailey] for M. Carey & son, 1819. 504 p. MWA;
MdCatS; NjR; PRosC; WM.   47515

Carlile, Thomas
An address, delivered before Essex Lodge on the
evening of 28th December, A. L. 1819. Salem, Mass.,
Pr. by W. Palfray, Jr., 1819. 13 p. MBFM; MSaE;
MWA; MiD-B; RPB.   47516

Carlisle, Sir Anthony
    An essay on the disorders of old age... Philadel-
phia, Pr. by W. Myer, for Edward Earle, 1819. 74 p.
DLC; MBM; MWA; MeB; MoSMed; NHun; NNNAM; NjR;
P; RPM.   47517

Carlisle Republican. Carlisle, Pa., Jacob R. Stine,
May 11, 1819, 1st issue. Weekly newspaper. MWA;
PHi.   47518

Carsons, Levi
    The dereliction and restoration of the Jews. A
sermon, preached in Park-Street Church, Boston, Sabbath, Oct. 31, 1819... Boston, Pr. by U. Crocker, for
Samuel T. Armstrong, 1819. 20 p. MiD-B.   47519

Cartwright, William
    Select poems; with a life of the author from Camp-
bell. (Bound with Drummond, W., Select poems)
Philadelphia, Mitchell, Ames & White, 1819. 11 p.
MS.   47520

Casey, Joseph P.
    The farmers' and gardeners' hive, shewing the ex-
pense and profit attending the cultivation of three hundred acres of land... Baltimore, Pr. by W. F. Redding,
1819. 24 p. DA; ICU; MdHi; PPL.   47521

Casket; or, The orphan's portion. Together with divine hymns. New Haven, Sidney's press, for J. Babcock and son, 1819. 35 p. CtHi.   47522

Castigator. Auburn, N.Y., James M. Miller, 1819,
1st issue. Weekly newspaper. N.   47523

A catechism of the New Testament. Salem, Mass.,
Pr. by John D. Cushing, 1819. 18 p. MSaE; MWA.
                                                  47524

Catharine Brown, the converted Cherokee; a missionary drama... New Haven, Pr. by S. Converse, 1819.
CtHi; CtY; MBC; MWA; NN; PHi.   47525

Catholic Church
    Ordo recitandi divini officii et missae celebrandae.
Ad usum...Baltimorensis.   Baltimore, 1819. Parsons
622.   47526

Catlin, Jacob
    Compendium of the system of divine truth.   Hart-
ford, 1819. 314 p. OO.   47527

Cause of and cure for hard times containing definition
of attributes and qualities indispensable in money as
medium of commerce and investigation of the facts of
banking system.   New York, 1819. 78 p.   47528

Cavallo, Tiberius
    Elements of natural and experimental philosophy...
with additional notes, selected from various authors by
F.X. Brosius. 2d Amer. ed.   Philadelphia, Thomas
Dobson, 1819. 2 v. ArLSJ; CtW; KyDC; MLow; MWA;
MdW; MiDSH.   47529

Cayuga County Bible Society
    Second annual report of the directors of the Cay-
uga County Bible Society, auxiliary to the American
Bible Society, presented January 27, 1819, with an ap-
pendix, containing extracts of correspondence, &c. &c.
Auburn, N.Y., Pr. by T.M. Skinner, 1819. 32 p.
NAuHi.   47530

Cayuga Republican.   Auburn, N.Y., Augustus Buckingham, Mar. 24, 1819, 1st issue. NAuHi.   47531

Cecil, Sabina.
    Little Charlotte...Philadelphia, Pr. by J.R.A.
Skerrett, for E. and R. Parker, 1819. MWA.   47532

-- Little Jane...Philadelphia, Pr. by J.R.A. Skerrett,
for E. and R. Parker, 1819. MWA.   47533

-- Little Mary; or, the picture-book...Philadelphia,
E. and R. Parker, 1819. 10 p. CtY.   47534

Centre College
    Charter of the Centre College: An act to incorpo-
rate the Trustees of the Centre College of Kentucky,
at Danville.   Approved January 21, 1819.   12 p. IEG.
                                                    47535
The Challenge accepted it is so well understood in
Frederick Town that Captain Williams, one of the Democratic candidates, was opposed to universal suffrage
... Frederick-Town, 1819.   Handbill. MdHi.   47536

Chalmers, Thomas
    Discourses on the Christian revelation... Mont-
pelier, Vt., E. P. Walton, 1819. 194 p. MB; MWA;
NNUT; NhD; OO; Vt; VtHi; VtU.   47537

-- The evidence and authority of the Christian revelation... Ed. 7.   Montpelier, Vt., E. P. Walton, 1819.
194 p. MB; MBAt; MWA; MH; OO; VtMiM; VtU. 47538

-- Sermons, preached in the Tron church, Glasgow...
New York, Pr. [by J. & J. Harper] ; Repr. by William. A. Mercein, for Kirk & Mercein, 1819. MWA.
                                                    47539
Chambers, A. H.
    Thoughts on the resumption of cash payments by
the bank.   1819.   MH-BA.   47540

Chambers, John
    A general history of Worcester.   Worcester, 1819.
ICT; OHi.   47541

Chandler, Jehu
    Memorial of Jehu Chandler, late printer to the
state, to the General assembly of Maryland, on the
subject of his claims for services in the years 1812,
'13, '14, '15 and '16, with proofs and documents.
[Annapolis? Pr. by Jehu Chandler?] 1819.   26 p.
MdHi.   47542

Channing, Edward Tyrrell
    Inaugural discourse, delivered in the Chapel of the
University in Cambridge, December 8, 1819... Cambridge, Pr. by Hilliard and Metcalf, for Cummings &

Hilliard, Boston, 1819. 31 p. MBC; MWA.   47543

Channing, William Ellery, 1780-1842
    A discourse on some of the distinguishing opinions
of Unitarians. Delivered at Baltimore in 1819. Ed.
14. Boston, Crosby, Nichols and Co., for the American Unitarian association, 1819. 47 p. ICMe; MH-AH;
OO; PPPrHi; RHi.   47544

-- An examination of passages of Scripture supposed
to prove the deity of Jesus Christ. Boston [1819?]
BrMus. Cat. 10. Chad: 192.   47545

-- A letter to Professor Stuart, in answer to his let-
ters to Rev. William E. Channing... Boston, Pr. by
Sylvester T. Goss, 1819. 22 p. ICMe; MHi; MiD-B;
NjR.   47546

-- Note for the second Baltimore edition, of the Rev.
Mr. Channing's sermon, delivered at the ordination of
the Rev. Jared Sparks. Together with a table of er-
rata, in the Baltimore and Boston editions of that publication. Boston, Repr. by Hews & Goss, 1819. 8 p.
CSmH; ICMe; MB; MBAt; MH; MNe; MWA.   47547

-- Objections to Unitarian Christianity considered.
[Boston, 1819] 18 p. MH-AH.   47548

-- Remarks on the character and writings of John Milton; occasioned by the publication of his lately discovered treatise on Christian doctrine. Boston, Pr.
by B. Perkins, 1819. 116 p. MMeT.   47549

-- A sermon delivered at the ordination of the Rev.
Jared Sparks, to the pastoral care of the first inde-
pendent church in Baltimore, May 5, 1819... Baltimore,
Pr. by Benjamin Edes, 1819. 63 p. MH; MWA; MdBP;
NIC; NjR.   47550

-- -- Ed. 2. Baltimore, Pr. by Benj. Edes, 1819. 71 p.
CBPac; CSt; ICMe; MB; MH; MdHi; NjPT; RHi.   47551

-- -- Ed. 2. Baltimore, Pr. by J. Robinson, 1819.

72 p. CSt; MBAU; MWA; MdBE; MdHi. 47552

-- A sermon delivered at the ordination of the Rev.
Jared Sparks...Boston, Repr. by Hews & Goss, 1819.
32 p. ICU; IEN; M; MBDiL; MH; MMeT-Hi; MNe;
MNF; MWeY; MWA; MiD-B. 47553

-- -- Boston, Repr. by Hews & Goss, 1819. 35 p.
A-Ar; CSt; DLC; MBC; MBeHi; MBr; MH; MHi; MMeT;
MWA; MdHi; MiD-B; NjR; OO. 47554

-- -- Boston, Pr. by Wells and Lilly, 1819. 53 p.
CBPac; CSt; Ct; CtY; IEN; ICP; MA; MH; MWA; MWiW;
MdHi; MeHi; MiD-B; MiU-C; NN; NjR; OClWHi; PHi;
PPL; RNHi. 47555

-- -- Springfield, Mass., Pr. by I. Daniels, 1819.
39 p. CSmH; CtY; MDeeP; MNF; MSHi; MWA; MWiW;
MdBE; NN; RHi. 47556

-- A sermon on war: delivered before the convention
of Congregational ministers of Massachusetts, May 30,
1816. Ed. 3. Boston, 1819. MB. 47557

-- Statement of reasons for not believing the doctrines
of Trinitarians respecting the nature of God and the
person of Christ. Occasioned by Prof. Stuart's letters
to Mr. Channing. Boston, 1819. RHi. 47558

-- Tract No. 85. Sermon on war delivered before the
convention of Congregational ministers of Massachusetts May 30, 1816. (With some abridgment) New
England Tract Society. Andover, Mass., 1819. 54 p.
MDeeP; MSaE; MeBat; RHi. 47559

-- Unitarian Christianity: a discourse on some of the
distinguishing opinions of Unitarians, delivered at Baltimore, May 5, 1819. Boston [1819?] 81 p. VtB.
47560

-- Das Vnitarische christenthum. Eine ordinationsrede
gehalten zu Baltimore 1819, Boston [1819?] 54 p.
IEG; MH-AH. 47561

Chapin, Seth
    Duty and dependence of sinners... Boston, Pr. by
U. Crocker, for Samuel T. Armstrong, 1819. 15 p.
CBPSR; MBAt; MBC; MH; MMeT; MWA; NNG; NjPT;
OO; PPPrHi.   47562

Chapin Stephen
    A series of letters on the mode and subjects of
baptism... Boston, Lincoln & Edmands, [1819] 76 p.
CBPSR; CSmH; CSt; CtSoP; MBAt; MBC; MBD; MH-AH;
MSaE; MWA; NNUT; NRAB; Nh; NjR.   47563

Chaplin, Jeremiah
    A sermon, delivered September 8, 1819, at the
ordination of the Rev. Stephen Chapin... Portland, Me.,
Pr. by Francis Douglas, 1819. 28 p. MA; MB; MH-AH;
MWA; MeHi; NjPT; NjR.   47564

Chapman, Ezekiel Jones
    Critical and explanatory notes, on many passages
in the New Testament, which to common readers are
hard to be understood... Canandaigua [N. Y.] Pr. by
James R. Bemis, 1819. CSfCW; CU; MBAt; MBC;
MMeT; MWA; MiD; N; NN; PPiW.   47565

Chapone, Mrs. Hester (Mulso)
    Letters on the improvement of the mind, addressed
to a young lady... Hagers-Town, Md., Pr. by William
D. Bell for Gabriel Nourse, 1819. 2 v. DLC; MH;
MWA; NcD; ViU.   47566

Chaptal [de Chauteloup, Jean Antoine Claude] comte,
1756-1832
    Des douanes et des prohibitions: par M. le comte
Chaptal... Philadelphia, M. Carey and son, 1819. 32 p.
DLC.   47567

Charlotte the vain little girl; and poems for children.
New-Haven, Sidney's press, for J. Babcock & son,
1819. 30 p. CtHi; NPV.   47568

Charleston, S. C., Circular church--Sabbath School no. 1.
    Reports of Sabbath school, no. 1... Charleston,

S. C., 1819. 14 p. MWA; N.   47569

Charlestown, Mass.
    Laws of the Commonwealth establishing and defining
the powers of the Charlestown board of health, with the
rules, orders and regulations of said board... Charlestown, Mass., 1819. 20 p. M.   47570

Charles Town, Va.
    To the public. [Charles Town, Va., 1819] Broad-
side. Norona & Shetler, 301.   47571

Charlestown Circulating Library
    Catalogue of the Charlestown circulating library.
Boston, Pr. by True & Weston, 1819. 56 p. MH;
MMeT.   47572

Chautauque Eagle. Mayville, N.Y., R.I. Curtis, May 15,
1819, 1st issue. Weekly newspaper. MWA.   47573

Chaucer, Geoffrey
    Select poems by Geoffrey Chaucer, with a life of
the author by Ezekiel Sanford. Philadelphia, 1819.
(British poets, v. 1) NjPT.   47574

Chazotte, Peter Stephen
    An introductory lecture on the metaphysics and phi-
losophy of languages... Philadelphia, pr. for the author,
1819. MWA; NHi.   47575

Cherry, Andrew
    The soldier's daughter, a comedy in five acts. Ed.
3. New York, D. Longworth, 1819. 82 p. MB; MBr;
MH; MWA; PU.   47576

Cherry-Valley Gazette. Vol. 1. Cherry-Valley, Tuesday Apr. 27, 1819. No. 30. Caption title of the earliest no. in NYPL 1920. NN.   47577

Chesterfield, Philip Dormer Stanhope, 4th earl of
    Principles of politeness... Pittsburgh, Pa., Eich-
baum & Johnston, 1819. MWA.   47578

Child, A. B.
   Better views of living; or, Life according to the
doctrine, of or whatever is right. Boston, Pr. by
Adams & Co., 1819. PPM.   47579

[Child, David Lee] 1794-1874
   An enquiry into the conduct of General Putnam, in
relation to the battle of Bunker, or Breed's Hill; and
remarks upon Mr. S. Swett's sketch of that battle.
Boston, Pr. by T. G. Bangs, 1819. 58 p.   CU; DLC;
M; MB; MH; MHi; MNF; MMal; MWA; MiD-B; MiU-C;
NN; NNP; Nh.   47580

Child, Griffin
   The trial balance of creeds and systems of faith...
Providence, Pr. at the Patriot office [J. Jones & Co.]
1819.   MWA.   47581

Children's hymn book: being a selection of hymns from
various authors... Newark, N. J., William Tuttle, 1819.
35 p.   MWA.   47582

The child's instructor.   Salem, N. Y., Dodd & Stevenson, 1819. 131 p. NNC-T.   47583

The Chillicothe almanac, 1820.   Chillicothe, O., Geo.
Nashee [1819] 48 p. OClWHi; OHi.   47584

Chillicothe.   Weekly Recorder.
   The carrier's address to the patrons of the Weekly
Recorder, Jan. 1st, 1820. [Chillicothe, 1819] Broad-
side.   OClWHi.   47585

Chittenden County Agricultural Society
   Cattle show at Burlington, on Tuesday and Wednesday, the 28th and 29th of September, 1819, to com-
mence at 10 o'clock, A. M. on each day... Sandford
Gadcomb, Sec. [1819] Broadside. VtHi.   47586

Chitty, Joseph, 1776-1841
   A practical treatise on bills of exchange, checks on
bankers, promissory notes, bankers' cash notes, and
bank notes... A new ed., from the last London ed.

Brookfield, Mass., Pr. by E. Merriam and Co., 1819.
477 p.   Ct; MH-L; MWA; NIC-M; WaU.   47587

-- A practical treatise on the criminal law...v. 1-3.
Philadelphia, Pr. by William Brown, for Edward Earle,
1819. IaU-L; MWA; NjR.   47588

-- -- v. 4.   Philadelphia, Pr. by Adam Waldie, for
Edward Earle, 1819. IaU-L; MWA; NjR.   47589

-- -- v. 1.   Philadelphia, Pr. by Clark & Raser, for
Isaac Riley, 1819. Ct; MWA; NIC-L.   47590

-- -- v. 2, part 1-2.   Philadelphia, Pr. by G. L. Austin, for Isaac Riley, 1819. Ct; MWA; NIC-L.   47591

-- A treatise on the parties to actions...v. 1. 3d
Amer. ed.   Philadelphia, I. Riley, 1819. 530 p. In-SC;
MWA; NLitf.   47592

-- A treatise on pleading...v. 2.   3d Amer. ed. Philadelphia, I. Riley, 1819. 611 p. MWA; NLitf.   47593

Choice Emblems, for the improvement and pastime of
youth.   Woodstock, Pr. by David Watson, 1819. 31 p.
McCorison List.   47594

The Christian Disciple and Theological Review. Boston,
Wells & Lilly, 1819-(1821). Vol. 1. NjR; WM; ViRU.
                                                   47595

Christian Disciple Society
     An essay on conversion...Boston, Pr. by Wells &
Lilly, 1819. 20 p. MA; MBC; MWA; NNUT.   47596

-- An essay on the meaning of the phrase, "Holy Spirit." Boston, Pr. by Wells and Lilly, for the Christian
Disciple Society, 1819. MA; MH; MWA; NNUT. 47597

The Christian messenger---edited by Rev. Abner Kneeland...Vol. 1.   Philadelphia, Pr. for the proprietors,
1819-20.   MdBD; NCaS.   47598

Christian Orator.   Ed. 3. Charlestown, S. Etheridge,

1819. MWA.   47599

The Christian Pilgrim, containing an account of the
wonderful adventures and miraculous escapes of a
Christian in his travels from the land of destruction to
the New Jersalem. [sic] Boston, 1819. KyBgW. 47600

Christian resignation, a sermon delivered at Martins-
burgh, Jan. 10, 1819...Martinsburgh, Va., Pr. by
John Alburtis, 1819. 22 p. NjPT.   47601

Christian Spectator. New Haven, Howe & Spalding,
Jan., 1819, 1st issue. Monthly periodical. Ct; CtHi;
DLC; NNG; OWoC.   47602

Christian Watchman. Boston, True & Weston, May 29,
1819, 1st issue. Weekly newspaper. MBC; MWA. 47603

The Christian world unmasked; or, An inquiry into the
foundation of Methodist camp meetings, with a plan for
their correction and improvement...Watertown, N. Y.,
Pr. for the author, 1819. 72 p. MWA; NjR.   47604

Christianity and infidelity contrasted. Philadelphia, Pr.
[by J. R. A. Skerrett] for Benjamin & Thomas Kite...
1819. MWA.   47605

The Christian's daily companion...Georgetown, D. C.,
Pr. by Clark & Raser, for Elijah Weems, and Gabriel
Nourse, Sharpsburg, Md., 1819. 292 p. MWA; MdHi;
PLT; RNR.   47606

Christmas, Joseph Stibbs
    The artist...Washington, Pa., Pr. by John Gray-
son, 1819. MWA.   47607

Church, John Hubbard
    The reign of Messiah...Concord, N. H., Pr. by
George Hough, 1819. 32 p. DLC; MBC; MWA.   47608

Church, Rodney J.
    Oration at Clermont, July 5. Hudson, N. Y., 1819.
MBAt.   47609

Church catechism broke into short questions. 2d Amer.
ed. improved. Hartford, Pr. by G. Goodwin & sons,
1819. 24 p. CtHi. 47610

Churchill, Charles
Select poems. Philadelphia, 1819. NjPT. 47611

Churchill, Juvenal
Magazine of wonders addressed to the people of
the state of New York. No. 1. New York, the author,
1819. 11 p. MB. 47612

No entry. 47613

The Cincinnati almanac: No. 1:...for the year of our
Lord 1820...By Samuel Burr, philo. [Cincinnati, O.]
Mason & Palmer [1819] 53 p. DLC; ICN; MWA; OC.
47614

Cincinnati. Christ Church.
The constitution, and rules of the Sunday School Society of Christ Church. Cincinnati, O., Pr. at the office of the Inquisitor, 1819. 7 p. CSmH. 47615

The Cincinnati directory, containing the names, profession and occupation of the inhabitants of the town, alphabetically arranged; with the number of the building occu-
pied by each...[Cincinnati] Pr. by Morgan, Lodge &
Co., for Oliver Farnsworth, 1819. 155 p. CSmH; DLC;
MHi; MWA; NN; OC; OClWHi; OCHP; WHi. 47616

Cincinnati. House carpenters and joiners.
The book of prices...adopted, Monday, Jan. 4,
1819. Cincinnati, Pr. by Mason and Palmer, 1819.
32 p. OCU. 47617

-- Inquisitor and Cincinnati Advertiser.
A New-Years Lay, for 1820...[Cincinnati, 1819]
11 p. OClWHi. 47618

Cincinnati Miami Bible Society.
Fifth annual report...Cincinnati, Pr. for the Soci-

ety by Mason and Palmer, 1819. 24 p. OCHP; PPP.

47619

Cincinnati University
Laws and regulations of the Cincinnati college.
Cincinnati, O., Pr. by Cooke, Powers, and Penney,
1819. MWA. 47620

Citizen and farmer's almanac for 1820. By David
Young. Morris-Town, N.J., Jacob Mann [1819] [36] p.
DLC; MWA; NjHi; NjMo; NjR. 47621

Claiborne, Nathaniel Herbert
Notes on the war in the South...Richmond, Va.,
William Ramsay, 1819. 112 p. CU; CSmH; CtSoP; CtY;
DeWI; DLC; FStP; GHi; GU-De; IC; ICN; IU; IaU; InHi;
KyU; LNH; MB; MWA; MWiW; MdHi; MiD; MnHi;
MoSH; MsJS; O; OC; OClWHi; OMC; P; PHi; PPL-R;
T; TKL; TNP; TxU; Vi; ViL; ViHi; ViU. 47622

Clark, Aaron
List of all the incorporations in the state of New-
York, except religious incorporations...Albany, Pr. by
Jesse Buel, printer to the state, 1819. 106 p. NN;
NNS. 47623

-- An oration. A project for the civilization of the
Indians of North America. Delivered before the P.B.
Ph. Society, Schenectady, July 22, 1816...Albany, Pr.
by Packard & Van Benthuysen, 1819. 24 p. DLC; NN.

47624

Clark, John, 1766-1832
Considerations on the Purity of the Principles of
William H. Crawford, Esq., deducible from his conduct
in connexion with that of Charles Tait, Esq., towards
the author of this publication. Augusta, Ga., Pr. at
the Georgia Advertiser Office, 1819. 208 p. GU-De.

47625

Clark, Orin, 1788-1828
Address, delivered in Trinity church, Geneva...
Geneva, N.Y., Pr. at the office of the Geneva Gazette,
1819. 12 p. CSmH. 47626

Clark, Victorianus
　　Rhyming geography; or, a poetic description of the
United States of America...Hartford, Peter B. Glea-
son & co., 1819. 167 p.　CSmH; CtHT-W; CtHi; CtY;
MWA; OClWHi; RPB.　　　　　　　　　　　47627

Clarke, Adam
　　Dissertation on the use and abuse of tobacco.
Wherein the advantages and disadvantages attending the
consumption of that entertaining weed are particularly
considered...New-York, Pr. by C. S. Van Winkle,
1819.　24 p.　CtHi; DLC; NHi; NNG; NNS.　　47628

-- The doctrine of salvation by faith proved...New
York, Pr. by J. C. Totten, for J. Soule and T. Mason
...1819.　32 p.　MWA; NNMHi; NjR.　　　　　47629

-- -- Salem, N. J., Pr. by Elijah Brooks, 1819. 35 p.
NjR.　　　　　　　　　　　　　　　　　　47630

-- -- Urbana, O., Pr. by Allen M. Poff, 1819.　45 p.
MWA; OCHP; OClWHi.　　　　　　　　　　　47631

-- A letter to a Methodist preacher, on his entrance
into the work of the ministry...Nashville, Tenn., Pr.
by G. Wilson, 1819.　36 p.　T.　　　　　　　47632

-- Memoirs of the late Mrs. Mary Cooper...Boston,
Wells and Lilly, 1819.　276 p.　MNan; MWA; ScNC.
　　　　　　　　　　　　　　　　　　　47633

Clarke, Matthew St. Claire and D. A. Hall
　　Constitutional law.　Washington, D. C., Gales and
Seaton, 1819.　360 p.　NcG.　　　　　　　　47634

Clarke, Samuel
　　A Masonic address, delivered before a convention
of five lodges, Morning Star, Olive Branch, Fredonia,
Charity, and King Solomon's.　Assembled at Grafton,
June 24, A. L. 5819.　Worcester, Mass., Wm. Man-
ning, 1819.　18 p.　DLC; ICMe; IaCrM; MBFM; MH;
MWA; PMA.　　　　　　　　　　　　　　47635

Clarksville Gazette.　Clarksville, Tenn., John Fitz-

gerald, May, 1819, 1st issue. Weekly newspaper.
DLC. 47636

Clavis universalis...Ephrata, Pa., Pr. by Joseph
Bauman, 1819. 224 p. MWA. 47637

Clay, Henry, 1777-1852
Speech of the Hon. Henry Clay, in the House of
representatives of U.S. on the Seminole war. [Washington, D.C., 1819] 30 p. CtY; DLC; KyRE; MH; MHi;
MWA. 47638

Clayton, Augustin Smith
The office and duty of a justice of the peace...
Milledgeville, Ga., S. Grantland, 1819. 463 p. GU-De;
MWA. 47639

Clear and concise statement of New York and surrounding country; containing a faithful account of many of
those base impositions...constantly and uniformly practised upon...emigrants...New York, John Wilson,
1819. 32 p. ICU; NN; NSyHi. 47640

Cleaveland Herald. Cleaveland, Ohio, Z. Willis & Co.,
Oct. 19, 1819, 1st issue. Weekly newspaper. DLC;
OClWHi. 47641

No. XII. The clergyman's almanack...1820...Boston,
Pr. by Parmenter & Balch, for Lincoln & Edmands,
[1819] [48] p. MWA; MeHi; NjR; RPB. 47642

Clergyman's minor almanack for 1820. Boston, Lincoln & Edmands, [1819] MWA. 47643

The clerk and magistrate's assistant...Poughkeepsie,
N.Y., Paraclete Potter and S. Potter, & Co., Philadelphia, 1819. MWA. 47644

Clifton, Arthur
An original collection of psalm tunes, extracted
from the most beautiful works, (chiefly sacred) of the
most celebrated ancient and modern composers...Baltimore [1819] 87 p. CtY. 47645

Clinton, C. A.
    Oration, delivered on the 43d anniversary of Amer-
ican independence. By appointment of the Albany Military Association. Albany, Cales, 1819. 16 p. MB.
                                                    47646

Clinton, DeWitt
    The Martling-man; or Says I to myself how is this?
From the New-York Columbian of March, 1819. New-
York, 1819. 23 p. MBat; MH; N.   47647

[Clopper, Jonas]
    Fragments of the history of Bawlfredonia: contain-
ing an account of the discovery and settlement of the
great southern continent, and of the formation and
progress of the Bawlfredonian commonwealth. By
Herman Thwackius [pseud.]...[Baltimore?] Pr. for the
American booksellers, 1819. 164 p. CtY; DeGE; DLC;
MH; MWA; MdHi; NjR.   47648

Cobb, Thomas W.
    Debate, in the House of Representatives of the U-
nited States, on the Seminole war. (Speech of Mr.
Cobb) [Washington, D.C., 1819] 12 p. MB.   47649

Cobbett, William
    The American gardener; or, A treatise on the sit-
uation, soil, fencing and laying-out of gardens; on the
making and managing of hot-beds and green-houses;
and on the propagation and cultivation of... vegetables,
herbs, fruits and flowers. By William Cobbett. Claremont, N.H., Manufacturing Co., Simeon Ide [1819]
230 p. KyLxT; NbU; NjP; NjR.   47650

-- List of field seeds and garden seeds...[New York]
Pr. by Clayton & Kingsland, 1819. MWA.   47651

-- A year's residence in the United States of America
...Parts II-III. New York, Pr. by Clayton and Kings-
land, sold at No. 53 Vesey-street, 1819. 432 p. DLC;
MWA; NjR; OCHP; OClWHi.   47652

Cochranism delineated; or, A description of, and specific for a religious hydrophobia, which was spread,

and is still spreading in a number of towns in the
counties of York and Cumberland, District of Maine...
Boston, Pr. by Hews & Goss, 1819. 16 p. DLC; MBr;
MWA.   47653

[Cocke, John] 1772-1854
    Letter to the Honorable John H. Eaton, Dec. 16,
1818. Knoxville, Tenn., Pr. by Heiskell & Brown,
1819. 16 p. DLC; MB; MWA; Nh; T.   47654

-- To the Hon. John H. Eaton, June 26, 1819. Knoxville, Tenn., Pr. by Heiskell & Brown, 1819. 31 p.
MB; T.   47655

Cogswell, Jonathan, 1782-1864
    A sermon delivered in Augusta, June 23, 1819; be-
for the Maine missionary society, at their twelfth anniversary...Hallowell, Me., Pr. by E. Goodale, 1819.
40 p. DLC; MWA; MeHi; NN.   47656

-- The support of the gospel, an important duty...
Kennebunk, Me., Pr. by James Remich, 1819. 20 p.
MBC; MWA; MeB; MeHi.   47657

Cogswell, William
    Nature and evidence of the inspiration of the Sacred
Scriptures. A sermon before Adoniram R.A. Chapter,
Montgomery, Constellation, Rising Star and St. Alban's
Lodges. At Walpole, June 24, A.L. 5819...Dedham,
Mass., H. & W.H. Mann [1819] 34 p. CtY; MBAt;
MBFM; MWA; MWiW.   47658

Colby, John
    The life, experience, and travels of John Colby...
Vol. II...Andover, N.H., Pr. by Ebenezer Chase,
1819. 66 p. MH; MWA.   47659

Colden, Cadwallader David, 1769-1834
    A vindication by Cadwallader D. Colden, of the
steamboat right granted by the state of New-York [to
Livingston and Fulton] in the form of an answer to the
letter of Mr. Duer, addressed to Mr. Colden. New-
York, Pr. by W.A. Mercein, 1819. 96 p. DLC; MWA;

MoK.   47660

Coleman, Eliphalet Beecher
    The Sabbath school catechism...Ed. 5.   New
Haven, Pr. at the office of the Religious Intelligencer,
1819. 48 p. CSmH; ICP; PPiW.   47661

-- The Sunday-School Catechism, containing questions
on the historical part of the New Testament...In three
numbers. (No. II) Ed. 2.   Middlebury, Vt., Francis
Burnap, 1819. 48 p. VtU-W.   47662

-- -- In three numbers. Ed. 3.   New Haven, Pr. at
the office of the Religious Intelligencer, 1819. 48 p.
CtHi; MShr; MWA; NIC; PPiW.   47663

-- -- Ed. 6.   New-Haven, Pr. at the office of the Religious Intelligencer, 1819. 48 p. (In three numbers -
No. I.)   CtHi; CtSoP; NN; OO.   47664

A collection of hymns for the use of the Protestant
Church of the United Brethren.   New and revised ed.
Philadelphia, Pr. by Conrad Zentler, 1819. 400 p.
MWA.   47665

Collier, William
    The minister's hope; and its influence on his
preaching and character.   A sermon delivered in Lyme,
Connecticut, at the ordination of Brother George W.
Appleton...Boston, Pr. by Hewes & Goss, 1819. 24 p.
CSt; CtSoP; DLC; M; MB; MBAt; MBAU; MBC; MBDiL;
MH-AH; MWA; MiD-B; NN; NRAB; NjR; OClWHi; PPM;
RPB.   47666

Colman, Benjamin
    Sermon before General Court.   Boston, 1819.
CtHT.   47667

Columbia Review.   Columbia, Tenn., J. Walker and A.
C. Hays, 1819, 1st issue. Newspaper. T.   47668

Columbian.   Columbia, Pa., William Greer, July 24,
1819, 1st issue. Weekly newspaper. Lancaster County

Historical Society.   47669

-- Kittanning, Pa., F. Rohrer, 1819. Newspaper.
Brigham, p. 864.   47670

Columbian Advocate. Germantown, Pa., C. Tietjen &
Co., July 23, 1819, 1st issue. Weekly newspaper.
MWA.   47671

The Columbian calendar, or New-York and Vermont al-
manack, for...1820...Troy, N.Y., Pr. by Francis
Adancourt...[1819] 36 p. MWA; NHi; NN; NT; PPL-R.
                                                   47672
-- By Andrew Beers...Troy, N.Y., Pr. by Francis
Adancourt, for Tracy & Bliss [1819] 36 p. MWA.
                                                   47673
-- Troy, N.Y., Pr. by Francis Adancourt, for William
S. Parker [1819] 36 p. MWA; OClWHi; PPL.   47674

Columbian Herald. Woodbury, N.J., Philip J. Gray &
Co., Sept. 23, 1819, 1st issue. Weekly newspaper.
Camden County Historical Society, Camden, N.J. 47675

Columbian Telescope. Alexandria, Va., Samuel H.
Davis, June 16, 1819, 1st issue. Weekly newspaper.
DLC; PHi.   47676

Columbian spelling book. Providence, Miller & Hutchens, 1819. MWA.   47677

Columbus. Ohio Monitor
    The carrier of the Monitor, to his patrons...[Co-
lumbus, O., 1819] Broadside. Ernest J. Wessen,
Mansfield, Ohio.   47678

Colvin, John B.
    The magistrate's guide...Ed. 2. Georgetown,
D.C., Pr. by E. de Krafft, for Elijah Weems... 1819.
479 p. MWA; MdBP; MdU.   47679

Comly, John
    English grammar, made easy to the teacher and
pupil, originally compiled for the use of West-town

Boarding School, Pennsylvania. Ed. 10, rev. and cor.
Philadelphia, Pr. by William Fry, for Kimber and
Sharpless, 1819. 104 p. MWA; NcWsS; PLFM. 47680

-- A new spelling book. Philadelphia, 1819. PSC-Hi.
                                                     47681
Commercial Advertiser. Mobile, Ala., Miller & Fitz-
gerald, 1819. Brigham, p. 6.   47682

The common prayer book or the pious county parish-
ioner. Being directions how a Christian may manage
every day, through the whole course of his life, with
safety and success...2d Amer. ed. Frederick-Town
[Md.] Pr. by Matthias Bartgis, 1819. 194 p. DLC;
MWA; MdBD; MdHi.   47683

Common Prayer Book Society of Pennsylvania.
     The first annual report of the managers of the Com-
mon prayer book society of Pennsylvania. Philadelphia,
Pr. by William Fry, 1819. 16 p. MBD.   47684

Communication made to the Committee appointed to inspect the books and accounts of the Miami University.
[Hamilton, O., 1819] 5 p. MiU; NN; OClWHi.   47685

A compendious account of the late war, to which is
added, The curious adventures of Corporal Samuel
Stubbs...Boston, Pr. by W. Walter, 1819. RPB. 47686

Comyn, Samuel
     A treatise of the law relative to contracts...Brook-
field, Mass., Pr. by E. Merriam & Co., for Elisha
Hammond, 1819. 2 v. MWA; MiD-B; NcWfC.   47687

-- -- 2d Amer. ed. New York, Gould and Banks and
William Gould, 1819. 2 v. Ct; MWA; PLL.   47688

Concise narrative of the Seminole campaign. By an of-
ficer, attached to the expedition. Nashville, Tenn.,
Pr. by M'Lean & Tunstall, 1819. 41 p. CtHT-W;
CtSoP; DLC; MB; MBAt.   47689

A concise sketch of the execution of J. Williams. Boston, 1819. MB.   47690

Concord Observer. Concord, N. H., George Hough,
Jan. 4, 1819, 1st issue. Weekly newspaper. DLC;
NhD.   47691

Condy, Thomas D.
    An oration, delivered, in St. Philip's Church, be-
fore an assemblage of the inhabitants of Charleston,
South-Carolina, on the 5th day of July, 1819...Charles-
ton, S. C., Pr. by A. E. Miller, 1819. 21 p. DLC;
MiD-B; PPL-R; ScU.   47692

No entry.   47693

Congregational Churches in Connecticut. General Asso-
ciation.
    Proceedings, June, 1819. Hartford, Peter B.
Gleason & Co., 1819. 20 p. MWA; MWiW; NcMHi.
                                              47694
Congregational Churches in Massachusetts. General As-
sociation.
    Extracts from the minutes of the General associa-
tion and Domestic missionary society of Massachusetts
proper, assembled at Pittsfield, June 22, 1819.
Charlestown, Mass., Pr. by S. Etheridge, for the
General association, 1819. 34 p. CSt; GDC; MHi;
MiD-B; NjPT.   47695

Congregational Churches in New Hampshire. General
Association.
    Extracts from the minutes of the General associa-
tion of New Hampshire, convened at Haverhill, September 21, 1819. Concord, N. H., Pr. by George Hough,
for the General association, 1819. 23 p. MMonsA;
MWA.   47696

Congregational Churches in Vermont. General Convention of Congregational and Presbyterian Ministers.
    Extracts from the Minutes of the General Conven-

tion of Congregational and Presbyterian Ministers in Vermont, at their session at Burlington, September, 1819. Middlebury, Vt., Pr. by Francis Burnap, 1819. 16 p. DLC; MWA; NN.   47697

Connecticut (State)
    New index to the Statutes Book I. Hartford, 1819. [13] p. MH-L.   47698

-- The public statute laws of the state of Connecticut. Book II. Commencing October session, 1808. Hartford, Pr. by Hudson and co. [1819] 379 p. CtMMHi; CtSoP; CtY-L; DLC; Ia; Nb; OCLaw.   47699

-- Report of the committee on the subject of taxation. [New Haven] Flagg and Gray [1819] 8 p. CtHi. 47700

-- Reports, May and Oct. 1818, and May, 1819; Two reports of the joint committee of the General Assembly, May, 1819... together with the explanations and exhibits of the Commissioner of the school fund, made on Friday the 4th of June. New-Haven, Osborn and Baldwin, 1819. 40 p. Ct; CtHC; DLC; MB; MdBJ; PPAmP; PPL.   47701

-- ...A sketch of a bill providing for the assessment and collection of taxes in this state, together with an explanation of the principles on which the bill is founded... [Hartford, 1819] 46 p. CtY.   47702

-- State ticket, 1819. Hartford, G. Goodwin & Sons, [1819] MWA.   47703

-- To the Senate and House of Representatives of the state of Connecticut... [Hartford, Pr. by E. Babcock & Son, 1819] MWA.   47704

The Connecticut almanac, for the year 1820... New-Haven, Sidney's press, for John Babcock and son [1819] [22] p. CtY; MWA; NjR.   47705

Connecticut Asylum for the Education and instruction of Deaf and Dumb Persons.
    Third report...May 15, 1819. Hartford, Pr. by Hudson and Co., 1819. 19 p. CSmH; Ct; DLC; KHi; NN.   47706

Connecticut Bible society.
    Report of the Directing committee...May 5, 1819. Hartford, Pr. by Hudson & Co., 1819. MWA; MWiW.
                                                   47707
-- Tenth report of the Connecticut Bible Society. Hartford, Pr. by Hudson & Co., 1819. 13 p. MBC.
                                                   47708
Connecticut medical society.
    Proceedings of the president and fellows of the... at their annual convention, in October, A.D. 1819... together with the incorporating acts, and the by-laws of the society. New-Haven, Pr. by S. Converse, 1819. 15 p. CtHi.   47709

The Connecticut Register and United States Calendar for 1820. By Nathan Daboll. New London, Conn., Samuel Green, 1819. [176] p. CtHi; MWA; RNHi. 47710

Connecticut Reserve Bible Society.
    Fifth annual report...presented May 5, 1819. Warren [Ohio] Pr. by Hapgood & Andrews, 1819. 16 p. CSmH; MBC.   47711

Connecticut river steam-boat company.
    Copy of a petition about to be presented to the legislature of Connecticut...[Hartford, 1819] 7 p. CSmH; MWA.   47712

Connecticut society auxiliary to the Baptist board of foreign missions.
    The fourth report...Hartford, Pr. by F.D. Bolles & Co., 1819. MWA.   47713

Considerations in favour of the appointment of Rufus King...[1819] MWA.   47714

Constitution of the Society in Roxbury, Brookline and

Brighton, for apprehending horse thieves. Boston, Pr.
by Sewell Phelps, 1819. 12 p. MBNEH.   47715

Constitutional law: comprising the Declaration of independence; the Articles of confederation; the Constitution of the United States; and the constitutions of the
several states...Washington City, Gales and Seaton,
1819. 360 p. CoCsc; CtSoP; CtY; DGU; DLC; MA;
NIC; NNLI; PPL-R; PPTU.   47716

The controversy, originating from the publication of
an article entitled, "Sunday Police." Ballston-Spa,
N. Y., Pr. by U. F. Doubleday, 1819. 35 p. DLC;
MWA.   47717

Convention of delegates of the several moral societies,
in the state of New-York, Albany, 1819.
        Transactions...13th January, 1819...Albany, Pr.
by E. and E. Hosford, 1819. MWA.   47718

Conversation in a boat between two seamen. Ed. 2.
Andover, Mass., Pr. by Flagg & Gould, 1819. 24 p.
MMeT.   47719

Converse, James, 1772-1839
        A sermon, delivered on the day of general election,
at Montpelier, October 14, 1819. Before the honourable Legislature of Vermont...Montpelier, Vt., Pr. by
E. P. Walton, 1819. 27 p. CSmH; CtHT; DLC; MBC;
MWA; MiD-B; NjPT; OCHP; Vt; VtMiM; VtU-W. 47720

Conway, James H.
        The North Carolina Calculator; or, new practical
arithmetic...Salisbury, N. C., Pr. by J. Krider, 1819.
238 p. NcU.   47721

Cook, Thomas
        The new universal letter writer. Containing let-
ters on duty, amusement, love, courtship, marriage...
and other useful subjects...Baltimore, Pr. by R. J.
Matchett, for John J. Harrod, 1819. 275 p. MH;
MdHi; VtStjf.   47722

Cooke, Increase
The American orator. New Haven, Sidney's press, for J. Babcock & son and S. & W.R. Babcock, 1819. 408 p. CtHT; CtY; DLC; IC; IaHi; KyLxT; MB; MBAt; MH; MScitHi; MWA; MWiW; MeBaT; NCH; PWW; TNP; ViU.   47723

-- To the youth of America, with a view to their general excellence of knowledge, taste and virtue. New Haven, Sidney's press, 1819. 407 p. IHi.   47724

Cooper, Ezekiel
The substance of a funeral discourse, delivered... on Tuesday, the 23d of April, 1816, in St. George's church, Philadelphia; on the death of the Rev. Francis Asbury... Philadelphia, Jonathan Pounder, 1819. 230 p. IEG; MWA; NIC; NNMHi; NjPT; NjR.   47725

Cooper, Thomas, 1759-1840
Appeal to the government and congress of the United States against the depredations committed by American privateers on the commerce of nations at peace with us, by an American citizen. New York, 1819. PPAmP.   47726

-- Tracts on medical jurisprudence... Philadelphia, Pr. by Thomas Town, for James Webster... 1819. 456 p. CoU; In-SC; MB; MWA; Mi; NBMS; NIC-L; NNNAM; OCLaw.   47727

Copia eines Briefs; Welchen ein ungenannter Freund an seinen Freund gesandt hat. Enthaelt eine Wahre Erklaerung von dem Beyfalls - oder His - torischen Glauben, und dem Wahren u. Seligmachende Glauben. Siehe Jacobs Cop. 2, Ephrata: Joseph Bauman, 1819. 35 p. P; PHi; PPG.   47728

Coppinger, Joseph
On the construction of flat roofed buildings, whether of stone, brick, or wood, and the mode of rendering them fire proof. New York, Pr. by C.S. Van Winkle, for the author, 1819. 23 p. DLC; MSaE; NN.   47729

Cordier, Mathurin, 1479-1564
    Corderii colloquia; or, Cordery's colloquies; with
a translation of the first forty...Ed. 4, rev. and cor.
by the author. New York, George Long, 1819. 166 p.
KyLoP; MWA; NNC.   47730

Cornell, Stephen
    The traders ready reckoner...Hudson, N. Y., Pr.
by Ashbel Stoddard, for the author, 1819. 186 p.
CSmH; MWA; OClWHi.   47731

Corner stone of a new church in Boston. Extract from
the Boston Recorder, June 26, 1819. [Boston, 1819?]
Broadside. MH; NN.   47732

The Cottager's wife. A narrative written by a clergyman of the Church of England. Taken, with some
omissions, from the Christian Observer. Ed. 4.
Andover, Mass., Pr. by Flagg & Gould, 1819. 24 p.
MMeT.   47733

Cotterill, Thomas
    Family prayers, composed principally in expres-
sions taken from the Holy Scriptures, and from the established services of the Church of England...1st Amer.
from 2d London ed. New York, Pr. by Thompson &
Farrand, for J. Eastburn and Co., 1819. 286 p. CoGr;
MWA.   47734

Cottin, Mme. Sophie (Ristaud)
    Elizabeth; or, the exiles of Siberia, a tale...Balti-
more, Pr. by J.D. Toy, for F. Lucas, 1819. 151 p.
CtHT-W; DLC; MWA; MdHi.   47735

Cottom's new Virginia almanack, for...1820...by Joseph
Cave...Richmond, Peter Cottom [1819] [32] p. ViU.
                                                    47736
A count and conjecture or two on the number of the
beast...New York, Pr. by William A. Mercein, 1819.
19 p. NjR.   47737

Coventry, Alexander
    Address to the Agricultural Society of the county of

Oneida; delivered at Whitestown, on the 27th day of
Sept. 1818... Utica, N. Y., Pr. by William Williams,
1819. 30 p. CSmH; MBAt; MBHo; NCH; NUt; NUtHi.
47738

Cowper, William, 1731-1800
The task; a poem, in six books... Boston, Pr. by
Thomas Badger, jun., 1819. 232 p. CSt; CtHT-W;
DLC; IU; IaDm; MBBC; MBev; MH; MWA; MeB; NN;
NSchU; NjMo; RPB; ViU; VtMiS; WRac.   47739

Crabb, George
English synonymes explained. 1st Amer., from
the 2d London ed. Boston, C. Ewer, 1819. 1006 p.
CoD; CtHC; DLC; GDC; InCW; MB; MBAt; MBC; MBrid;
MH; MW; MWiW; NDunk; NWM; NhD; NjP; NjPT; NjR;
OClW; OClWHi; OCoSD; P; TSewU; TxShA; ViAl; ViPet.
47740

Crabbe, George
Tales of the hall. Boston, Wells & Lilly, 1819.
2 v. KyLx; MBAt; MBev; MBL; MH; MWA; MeB; NcU;
NcWsS; NjP; PPL-R; ScC; ViAl.   47741

Crafts, William
Eulogium on Keating Lewis Simons, (late commanding the 29th Regt. of South-Carolina militia)... Charleston, S. C., Pr. by A. E. Miller, 1819. 31 p. PHi; ScC.
47742
-- -- Charleston, S. C., Repr. by A. E. Miller, 1819.
31 p. DLC; MBAt; MWA.   47743

[--] The Sea serpent; or, Gloucester hoax. A dra-
matic jeu d'esprit, in three acts... Charleston, S. C.,
A. E. Miller, 1819. 34 p. CtY; MBAt; MWA; MH;
NN; RPB.   47744

Craig, John D.
An introductory lecture to a course on Experiment-
al philosophy, delivered Nov. 5, 1819. Baltimore,
Lucas, 1819. 20 p. MdBE.   47745

Cramer's Deutscher Pittsburger für die Westliche ein-
gerichteter Calendar, 1820. Pittsburgh, Pa., Cramer
und Spear [1819] MWA.   47746

Cramer's magazine almanack for 1820.   By Rev. John
Taylor.   Pittsburgh, Pa., Cramer & Spear [1819]
MWA; PHi.   47747

Cramer's Pittsburgh almanack for 1820.   Calculations
by Rev. John Taylor.   Pittsburgh, Pa., Cramer and
Spear [1819]   MWA; OHi.   47748

Crane, J. C.
    [Spelling book in Tuscarora dialect.   Buffalo, N. Y.,
1819?]   15 p.   MWA.   47749

The cries of London.   Cooperstown, N. Y., H. & E.
Phinney, 1819.   29 p.   MWA.   47750

The crisis.   To the people of Connecticut.   [Hartford,
1819?]   16 p.   Ct; CtY; DLC; MWA; MiD-B; MBAt; NHi.
                                                   47751
Croes, John, bp.
    A charge to the clergy of the Protestant Episcopal
Church, in the state of New-Jersey, delivered in Trin-
ity-Church, at Swedesborough, on Wednesday, Aug. 18,
1819, at the annual convention of the church in said
state.   New Brunswick, N. J., Pr. by William Myer,
1819.   16 p.   MBDiL; MWA; NHi; NNG; NjR; PHi.
                                                   47752
Cross, Jeremy L.
    The true masonic chart, or Hieroglyphic monitor,
containing all the emblems explained in the degrees...
New Haven, Flagg, Gray, 1819.   354 p.   CSmH; Ct;
CtY; IaCrM; MBFM; MH; MiD-B; NIC; NdFM; OCM.
                                                   47753
[Croswell, Harry]
    A sober appeal to the Christian public... New
Haven, Flagg & Gray, and J. Babcock & son, 1819.
23 p.   CSmH; Ct; CtHi; CtY; MMeT; MWA; MiD-B.
                                                   47754
Crowther, Jonathan, 1760-1824
    Portraiture of Methodism, consisting of their be-
lief, and the doctrine which they preach; also a sum-
mary account of the life and travels of the Rev. John
Wesley... Frederick-town, Md., G. Kolb, 1819.   156 p.
IEG; IaDL; IaMrC; MdBAHi; MdBP.   47755

Cruse, P. H.
　　The Red book...Baltimore [1819] DLC.　　　47756

Cummings, Hooper
　　The Christian's Vade-Mecum...Albany, E. & E.
Hosford, 1819. 227 p. CtY; NjPT.　　　　　47757

Cummings, Jacob Abbot, 1773-1820
　　An easy selection of geography...New-York, T. &
J. Swords, 1819. 180 p. N.　　　　　　　47758

-- First lessons in geography and astronomy...Boston,
Cummings & Hilliard, 1819. 82 p. CLSU; MB; MHa;
MWA; MiD-B; NNC.　　　　　　　　　47759

-- The pronouncing spelling book, adapted to Walker's
critical pronouncing dictionary...Boston, Cummings &
Hilliard, 1819. 205 p. DLC; MLow; MWA; MtUrAc.
　　　　　　　　　　　　　　　　　47760
Cummins, Ebenezer Harlow
　　A summary geography of Alabama...Philadelphia,
Pr. by William Brown, 1819. 24 p. LU; MSaE; MWA.
　　　　　　　　　　　　　　　　　47761
Curtis, Samuel
　　A valuable collection of recipes, medical and mis-
cellaneous...Amherst, N.H., Pr. by Elijah Mansur,
1819. 70 p. MBM; MWA; NhD; OC.　　　　47762

Cushing, John
　　An Half Century sermon, delivered at Ashburnham,
Nov. 3, 1818...Ed. 2. Worcester, Mass., Pr. by
William Manning, 1819. 24 p. MSaE; MWA; MWHi;
Nh; Nh-Hi.　　　　　　　　　　　　　47763

-- A sermon, delivered at Ashburnham, April 4th,
1819, at the interment of Miss Rebecca Meriam...
Worcester, Mass., Pr. by William Manning, 1819.
14 p. CSt; MWA; NjR.　　　　　　　　　47764

D
Daboll, Nathan, 1750-1818
　　Daboll's Schoolmaster's assistant: improved and en-

larged...Stereotype ed.   New London, Conn., S.
Green, 1819. 240 p. MnU.   47765

-- Daboll's Schoolmaster's assistant. Being a plain
practical system of arithmetic; adapted to the United
States.   Ed. 3.   Norwich, Conn., R. Hubbard & Mar-
vin, 1819.   240 p. CtHT-W; CtHi; MH; MWA; MB.
                                                   47766
Daggett, Herman
     An inauguration address delivered at the opening of
the Foreign mission school...Elizabeth-Town, N.J.,
Pr. by J. & E. Sanderson, for Edson Hart, agent of
the Foreign mission school, 1819.   8 p. MWA.   47767

-- -- New Haven, Pr. by S. Converse, for Nathan
Whiting, agent of the Foreign mission school, 1819.
8 p.   CSt; CU; CtY; Ct; CtHi; DLC; ICN; MH-AH;
MSaE; MWA; NRAB; NcD; OClWHi; RP; ViU.   47768

Dalzel, Andrew
     ANAΛEKTA 'EΛΛHNIKA MEIZONA sive collectanea
Graeca majora...Editio tertia Americana...Sumptibus
J. A. Cummings et W. Hilliard.   Hilliard et Metcalf
Typographis.   Cantabrigiae, [Cambridge, Mass.] 1819-
20.   2 v.   MWA.   47769

-- -- Editio quarta Americana...sumptibus J. A. Cummings et W. Hilliard.   Hilliard et Metcalf Typographis.
Cambridge, Mass., 1819. MWA.   47770

-- Collectana Graeca minora...6th Amer. ed.   New
York, W. E. Dean, 1819. 299 p. MdBD.   47771

[Damphoux, Edward?]
     Latin prosody; containing the rules of quantity and
the principles of Latin versification.   For the use of
St. Mary's college.   Baltimore, Pr. by J. Robinson,
for F. Lucas, Jr., 1819.   72 p. DGU; MWA; MdBS;
MdW.   47772

Dana, Daniel
     The deity of Christ...Ed. 2.   Newburyport, Mass.,
Pr. by W. & J. Gilman, 1819.   32 p. MNe; MWA;

MeB.   47773

-- -- Ed. 2. Newburyport, Mass., Pr. by W. & J.
Gilman, for Charles Whipple, 1819. MWA.   47774

[--] The Latin tutor... accommodated to Adam's grammar, and Smith's N. H. L. grammar... Boston, Pr. by
Hilliard & Metcalf, on the University press, for Cummings and Hilliard, 1819. 286 p. MH; NNC.   47775

-- A sermon delivered at the installation of the Rev.
Henry Blatchford... Newburyport, Mass., Pr. by Ephraim W. Allen, 1819. 20 p. MWA; MiU-C.   47776

-- A sermon preached December 30, 1819, at the dedication of the house of worship erected for... the First
church in Dedham... Dedham, Mass., Pr. by H. & W.
H. Mann [1819] 16 p. M; MA; MAtt; MB; MBAt; MdHi;
MH-AH; MSaE; MWA; MeHi; NN; PLT.   47777

-- -- Ed. 2. Dedham, Mass., Pr. by H. & W. H.
Mann [1819] 16 p. CSt; ICMe; MBNMHi; MHi; MWA;
MiU-C.   47778

Dana, Edmund
    A description of the bounty lands in the state of
Illinois... Cincinnati, O., Pr. by Looker, Reynolds &
Co., 1819. 108 p. CtY; DLC; MBAt; MWA; NHi;
OClWHi; WHi.   47779

-- Description of the principal roads and routes... of
the United States... Cincinnati, O., Pr. by Looker,
Reynolds & Co., 1819. MWA.   47780

-- Geographical sketches on the western country...
Cincinnati, O., Pr. by Looker, Reynolds & Co., 1819.
312 p. CSmH; CtY; DLC; MBAt; MWA; NBLiHi; NHi;
NN; OClWHi; WHi.   47781

Danforth, Thomas
    Danforth papers. Boston, Massachusetts Historical
Society Collections, 1819. (Vol. 8, series 2, p. 46-
111) MoSM; RPB.   47782

The danger of delay- [Hymn- Prayer of a repenting
sinner] [Ed. 3. Andover, Mass., 1819] 8 p. (In
New England tract soc. Publications, V. 4, no. 80)
CBPac.   47783

Daniel, Samuel
    Select poems, by Samuel Daniel; with a life of the
author by Ezekiel Sanford. Philadelphia, 1819. 2 v.
MH; NjPT.   47784

Daniels, Thomas H.
    Some particulars of the life of Thomas H. Daniels,
alias Daniel H. Thomas, who was apprehended in Newport on the 29th November, on suspicion of being concerned in the robbery and murder of Mr. Jacob Gould,
of Stoneham... Boston, William Chamberlain, 1819.
24 p. DLC; MH-L; MDovC; MWA; MiD-B; RHi. 47785

Darby, William, 1775-1854
    A tour from the city of New-York, to Detroit.
New-York, Kirk & Mercein, for the author, Pr. by E.
Worthington, 1819. 228 p. CSmH; DLC; MWA; MWiW;
MiU-C; MnM; NCanHi; NPStA; NRU; ScU.   47786

D'Arcy, Uriah Derick
    The black vampyr≤; a legend of St. Domingo...
New York, 1819. 72 p. RPB.   47787

Darrow, Pierce
    The artillerist... Hartford, Pr. by Peter B. Glea-
son & Co, 1819. 144 p. CtY; MWA.   47788

Dartmouth College
    Catalogue of the officers and students of Darmouth
College, Hanover, Oct. 1819... Concord, N.H., Pr.
by George Hough [1819] Broadside. MH.   47789

D'Arusmont, Mme. Frances (Wright), 1795-1852
    Altorf, a tragedy, by Frances Wright. Philadel-
phia, M. Carey & son, 1819. 83 p. CtY; MWA; RPB.
                                                         47790
Davenport, James
    To the Rev. J.D.; on his departure from Boston,

by way of a dream... To which is added a postscript to
the Rev. ...A. Croswell. By a female friend. (In
verse) Boston, repr., 1819. BrMus Cat 13 Dant: 215.
                                            47791
Davie, William R.
   An address delivered before the South Carolina Agricultural Society, at their anniversary meeting, held
in Columbia, on the 8th of December, 1818... Columbia,
S.C., Pr. at the Telescope Press, 1819. 29 p. NcD.
                                            47792
Davies, Benjamin
   A new and concise system of book-keeping, accord-
ing to the Italian method of double entry... Ed. 2, with
additions and improvements. Philadelphia, Benjamin
Johnson, 1819. 286 p. MH; MWA; NjR.   47793

Davison, Asa Lee
   An oration, delivered at Alfred [N.Y.] on the 4th
of July, 1816, in commemoration of the independence of
the United States. Auburn [N.Y.] Pr. by Skinner &
Crosby, 1819. 12 p. NAuHi.   47794

Davy, Sir Humphry, bart, 1778-1829
   Elements of agricultural chemistry, in a course of
lectures for the Board of Agriculture...2d Amer. ed.
Hartford, Pr. by Hudson & Co., 1819. 304 p. Ct;
CtY; ICU; IU; MBC; MB-FA; MBHo; MH; MWA; MeU;
Mi; NT; NhPat; NjP; OCU-M; OHi; NRom; NSyHi; OMC;
PPL-R; PHC; RNR; UPB; ViU; WU.   47795

Day, Jeremiah
   An introduction to algebra... New Haven, Pr. by
Flagg & Gray, for Howe & Spalding, 1819. 219 p. CU;
KyLxT; MA; MB; MH; MoU; NNMer; PU; RJPHL; RPB.
                                            47796
[Day, Thomas]
   The forsaken infant; or, entertaining history of
Little Jack. New York, J.C. Totten, 1819. 46 p. CtY;
DLC; MWA; NN; NNS; PP.   47797

Dean, Paul, 1789-1860
   A discourse delivered before the African society,
at their meeting-house, in Boston, Mass. on the aboli-

tion of the slave trade by the government of the United
States of America, July 14, 1819...Boston, Pr. for
Nathaniel Coverly, 1819. 16 p. DLC; ICMe; MB; MBAt;
MHi; NN; OClWHi; WHi.   47798

-- An eulogy, delivered in Boylston Hall, Boston...on
the character of...Thomas Smith Webb...Boston, E.G.
House, 1819. 16 p. DLC; IaCrM; MB; MWA; RHi.
                                                   47799
-- -- Ed. 2. Boston, E.G. House, 1819. 16 p. DLC;
M; MB; MH; MHi; MWA.   47800

[Dearborn, Henry] 1751-1829
    An enquiry into the conduct of General Putnam, in
relation to the battle of Bunker, or Breed's Hill: and
remarks upon Mr. S. Swett's sketch of that battle...
Boston, Pr. by Thomas C. Bangs, 1819. 58 p. MB;
PU; WHi.   47801

Dearborn, Henry Alexander Scammell, 1783-1851
    A memoir on the commerce and navigation of the
Black sea, and the trade and maritime geography of
Turkey and Egypt...Boston, Wells & Lilly, 1819. 2 v.
DLC; FTU; MB; MBL; MBev; MNe; MWA; MWiW; NN;
NNA; NNS; NT; PPA; PPAmP; PPL-R; PU.   47802

[Defoe, Daniel]
    The history of Robinson Crusoe...Woodstock, Vt.,
Pr. by David Watson, 1819. MWA.   47803

-- The life and most surprising adventures of Robinson
Crusoe...A new ed. New York, George Long, 1819.
MWA; NcC.   47804

[--] New Robinson Crusoe: designed for youth...New
Haven, Sidney's press, for J. Babcock & son, 1819.
36 p. CtHi.   47805

Degrand, Peter Paul Francis
    To each member of the Senate and of the House of
Representatives of Massachusetts. Boston, 17 June,
1819. ...Broadside. NN.   47806

-- Tariff on duties, on importations into the United
States.   Compiled...under the direction of H. A. S.
Dearborn.   Boston, 1819. 64 p. MB.   47807

Degrand's Boston weekly report of public sales and of
arrivals.   [Boston] Vol. 1-9.   [1819-28]   MB; MH.
47808
Dehon, Theodore, bp.
   A discourse delivered before the General convention of the Protestant Episcopal church...on the 21st
of May, 1814...Boston, Pr. by E. G. House, for R. P.
& C. Williams, 1819. 36 p.   MB; MBDiL; MHi; MWA;
MdBD; NNG; NcD; Nh; PPL; PPM; RHi; RPB.   47809

Delaware (State)
   Journal of the House of Representatives of the
state of Delaware, Jan. ...1819...Dover, Pr. by J.
Robertson, 1819.   336 p. DLC; DeHi.   47810

-- Journal of the Senate of the state of Delaware...
Jan. ...1819...Dover, Pr. by J. Robertson, 1819.
184 p. DLC; DeHi.   47811

-- Laws of the state of Delaware, passed at a session
of the General Assembly, begun and holden at Dover,
on Tuesday the fifth day of January, in the year of our
Lord 1819...Dover, [Del.]   Pr. by J. Robertson, 1819.
527 p.   DLC; Ia-L; In-SC; MdBB; MiL; MiU-L; Nb; Nj;
O; T; Wa-L; W.   47812

-- A report of the finances of the state of Delaware,
for the year 1818.   [Dover, Pr. by John Robertson,
1819] 93 p. DLC.   47813

Delaware Gazette.   Delhi, N. Y., J. J. Lappon, Nov.
18, 1819, 1st issue.   Weekly newspaper. Cannon Free
Library, Delhi.   47814

Delectus sententiarum et historiarum, ad usum tironum
accommodatus...Bostoniae: Wells et Lilly, 1819. 110 p.
CtHT-W; MWA; NNC; NjR; PPL.   47815

Delectus Sententiarum Graecarum.   2d Amer. ed. Cam-

bridge, J. A. Cummings & W. Hilliard, 1819. MWA.
47816

Dellon, Gabriel, b. ca. 1649
An account of the inquisition at Goa, in India;
translated from the French of M. Dellon...Pittsburgh,
Pa., Pr. by Butler & Lambdin, for R. Patterson and
Lambdin, 1819. 208 p. MA; PPi; RPB.   47817

Democratic Party. Cayuga County, N. Y.
Proceedings of the Cayuga County Republican convention of delegates, held at Lynch's Inn, in Auburn,
January 7, 1819. Auburn, N. Y., Pr. by D. Rumsey,
1819. 8 p. N.   47818

-- New York.
Address, of the Republican members of the Legislature friendly to the administration of the state government, to their constituents. Albany, April 13, 1819.
Levi Adams, Stephen Bates. Broadside. NHi.   47819

-- -- Republican senatorial nominations...[April 9,
1819] 16 p. NjR.   47820

Description of an ancient carved box, in the museum of
the East-India marine society, in Salem. [Salem,
Mass., 1819] 7 p. DLC.   47821

Deutsche Freund. New York, Edward Schaffer, 1819.
Newspaper. Seidensticker, p. 208.   47822

Devotional exercises, chiefly designed for use of families on the Sabbath. By Gentlemen of the clergy on
Piscataqua River. Boston, 1819. 272 p. MBC. 47823

Dewees, William Potts
An essay on the means of lessening pain, and fa-
cilitating certain cases of difficult parturition...Ed. 2.
Philadelphia, Pr. by William Fry, for Thomas Dobson,
1819. 156 p. ICU-R; MH-M; MWA; NNNAM; NRU-M;
PPiAM.   47824

[DeWitt, Simeon]
Considerations on the necessity of establishing an

agricultural college and having more of the children of
wealthy citizens educated for the profession of farming.
Albany, Webster & Skinner, 1819. 42 p. MWA; N;
NIC; NN; NTRPI; NjR.   47825

Dexter, Franklin, 1793-1857
    An oration, delivered July 4, 1819, at the request
of the selectmen of the town of Boston... Boston, Joseph
T. Buckingham [1819] 19 p. CSmH; CSt; CtY; DLC; M;
MB; MBB; MBC; MH; MMal; MWA; NN.   47826

Dialogue on Saturday Evening- No. 102. N. E. Tract
Soc. 1st ed. [Andover, Mass., Flagg & Gould, 1819]
MWA.   47827

Dibdin, Charles
    From childhood's down to noon of youth. Addition-
al air in Lionel and Clarissa; as sung by Mr. Philipps.
Boston, G. Groupher & Co. [1819] MHi.   47828

Dibdin, Thomas John, 1771-1841
    The heart of Mid-Lothian.... Baltimore, 1819. 47
p. NN.   47829

-- The ninth statue; or, The Irishman in Bagdad; a
musical romance... New York, D. Longworth, 1819.
DLC; MH; MWA; RPB; TxU.   47830

Dill, James
    A new conductor generalis: being a summary of the
law relative to the duty and office of the justice of the
peace, sheriff, coroner, constable, juryman, overseer
of the poor... Albany, E. F. Backus, 1819. 482 p.
(Private collection of W. H. Lester, Desha, Ark.)
                                                47831
Dilworth, H. W.
    The complete letter-writer: or, Young secretary's
instructor. Containing a great variety of letters. ...
Baltimore, Pr. by Wm. Warner, 1819. 108 p. DGU;
MdHi.   47832

Dilworth, Thomas
    A new guide to the English tongue... Philadelphia,

John Bioren, 1819.   CtHT-W; MWA.   47833

The directory and stranger's guide, for the city of
Charleston; also, a directory for Charleston Neck, be-
tween Boundary-street and the lines, for the year 1819
...[Charleston, S.C.] Pr. by A.E. Miller, 1819. 154 p.
DLC.   47834

A discourse, delivered before the New Jerusalem
Church, in Boston, on Christmas Day, December 25,
1818.   Boston, Pr. by Parmenter & Balch, for Cummings & Hilliard, 1819.   23 p. DLC; LNH; MMeT;
MNe; MWA; MeHi; NN; NjPT; PHi; PPL.   47835

District of Columbia
      Code of laws for the District of Columbia: pre-
pared under the authority of the Act of Congress of the
29th of April, 1816...Washington, D.C., Pr. by Davis
& Force, 1819.   575 p. CSfLaw; Ct; DLC; IaU-L; In-
SC; M; MB; MdBB; MH-L; NIC-L; OCLaw; RPL; W.
                                                47836
Dixon, Joshua
      Scriptural examinations on the church catechism,
revised by George A. Smith, Ed. 4.   Philadelphia,
H. Hooker [1819?] CtHC.   47837

Doddridge, P.
      The family expositor, abridged; according to the
plan of its author...Hartford, Silas Andrus, 1819.
416 p. NjR; NCoxhi; PLT.   47838

Dodge, Nehemiah
      A description of gospel ministers...Exeter, N.H.,
Josiah Richardson, 1819.   MWA.   47839

Dodsley, Robert
      The toy-shop...Middlebury, Vt., Pr. by Copeland
& Allen, for H. Richardson, 1819. 34 p. MWA; PP;
VtMiS; VtU.   47840

Domestic industry: a poem, in a dialogue between a
farmer and a manufacturer...[Philadelphia? 1819?]
NHi; RPB.   47841

Dow, Daniel
    Ministers of the gospel should take heed... Lei-
cester, Mass., Pr. by Hori Brown, 1819. MWA.
                                              47842

[Drake, Joseph Rodman]
    Poems, by Croaker, Croaker & Co., ... New York,
pub. for the reader, 1819. MWA; RPB.   47843

Drelincourt, Charles
    The Christian's consolations against the fears of
death... Philadelphia, Simon Probasco... 1819. 612 p.
GDC; MWA; PLT.   47844

Drew, Samuel, 1765-1833
    The life of the Rev. Thomas Coke... New York,
Pr. by A. Paul, for J. Soule and T. Mason, 1819.
341 p. GAuY.   47845

-- Scriptural and philosophical arguments, to prove the
divinity of Christ, and the necessity of His atonement.
1st Amer., from 3d London ed. Baltimore, Pr. by
John D. Toy, for J. Kingston, 1819. 48 p. CBPac;
IEG; MdBD; NNG.   47846

[Duer, John]
    Dick Shift, or The state triumvirate. A political
tale in imitation of Swift. New-York, 1819. 31 p. CtY.
                                           47847
[--] Dick Shift; or, The state triumvirate, a political
tale in imitation of Swift... Ed. 2. Sandy-Hill, N.Y.,
Pr. at the office of the Times, 1819. 24 p. CSmH.
                                           47848
[--] The state triumvirate, a political tale: and the
epistles of Brevet Major Puff [pseud.]... New York, Pr.
by J. Seymour, for W.B. Gilley, and the author, 1819.
215 p. NjP.   47849

Duer, William Alexander, 1780-1858
    A reply to Mr. Colden's vindication of the steam-
boat monopoly. With an appendix, containing copies of
the most important documents referred to in the argument... Albany, E. and E. Hosford, 1819. 211 p.
CSmH; CtHC; DLC; MBNEH; MWA.   47850

Dunbar, Elijah
    A sermon, preached at Dublin, on ...Dec. 18,
1817; at the interment of Rev. Edward Sprague...Keene,
N.H., Pr. by John Prentiss, 1819. 19 p. MWA; Nh;
Nh-Hi; NjPT.   47851

Duncan, Andrew
    Observations on the distinguishing symptoms of...
pulmonary consumption...1st Amer. ed.   Philadelphia,
Pr. by W. Brown, for Collins & Croft, 1819. 155 p.
CSt-L; MWA; MdBJ; NBMS; NIC; NNNAM; OCGHM.
                                                   47852

Dunham, Josiah
    Address delivered in publick, at the first quarterly
meeting of the Windsor Union Sunday-school society,
January 1, 1819...Windsor, Vt., Pr. by W. Spooner,
1819. 15 p. MWA; OCHP; VtU.   47853

Dunlap, Andrew
    An oration, delivered at Salem, on Monday, July
5, 1819...Salem, Mass., Pr. by Warwick Palfray,
Jun., 1819. 15 p. CSmH; DLC; MB; MBC; MH; MHi;
MWA; MiD-B; NN.   47854

Dutchess County, N.Y.
    Rules and orders of the Court of Common Pleas
of the County of Dutchess, made and published by the
judges of the said court, January term 1819. Poughkeepsie, P. Potter, 1819. 32 p. MH-L; NP.   47855

Duties payable on goods, wares and merchandise, imported into the United States of America, from and after June 30, 1816, with the letter of instructions, from
the comptroller to the collectors respecting the altera-
tions and additions to the tariff, agreeably to acts of
Congress of April 20, 1818...Ed. 2, improved and enlarged. New-York, Day & Turner, 1819. 60 p. DLC.
                                                   47856

Dutton, Salmon
    An examination of the modern doctrine of future
punishment...Boston, Pr. by Henry Bowen, 1819. 64 p.
DLC; MBC; MMeT; MWA.   47857

Dutton, Warren, 1774-1857
An address delivered to the members of the bar of Suffolk, at their annual meeting, in September, 1819. Boston, Pr. by S. Phelps, 1819. 18 p. CSmH; Ct; DLC; ICLaw; IEN-L; MBS; M; MH-L; MHi; MMeT; MWA; MiD-B; NGH; NIC-L; NN; NjPT. 47858

[Dwight, Edwin Welles]
Memoirs of Henry Obookiah...Elizabethtown, N. J., Pr. by J. & E. Sanderson, for Edson Hart, agent of the Foreign mission school, 1819. MWA. 47859

[--] -- New Haven, Pr. by S. Converse, for Nathan Whiting, agent of the Foreign mission school, 1819. 129 p. CU-B; CtWins; CtY; ICN; MH; MWA; NRAB; NcD; Nh-Hi; OC; OClWHi; OMC; OO; RHi; RP; RRu; ScU; ViU. 47860

[--] -- ...A native of Owhyee. New York, 1819. MB; MSaE. 47861

Dwight, Sereno Edwards
A sermon, delivered at the funeral of Rev. Joshua Huntington...Boston, Pr. by U. Crocker, for Samuel T. Armstrong, 1819. 44 p. CBPSR; DLC; ICN; MB; MBAt; MBC; MDeeP; MH; MHi; MSaE; MW; MWA; MdBE; MeB; MiD-B; Nh-Hi; NjPT; NjR; OO; PHi. 47862

Dwight, Timothy, comp.
Hymns selected from Dr. Watts, Dr. Doddridge, and various other writers. According to the recommendations of the joint committee of the General Association of Connecticut, and the General Assembly of the Presbyterian Church in America...Hartford, Geo. Goodwin and Sons, 1819. [303]-573 p. CtHi. (Bound with Isaac Watts' Psalms of David imitated in the language of the New Testament) 47863

Dyer, Joseph
A compendious narrative, elucidating the character, disposition and conduct of Mary Dyer, from the time of her marriage, in 1799, till she left the society called Shakers, in 1815...Concord [N. H.] Pr. by Isaac Hill,

for the author, 1819. 88 p. CtHT-W; DLC; MB; MBAU;
MH; MWA; MWiW; Nh; Nh-Hi; OClWHi.   47864

Dyer, Samuel
    A new selection of sacred music, consisting of
nearly two hundred and fifty approved psalm and hymn
tunes...Ed. 2, improved and enlarged.   Baltimore,
Pr. by J. Robinson, for Joseph Robinson and the author [1819?] xx p. 244 numbers. MWA.   47865

                         E
Early instruction recommended in a narrative of the
life of Catherine Haldane; with an address to parents on
the importance of religion.   New-Haven, Sidney's press,
for J. Babcock & son, 1819. 36 p. CtHi; MWA. 47866

East, T.
    The memoirs of the late Emma Humphries, with a
series of letters to young ladies, on the influence of
religion; and to parents, on the religious education and
the bereavement of their children.   Boston, S. T. Armstrong, 1819. 236 p.   MB; MBC; MNan; MSwe; MWA;
OAsht; PRea; WBeloC.   47867

East-Tennessee Patriot.   Jonesborough, Tenn., J.
Howard, Nov. 23, 1819, 1st issue. Weekly newspaper.
NHi.   47868

Eastburn, James & Co., firm, booksellers, N. Y.
    Supplement to a catalogue of books for 1818; in-
cluding many rare and valuable articles in ancient and
modern literature now on sale by James Eastburn &
co. ...New-York, Pr. by Abraham Paul, March, 1819.
285 p.   MWA; N; NjPT.   47869

Eaton, Amos
    Botanical dictionary.   Ed. 2. New Haven, Pr. by
Clark & Lyman, for Howe & Spalding, Middletown, 1819.
MWA.   47870

Eaton, Peter, 1765-1848
    A sermon, delivered before His Excellency John

Brooks, esq., governor; His Honor William Phillips, esq., lieutenant governor; the Honorable council; and the two houses composing the legislature of Massachusetts, on the anniversary election, May 26, 1819... [Boston] Pr. by Russell and Gardner, for Benjamin Russell, 1819. 25 p. CBPac; CSmH; CSt; Ct; CtHC; CtSoP; DLC; ICT; M; MA; MBC; MBNMHi; MBr; MH; MHi; MMeT; MSaE; MW; MWA; MeHi; MiD-B; MnHi; NN; NjR; OClWHi; RPB.   47871

-- A sermon, preached at the installation of the Rev. Humphrey C. Perley...Salem, Mass., Pr. by Warwick Palfray, Jun., 1819. 14 p. MH-AH; MSaE; MWA.
47872

Eddy, Samuel, 1769-1839
    Reasons offered by Samuel Eddy, esq., for his opinions...Ed. 3. [Providence] Jones & Wheeler, 1819. 16 p. CtHi; MWA.   47873

-- Reasons offered for his opinions, to the First Baptist Church in Providence, from which he was compelled to withdraw for heterodoxy. With the Review of reasons offered. Ed. 4. Baltimore, Pr. by J. Robinson, 1819. 36 p. MBAU; MH; MdHi.   47874

Eddy, Thomas
    Memoir of the late John Murray, Jun. New York, Pr. by E. Conrad, 1819. 17 p. MWA; NHi; NNNAM.
47875

Edgeworth, Maria
    Birth day present...Boston, Wells and Lilly, 1819. MWA.   47876

-- Little merchants...Boston, Wells and Lilly, 1819. MWA.   47877

-- Moral tales for young people. New York, Pr. by W. B. Gilley, 1819. 3 v.   47878

-- Popular tales...v. 1. 3d Amer. ed. Philadelphia, Collins & Croft, 1819. 295 p. MWA; NjR.   47879

-- The white pigeon by Miss Edgeworth. Boston,

Wells & Lilly, 1819. 20 p. MH.   47880

Edwards,
A poem on the mineral waters of Ballston and
Saratoga. With notes. [By Mr. ... Edwards] New
York, 1819.   Sabin 63089.   47881

Edwards, Jonathan, 1703-1758
Account of Abigail Hutchinson, a young woman
hopefully converted at Northampton, Mass. 1734. ...
Andover, Mass., Pr. by Flagg and Gould, for the New
England Tract Society, 1819. 8 p. CtHi; CBPac;
MNF; MWA.   47882

-- Thoughts on the revival of religion in New-England
... Northampton, Mass., Pr. by J. Metcalf, for Simeon
Butler, 1819. 360 p. CSmH; MNF; MWA; NSyU; Nh;
OClW; PAtM; TWcW.   47883

Edwardsville Library.
A complete catalogue of all the books now in, or
belonging to, the Edwardsville library... Drawn for the
use of the share-holders, at the library room, Edwardsville, Nov. 30, 1819. John H. Randle, librarian.
Edwardsville, Ill, Pr. by H. Warren [1819] Broadside.
IEd.   47884

Edwardsville Spectator. Edwardsville, Ill., Hooper
Warren, May 29, 1819, 1st issue. Weekly newspaper.
DLC; MoSM.   47885

Election. To the independent electors of Hamilton
County... [Cincinnati, O., 1819] Broadside. MWA.
                                                  47886
Elegentiae Latine, from 5th English ed. New Haven,
Howe & Spalding, 1819. MWA.   47887

Elegiac Stanzas. Salem, Mass., 1819. Broadside.
(On the death of John Emery Abbot, minister of the
North Church, Salem, 1819) MSaE.   47888

An elegy on the death of Philo S. White, son of Mr.
Noah White of Sutton, who died August 16, 1819, aged

one year... [1819?] Broadside. McCorison List. 47889

Eliot, Andrew
    A sermon, preached on the day of the general
election, at Hartford, in the state of Connecticut, May
5th, 1819. Hartford, Pr. at the Times office, 1819.
20 p. CBPSR; Ct; CtHC; CtSoP; CtHi; CtY; DLC; M;
MBC; MH-AH; MHi; MWA; MWiW; MiD-B; NAuT; NN;
OClW; VtMiM.   47890

Ellen: a tale... Philadelphia, Pr. by Clark & Raser,
1819. MWA.   47891

Elliott, John, 1768-1824
    A sermon delivered on the next Lord's day after
the death of Jonathan Todd, esquire, who departed this
life February 10, 1819... Hartford, Pr. by George
Goodwin & sons, 1819. 31 p. CSmH; CtHi; CtY; MH-
AH; MWA; MiD-B; NjR; RPB.   47892

Elliott, Mrs. Mary (Belson)
    Grateful tributes... New York, Samuel Wood & sons,
and Samuel S. Wood & Co., Baltimore, 1819. MWA.
                                              47893
[--] My brother... Philadelphia, Wm. Charles, 1819.
MWA.   47894

-- The orphan boy... New York, Pr. by N. Van Riper,
for B. Gilley, 1819. MWA; NN.   47895

Elliott, Moses, 1775-1849
    A sermon delivered at Pittsfield, Vt. on a day of
thanksgiving, December 3, 1818... Windsor, Vt., Pr.
by Ide & Aldrich, 1819. 14 p. RPB; Vt; VtU-W.
                                              47896
Ely, Alfred
    A sermon, preached at Northampton, before the
Hampshire missionary society... Northampton, Mass.,
Pr. by Thomas W. Shepard & co., 1819. 40 p. MBAt;
MBC; MH-AH; MHi; MNF; MWA; NjPT; NjR; OClWHi.
                                              47897
Ely, Ezra Stiles
    Conversations on the science of the human mind...

Philadelphia, Pr. by William Fry, for A. Finley, 1819.
228 p. CtHC; LU; MWA; NjPT. 47898

[Ely, John]
The child's instructor... New York, Evert Duyckinck... 1819. MWA. 47899

Emerson, Brown
Departed Saints with Christ, a sermon. Preached
at Essex, Dec. 15, 1818, at the interment of Mrs.
Hannah Crowell... Salem, Mass., Pr. by John D. Cush-
ing, 1819. 19 p. MBC; MMch; MSaE; MWA; NjPT;
RPB. 47900

-- Excellence of the Bible; a sermon, in Salem, before
the Bible society of Salem and vicinity on the anniversary June 9, 1819, (with 8th report of the society).
Salem, Mass., John D. Cushing, 1819. 15 p. CtHC;
MSaE; MWA; NjR; RPB. 47901

Emerson, Joseph, 1777-1833
The evangelical primer, containing a minor doc-
trinal catechism; and a minor historical catechism; to
which is added the Westminster assembly's Shorter
catechism... Ed. 10. Boston, Pr. by Samuel T. Armstrong, 1819. 72 p. DLC; MC; MS; MWA; MdBE;
MiD-B; NNC; NNT-C; NNUT; Nh-Hi. 47902

-- General topics of a course of astronomical lectures
... Boston, Pr. by U. Crocker, 1819. MWA. 47903

-- Outline of a course of astronomical lectures... Boston, Pr. by U. Crocker, for Samuel T. Armstrong,
1819. 64 p. MBAt; MWA; NjPT. 47904

Emory, John
The divinity of Christ, vindicated... Philadelphia,
Pr. by Anderson & Meehan, for Thomas and William
Bradford, 1819. MWA. 47905

English, Clara
The affecting history of the children in the wood.
Hartford, George Goodwin & Sons, 1819. 54 p. CtHi;

MB.   47906

English, George Bethune
A narrative of the expedition to Dongola and Sen-
naar, under the command of his excellence Ismael
Pasha. Boston, Pr. by Wells & Lilly, 1819. 177 p.
MMeT.   47907

An enquiry into the causes of the present commercial
embarrassments in the United States. With a plan of
reform of the circulating medium. In two letters, addressed to the Secretary of the Treasury, by an anti-
bullionist. [1819?] 44 p. DeGE.   47908

An enquiry into the conduct of General Putnam, in relation to the Battle of Bunker, or Breed's Hill: and remarks upon Mr. S. Swett's sketch of that battle. Boston, Pr. by Thomas G. Bangs, 1819. 58 p. MBNEH;
Nh-Hi.   47909

Erie Reflector.   Erie, Pa., John Morris, Sept. 29,
1819, 1st issue.   Weekly newspaper.   MWA.   47910

An essay on The inability of sinners. From the Evangelical guardian and review, for February and March,
1818, printed at New York. Ed. 2. By a Presbyterian. Philadelphia, J.W. Scott, 1819. 24 p. MWA;
NNG; NjR; ViRut.   47911

Essex Agricultural Society
Premiums offered by the Essex Agricultural Soci-
ety, December 7, 1819. Salem, Mass., Pr. by T.C.
Cushing [1819] 7 p. MSaE.   47912

Essex County, Massachusetts
Rules and regulations of the Bar of the County of
Essex; agreed upon at March term, 1806. Salem,
Mass., Pr. by John D. Cushing, 1819. 28 p. MH-L;
MSaE; MWA.   47913

Essex Register
Carriers' New Year address. Salem, Mass.,
1819. Broadside. (Pr. on silk) MSaE.   47914

Estabrook, Joseph
A good life the best evidence of a pious heart. A
discourse, delivered Feb. 22, 1819, at the interment
of the Rev. Joseph Lee...Worcester, Mass., Pr. by
William Manning, 1819. 19 p. MBC; MTemNHi; MW;
MWA; MWHi; MWo; MiD-B; NN. 47915

Eternity of future punishment of the wicked. By a
clergyman of Massachusetts. Worcester, Mass., Wm.
Manning, 1819. 12 p. MWA; MWHi. 47916

[Etheridge, Samuel] comp.
The Christian orator, or A collection of speeches,
delivered on public occasions, before religious benevolent societies. To which is prefixed an abridgment of
Walker's Elements of elocution. Designed for the use
of colleges, academies and schools. By a gentleman
of Massachusetts. Ed. 3. Charlestown [Mass.] Pr.
by S. Etheridge, for Cushing & Jewett, and F. Lucas,
Baltimore, 1819. 298 p. CtHT; DLC; MdBLC; NUtHi;
ViRut. 47917

Euclides
Elements of geometry, containing the first six
books of Euclide...New York, Pr. by G. Long, for
James Eastburn and Co., 1819. 333 p. CtY; MA; MH;
MW; MWA; WyU. 47918

Evadne; or, the statue: a tragedy. From the 1st London ed. of 1819. New York, Longworth, 1819. 63 p.
MBr; NIC. 47919

Evangelical Lutheran Church
Plan. Entwurf zu einer central verbindung der
Evangelisch Lutherischen kirche in dem Vereinigten
Staaten von Nord Amerika. Baltimore, Gedruckt bei
Schaeffer und Maund, 1819. 7 p. MoSC; PPLT. 47920

-- Ohio and adjacent states.
Verrichtungen der ersten General Conferenz...
Lancaster, O., Pr. by Johann Herman, 1819. 32 p.
OCHP; OCoC. 47921

-- Verrichtungen der zweyten General-Conferenz...
Lancaster, O., Pr. by Johann Herman, 1819. 16 p.
OCoC.   47922

-- Synod of Pennsylvania.
Verhandlungen der Deutsch-Evangelisch-Lutherischen
Synode von Pennsylvanien und den benachtenbarten Staaten
gehalten zu Baltimore den 6ten Juni, 1819. Allentown, Pa.,
Pr. by Carl L. Hutter, 1819. 18 p. PHi; PLT; PAtM; PGL.
                                                   47923

Evangelical missionary society of Massachusetts
A brief history of the Evangelical missionary so-
ciety of Massachusetts...[1819] 7 p. CBPac; MH;
MWA.   47924

Evans, Estwick, 1787-1866
A pedestrious tour, of four thousand miles through
the western states and territories, during the winter
and spring of 1818...Concord, N.H., Pr. by Joseph C.
Spear, 1819. 256 p.   DLC; MH; MWA; Md; MdHi;
Nh-Hi; OClWHi; OT.   47925

Everest, Cornelius B.
A defence of the Gospel a ministerial duty. A sermon, delivered at Windham [Conn.] July 28, 1816...
Ed. 2. Windham, Conn., Pr. by J. Byrne, 1819.
46 p. CSmH; CtHi.   47926

Ewell, James
Just published, Ewell's celebrated family physician.
[1819] 2 p. DLC.   47927

-- The medical companion...with a dispensatory and
glossary...Ed. 5, greatly improved. Philadelphia, Pr.
for the author, 1819. 698 p.   DNLM; ICJ; LNT-M;
MBM; MWA; MdBJ; MoSU; NcWfC; PPC; PU.   47928

Ewell, Thomas
Statement of improvements in the theory and prac-
tice of the science of medicine...Philadelphia, Pr. by
John Bioren, 1819. 168 p. MBM; MWA; P.   47929

Ewer, Charles
    Books and stationary... Charles Ewer, No. 51
Cornhill... Boston. Informs his friends and the public,
that he has recently made large additions to his stock
of books, which now comprises an extensive assort-
ment of approved standard works... [1819] [12] p.
MWA.   47930

An examination of the case of the people, vs. Edward
Robbins and John Sheffield, tried at the general sessions in and for the city and county of New-York, January 4th, 1819... By a member of the Bar. New-York,
1819. 40 p. NNG.   47931

An expose of facts, concerning recent transactions, relating to the corps of cadets of the United States' Military academy, at West-Point, New-York. Newburgh,
N.Y., Pr. by Uriah C. Lewis, 1819. 106 p. DLC;
MWA; N; R.   47932

                              F
Facts and considerations on the question Why is steam-
boat navigation interesting to Connecticut? Hartford,
George Goodwin & Sons, 1819. 8 p. CtHi; CtY; MWA.
                                                   47933
Fair play is a jewel. New-York, Pr. by J. Seymour,
for Elam Bliss, 1819. 15 p. DNLM; MBM; NNNAM;
PPAmP.   47934

A faithful account of the massacre of the family of
Gerald Watson, of Fayetteville County, N.C., by John
Jackson, the father-in-law of said Watson, which hor-
rid catastrophe took place in July last... Boston, N.
Coverly, 1819. 24 p. DLC.   47935

Faithful statement of the correspondence between the
Rev. Mr. Brady, and the Rev. Leonard Edelen. Wash-
ington City, Pr. by Davis & Force, 1819. 43 p.
MdBLC.   47936

The family receipt book, containing eight hundred valuable receipts in various branches of domestic economy;

...2d Amer. ed. Pittsburgh, Pa., Randolph Barnes,
1819. 408 p. ArU; CSmH; CtHT-W; CtY; DLC; MCM;
MH; MWA; NGlf; NUtHi; OMC; OO; P; PP; PPL; PPi;
Vi.   47937

Family record of the Thomas'. 1819 (Facsimile copy)
MWA.   47938

Farmer, Henry Tudor
    Imagination; The maniac's dream, and other po-
ems;...New York, Kirk & Mercein, 1819. 163 p.
DLC; MB; MWA; NN; NNebg; NSchU; RPB; ViHaI.
                                                       47939
Farmer. Springfield, Ohio, George Smith, Feb. 13,
1819, 1st issue. Weekly newspaper. OCHP.   47940

Farmer's almanac for 1820. Astronomical calculations
by John Sharp. Baltimore, William Warner [1819]
DLC; MWA; ViAl.   47941

Farmer's almanac for the year...1820. By Joshua
Sharp. Baltimore, J. Robinson [1819] MWA; PHC.
                                                       47942
-- By Joshua Sharp...Baltimore, Cushing & Jewett
[1819] [36] p. MdHi.   47943

The farmer's almanack, calculated on a new and im-
proved plan, for the year of our Lord 1820...No. 28.
Established in 1793 by Robert B. Thomas...Boston,
Carter, Hendee & co.,...[1819] CU.   47944

The farmer's almanack, for the year of our Lord,
1820. Boston, Pr. by J.H.A. Frost, for West, Rich-
ardson & Lord...Boston [1819] 48 p. CSmH; CL;
InStmaS; MBB; MBilHi; MBNEH; MHa; MMal; MMeT;
MNF; MPeHi; MS; MWA; MTemNbli; MdHi; MeBa;
MeHi; MiGr; NjR; RNHi; RPB; WHi.   47945

The farmers' almanac, for...1820...By Samuel Burr.
Cincinnati, O., Pr. by Reynolds & co., for Phillips &
Speer Looker [1819] 32 p. DLC; MWA; OCHP;
OClWHi.   47946

-- Hartford, Geo. Goodwin & Sons, [1819] [48] p.
CtHi; MWA.   47947

-- Portland, Me., A. Shirley & F. Douglas [1819]
MH; MWA; MeHi.   47948

-- By Andrew Beers. Poughkeepsie, N.Y., P. & S.
Potter [1819] [36] p. MWA.   47949

The farmer's almanac, for the year of our Lord 1820.
...Calculated for the horizon and meridian of Phila-
delphia...By Andbew [sic] Beers...Wheeling [Va.] S.
Potter & Co. [1819] [28] p.   47950

Farmer's calendar, or Ontario and Genesee almanac,
for...1820...By Andrew Beers...Rochester, N.Y., E.
Peck & co. [1819] 36 p. NRHi.   47951

The farmer's calendar: or Utica almanack, for 1820...
by Andrew Beers...Utica, N.Y., Pr. by William Williams [1819] 36 p. DLC; NUtHi; NjR.   47952

The farmer's diary, or Beer's Ontario almanack, for
the year of our Lord 1820...By Andrew Beers,...
Canandaigua, N.Y., J.D. Bemis & Co. ...[1819]
[36] p. MWA; NBuHi; NCH; NCanHi; NRMA; WHi.
                                                    47953
Farmer's diary or Catskill almanack for...1820...By
Andrew Beers...Catskill, N.Y., Pr. by Croswell &
son, for J.S. Lewis [1819] [36] p. DLC.   47954

-- By Andrew Beers...Catskill, N.Y., Pr. by Croswell & son, for Nathan Elliott [1819] [36] p. NjR.
                                                    47955
Farmer's diary; or Columbia almanack for...1820...
By Andrew Beers...Hudson, N.Y., Ashbel Stoddard
[1819] [36] p. NHi.   47956

Farmer's diary; or Kingston almanack, for...1820...
By Andrew Beers...Kingston, N.Y., Pr. by Croswell
& son, for John Tappen, [1819] [36] p. NjR.   47957

Farmer's diary; or Newburgh almanack, for...1820...

By Andrew Beers...Newburgh, N.Y., Benj. F. Lewis
& co. [1819] [36] p. NBLiHi; NjR.   47958

Farr, Samuel
    Elements of medical jurisprudence to which are
added directions for preserving public health...Phila-
delphia, Pr. by Thomas Town, for James Webster,
1819. 554 p. OCLaw.   47959

Farrar, Timothy
    Report of the case of the trustees of Dartmouth
college against Wm. H. Woodward. Portsmouth, N.H.,
Pr. by J.J. Williams, for John W. Foster, 1819.
406 p. CSf; DLC; ICLaw; Ia; LNT-L; M; MA; MB;
MBAt; MH; MPeaI; MS; MW; NB; NCH; NN; NNG; MnU;
NbU; Nj; NjR; OCLaw; PP; PPi; Vt; WHi.   47960

The fashionable letter writer; or, art of polite correspondence...with forms of complimentary cards, and a
new and easy English grammar...New-York, George
Long, 1819. 151 p. MPeHi; MWA.   47961

Fearne, Charles
    An essay on the learning of contingent reminders
and executory devises...1st Amer. from 6th London
ed., with notes, and an analytical index, by Charles
Butler, esq. ...Philadelphia, Pr. by T.H. Palmer,
for Philip H. Nicklin, 1819. 618 p. ICLaw; MWA;
NNC-L; NcD; OrSC.   47962

Federal party--Connecticut
    State ticket...[Hartford, Pr. by G. Goodwin &
sons, 1819] MWA.   47963

Federal Republican and Baltimore Telegraph
    Baltimore. March 1819. Dear Sir. As one in-
terested in the advancement of sound and hearty fed-
eralism - the "good old cause" of the Revolution, we
take the liberty to address you on a subject extremely
interesting, not only to ourselves, but to that cause,
and we hope to you also. It is this:- We are about
giving a more animated and generally interesting character to our country paper...(Signed) B. Edes and J.P.

Heath, 1819. 1 p. Broadside. DLC.   47964

Felch, Cheever
    An address, delivered on the Festival of the Na-
tivity of St. John the Baptist, at Walpole, Mass. June
24, A. L. 5819, before Andoniram R. A. Chapter,
Montgomery, Constellation, Rising Star and St. Alban's
Lodges...Dedham, Mass., Pr. by H. & W. H. Mann
[1819] 23 p. CtY; MBAt; MBFM; NNFM; PPFM.47965

Female Mission Society
    The constitution of the Female Mission Society
auxiliary to the New Hampshire Baptist Domestic Mission Society. Concord, N. H., Pr. by Hill & Moore,
1819. 4 p. DLC.   47966

Female Missionary Society of the Western District
    The 2d annual report of the trustees of the Female
Missionary Society of the Western District. Utica,
N. Y., Pr. by William Williams, for the Society, 1819.
8 p. NUtHi.   47967

-- The third annual report of the trustees of the Female missionary society of the Western district, presented Sept. 7, 1819. Utica, N. Y., Pr. by W. Williams, for the Society, 1819. 32 p. N; NUtHi.   47968

Female society of Boston and its vicinity, auxiliary to
the American education society.
    Constitution and circular address...Boston, Pr.
by Ezra Lincoln, 1819. 12 p. CSt; MWA; PHi.   47969

Fenelon, François de Salignac de la Mothe
    Dialogues concerning eloquence in general; and
particularly that kind which is proper for the pulpit.
Boston, 1819. InCW.   47970

-- Pious reflections for every day of the month...
Baltimore, Thatcher & Co., 1819. MWA.   47971

-- -- Boston, Lincoln & Edmands, 1819. 54 p.
MDedHi; MDeeP; MWA; NN; NcD.   47972

Fenning, Daniel
    The universal spelling book; or, A new and easy
guide to the English language...Baltimore, 1819. 168 p.
IU.   47973

Ferguson, Adam
    An essay on the history of civil society...Ed. 8.
Philadelphia, Pr. by William Fry, for A. Finley,
1819. 506 p. ICP; IaFairP; MH-AH; MWA; MsJS;
NICLA; Nj; OC; PFal; TNP; TxU.   47974

Ferguson, James
    An easy introduction to astronomy for young gentle-
men and ladies...Philadelphia, Pr. by William Greer,
for Benjamin Warner, 1819. 177 p. ILebM; MH;
MWA; MdBS; NNT-C; ViU.   47975

No entry   47976

A few remarks on Prof. Stuart's reply to Mr. Channing's sermon, by a layman. [Boston, Pr. by Sylvester T. Goss, 1819?] MWA.   47977

Field, David Dudley, 1781-1867
    A statistical account of the county of Middlesex, in
Connecticut...Middletown, Conn., Pr. by Clark & Lyman, for the Connecticut academy of arts and sciences,
1819. 154 p. CtHi; CtHT-W; DLC; MWiW; NUtHi;
Nh; OClW.   47978

-- Statistical account of the county of Middlesex, in
Connecticut...Middletown, Conn., Pr. by Clark & Lyman, 1819. 7 pams. in 1 v. CtHi.   47979

Filangieri, Gaetano, 1752-1788
    La scienza della legislazione...Filadelfia, Stam-
peria delle provincie unite, 1819. 5 v. CU-Law; NHi;
NNU.   47980

The financiers A, B, C respecting currency. Washing-

ton, D. C., Pr. by DeKrafft, 1819. 24 p. PPAmP.
47981

Findly, Samuel
A funeral sermon delivered on the death of Henry
P. Smith... Frankfort, Ky., Kendall & Russell, 1819.
34 p. ICU.   47982

The first principles of religion, and the existence of a
diety... New Haven, A. B. Goldsmith, and N. & S. S.
Jocelyn, 1819. 56 p. NNUT.   47983

Fisk, Elisha
A sermon, preached in Braintree, before the Nor-
folk auxiliary society for the education of pious youth
for the gospel ministry... Dedham, Mass., Pr. by H.
& W. H. Mann [1819] 36 p. CSmH; ICMe; MB; MBAt;
MBC; MWA; NhD.   47984

Fisk, Ezra
Consolation in death. A sermon, preached at the
funeral of the Rev. George Stewart, Blooming-burgh,
Sept. 21, 1818... Goshen, N. Y., Pr. by T. B. Crowell,
1819. 33 p. DLC; MWA.   47985

-- Sin finds out the criminal. A sermon, delivered at
the execution of James Teed and David Dunning... April
16, 1819... Goshen, N. Y., Pr. by T. B. Crowell, 1819.
30 p. CSmH; MBC; MWA.   47986

Fisk, Pliny
The Holy Land an interesting field of missionary
enterprise... Boston, Pr. by U. Crocker, for Samuel
T. Armstrong, 1819. (Bound with - Parsons, Levi.
The dereliction and restoration of the Jews... Boston,
1819) 39 p. CtHC; MBC; MH-AH; MWA; MiD-B; NIC;
NjPT; OCHP; OO.   47987

Fiske, Oliver
Address to the members of the American Antiquarian Society; together with the laws and regulations
of the institution, and a list of donations to the Society
since the last publication. Worcester, Mass., Pr. by
William Manning, 1819. 38 p. MWA; MWHi; NjR;

OCHP. 47988

Flagg, Joshua
A sermon, delivered on the evening of the first
Sunday in February, 1819...Salem, Mass., Pr. by
John D. Cushing, 1819. 16 p. MBC; MWA; NN. 47989

Flavel, John
A treatise on keeping the heart. Ed. 3. Boston,
N. Willis, 1819. MH. 47990

-- -- Ed. 3. Boston, Pr. by T. Badger, Jun., for
T. Bedlington, 1819. 203 p. CtY; MB; MH-AH; MHi;
MWA; MiD-B; MiOC; ScCMu; TWeW; UPB; VtWood.
47991

Fletcher, Alexander
Sermon at Kingston, Feb. 20, 1819, on the death
of Nancy Barlett, consort of Smith Bartlett. Kingston,
R. I., 1819. 22 p. RHi. 47992

Fletcher, John
Checks to Antinomianism...3d Amer. ed. New-
York, Pr. by Abraham Paul, for J. Soule and T.
Mason, and for the Methodist Episcopal church in the
United States. 1819-[20] 4 v. IaFayU; TNMPH. 47993

Flint, Abel, 1765-1825
Address delivered at the Baptist meeting house, in
Hartford, Apr. 27, 1819, at the annual meeting of the
Hartford Sunday School Society. Hartford, Pr. by Hud-
son and Co., 1819. 15 p. CtHi; CtSoP; NjPT. 47994

-- A sermon delivered at West Springfield, August 25,
1819; at the ordination of the Reverend William B.
Sprague...Hartford, Pr. by Peter B. Gleason & co.,
1819. 31 p. CSmH; CtHi; CtSoP; CtY; Ct; DLC; ICU;
KWiU; M; MA; MB; MBC; MDeeP; MH-AH; MHi; MSaE;
MSHi; MWA; MiD-B; MiU; NAuT; NcD; NjPT; NjR; OO;
PPL; PPPrHi; RPB. 47995

Flint, James
Report of the Jeffersonville and Ohio canal. [1819]
Broadside. Streeter. 47996

Florula Columbiensis, or a list of plants found in the
District of Columbia, arranged according to the Lin-
naean System...Washington, D.C., Pr. by Jacob Gideon, Jun., for the Washington Botanical Society, 1819.
MBHo.   47997

Floyd, Loammi
    Sermon in the Circular Church, Charlestown, De-
cember 17, 1819, at the ordination of the Rev. Jonas
King and the Rev. Alfred Wright.   Charlestown [1819?]
NHi.   47998

[Ford, Mrs. Sarah Endicott (Herrick)]
    Memoir of Mrs. Sally Fornis, who died at Beverly,
Massachusetts, July 31, 1817, AEt. 19.   Compiled
from private manuscripts written at the time by her
mother.   With remarks by H. Bingham.   Andover,
Mass., Flagg and Gould, 1819. 90 p. MWA; MdHi.
                                                       47999
Form used by Measurer of Wood. 18(19. in manuscript)
Salem, Mass., 1819. Broadside. MSaE.   48000

Forster, Anthony
    The Scripture doctrine of election.   A discourse
delivered on 21st February, 1819...Charleston, S.C.,
Pr. by J. Hoff, 1819. 21 p. MBev; MWA.   48001

Foster, Henry G.
    A discourse delivered before the New Jerusalem
Church, in Boston, on Christmas Day, December 25,
1818.   Boston, Pr. by Parmenter and Balch, for Cummings and Hilliard, 1819. 23 p. See [Worcester,
Thomas] DLC; MB; MHi; MSaE.   48002

Foxe, John, 1516-1857
    Book of martyrs...New York, 1819. PMA.   48003

Francis, Thomas, of Leeds
    Design and rules of the Bowdoinham Association.
1819. Noyes 853.   48004

Franklin, Benjamin
    Franklins Werke, Leben und Meynungen von Dr.

Benjamin Franklin. Mehrenteils von ihm selbet ges-
chrieben. Reading, Pa., Pr. by Johann Ritter & Co.,
1819. Seidensticker p. 209. 48005

Franklin Bank. Columbus, Ohio.
Rules and regulations...[Columbus] Pr. by P. H.
Olmsted, 1819. 17 p. CSmH. 48006

The Franklin magazine almanac for 1820. Calculations
by John Armstrong. Pittsburgh, Pa., Eichbaum &
Johnston, [1819] MWA; PSeW. 48007

Franklin Monitor. Charlestown, Mass., Bellamy &
Green, Jan. 2, 1819, 1st issue. Weekly newspaper.
MWA. 48008

Frederick, Francis
Lives and confessions of John Williams, Francis
Frederick, John P. Rog, and Peter Peterson, who
were tried at the U.S. Circuit Court in Boston, for
murder and piracy; sentenced to be executed Jan. 21,
1819...By Francis Frederick, murderer. Boston,
1819. 36 p. MB. 48009

Free Press. Lancaster, Pa., S.C. Stambaugh, May
10, 1819, 1st issue. Weekly newspaper. MWA. 48010

Free remarks on the spirit of the Federal constitution,
the practice of the Federal government, and the obligations of the union, respecting the exclusion of slavery
from the territories and new states. By a Philadel-
phian. Philadelphia, A. Finley, 1819. 116 p. MH-AH;
MWA; NjPT; RP; RPB; Vi. 48011

Free School Society, New York, N.Y.
By-laws of the Free School Society, of New-York,
as revised and adopted by The Trustees, 12 month,
(December), 1818. New York, Pr. by W. Treadwell,
1819. 24 p. MB. 48012

Freeman, James
Errors corrected in papers. Boston, 1819. MSaE.
48013

Freemasons.   Connecticut.
Constitution of the Grand council of Select masters of the state of Connecticut.   New London, Conn., S. Green, 1819. 7 p. Ct; LNMas; NNFM.   48014

-- Indiana. Grand Lodge.
Proceedings of the Grand Lodge of Indiana, begun and held at the Masons' hall in the town of Madison, on the second Monday in September, being the 13th day of the month, A. L. 5819, A. D. 1819. Madison, Ind., Pr. by Lodge & Arion [1819] 48 p. IaCrM; MBFM; NNFM.   48015

-- Kentucky. Grand Chapter.
Proceedings of the Grand Lodge of Kentucky, begun and held at the Masons' Hall in the Town of Lexington, on the last Monday of August, being the thirtieth day of the month, A. L. 5819, A. D. 1819. Lexington, Ky., Pr. by D. Bradford, at the Advertiser office, 1819. 96 p. KyHi; DSC; IaCrM; MBFM; NNFM.
48016
-- -- -- Proceedings of the Grand lodge of Kentucky, begun and held at the Masons' hall, in the town of Lexington, on the last Monday in November, being the 30th day of the month.   A. L. 5819.-A. D. 1819. Lexington, Ky., Pr. by Worsley & Smith, 1819. 94 p. MBFM; NNFM; OCM.   48017

Proceedings of the Grand Royal Arch Chapter of Kentucky, at a Grand Communication, begun and held at Frankfort, January 5th, A. D. 1819, A. L. 5819, Y. D. 2350. Shelbyville, Ky., Pr. at the Impartial Compiler Office, 1819. 12 p. NNFM.   48018

-- Louisiana. Grand Lodge.
Constitutions De L'Ancienne et Honorable Fraternitié Des Maçons Libres et Acceptés De L'Etat De La Louisiane. Redigees et Publiles Par Ordre De La Grande Loge De cet Etat. A La Nouvelle-Orleans. De L'Imprimerie De Roche Freres. A. L. 5819 [1819] 47 p. PPFM.   48019

-- Maine. Grand Lodge.
  Grand Lodge of Maine.   Convention of delegates.
Copy of a circular letter issued by Portland Lodge to
the several Lodges in the District of Maine.   Portland,
Me., Aug. 13th, 1819. 16 p. PPFM.   48020

-- Maryland. Grand Lodge.
  Extracts from the proceedings of the Grand Lodge
of Maryland, at their semi-annual communication, begun and held in the City of Baltimore, on Monday, the
1st day of November, A. L. 5819. [Baltimore, Pr.
by J. Robinson [1819] 4 p. MBFM; PPFM.   48021

-- Massachusetts. Grand Lodge.
  The act of Incorporation, by-laws, rules and regulations for the government and management of the
master, wardens and members, of the grand lodge of
Massachusetts.   Incorporated June 16, 1817. Adopted
Sept. 9, A. L. 5818.   Boston, Pr. by E. G. House,
1819.   32 p. MBFM; MH; PPFM.   48022

-- -- (Maine District)
  To the Rt. Worshipful Master, Wardens and Brethren of ... Lodge.   Brethren, as this portion of the
state will soon assume an independent rank in the Union, the attention of the Masonic Fraternity is naturally
and almost universally directed to a similar separation
of the Lodges in Maine from the jurisdiction of the
Grand Lodge of Massachusetts... Portland, Me., Aug.
13, 1819.   Broadside. MHi.   48023

-- New-Hampshire. Grand Lodge.
  Summary of the proceedings of the Grand Lodge
of New-Hampshire, at their General Assembly in Con-
cord, begun June 9, and continued by adjournment, to
June 10, A. L. 5819.   Amherst, N. H., Pr. by Richard
Boylston, 1819. DLC.   48024

-- New York. Grand Lodge.
  The constitution of the... Free and accepted Masons... of the state of New-York.   New York, Pr. by
Henry C. Southwick, for Thomas Longworth, 1819.
92 p. NNFM.   48025

-- -- -- Proceedings of the Grand Lodge of the fraternity of...Masons of ...New York, at the Quarterly communications and meeting of emergency, held between the 24th of A. L. 5818, and the 24th June, A. L. 5819. New York, Pr. by Bro. H. C. Southwick, for Bro. Thomas Longworth [1819] 69 p. MBFM; MWA; PPFM.   48026

-- -- -- Statement of the receipts and expenditures of the R. W. Grand Lodge of the state of New York, from the 27th Feb. A. L. 5806, to 26th May, A. L. 5819, made pursuant to an order of the Grand Lodge, passed on the 3d June, A. L. 5819. New York, T. Longworth and H. C. Southwick, 1819. 77 p. NIC.   48027

-- -- (City) Royal Arch Masons.
    By-laws of Independent Royal Arch Lodge, No. ... held in the City of New York, Nov. 23, 1818. New York, 1819. PHi.   48028

-- Ohio.
    Proceedings of the Grand lodge of Ohio. Columbus, Pr. by P. H. Olmsted, 1819. 116 p. CSmH; IaCrM; MBFM.   48029

-- Proceedings of the Grand lodge of Ohio, held at Columbus, Dec. 13, 1819...Worthington, Ezra Griswold, jr. [1819?] CSmH; IaCrM.   48030

-- -- American Union Lodge No. 1.
    Bye-laws...in the town of Marietta [O.] Marietta, Ohio, Pr. by Bro. R. Prentiss, 1819. 12 p. CSmH.
                                                         48031
-- -- Grand Chapter.
    Proceedings of the Grand Royal Arch Chapter of the state of Ohio...28th of December, 1818...Columbus, O., Pr. by P. H. Olmsted [1819] 23 p. ICS; MBFM.   48032

-- -- St. John's Lodge No. 13.
    By laws of St. John's Lodge, No. 13. Adopted Jan. 7, 1819...[Dayton, 1819] 8 p. IaCrM.   48033

-- -- Scioto Lodge, No. 6.
   By-laws of Scioto Lodge, No. 6, adopted A. L.
5808. By order of the Lodge. Chillicothe, Pr. by
Bros. Bailhache and Scott, 1819. 16 p. OCh.   48034

-- Pennsylvania. Grand Lodge.
   Grand lodge of the most ancient and honourable
fraternity of free and accepted Masons of Pennsylvania
...in the city of Philadelphia, on Monday, the 6th
December, anno Domini 1819, anno Lucis 5819. [Phila-
delphia, Pr. by T. S. Manning, 1819] 20 p. NNFM.
                                                48035
-- Royal Arch Masons. Connecticut. Grand Chapter.
   The general grand royal arch constitution for the
United States of America: and by-laws of the Grand
chapter of Connecticut. Hartford, Pr. by Lincoln &
Stone, 1819. 24 p. DLC.   48036

-- -- Kentucky.
   Proceedings of the Grand royal arch chapter of
Kentucky, at a grand communication, begun and held at
Frankfort, January 5th, A. D. 1819. Shelbyville, Ky.,
Pr. at the Imperial Compiler office, 1819. 12 p.
NNFM.   48037

-- -- Massachusetts. Grand Chapter.
   Grand royal arch chapter of Massachusetts...Bos-
ton, November, 1819. Boston, Pr. by comp. E. G.
House, 1819. 18 p. IaCrM; NNFM.   48038

-- -- New Hampshire. Grand chapter.
   Regulations of the Grand Royal arch chapter of...
New-Hampshire...Concord, N. H., Pr. by George
Hough, 1819. 17 p. MWA; NNFM.   48039

-- -- New York (City). Grand Chapter.
   Proceedings of General grand chapter, at a meet-
ing held in the city of New-York, Sept. 9, A. L. 5819.
[Boston, Pr. by E. G. House, 1819] 24 p. MWA;
NNFM.   48040

-- -- New York (State). Grand chapter.
   The constitution and regulations of the Grand

Royal arch chapter of the state of New York, adopted
at the city of Albany; on Feb. 7, 1805.   Albany, Pr.
by Packard and Van Benthuysen, 1819. 42 p.. IaCrM.
48041

-- South Carolina. Grand Lodge.
    Ordo Ab Chao.   Rules and regulations for the gov-
ernment of the Grand Lodge of Ancient Free-Masons
of South-Carolina, and the several lodges under it's
jurisdiction, ratified in Grand Lodge, on the 18th day
of June, A. L. 5819.   Charleston, S. C., Pr. by Archibald E. Miller, 1819. 26 p. MBFM.   48042

-- Tennessee. Grand Lodge.
    Proceedings... held at Nashville, from October,
A. L. 5818, to October, A. L. 5819, inclusive. Nashville, Tunstall & Norvell, 1819. 24 p. NNFM.   48043

-- Vermont.   Eastern Star Lodge, No. 43.
    By-laws of Eastern Star Lodge, No. 43, at Read-
ing.   Published by order.   Woodstock, Vt., Pr. by
David Watson, 1819. 24 p. VtHi; VtBFM.   48044

-- -- Grand Lodge.
    Grand Lodge of the Most Ancient and Honourable
Society of Free and Accepted Masons of the state of
Vermont.   Worshipful Lemuel Whitney, Grand Master.
Montpelier, Vt., Pr. by E. P. Walton [1819] 41 p.
IaCrM; MBFM; PPFM; VtBFM; VtHi.   48045

The Friend of peace, to which is prefixed A solemn
review of the custom of war; showing that war is the
effect of popular delusion, and proposing a remedy...
by Philo Pacificus.   Greenfield, Mass., Ansel Phelps,
1819.   231 p. KyLxT.   48046

-- No. XV; Vol. II. No. 8.   [Boston, Cummings and
Hilliard, 1819-20] 2 nos. CSmH.   48047

Friends of National Industry
    The proceedings of a convention of the Friends of
National Industry, assembled in the City of New York,
November 29, 1819... New York, Pr. by C. S. Van
Winkle... 1819.   22 p. MH-BA; PHi; PPM.   48048

Friends, Society of.
The pious instructor, being a selection in prose
and verse, from various authors eminent for virtue
and piety on moral and religious subjects, designed to
warn and to animate the zeal of all to piety and religion: but more particularly for the use of Friends,
schools... Hallowell, Me., William F. Laine, 1819.
214 p. ICT.   48049

-- Baltimore yearly meeting.
Report of the Committee on Indian concerns to the
yearly meeting held at Baltimore, 9th mo. 8th, 1819.
1819.   Folio,   1 1.   Sabin 34672.   48050

-- -- -- Another ed.   1 1.   Sabin 34672.   48051

-- Ohio yearly meeting, 1819.
The discipline of the Society of Friends, of Ohio
yearly meeting... Mountpleasant, O., Pr. by Elisha
Bates, [1819?] 102 p. CSmH; DLC; MWA; NN; NNUT;
OClWHi; PHC.   48052

-- -- Extracts from the minutes of Ohio yearly meeting, held at Mount-Pleasant, by adjournments, from
the 6th of the 9th mo. 1819 to the 11th of the same inclusive. [1819] Broadside. OClWHi.   48053

-- -- Report of the Committee on Indian concerns...
Signed: On behalf of the Committee, Lewis Walker,
Clerk, 9 mo. 8th, 1819. [1819] Broadside. OClWHi.
                                             48054
-- Philadelphia Yearly meeting.
Extracts from the minutes... 1819. [Philadelphia,
1819] 3 p. NjR.   48055

Frothingham, N. L.
Funeral sermon Apr. 19, '18. Death J. McKean.
Boston, J. T. Buckingham, 1819. MWA.   48056

                        G
[G., H.]
Interesting memoir of H.   G.,   of Philadelphia,

A striking instance of the influence of divine grace on the mind. Philadelphia, William Bradford, 1819. MWA. 48057

Gadsden, John
An eulogy, on the late Keating Lewis Simons... Charleston, S. C., Pr. by W. P. Young & son, [1819] DLC; MW; MWA; ScCC. 48058

Gage, Thomas
The history of Rowley, anciently including Bradford, Boxford & Georgetown from the year 1639 to the present time. Boston, Pr. by F. Andrews, 1819. 483 p. MMeT. 48059

Gales' North-Carolina almanack for the year of our Lord, 1820... By John Beasley. Raleigh, N. C., Pr. by J. Gales [1819] 34 p. NcD. 48060

Gallaudet, Thomas Hopkins, 1787-1851
An address, delivered at a meeting for prayer, with reference to the Sandwich mission, in the Brick church in Hartford, October 11, 1819... Hartford, Pr. by Lincoln & Stone, 1819. 15 p. CSt; CtHi; Ct; CtHC; CtHT-W; CtY; CtNwchO; CtSoP; DLC; GDC; ICT; IEG; M; MB; MBAt; MBC; MH; MHi; MH-AH; MSaE; MWA; N; NAuT; NCH; NHi; NN; NTEW; NcD; NjR; OClW; PPPrHi. 48061

Gallia Gazette. Gallipolis, Ohio. Joshua Cushing, May, 1919, 1st issue. Weekly newspaper. OMC. 48062

[Gallison, John] 1788-1820
A proposed Memorial to the Congress of the United States [on privateering] [Boston, May 1819] 7 p. CtY; DLC; MH; MHi; NN. 48063

Gallup, Joseph Adams
Pathological reflections on general diseased action ...Montpelier, Vt., Pr. by E. P. Walton, 1819. 20 p. CSmH; MB; MWA; NBMS; NNNAM; VtHi. 48064

Gardiner, William
A journal, of the external evidences of the Lord's gracious dealings, with Dr. William Gardiner... Philadelphia, Pr. by Simon Probasco, for Susannah Gardiner, 1819. 495 p. MWA; NjMF; ScNC.   48065

Gardner, Charles Kitchel
Compend of the United States system of infantry exercise and manoeuvres... New York, Pr. by William A. Mercein, 1819. 282 p. MWA; NN; NWM.   48066

Gates, Theophilus R.
A measuring reed; to separate between the precious and the vile: in two parts... Ed. 2, with additions. Philadelphia, Dickinson, 1819. 252 p. CtW.
48067
Der Gemeinnutzige Landwirthschafts- Calender. Auf das Jahr 1820.   Lancaster, Pa., Pr. by Anton Albrecht, 1819. Seidensticker p. 207.   48068

Geneva & France, Vol. 1-2.   Boston, Wells & Lily, 1819. ScSoh.   48069

Genlis, Stephanie Felicite Ducrest de Saint Aubin, Comtesse de, afterwards Marquise de Sillery, 1746-1830.
The history of the Dutchess of C...... From Adele and Theodore. Written by herself. Baltimore, Pr. for the booksellers, 1819. 103 p. MdBE; MdHi; MWA.   48070

No. II. The Gentleman's almanack, and annual register, for the year of our Lord 1820... By Zadock Thompson... Woodstock, Vt., Pr. by David Watson [1819] [48] p. MWA; NA; VtU-W.   48071

Georgia (State)
Acts of the General assembly of the state of Georgia, passed... Nov. and Dec., 1819... Milledgeville, Pr. by Camak & Hines, 1819. 176 p. DLC; GU-De.   48072

-- Journal of the Senate of the state of Georgia, at an

annual session...Nov. and Dec., 1819. Milledgeville,
Camak & Hines, [1819] 104 p. DLC.   48073

Georgia Advertiser. Augusta, T. S. Hannon, Mar.
1819, 1st issue. Tri-weekly and semi-weekly newspaper. DLC.   48074

Georgia Republican. Milledgeville, Jones & Denison,
September, 1819, 1st issue. Weekly newspaper.
Brigham, p. 120.   48075

Gibson, Robert
    Mathematical tables: difference of latitude and de-
parture: logarithms, from 1 to 10,000; and artificial
sines, tangents, and secants. Baltimore, F. Lucas,
1819. CoHi; CtY; LNH; NNC.   48076

Gile, Samuel
    A sermon, delivered in the Old South church,
Boston, before the Foreign mission society of Boston
and the vicinity...Boston, Pr. by Lincoln & Edmands,
1819. 28 p. CtSoP; DLC; ICMe; MB; MBC; MH;
MWA; MeLewB; MiD-B; NjPT; NjR.   48077

Gill, John
    Infant-baptism, a part and pillar of Popery...Ed.
4. Exeter, N.H., Josiah Richardson, 1819. MWA.
          48078
Gilles, John
    Life of George Whitefield...and Aaron C. Seymour
...Boston, Samuel T. Armstrong, 1819. 268 p. TxShA.
          48079
Gillet, Eliphalet, 1768-1848
    Thanksgiving. A discourse delivered at Hallowell,
on the day of the annual thanksgiving in Massachusetts,
Dec. 2, 1819...Hallowell, Me., Pr. by E. Goodale,
1819. 16 p. CSt; MWA; MeHi; NjPT.   48080

Gillett, Timothy Phelps, 1780-1866
    Causes which render the gospel ministry ineffectual,
stated and remedies suggested; a sermon delivered at
the installation of the Rev. Saul Clark...New Haven,
A. H. Maltby & Co., 1819. 18 p. CtHC; CtSoP; CtY;

ICN; NjPT. 48081

Gilley, William B.
Catalogue of recent publications, for sale by William B. Gilley, No. 92 Broadway, New-York. New-York, Pr. by J. Seymour, 1819. 36 p. CSmH. 48082

Gilman, Mrs. M.
My ten-rod farm; or, How I became a florist. Boston, 1819. PPM. 48083

Girod, John Francis
An exposition of the pretended title of the Marquis de Maison Rouge, to thirty leagues square of the river Ouachitta. Natchez, Miss., Pr. by R. C. Langdon, 1819. 32 p. DLC. 48084

Gleason, Benjamin
Anniversary oration, in commemoration of American independence... Charlestown, Mass., T. Green, 1819. 16 p. DLC; M; MB; MBAt; MWA. 48085

Gleninger, John W., M.D.
An essay in vindication of the unity of disease... Lebanon, Pa., Pr. by J. Hartman, 1819. 23 p. OCU-M. 48086

Gloucester Farmer. Camden, N.J., John A. Crane, Jan. 7, 1819, 1st issue, at Camden location. A weekly continuation of a paper formerly published at Woodbury. NjHi. 48087

[Godwin, William]
Baldwin's fables... New Haven, Sidney's press, for J. Babcock and son, 1819. 36 p. CtHi; MWA. 48088

Going, Jonathan
Outline of a plan for establishing a Baptist Literary and Theological Institution in New England. Worcester, Mass., 1819. MBAt. 48089

Goldsmith, Oliver
An abridgement of the history of England from

Julius Caesar to George II.   Hallowell, Me., Ezekiel
Goodale and S. K. Gilman, 1819.   371 p. MBrigStJ;
MMhHi; MWA; MeHi.   48090

-- -- ...Continued to the present time; by several literary gentlemen.   Newburgh, N. Y., B. F. Lewis and
Co., 1819. 348 p.   MSwe; MWA; MWiW.   48091

-- The deserted village...Middlebury, Vt., Pr. by
Francis Burnap, for H. Richardson, Jr., 1819. 108 p.
MB; MH; MWA; NN; VtMiS; VtU.   48092

-- The poems of Oliver Goldsmith.   Philadelphia,
McCarty & Davis, 1819. 144 p. NHav.   48093

-- The traveller...Hartford, Pr. by Lincoln and Stone,
for Samuel G. Goodrich, 1819. 166 p. CoPu; CtHT-W;
CtHi; CtY; DLC; MWA; NjR.   48094

-- -- Philadelphia, M'Carty and Davis, 1819. MWA.
                                                      48095
Golitsyn, Dmitri Dmitrievich, Kniaz.
    An appeal to the Protestant public, by Dametrius
A. Callitzin.   Ebensburg [Pa.] Pr. by Thomas Foley,
1819.   21 p. DGU; DLC; MdBS.   48096

-- A letter to a Protestant friend, on the Holy Scriptures: being a continuation of the "Defence of Catholic
principles. " Baltimore, F. Lucas, jr. [1819] 156 p.
DLC; MdHi; PPiU; PV.   48097

[Goodenow, John Milton] 1782-1838
    Historical sketches of the principles and maxims
of American jurisprudence, in contrast with the doctrines of the English common law on the subject of
crimes and punishments...Steubenville, O., Pr. by
James Wilson, 1819.   428 p. MBAt; MWA; NN;
OClWHi; PPB; PU.   48098

[Goodrich, Samuel Griswold]
    The youth's arithmetic.   Hartford, S. G. Goodrich,
1819. MH.   48099

Gorham, John
   The elements of chemical science. Boston, Cummings and Hilliard, 1819-20. 2 v.   CSfCMS; CtY; IGK; MA; MB; MH; MWA; MeLew; NHunt; NNNAM; NTRPI; NhD; OO; PPAmP; PPC; PPF; PPL-R; PU; RPM; ViU; VtU.   48100

[Gorman, John Berry] 1793-1864
   Dissertation on the nature and treatment of the typhus or nervous fever.   Milledgeville [Ga.] Pr. for the author, 1819. 32 p. DNLM.   48101

Gother, John
   A Papist misrepresented and represented, or, A twofold character of Popery... From the 19th London ed.   Revised by a Catholic clergyman of Baltimore. Baltimore, Fielding Lucas, Jun. [1819?] 36 p. DGU; DLC.   48102

Graham, Mrs. Isabella (Marshall)
   The power of faith... Ed. 3.   New York, Pr. by William A. Mercein, for Kirk and Mercein, 1819. MWA.   48103

-- -- Ed. 4.   New York, Pr. by William A. Mercein, for Kirk and Mercein, 1819.   336 p. MWA; NSpepF; RPB.   48104

-- -- Ed. 5.   New York, Pr. by William A. Mercein, for Kirk and Mercein, 1819.   336 p. MWA; NUtHi.
                                                          48105
[Granger, Gideon]
   The address of Epaminondas to the citizens of the state of New-York.   Albany, Pr. by Jeremiah Tryon, 1819. 51 p. CSmH; CSt; DLC; MBAt; MWA; MiD-B; VtMiS.   48106

Grant, Mrs.
   Letters from the mountains; being the real correspondence of a lady, between the years 1773 and 1807. By Mrs. Grant.   Boston, 1819. PPL-R.   48107

Graupner, Gottlieb, b. ca. 1740
    Rudiments of the art of playing on the piano forte
...Boston, G. Graupner...[1819] 40 p. CSmH. 48108

Gray, Thomas
    A sermon delivered before the ancient and honour-
able artillery company, in Boston, June 7, 1819. Be-
ing the 182d anniversary of their election of officers.
Boston, E. G. House, 1819. 22 p. CtHT-W; DLC;
ICMe; MB; MBC; MH; MHi; MWA; NCH; NjPT; NjR;
PHi; VtU.   48109

Graydon, William, 1759-1840
    The justices and constables assistant. Being a
general collection of forms of practice; interspersed
with various observations and directions...Harrisburgh,
Pa., Pr. by John Wyeth, for the author, 1819. 487 p.
DLC; MH-L; MWA; P.   48110

Great Britain
    Reports of cases argued and determined in the
courts of common pleas and Exchequer Chamber, from
Easter term 28th George III. 1788, to Hilary Term
36th George III. 1796...2d Amer., corr. from the
last London ed. Philadelphia, Philip H. Nicklin, 1819.
2 v. TJaU.   48111

-- Reports of cases argued and determined in the
Court of King's bench...By George Maule and William
Selwyn...Boston, Wells & Lilly, 1819-33. 6 v. In-SC;
KyLxT; LNT-L; MWA; OCoY; P; PU-L; ViU.   48112

Great truths in a little nut-shell...Pr. for the author,
1819. MWA.   48113

Green, Daniel L.
    Letter from Dr. Daniel L. Green, of Bethlehem,
to Dr. Samuel L. Mitchell, of New York, with the
answer. [on method of cure for deafness] [1819]
Broadside. MBM.   48114

Gregory, Charles
    A new and complete dictionary of arts and sci-

ences...New York, Collins and Co., 1819. 3 v. CtHT;
MWA; MsWJ.   48115

[Griffin, Edmund Dorr] 1804-1830
    J. Nelson's grammar school.   Prize poem--By
E. D. G.   [New York, 1819?] Broadside. NN.   48116

Griffin, Edward Dorr, 1770-1837
    The claims of seamen.   A sermon preached Nov.
7, 1819, in the brick church, New York, for the benefit of the Marine Missionary Society of the City.   New
York, J. Seymour, 1819.   30 p.   CtY; MWA; MWiW;
NjR; PMA.   48117

-- Foreign missions...New York, Pr. by J. Seymour,
1819.   27 p.   MB; MWA; MWiW; NjR; OC; RBr.   48118

-- An humble attempt to reconcile the differences of
Christian respecting the extent of the atonement.   New-
York, S. Dodge, 1819.   CtY; ICT; MWA; MWiW. 48118a

-- A sermon, in which is attempted a full and explicit
answer to the common and highly important question,
"What wilt thou have me to do?" delivered...August
1814...Brookfield [Mass.] Pr. by E. Merriam and co.,
1819.   12 p.   DLC; MWA; MiD-B; NjPT.   48119

[Griffin, John]
    Covey; or the converted sailor...Exeter, N. H.,
Josiah Richardson, 1819.   MWA.   48120

Grigg, Jacob
    Circular letter of the Dover Baptist association...
Exeter [N. H. ?] 1819.   MWA.   48121

Grimshaw, William
    History of England.   Philadelphia, B. Warner,
1819.   MWA.   48122

Grimshaw, William
    History of England, from the first invasion by
Julius Caesar, to the peace of Ghent; comprising every
political event worthy of remembrance...Philadelphia,

Lydia R. Bailey, 1819. 300 p. PMA.   48123

Gross, Thomas
    A sermon, delivered at Lisle...January 3, 1819
...Homer Village, N.Y., [John W. Osborn, for Jesse
Searl] Pr. at the Repository office, 1819. MWA. 48124

-- A sermon, delivered at Lisle, county of Broome
(state of New York) ...January 3, 1819...[Norwich,
N.Y., Pr. by J.F. Hubbard, 1819] MWA.   48125

The Guardian, or, Youth's religious instructor: a
monthly publication...New Haven, Nathan Whiting, at
the office of the Religious intelligencer, 1819-27. Vol.
1-9. MBC; MNoanHi; NjR; OO; RPB.   48126

Guerri de Maubreuil, Marie Armand, Marquis d' Ors-
vault, 1782-1855.
    Lettre interéssante adressée a S.A.R. le prince
régent d' Angle-terre par M. Marie-Armand de Guerry
de Maubreuil, marquis d' Orvault...Philadelphie, 1819.
15 p. CtY.   48127

                        H
Habermann, Johann
    Christliche Morgen-und-Abend-Gebeter...Baltimore,
Pr. by Schäffer und Maund, 1819. 54 p. DLC; MWA;
MdBE; PPLT.   48128

Hack, Maria
    Affection's gift to a beloved god-child by M.H.
from the London ed. Boston, Wells and Lilly, 1819.
148 p. MB.   48129

[Haines, Charles Glidden]
    An appeal to the people of the state of New-York,
on the expediency of abolishing the Council of Appointment. New-York, Pr. by E. Conrad, 1819. 83 p.
MBAt; MWA; MiD-B; NbU.   48130

[Haldane, James Alexander]
    Early instruction recommended in a narrative of

the life of Catherine Haldane... Boston, Lincoln & Edmands, 1819. MWA. 48131

[--] -- New Haven, Sidney's press, for J. Babcock and son [sold by S. & W.R. Babcock] 1819. 36 p. DLC; MWA; RPB. 48132

[--] -- Portland, Me., Pr. by A. Shirley, for William Hyde, 1819. 24 p. MWA. 48133

Hales, John G.
Map of Boston and its vicinity... Boston, 1819. PPAmP. 48134

[Hall, Richard]
To the publick... [New Ipswich, N.H.?] 1819. MB; MWA. 48135

Hall, Robert
The work of the Holy Spirit... [Andover, Mass., 1819] MB. 48136

[Halleck, Fitz-Greene] 1790-1867
Fanny... New-York, Pr. by Clayton & Kingsland, for C. Wiley & co., 1819. 49 p. CSt; DLC; DeGE; ICU; MWA; RPB. 48137

Hallowell collections of sacred music... Ed. 2. Hallowell, Me., E. Goodale, 1819. 215 p. MHi; MWA; MeBa; RPB. 48138

Hamilton, Elizabeth
Translation of the letters of a Hindoo Rajah... Boston, Wells and Lilly, 1819. 2 v. CSmH; MH; MSaP; MWA; MdBP; NN; PMA; PPA; PPL-R; RJa; RNR. 48139

Hamilton, James
The life and dying confession of James Hamilton... [Albany, 1819] MWA. 48140

Hamilton College
Catalogue of the faculty and students of Hamilton College, December 1, 1819. Utica, N.Y., Pr. by

William Williams, 1819. [8] p. NCH.   48141

Hamilton Gazette. Hamilton, Ohio, Camron & Murray, Oct. 12, 1819, 1st issue. Weekly newspaper.
OHi.   48142

Hamilton Recorder. Hamilton, N. Y., Condery & Smead, June 11, 1819, 1st issue. Weekly newspaper.
MWA.   48143

Hammond, Abijah
    An address delivered before the Westchester Agricultural Society on the 27th of October, 1819... New York, 1819. 15 p. MHi.   48144

Hampden-Sidney College, Hampden-Sidney, Va.
    Laws of Hampden-Sidney college. [Richmond, Pr. at the Franklin press, 1819?] 15 p. DLC.   48145

Hampshire Education Society
    The annual report of the committee to the Hampshire Education Society... Nov. 3, 1819... Northampton, Mass., Pr. by Thomas W. Shepard and co., 1819.
12 p. MWA.   48146

Handbuch fur Deutsche; enthaltend formen zu handschriften, welche den deutschen burgern der Vereinigten Staaten nuzlich und dienlich seyn kounen... Reading [Pa.] Gedruckt und hrsg. von Johann Ritter und comp., 1819. 112 p. CSt; DLC; MH; MWA.   48147

Handel and Haydn Society
    The creation, a sacred oration, in three parts, to be performed on the evening of the 2d of March, at Boylston Hall, by the Handel and Haydn Society. Boston, Pr. by Thomas Badger, Jr., 1819. DLC; MB.
48148
-- Oratorio in two parts, to be performed on the evening of the 1st of July, at Boylston Hall, by the Handel and Haydn Society. Assisted by the celebrated vocal performer Mr. Incledon. Boston, Pr. by Thomas Badger, Jr. [1819?] DLC.   48149

-- Oratorio, selected from the words of Handel, and other eminent authors, to be performed on the evening of the 1st of April, at Boylston Hall by the Handel and Haydn Society. Boston, Pr. by Thomas Badger, Jr., 1819. DLC.   48150

Hannam, Thomas
      An analysis, or outlines of sermons...Haverhill, Mass., Repr. by P. N. Green, for John Briggs, 1819. 312 p. MBNMHi; MHaHi; MWA.   48151

Happy poverty, or the story of poor blind Ellen... Philadelphia, Religious tract society, 1819. 12 p. NjR.
                                                       48152
The Happy waterman; or Honesty the best policy. To which are added, The boy of Dundee, and The Gardener and rose tree. Boston, Lincoln & Edmands, 1819. 24 p. MH; MWA.   48153

Harby, Isaac
      Alberti, A play in five acts...Charleston, S. C., Pr. by A. E. Miller, for the author, 1819. 55 p. CSmH; MB; RPB.   48154

Hardcastle's annual masonic register and pocket magazine, for the year of masonry, 5819. New York, Pr. by Southwick & Pelsue for Bro. J. Hardcastle, 1819. 72 p. NHi.   48155

Hardie, James
      A dictionary of the most uncommon wonders of the works of art and nature...New York, Pr. by Samuel Marks, 1819. 336 p. CtW; MWA; NB; NjR.   48156

-- The new freemason's monitor. Ed. 2. New York, George Long, 1819. 346 p. MH; MWA; NNFM; OCM; TxWFM.   48157

[--] Selecta e profanis scriptoribus...Nova editio... Andover, Mass., Pr. by Flagg & Gould, for M. Newman, 1819. MWA.   48158

[--] -- Philadelphia, Pr. by Lydia R. Bailey, 1819.

299 p.   MWA; PPL; PReaHi; PV.   48159

[--] -- Philadelphia, E. & R. Parker, 1819. MWA.
48160
[--] -- Philadelphia, M. Carey & Son, 1819. MWA.
48161
Harding, Benjamin
    A tour through the Western Country, A.D. 1818
and 1819.   Published for the use of emigrants. New-
London, Pr. by Samuel Green, for the author, 1819.
17 p.   DLC; MWA; NN.   48162

[Harding, Mrs. Anne Raikes] 1780-1858
    Decision.   A tale.   By the author of Correction,
&c. ... New York, A. T. Goodrich & co. ... 1819. 2 v.
DLC; MH.   48163

Hardy, Charles
    Commodore Charles Hardy, to his kind patrons,
whom he has served, by sweeping the streets for nineteen years, a good old faithful servant, and who wishes
his kind customers health, wealth, long life and happy
New Year.   Boston, 1819.   Broadside. MB.   48164

Hare, Joseph Thompson, 1780-1818
    Confessions of a highwayman.   Baltimore, Pr. for
the publisher [E.J. Coale] [1819?] 23 p. PPL. 48165

[Hare, Robert]
    Defence of the American character... Philadelphia,
1819.   MWA.   48166

Hare, Robert, 1781-1858
    A new theory of galvanism, supported by some ex-
periments and observations made by means of the cal-
orimotor, a new galvanic instrument.   Also, a new
mode of decomposing potash extemporaneously. Read
before the Academy of Natural Sciences, Philadelphia
... Philadelphia, M. Carey, 1819. 17 p. DeGE; MBM;
MHi; MWA; P; RPB.   48167

The Harp; or, Songster's companion: being a choice
selection of sentimental and entertaining songs. Ro-

chester, N. Y., E. Peck & Co., 1819. 50 p. CtNwchA.
48168

Harris, Thaddeus Mason
Discourses, delivered on public occasions, illus-
trating the principles, displaying the tendency, and
vindicating the design, of Free masonry...Philadelphia,
G. Howorth, and M'Carty & Davis [1819] 376 p. DLC;
MdBS.   48169

Harrison, Elisha
To the free and independent electors of the 10th
senatorial district of the state of Indiana, composed of
the counties of Posey, Vanderburgh, Warwick, Spencer
and Perry. Fellow-citizens...I have been induced to
offer myself as a candidate to represent you in the ensuing general assembly...Evansville, 7th July, 1819.
Broadside. In.   48170

Harrison, Susannah
Songs, in the night: by a young woman under
heavy afflictions...New Brunswick, N. J., 1819. 215 p.
KyLoS.   48171

[Harrod, John J] comp.
Special and camp-meeting songs, for the pious...
Ed. 3. Baltimore, John J. Harrod, 1819. 216 p.
NNUT.   48172

Hart, Cyrus Wadsworth
Political dissertations and essay, and a third and
concluding epistle to a departed spirit...Newlisbon (O.)
Pr. by William D. Lepper, for the author, 1819. 24 p.
OClWHi.   48173

Hart, W. Jillard
An introduction to the study of chronology, and
universal history, in question and answer. Philadelphia, M. Carey and son, 1819. 181 p. KyDC; RLa.
48174

Hart, William H.
A sermon, preached before the Masonic societies
of Richmond and Manchester, on St. John's day, December 27, A. L. 5818. Richmond, Pr. by John War-

rock, 1819. CSmH.   48175

Hartford Auxiliary Colonization Society
    Constitution of the Hartford Auxiliary Colonization
Society: A list of officers chosen at the organization
of the society; together with an address to the public.
Hartford, Pr. by Lincoln & Stone, 1819. 16 p. CtHC;
CtHi; CtHT-W; CtSoP; DLC; ICN; MB; MWA.   48176

Hartford, Conn. Society for Savings
    Constitution, object and by-laws...Hartford, 1819.
11 p. CtY.   48177

Harvard University. Boylston Medical Society.
    Catalogue of members...Feb. 1, 1819. Boston,
T. Badger, Jr., 1819. 8 p. NNNAM.   48178

Harvey, Joseph, 1787-1873
    The banner of Christ set up...Elizabeth-Town,
N. J., Pr. by J. & E. Sanderson, for Edson Hart,
agent of the Foreign mission school, 1819. MWA.
                                                48179
-- --...Delivered at the inauguration of the Rev. Her-
mon[!] Daggett, as principal of the Foreign Mission
school in Cornwall, Connecticut, May 6, 1818...New-
Haven, Pr. by S. Convers, for Nathan Whiting, agent
of the Foreign Mission school, 1819. 32 p. CSf; CSt;
CU; Ct; CtHi; CtY; MH; MWA; NcD; OClWHi; NRAB.
                                                48180
-- A reply to the statements of Mr. Daniel Parker, in
a late publication, entitled "Proscription delineated."
Hartford, Gleason & Co., 1819. 112 p. CtHC; CtY;
MB; MBC; MH; MH-AH; MWA; NN; NjR.   48181

Harwood, Edward
    The life and character of Jesus Christ delineated
...Philadelphia, Pr. by Wm. Fry, 1819. MWA. 48182

Haseltine, Samuel
    Experience of, written by himself, with fragments
of the Exercise of his mind to the closing scene and
an elegy on the death of his brother, to which is prefixed A sketch of his life. (Motto) Hanover, Pr. by

Charles Spear, 1819.   48183

Haskel, Daniel
    A sermon, delivered in Randolph, at the annual
meeting of the Vermont juvenile missionary society...
Middlebury, Vt., Pr. by Francis Burnap, 1818. 40 p.
CtY; MBC; MWA; MiD-B; NNUT; OO; VtHi; VtMiM;
VtMiS; VtU.   48184

Hastings, Thomas, 1784-1872
    The musical reader: or practical lessons for the
voice...Rev. and enl.   Utica [N.Y.] Pr. typographical-
ly by William Williams, 1819. 84 p. CSmH; CtHT-W; LNH;
MWA; NNUT; NRU; N; PPi.   48185

-- Musica sacra: or Springfield and Utica collections
united: consisting of psalm and hymn tunes, anthems
and chants...Ed. 2, rev.   Utica, N.Y., William Williams, 1819. 277 p. CSmH; CtHT-W; CtW; CtY; DLC;
ICN; IEG; IGK; MB; MH; MNF; MS; MWA; MdLuW;
MiD-B; N; NAnge; NBu; NFred; NN; NUt; NUtHi; NNUT;
NRU; NSyHi; NjP; NjPT; OClWHi; RPB; VtMiS.   48186

Haswell, Anthony
    Haswell's easy and instructive lessons...Ed. 2.
Bennington, Vt., Pr. by Darius Clark, 1819. 83 p.
CSt; MWA; Vt.   48187

Hatch, Roger C.
    Articles of faith- Nov. 25, '18.   Hopkinton. Con-
cord, N.H., Hill & Moore, 1819. MWA.   48188

[Haven, Samuel]
    A statement of the proceedings in the First church
and parish in Dedham...Cambridge, Pr. by Hilliard &
Metcalf, 1819. MWA; MWiW.   48189

Hawker, Robert
    The poor man's morning portion... 1st Amer. ed.
New York, Pr. by Jansen & Ritter, for Robert Wau-
chope, 1819. 340 p. MWA; MnHi; NRAB.   48190

-- Zion's pilgrim... Baltimore, Pr. by John D. Toy,
for Mordecai Stewart, 1819. MWA.   48191

[Hawley, Gideon]
    Instructions for better government and organiza-
tion of common schools. Albany, Websters and Skinners, 1819. MWA.   48192

Hawley, William Agur
    The death of saints an important event... Pittsfield,
Mass., Pr. by Phinehas Allen, 1819. 15 p. MB; MWA;
VtMiM.   48193

Haynes, Lemuel
    Universal salvation a very ancient doctrine... New-
burgh, N.Y., B.F. Lewis and Co., 1819. MWA. 48194

-- -- Newburyport, Mass., Pr. by W. & J. Gilman,
1819. MNe; MWA.   48195

Haynes, Sylvanus
    The Bible method of supporting the gospel minis-
try... Exeter, N.H., Josiah Richardson, 1819. MWA.
                                            48196

[Haywood, John]
    The Christian advocate... By a Tennesseean...
Nashville, Tenn., Thomas G. Bradford, 1819. 357 p.
CSmH; DLC; ICN; KyLxT; MB; NN; TCh; TKL-MC;
TxU.   48197

-- A manual of the laws of North Carolina, arranged
under distinct heads in alphabetical order... Ed. 4.
Raleigh, N.C., Pr. by J. Gales, 1819. 877 p. C;
CSt; DLC; ICN; Ia; IaU-L; In-SC; M; NcAS; NcWfC.
                                            48198

Hazlitt, William
    Lectures on the English comic writers... Philadel-
phia, Pr. by T.H. Palmer, for M. Carey and son,

1819.   343 p.   CtY; MBBC; MH-AH; MWA; MWH;
NNCoCi.   48199

[Heald, Henry]
    Western tour, in a series of letters; written dur-
ing a journey through Pennsylvania, Ohio, Indiana, and
into the states of Illinois and Kentucky: - giving an account of the soil, face of the country, antiquities and
natural curiosities, etc. [Wilmington, Del., J. Wilson, 1819] 91 p. DeHi; DeWI; NN.   48200

Healy, Joseph
    An appeal to the public, by Joseph Healy, in vindi-
cation of his own character, against the aspersions
which have gone abroad through the slanderous abuse
of Ebenezer Paine.   Also, an exposition of some of the
prominent features in the character of Ebenezer Paine.
Boston, N. Coverly, 1819. 44 p.   MBr.   48201

Heartte, Isaac T.
    Ars navigandi: or, Tables of longitude, for cor-
recting the effects of parallax and refraction, on the
distances observed between the sun and moon, or moon
and star...Baltimore, Pr. by B. Edes, for the author,
1819.   39 p.   DLC; MB; MdBMAS; MdHi.   48202

Heath, John D.
    A masonic oration, delivered in Lodge No. 39,
Columbia...Columbia, S.C., Pr. by D. Faust, 1819.
14 p. N.   48203

Heckwelder, John Gottlieb Ernestus
    An account of the history, manners, and customs
of the Indian nations.   By Rev. John Heckwelder.
Philadelphia, Abraham Small, 1819.   465 p. DLC; MH;
PEdg.   48204

[Hedge, Levi]
    A sketch of the life and character of Rev. Joseph
McKean, D.D., LL.D., late Boylston professor in
Harvard university.   Massachusetts historical society
collections.   Boston, 1819. MA; MoSM.   48205

Hemphill, Joseph, 1770-1842
Speech of Mr. Hemphill, on the Missouri question.
In the House of representatives of the United States.
[Washington, D. C., ? 1819] 27 p. CSmH; MH; N;
OClWHi; PPL.   48206

Henderson's almanack for 1820. By Joshua Sharp.
With J. Beasley's weather predictions. Raleigh, N. C.,
Thomas Henderson [1819] MWA.   48207

Hendley, George
A memorial for Sunday school girls... 1st Amer.
ed. Boston, Pr. by U. Crocker, for Samuel T. Armstrong, 1819. MWA.   48208

Henkel, Ambrose, 1786-1870
Das kleine A B C-buch, oder erste Anfangs-buch-
lein, mit schoenen bildern und deren namen... 2. aufl.
New-Market, Schenandoah County, Va., Pr. in Salo-
mon Henkel's druckery, 1819. 36 p. CSmH; CtHT-W;
DLC; MWA; NN; NcD; PHi; PPLT; Vi; ViU; ViLxW;
ViW.   48209

Henry, Matthew
The communicant's companion... New York, Pr.
by Nichols & Price, for L. & F. Lockwood, 1819.
285 p. MWA; MoKiT.   48210

-- A method for prayer; with scripture expressions,
proper to be used under each head. New-York, Pr.
by C. N. Baldwin, for N. B. Holmes, 1819. 234 p.
MeBat; N; TChU.   48211

Henry, Philip
Fragments. (Tract no. 119) New-York, J. Seymour, 1819. 4 p. PPiXT.   48212

Henry, William
The elements of experimental chemistry... 1st
Amer., from 8th London ed. Philadelphia, Robert De-
silver, 1819. 2 v. MOra; MdU; MeHi; NBMS.   48213

Henry Goodwin; or The contented man. By the author

of "William's Return," and "The Twin Brothers."
Boston, Pr. by Wells and Lilly, 1819. 98 p. MPlyA;
MWA.   48214

Hermann, L. J.
  Catechismus der glaubenslehren lebenspflichten der
Christlichen religion.   Reading, Pa., 1819. 70 p.
MWA; P; PPLT.   48215

The hermit of the forest... Cooperstown, N.Y., H. &
E. Phinney, 1819. 28 p. MWA.   48216

Herr, John
  Eine Kurze und Apostolische Antwort... 1819.
MWA.   48217

[Hersey, Thomas]
  A voice from the grave; or a letter from the dead
to the living,... Philadelphia, William Bradford, 1819.
12 p. MWA; NRAB.   48218

Herttell, Thomas
  An expose of the causes of intemperate drinking,
and the means by which it may be obviated.   New
York, E. Conrad, 1819. 56 p. MH; MWA; NNS;
PPL-R.   48219

Hesitation; or, To marry, or not to marry? By the
author of the Balance of comfort, Bachelor and mar-
ried man, &c ... New-York, Pr. by C. S. Van Winkle,
for W.B. Gilley, 1819. 2 v. CtHT-W; MB; MWA; NN;
NcD.   48220

Heuzet, Jean
  Selectae profanis scriptoribus, adjectis notis.
Novo editio expurgata et emendata.   Andover, Mass.,
Pr. by Flagg & Gould, for M. Newman, 1819. 276 p.
CtY; MB; MBC; MMonsA; KyBC; NNC.   48221

-- Selectae profanis scriptoribus historiae quibus ad-
minata sunt varia honeste vivendi praecepta, ex hisdem
scriptoribus deprompta... Philadelphia, Benjamin Warner, 1819. DLC.   48222

Heythuysen, F. Van
    The equity draftsman; being a collection of prece-
dents drawn by some of the leading men at the equity
bar... Selected by F. Van Heythuysen... 1st Amer. ed.
New York, Gould and Banks, 1819. 658 p. MoU;
VtBaT.   48223

Hill, William
    Ministerial parity, or an equality of grade, office,
and authority, among the Christian clergy, vindicated
and proved in a sermon, delivered in Winchester, October 21st, 1819... Winchester, Va., J. McGlassin,
1819. 71 p. CSmH; CtSoP; DLC; NjPT; NjR; Vi; ViU.
                                                 48224
Des Hintenden Bolten Americanischer calender.   Auf
das jahr... 1820... Baltimore, Schaeffer und Maund
[1819] [36] p. MdHi.   48225

Hippocrates
    The prognostics and crises of Hippocrates, trans-
lated from the Greek; with critical and explanatory
notes... By Henry William Ducachet... New-York, J.
Eastburn and co., 1819. 126 p. DLC; MBM; MWA;
NBMS; NNNAM.   48226

Historical sketch First Baptist Church.   Boston, 1819.
47 p. MWA.   48227

The history of Don Francisco De Miranda's attempt to
effect a revolution in South America, in a series of
letters, by a Gentleman who was an officer to that
General, to his friend in the United States.   Ed. 2.
Boston, Edward Oliver, 1819. 312 p. MPlyP.   48228

The history of Fanny Beverly, and her dog Fido...
New Haven, Sidney's press, for J. Babcock & son,
1819. 31 p. MWA.   48229

History of Henry Fairchild and Charles Trueman.
Philadelphia, Pr. by Clark & Raser, 1819. MWA.
                                                 48230
The history of Joseph, the son of Israel.   Woodstock,
Vt., Pr. by David Watson, 1819. 31 p. MWA.   48231

History of Little Henry and his bearer. From 8th
London ed. New York, J.C. Totten, 1819. 58 p.
MWA.   48232

-- Newburyport, Mass., W. & J. Gilman, 1819. 50 p.
MWA.   48233

History of Mr. S....and David Thomson. New York,
Pr. by Religious tract society, 1819. PPPrHi. 48234

The history of Ralph Raymond...Hartford, Pr. by
Roberts & Burr, for S.G. Goodrich, 1819. MWA.
                                                  48235
A history of the Bible. 1819. 72 p. MWA.   48236

History of the Bible. Boston, Pr. by Parmenter and
Balch, for T. Bedlington, 1819. 254 p. MAshlHi; MB;
MH; MHaHi; MWA; NjR; PP.   48237

The history of the Dutchess [sic] of C.....From Adele
and Theodore. Written by herself. Baltimore, Pr.
for the booksellers, 1819. 103 p. MWA; MdHi. 48238

The history of Tommy Two-shoes...Woodstock, Vt.,
Pr. by David Watson, 1819. 31 p. MWA.   48239

History of William Black, the chimney sweeper. New
York, Pr. by Religious tract society, 1819. PPPrHi.
                                                  48240
Hitchcock, Silas
    A small collection of practical and experimental
hymns, original and selected...Sangerfield, N.Y., Pr.
by Joseph Tenny, 1819. 64 p. MWA; RPB.   48241

Hoare, Prince
    My grandmother; a musical farce in two acts.
New York, T. Longworth, 1819. 22 p. CSmH; MH;
RNR.   48242

-- No song no supper; an opera...New-York, David
Longworth, 1819. 33 p. MH; N; NN.   48243

Hobart, John Henry, bp.
    Address in convention of the Protestant Episcopal
Church of Connecticut.   New Haven, Oct. 1819. p. 25-
36.   CtHC; NjR.   48244

-- The candidate for confirmation instructed in a sermon explaining the office confirmation... New York,
stereotyped by James Conner, for the Protestant Episcopal Tract Society, 1819. 56 p.   MHi; MWA; NjR; OC.
                                                        48245
-- The Churchman. The principles of the Churchman
stated and explained, in distinction from the corrup-
tions of the Church of Rome, and from the errors of
certain Protestant sects... New-York, Pr. by T. & J.
Swords, 1819. 32 p.   MB; MBDiL; MWA; NIC; NNG;
NjPT; NjR.   48246

-- A companion for the altar... Ed. 4.   New York,
T. & J. Swords, 1819. 222 p.   MWA; NjR.   48247

Der Hoch-Deutsche Americanische Calender, auf das
Jahr 1820... Germantaun, Pa., M. Billmeyer [1819]
[40] p. NjR.   48248

Hoch Deutsches Lutherisches A B C und namen büchlein
... Germantown, Pa., M. Billmeyer, 1819. MWA.
                                                        48249
Hoch-Deutsches Reformirtes A B C und Namen-Büch-
lein... Germantwown, Pa., M. Billmeyer, 1819. MWA.
                                                        48250
Hoff's agricultural and commercial almanac, calculated
for the states of Georgia and the Carolinas, for the
year of our Lord, 1820... Calculated by Joshua Sharp.
Charleston, S. C., Pr. by J. Hoff, [1819] 36 p. DLC.
                                                        48251

Hoff's commercial or City almanac... 1820-
Charleston, S. C., 1819.   ScC.   48252

Hofland, Mrs. (Barbara Wreaks Hoole)
    The affectionate brothers; a tale by Mrs. Hofland.
New York, W. B. Gilley, 1819. 150 p. MH; PPL.
                                                        48253
-- Ellen, the teacher... New York, Pr. by N. Van

Riper, for W. B. Gilley, 1819. 189 p. CtHi; MDeeP;
MH; MWA; RPB.   48254

Hoge, John Blair
 The Heavenly rest; a sermon, delivered at Mar-
tinsburgh, July twenty-first, 1819, on occasion of the
death of Mrs. Ann Boyd...Martinsburgh, Va., Pr. by
J. Alburtis, 1819. 35 p. PPPrHi.   48255

Hohman, Johann George
 Eine schöne, anmuthige und lesenswürdige Ge-
schichte von der Geduldigen Helena...Reading, Pa.,
Pr. by Carl A. Bruckman, 1819. MWA.   48256

-- Eine schöne, anmuthige und lesenswürdige Ge-
schichte ...von Genovefa...Reading, Pa., Pr. by C.
A. Bruckman, 1819. MWA.   48257

-- Das Evangelium Nicoldemus oder Gewisser Bericht
von dem leben, leiden und Sterven Unsers Heilands
Jesu Christi...gegeben von Johann George Hohman...
Reading, Pa., Pr. by W. Bruckman, 1819. DLC;
MWA; NjR; P.   48258

-- Der lange verborgene freund, oder: Getreuer und
christlicher unterricht fur jedermann... 2. und ver-
besserte aufl. [Reading? 1819] 87 p. DLC.   48259

-- The long lost friend, containing mysterious and in-
valuable arts and remedies, for man as well as animals...Lancaster, Pa., 1819. 127 p. Bausman, p.
63.   48260

Holcombe, Henry
 A reply to Thomas Roberts and W. E. Ashton as
moderator and clerk of the Philadelphia Baptist association. Philadelphia, 1819. 25 p. RPB.   48261

Holcroft, Thomas
 The road to ruin...2d Amer. ed. New York,
David Longworth, 1819. MB; MBr; MH; MWA.   48262

Holley, O. L.
New-York, February 9, 1819. Gentlemen, having made some new arrangements for the ...and punctual publication of the American ...magazine and critical review, I have to request forthwith transmit a statement of your account...E. Biglow and O. L. Holley, and with O. L. Holley and Benjamin G. Jansen, of this city, to whom is transferred the debts due on account of the ...yours, &c. [O. L. Holley in Ms.] [Addressed to Messrs. Worsley & Smith] Lexington, Ky., 1819. Broadside. WHi.   48263

Holmes, Abiel
A sermon delivered before the Convention of the Congregational ministers of Massachusetts...Cambridge, Pr. by Hilliard and Metcalf, 1819. 36 p. MWA; NjR.
48264

Home, John
Douglas...a tragedy...Ed. 3. New York, Thomas Longworth, 1819. 56 p. MH; MWA; RNR.   48265

Homerus
The Iliad of Homer...Baltimore, Pr. by J. Robinson, for F. Lucas, Jun., and N. G. Maxwell, 1819. 2 v. DeGE; MB; MWA; MdW; NcWsS.   48266

-- The Illiad and Odyssey of Homer; trans. into English blank verse by the late William Cowper. Boston, Joseph T. Buckingham, 1819. OAU.   48267

Hooper, John
The advantages of early piety displayed, in a memoir of Mr. John Clement...Boston, Pr. by U. Crocker, for Samuel T. Armstrong, 1819. 200 p. IaGG; MB; MWA; PMA.   48268

Hooper, William
An address delivered before the North Carolina Bible Society, Dec. 1819. Fayetteville, N. C., 1819. 8 p. Cadmus Book Shop Cat. 114, 1933.   48269

-- A short system of Latin prosody: containing all the necessary rules and directions for scanning hexameter

verse, and Horace's lyrics, with ease and advantage.
Philadelphia, Pr. by L.R. Bailey, for the author,
1819. 36 p. NcU; P.   48270

[Hopkins, Samuel]
   The trial: Calvin and Hopkins versus the Bible
and commonsense. By a lover of the truth. Boston,
1819. 2 ed. RHi.   48271

Hopkins, Samuel Miles
   An address to the Agricultural society, of the
county of Genesee... Batavia, N.Y., Pr. by Miller &
Blodgett, 1819. 24 p. DLC; MB; MWA; N.   48272

Hopkinton, N.H.--First Congregational church.
   Articles of faith... Concord, N.H., Pr. by Hill &
Moore, 1819. 8 p. MWA; Nh-Hi; NjR.   48273

[Hornyhold, John Joseph, bp.]
   The real principles of Catholics; or, A catechism
of general instruction for grown persons... Philadelphia,
Bernard Dornin, 1819. 326 p. MdBS; MdW.   48274

Hosack, David, 1769-1835
   A biographical memoir of Hugh Williamson...
member of the New-York Historical Society... delivered
on the first of November, 1819... New-York, Pr. by
C.S. Van Winkle, 1819. 91 p. NNS.   48275

-- Course of studies designed for the private medical
school established in New-York, by David Hosack...
New York, C.S. Van Winkle, 1819. 7 p. DNLM. 48276

House carpenters' book of prices, and rules, for measuring and valuing all their kinds of work. Philadelphia, 1819. 50 p. CtY.   48277

Housewrights rules of work for the town of Portland,
1819. Portland, Me., Pr. by A. & J. Shirley, 1819.
24 p. MeHi.   48278

Howard Benevolent Society
   Howard Benevolent Society, organized in Boston,

June 1, 1812. Incorporated, Feb. 16, 1818. Boston,
Pr. by Ezra Lincoln, 1819. 24 p. MWA.   48279

Howe, John
    An address, delivered at the installation of offi-
cers in Washington Lodge, Roxbury, December 6th,
A. L. 5819... Boston, Pr. by Joseph T. Buckingham,
1819. 31 p. ICN; MH; MHi; MMeT; NNFM; PHi;
PPFM.   48280

Howe, Nathanael
    The design of John's baptism... Andover, Mass.,
Pr. by Flagg & Gould, 1819. 24 p. CBPSR; MBDiL;
MWA; NN; NRAB.   48281

Howell, M. E.
    Dr. Abraham Howell's genuine tetter ointment, pre-
pared and sold by M. E. Howell at 63 North Eighth
Street, Philadelphia. Philadelphia, 1819. Broadside.
(William B. Pennebaker, 1634 Old York Road, Harts-
ville, Pa.)   48282

Howe's genuine almanac for the year 1820. By J.
Howe. Enfield, Mass., 1819. 24 p. MHi; MWA; WHi.
                                             48283
Hoyle, Edmond, 1672-1769
    Hoyle's games improved, containing whist, piquet
... draughts... chess... New York, G. & R. White, 1819.
272 p. OCl.   48284

Hubbard, William
    An introductory address preceding a sermon
preached at Goshen, in January, 1819... Goshen, Mass.,
Pr. by Ephraim Whitman, 1819. 40 p. MWA; MiD-B.
                                             48285
Hubbard, William
    An introductory address... Goshen, Mass., Pr.
by Ephraim Whitman, 1819. (Type and set-up of title
varies) MWA.   48286

[Hughs, Mrs. Mary (Robson)]
    Henry Goodwin... Boston, Pr. by Wells & Lilly,
1819. MWA.   48287

[--] -- Philadelphia, 1819. MWA.   48288

Hull, Joseph Hervey
    A guide to the English language: containing the
powers of the English alphabet...Rev. impression.
Utica, N.Y., William Williams, 1819. 167 p. DLC;
NBuG; NCH; NUtHi; OClWHi.   48289

An humble attempt to reconcile the differences of
Christians respecting the extent of the atonement by
showing that the controversy which exists on this subject is chiefly verbal...New York, Stephen Dodge,
J. Seymour, 1819. 449 p. KyLoP.   48290

Humphrey, Heman, 1779-1861
    The promised land. A sermon, delivered at
Goshen, [Conn.] at the ordination of the Rev. Messrs.
Hiram Bingham & Asa Thurston, as missionaries to
the Sandwich Islands, Sept. 29, 1819...Boston, Pr. by
U. Crocker, for Samuel T. Armstrong, 1819. 40 p.
CSmH; CtHT-W; CtY-D; DLC; ICN; IEG; MB; MBC;
MBDiL; MBev; MDeeP; MH; MNe; MWA; MWiW;
MiD-B; MnHi; NCH; NN; NNC; OClWHi; PLT; RBr;
VtMiM.   48291

Hunt, Gilbert J.
    The historical reader; containing "The late war be-
tween the United States and Great Britain, from June,
1812, to February, 1815...Ed. 3. New York, Daniel
D. Smith, 1819. 233 p. DLC; MWA; MiD-B.   48292

-- -- Ed. 3. New-York, David Longworth, 1819.
233 p. DLC; MWA; NSmB.   48293

-- -- Ed. 3. New York, Richard Scott, 1819. MWA.
                                                        48294
-- The late war, between the United States and Great
Britain...Ed. 3. New York, B. Crane, 1819. MWA.
                                                        48295
-- -- Ed. 3. New York, D. Longworth, 1819. 233 p.
DLC; MiU; ViRu.   48296

-- -- Ed. 3. New York, Daniel D. Smith, 1819.

MWA.   48297

-- -- Ed. 3. New York, G. J. Hunt, 1819. MWA.
                                                   48298
-- -- Ed. 3. New York, Scott & Seguine, 1819.
233 p. MH; MWA; OClWHi.   48299

Hunt, Richard
    An address, delivered before the Female juvenile
benevolent society... in Attleborough... Providence,
Pr. by Miller & Hutchens, 1819. MWA.   48300

Hunt, William Gibbes
    A masonic eulogy on the character and services of
the late Thomas Smith Webb, Esq. ... Lexington [Ky.]
Pub. by request, 1819. CSmH; DSC; IaCrM; MBAt;
MBFM; N.   48301

Huntington, Daniel
    A poem, on the pleasures and advantages of true
religion. Providence, Pr. [by William G. Goddard
and James D. Knowles] at the Rhode-Island American
office, 1819. DLC; MWA; RPB.   48302

Huntington, Eleazer
    Introduction to the art of penmanship: or, A new
and improved system of round and running hands.
For the use of schools in the United States... Hartford,
Pr. by B. & J. Russell, for the author, 1819. 18 p.
CtHi; MWA.   48303

Huntington, William
    God the guardian of the poor, and The bank of
faith: or, A display of the providences of God, which
have at sundry times attended the author... From the
7th London ed. Baltimore, Pr. by B. Edes, for
Paris Davis, 1819. 286 p. CtY; MdBP; MdHi.   48304

Huntsman, Adam
    Murfreesborough, Nov. 27, 1819. Fellow citizens,
the important session of 1819 is now drawing to a
close... [Murfreesborough, Tenn., 1819] Broadside.
MWA.   48305

Hutchin's revived almanack, 1820. New York, C. N.
Baldwin [1819] MWA. 48306

Hutchins' revived for 1820. New York, Daniel D.
Smith [1819] MWA. 48307

-- By William Collom. New York, George Long
[1819] 36 p. MWA; NHi; NN. 48308

-- -- Poughkeepsie, N. Y., Isaac T. Doughty [1819]
36 p. MWA; WHi. 48309

Hutton, Catherine
Oakwood Hall... Philadelphia, Pr. [by Asher Mi-
ner] for M. Carey & Son, 1819. 2 v. MWA. 48310

Hyde, Alvan, 1768-1833
The ambassador of Christ encouraged to be faithful. A sermon delivered September 1st, 1819, at the
ordination of the Rev. Alvan Hyde, junr. to the pastoral care of the church in Madison, County of Ge-
auga, Ohio...Stockbridge [Mass.] Pr. by C. Webster,
1819. 19 p. M; MB; MPiB; NjR; OClWHi; RPB. 48311

-- Sketches of the life, ministry and writings of the
Rev. Stephen West...Stockbridge [Mass.] Pr. by
Charles Webster, 1819. 18 p. CSmH; MBAt. 48312

Hyde, Jabez Backus
Kianasa, nana nonedowaga neuwenuda. Hymns in
the Seneca language. Buffalo, N. Y., Pr. by H. A.
Salisbury, 1819. 40 p. MWA; NBuHi. 48313

Hymns and songs of praise, for the use of children in
general...New Haven, Sidney's press, for J. Babcock
& Son, 1819. 36 p. CtHi; MWA; NjR. 48314

Hymns for infant minds. By the author of original
poems...Ed. 7. To which are added lines on the
death of Mrs. Harriet Newell and the Twins. Boston,
Pr. by U. Crocker, for Samuel T. Armstrong, 1819.
71 p. DLC; MWA. 48315

-- Hanover, Pr. by Charles Spear, 1819. 72 p. MWA.
48316

Hymns for little children. New York, Samuel Wood &
sons, and Samuel S. Wood & Co., Baltimore, 1819.
MWA; RPB.   48317

Hymns for use of children. Tract & Book Soc. of the
Evangelical Lutheran Church. Philadelphia, W. Fry,
1819. 24 p. MWA.   48318

                              I
Ide, Jacob
    The nature and tendency of balls...Dedham, Mass.,
Pr. by H. & W.H. Mann [1819] 50 p. CSmH; MWA.
48319
-- A sermon, delivered December 29, 1819, at the
ordination of the Rev. David Brigham, as pastor of
the Second Congregational church in Randolph...Bos-
ton, Pr. by Lincoln & Edmands, 1819. 28 p. KTW;
MB.   48320

Illinois (State)
    Journal of the House of Representatives, of the
second session of the General Assembly, of the state
of Illinois, begun and held in the town of Kaskaskia,
on Monday the eighteenth day of January, A.D. 1819.
Kaskaskia, Ill., Blackwell & Berry, 1819. 192 p. I;
IHi; NN.   48321

-- Journal of the Senate, of the second session, of
the General Assembly, of the state of Illinois, begun
and held in the town of Kaskaskia, on Monday the
eighteenth day of January, A.D. 1819. Kaskaskia, Ill.,
Blackwell & Berry, 1819. 224 p. I; IHi.   48322

-- Laws passed by the first General Assembly, of the
state of Illinois, at their second session, held at Kaskaskia, Pr. by Blackwell & Berry, 1819. 445 p. DLC;
ICHi; ICN; IHi; IU; IaU-L; In-SC; InU; OCLaw.   48323

Illinois Gazette. Shawneetown, Eddy & Kimmel, Sept.
25, 1819, 1st issue with this title. A weekly continu-

ation of the "Illinois Emigrant." DLC. 48324

The imitation of the Blessed Virgin; composed on the plan of the imitation of Christ. From the French. Philadelphia, Bernard Dornin, 1819. 386 p. DGU; NPStA. 48325

Improved New-England almanack for 1820. By Nathan Wild. Keene, N. H., John Prentiss [1819] [48] p. MH; MWA; Nh-Hi; OCHP. 48326

In consequence of some remarks on the Layman, he offers the following arguments...[1819] MWA. 48327

Inchbald, Mrs. Elizabeth (Simpson) 1753-1821
    The wedding day, a comedy, in two acts...New York, David Longworth, 1819. 31 p. C; DLC; MH; MWA. 48328

Independent Chronicle & Boston Patriot. Semi-weekly ...Boston, Ballad & Wright, 1819. DLC. 48329

Independent Examiner. Vevay, Ind., Stephen C. Stevens, 1819. Brigham, p. 142. 48330

Independent Press. Natchez, Miss., Peter Isler, Mar. 24, 1819, 1st issue. Weekly newspaper. DLC. 48331

Independent Republican. Watertown, N. Y., S. A. Abbey, Apr. 5, 1819, 1st issue. Weekly newspaper. MWA. 48332

Independent Virginian. Clarksburg, Va., William M'Granaghan, Aug. 4, 1819, 1st issue. Weekly newspaper. DLC. 48333

Indiana (State)
    Journal of the House of Representatives of the state of Indiana, being the third session of the General Assembly, begun and held at Corydon...seventh day of December, 1818. [Corydon] Pr. by A. & J. Brandon, 1818[!] [1819] 185 p. In. 48334

-- Journal of the House of Representatives of the
state of Indiana, being the fourth session of the General Assembly begun and held at Corydon... sixth day
of December - 1819. Corydon, Pr. by Brandon &
M'Cullough, 1819-'20. 383 p. In.   48335

-- Journal of the Senate of the state of Indian, being
the 3d session of the General Assembly, begun and
held at Corydon... the 7th day of December, 1818
[Corydon] Pr. by A. & J. Brandon, 1818[!] [1819]
120 p. In.   48336

-- Journal of the Senate of the state of Indiana, being
the fourth session of the General assembly, begun and
held at Corydon... sixth day of December, 1819.
Corydon, Brandon & M'Cullough, prs., 1819-'20.
274 p. In.   48337

-- Laws of the state of Indiana, passed and published
at the 3d session of the General assembly, held in
December, 1818... Corydon, A. & J. Brandon, 1819.
152 p. DLC; In; InHi; InU; N.   48338

Indiana Oracle. Laurenceburg, Dunn & Russell, Sept.
1, 1819, 1st issue. Weekly newspaper. In.   48339

The infant preacher... New Haven, Pr. [by Nathan
Whiting] at the office of the Religious intelligencer,
1819. 32 p. MWA.   48340

-- ...Or the story of Henrietta Smith. [Philadelphia]
1819. 12 p. MWA; NHi.   48341

The infantry exercise of the United States Army,
abridged for the use of the militia of the United States.
Ed. 3, cor. and improved. Poughkeepsie, N. Y.,
H. Potter and S. Potter & Co., Philadelphia, 1819.
156 p. ICJ; MWA; NBatHL.   48342

Informer. Shepherdstown, Va., W. Sappington & Co.,
Aug. 5, 1819, 1st issue. Weekly newspaper. Brigham,
p. 1174.   48343

Ingersoll, Samuel Bridge
  Address, delivered before the Marine Bible society of New-Haven,...New Haven, Pr. at the office
of the Religious intelligencer, 1819. 24 p. CtY; MB;
MWA; MiD-B; NjPT.   48344

Instances of filial intrepidity and tenderness. Boston,
Lincoln & Edmands, 1819. 8 p. CSt; MAShlHi; MWA.
                                                       48345
The interesting conversion and exemplary life of Mrs.
Tooly. Ed. 2. Andover, Mass., 1819. (N.E. Tract
Soc. Tract no. 94) MSaE.   48346

Interesting memoir of H - G - of Philadelphia...Phila-
delphia, William Bradford, agent, 1819. MWA. 48347

Ireland, James, 1748-1806
  The life of the Rev. James Ireland, who was, for
many years, pastor of the Baptist church at Buck
Marsh, Waterlick and Happy Creek, in Frederick and
Shenandoah counties, Virginia. Winchester, Va., Pr.
by J. Foster, for the pub., 1819. 232 p. CSmH; DLC;
ICU; MWA; RPB; TxU; Vi; ViU.   48348

Ironside, J., pseud.
  The Truth no. 1-2. By J. Ironside (pseud.) New-
Haven, 1819. CtHi; CtY; MHi; MWA.   48349

[Irving, Washington] 1783-1859
  A history of New-York...Ed. 3. Philadelphia,
v. 1. Pr. by J. Maxwell, v. 2. Pr. by W. Fry, for
M. Thomas, 1819. 2 v. CSmH; CtY; MWA; MdW;
MiDW-M; ViSwc.   48350

[--] Salmagundi. 1st-2d series. Philadelphia, M.
Thomas...1819. 4 no. CSmH.   48351

-- -- 2d series, by Washington Irving. New York,
Pr. by J. Maxwell, for Haley & Thomas, 1819. 3 v.
NjR.   48352

[--] -- Vol. II. New York, Pr. by J. Maxwell, for
Hall & Thomas, 1819. 230+ p. MdHi; NjR.   48353

[--] -- 2d series. By Launcelot Langstaff, esq.
[pseud.] Philadelphia, Pr. by J. Maxwell, for M.
Thomas, J. Hale and C. Thomas, New York, 1819.
58 p. CSmH; NjR.   48354

[--] The sketch book of Geoffrey Crayon, gent. New
York, Pr. by C. S. Van Winkle, 1819-20. 7 pts. in 2 v.
ICBB; MWA; MWiW; NjR; RP; RPB.   48355

[--] -- No. I. [Ed. 2] New York, Pr. by C. S. Van
Winkle, 1819. 94 p. MWA; NjR.   48356

Isaac, Daniel
    The doctrine of universal restoration examined...
New York, Pr. by A. Paul, for J. Soule and T. Mason, 1819. 160 p. MWA; NNMHi; NNUT; NcD; PMA.
                                               48357
Isabella; or, the fatal marriage. A tragedy in five
acts. New York, the Longworths, 1819. MWA. 48358

Isaiah Thomas's town and country almanack, or Complete farmer's calendar...1820...Worcester, Mass.,
Pr. by Manning & Trumbull, for George A. Trumbull...
[1819] [44] p. CSmH; MDedHi; MWA; MWeA; MWHi;
WHi.   48359

                         J
Jack-the-Giant-Killer, pseud.
    A book with the title in the right place. [A poke
in the ribs to all who hate controversies; or, The necessity and importance of writing pamphlets vindicated...New Haven, Pr. by Flagg & Gray, 1819] 11 p.
NN.   48360

Jackman, Joseph
    The sham-robbery, committed by Elijah Putnam
Goodridge, on his own person, in Newbury, near Essex bridge, Dec. 19, 1816...Concord, N. H., Pr. for
the author, 1819. 151 p. MWA; MNe; Nh; OClWHi.
                                               48361
Jackson
    New vade mecum: or a pocket companion for law-

yers, deputy sheriffs and constables... By Publicola
[pseud.] of Gilmanton, N. H. Boston, 1819. MB. 48362

Jackson, Andrew
    Correspondence between Major General Jackson
and Brevet Major General Scott, on the subject of an
order, bearing date the 22nd April, 1817; published by
the former, to the troops of his division. [Richmond]
1819. 16 p. N.   48363

Jackson, James
    James Jackson ex dem. Abraham Houseman and
others, vs. Jacob I. Sebring and Thomas Carpenter.
In the Court for the trial of impeachments and the correction of errors. Albany, Pr. by I. W. Clark, 1819.
24 p. N.   48364

Jackson, John
    A faithful account of the massacre of the family of
Gerald Watson... Boston, N. Coverly, 1819. 24 p.
MSaE.   48365

James, John Angell
    The Sunday school teacher's guide... With an ap-
pendix. Baltimore, Pr. by John D. Toy, for Cushing
& Jewett, 1819. 150 p. MH; MdHi.   48366

-- -- Boston, Lincoln & Edmands, 1819. 175 p. MWA;
RPB.   48367

Janes, Walter
    A masonic poem... Brookfield, Mass., Pr. by E.
Merriam & Co., 1819. 24 p. MBFM; MWA; NcS; RPB.
                                                   48368
[Janeway, Jacob Jones]
    An essay on the inability of sinners. From the
Evangelical Guardian, and Review, for Feb. & March,
1818. Ed. 2. Philadelphia, 1819. 24 p. CtY; MH-AH.
                                                   48369
[Jeffreys, George W.]
    A series of essays on agriculture and rural affairs,
in forty-seven numbers. By "Agricola," a North-Caro-
lina farmer... Raleigh, N. C., Joseph Gales, 1819. 223 p.

AFlT; CSmH; CLM; ICJ; MWA; NjR; NN; Nc; NcAS; NcD; NcU; NcWfC.   48370

Jenkins, Joseph
    An address delivered before the Massachusetts charitable mechanick association, December 17, 1818, being the anniversary of the choice of officers...Boston, Pr. by Munroe & Francis, 1819. 24 p. CtHT-W; DLC; MBAt; MBr;   MH; MHi; MMeT; MWA; MnHi; PHi.   48371

Jenks, Benjamin
    Prayers and offices of devotion for families... Boston, Pr. by U. Crocker, for Samuel T. Armstrong, 1819. 290 p. MBAt; MNe; MWA; MWiW; MWborHi; NRAB; PPM; VtMiS.   48372

-- -- Philadelphia, M'Carty & Davis, 1819. 323 p. MWA; ViRut.   48373

-- -- Philadelphia, G.W. Mentz, 1819. MH; MWA.
                                                   48374
Jess, Z.
    American tutor's assistant. Ed. 12. Philadelphia, M'Carty & Davis, 1819. MWA.   48375

Jewett, Luther
    A discourse, delivered at St. Johnsbury, December 3, 1818...Danville, Vt., Pr. by Ebenezer Eaton, 1819. 15 p. MHi; MWA; VtHi; VtMiM.   48376

Johnson, Hon. Mr. of Kentucky
    Review of a report of the Committee...on the subject of mails on the Sabbath, presented to the Senate of the United States...Boston, 1819. PPM.   48377

Johnson, Charles Britten
    Letters from the British settlement in Pennsylvania. To which are added, the constitutions of the United States, and of Pennsylvania: and extracts from the laws respecting aliens and naturalized citizens... Philadelphia, H. Hall, 1819. 192 p. CtHi; CtY; DLC; MB; MnHi; MoSM; MdBJ; P; PPins.   48378

Johnson, John
A mathematical question, propounded by the Vice-
gerent of the World; answered by the King of Glory,...
Kennebunk, Me., Pr. by James K. Remich, 1819.
79 p. MB; MFiHi; MWA. 48379

Johnson, Robert Wallace
The nurse's guide, and family assistant; 2d Amer.
ed., cor. Philadelphia, Pr. by A. Small, for Anthony
Finley, 1819. 180 p. DLC; DNLM; MWA. 48380

Johnson, Samuel, 1709-1784
A dictionary of the English language. 1st Amer.
from the 11th London ed. To which are added, Walker's principles of English pronunciation. Philadelphia, J. Maxwell, Moses Thomas, 1819. 2 v. GU;
MWA; MoS; NcU; NjR. 48381

-- ...Johnson's dictionary of the English language in
miniature...1st New York, from the last English ed.
New-York, G. Long, 1819. 295 p. CtY; MWA. 48382

-- The lives of the most eminent English poets...
Philadelphia, Pr. [by A. Fagan] for Benj. C. Buzby &
Benjamin Warner, 1819. 3 v. CBPSR; CoGrS; MWA;
MnHi; ScY. 48383

-- -- Philadelphia, Pr. [by A. Fagan] for Benj. Warner and Benj. C. Buzby, 1819. 3 v. CtW; MWA; ViRu;
ViSwc. 48384

-- Rasselas: a tale...Baltimore, Pr. by J. Robinson,
for Fielding Lucas, Jr., 1819. 176 p. MB; MWA.
48385

Johnston, William
A discourse on the divine Trinity...Wilmington,
Del., Pr. by J. Wilson, 1819. 12 p. MWA. 48386

Jones, Elizabeth C.
Poems on different subjects...Providence, Pr. by
H. H. Brown, 1819. DLC; MWA; RPB. 48387

Jones, Richard, 1779-1851
The green man; a comedy, in three acts... New-
York, David Longworth, 1819. 68 p. DLC; MWA; NN.
48388

Jones, Samuel
A selection of psalms and hymns, done under the
appointment of the Philadelphia Association. Ed. 4.
Philadelphia, Pr. by Joseph Rakestraw, for Theophilus
Harris, 1819. 410 p. MWA.   48389

-- -- ... By Samuel Jones, D.D. and Burgiss Allison,
A.M. Ed. 4. Philadelphia, Pr. by Joseph Rakestraw,
for Theophilus Harris, 1819. 410 p. MH-AH; NRAB;
NjPT.   48390

Jones, William
The Catholic doctrine of a Trinity... Urbana, O.,
Repr. by A.M. Poff, 1819. 94 p. DLC; MWA; OClWHi;
OHi.   48391

Josephus, Flavius
The wonderful and most deplorable history of the
latter times of the Jews... Bellows Falls, Vt., Pr. by
Bill Blake & Co., 1819. 299 p. CSt; CtY; CtW; DLC;
MMeT; MWA; NCaS; NN; NNUT; Nh-Hi; RPB; ScU;
VtHi; VtU.   48392

Journal of Belles Lettres. Lexington, Ky., Nov. 20,
1819, 1st issue.   48393

Joyce, J.
A system of practical arithmetic, for the use of
schools... Baltimore, N.G. Maxwell, 1819. 287 p.
CSmH; ICBB; MH; MWA; MdHi; NCH.   48394

Joyce, Jeremiah
Scientific dialogues... New ed. Philadelphia, Pr.
by T.H. Palmer, for M. Carey... 1819. V. 2-3.
MWA.   48395

Judd, Bethel
Address, delivered at St. James' Church, New
London, on the 24th of June, 1819. To the members

of Union Lodge. By...rector of St. James' Church.
New-London, Samuel Green, 1819. 16 p. CtHi; MBFM.
48396

Judson, Andrew T.
Letter to James Thomas, esq. comptroller. New
London, Conn., Clapp & Francis, 1819. 46 p. Ct;
DLC. 48397

Juvenile history of beasts. Part I. ... Philadelphia,
Pr. by J. R. A. Skerrett, for E. and R. Parker, 1819.
MWA. 48398

The juvenile instructor... Philadelphia, Pr. by J. R. A.
Skerrett, for E. and R. Parker, 1819. MWA. 48399

Juvenile piety... Boston, Lincoln & Edmands, [1819]
33 p. MWA. 48400

The juvenile story-teller... New Haven, Sidney's press,
for J. Babcock & son, 1819. 30 p. CtHi; MWA. 48401

The juvenile trial... New Haven, Sidney's press, for
J. Babcock & Son [S. & W. R. Babcock, Charleston,
S. C.] 1819. 35 p. CtHi; MWA. 48402

-- New Haven, Sidney's press, for J. Babcock & son,
1819. (Varied ed.) 35 p. CtHi; MWA. 48403

K

Kames, Henry Home, lord.
Elements of criticism... New York, Pr. by J.
Oram, for Collins and Co., 1819. MWA. 48404

-- -- 3d Amer. ed. New York, Pr. by J. Oram, for
Collins and Hannay, 1819. 2 v. CtHC; MWA. 48405

-- -- 3d Amer. ed. New York, Pr. by J. Oram, for
Evert Duyckinck, 1819. MWA. 2 v. 48406

[Keely, George]
The nature and order of a Gospel church, and the
obligations of its members, stated in a sermon

preached at the Baptist meeting-house, Haverhill,
Mass., 29th Nov. 1818...Haverhill, Mass., P.N.
Green, 1819. 27 p. CSt; MHa; MHaHi; MWA; MWo;
NRAB.   48407

-- A sermon preached at the Baptist meeting house in
Haverhill, Thanksgiving day, Dec. 2, 1819...[Haver-
hill, Mass.] Pr. by P.N. Green, 1819. 15 p. MHa;
MWA.   48408

Keith, Thomas
    A new treatise on the use of globes...3d Amer.
ed.   New York, Samuel Wood & Sons and Samuel S.
Wood & Co., Baltimore, 1819. 352 p. GDC; MH;
MWA; MdBD; NNA; OCU.   48409

Kelly, John
    Solemn and important reasons against becoming a
Universalist.   Exeter, N.H., Josiah Richardson, 1819.
MWA.   48410

[Kendrick, William]
    The whole duty of woman.   A new ed., with con-
siderable improvements.   Rochester, N.Y., E. Peck
& Co., 1819.   118 p. MH; MWA; NRU.   48411

Kentuckian.   Lancaster, Ky., 1819. Newspaper. Brig-
ahm, p. 161.   48412

Kentucky (State)
    Acts passed at the first session of the twenty-
seventh General assembly for the Commonwealth of
Kentucky, begun and held in the town of Frankfort, on
Monday the seventh day of December 1818...Frankfort,
Ky., Pr. by Kendall & Russells, 1819. 594-802 p.
CSfLaw; DLC; In-SC; KyHi; KyLoF; PU; Wa-L.   48413

-- Decisions (Marshall, reporter) of the court of appeals of Kentucky, commencing with the Fall term,
1817...Washington, Ky., 1819 [-1823] v. 1-3. Az;
CSjoSCL; DLC; IU; KyBgW; MH-L; MBS; Nc-S; PPB.
                                               48414
-- Journal of the House of Representatives of the Com-

monwealth of Kentucky, begun...seventh day of December, 1818...Frankfort, Pr. by Kendall and Russells, 1818[!] [1819] 325 p. DLC; ICU; KyLoF; KyLxT.48415

-- Journal of the Senate of the Commonwealth of Kentucky, begun...7th day of December, 1818...Frankfort, Pr. by Kendall and Russells, 1818[!] [1819] 288 p. DLC; ICU; KyLo; KyLxT; KyU; WHi. 48416

-- The opinion of the Court of appeals, for the Commonwealth of Kentucky; in the case of the Commonwealth vs. James Morrison...Frankfort, Ky., Pr. by J. H. and W. B. Holeman, 1819. 27 p. CSmH; ICU; KyHi; MBAt; MWA; NN. 48417

The Kentucky almanac, for the year of our Lord 1820: ...By John Bradford, Esq., Lexington, Ky., Pr. by Thomas Smith, at the office of the Kentucky Reporter, [1819] 36 p. CSmH; DLC; ICU; KyLo; KyLx; MWA; MoHi; WHi. 48418

Kentucky patriot. Glasgow, Ky., A. A. James, Aug. 1819, 1st issue. Weekly newspaper. Brigham, p. 158. 48419

Kentucky Republican. Hopkinsville, Ky., Putnam Ewing, 1819, 1st issue. Weekly newspaper. OHi. 48420

Kett, Henry
    The flowers of wit; or, A choice collection of bon mots, ancient and modern...Boston, 1819. 2 v. PPL-R. 48421

A key to knowledge...New York, Pr. by J. Van Riper & Co., for W. B. Gilley, 1819. MWA; MnU; NcWsS; RPB. 48422

Kilbourn, John, 1787-1831
    The Ohio Gazetteer, or topographical dictionary; ...Ed. 6, improved. Columbus, Pr. by Bailhache & Scott, for J. Kilbourn, 1819. 176 p. CSmH; CtY; DLC; ICN; MWA; NHi; NN; OClWHi; PPL; PU; WHi. 48423

Kimball, Daniel
    A sermon, preached before the Hingham peace so-

ciety, December 2, 1819...Boston, Pr. by Lincoln &
Edmands,[1819] 12 p. ICMe; MH; MHi; MNBedf;
MWA; NjPT; PPL. 48424

Kimball, David Tenney
The obligation and disposition of females to pro-
mote Christianity...Newburyport, Mass., Pr. by
Ephraim W. Allen, 1819. 15 p. MB; MH-AH; MSaE;
MWA; NjPT; NjR. 48425

Kimber, E.
Arithmetic. Ed. 7. Philadelphia, Pr. by Dickinson, for Kimber & Sharpless, 1819. MWA. 48426

Kimber & Conrad's A B C book...Philadelphia, Kimber
& Conrad [1819?] DLC. 48427

King, G. B.
Commercial swift writer. New York, Collins &
Co., [1819] MWA. 48428

King, Rufus, 1755-1827
Papers relative to restriction of slavery. Speeches
of Mr. King and Messrs. Taylor & Talmage. Philadelphia, Hall & Atkinson, 1819. 35 p. DeWI; RPB.
48429
-- Substance of two speeches, delivered in the Senate
of the United States, on the subject of the Missouri
bill...New-York, Kirk & Mercein, 1819. 32 p. CSfCW;
CtY; DLC; MWA; MWiW; NSmB. 48430

King, William, 1685-1763
Political and literary anecdotes of his own times.
Boston, Wells and Lilly, 1819. 187 p. CSfCW; CtY;
DLC; IC; MBAt; MBC; MBL; MH; MHi; MMeT; MSaE;
MWA; MdBJ; PHi; PP; PPL-R; RNR; RPM; ScU. 48431

Kings County Society for Promoting Agriculture and
Domestic Manufactures.
Constitution. Brooklyn, N.Y., 1819. NBLiHi.
48432
[Kinloch, Francis] 1755-1826
Letters from Geneva and France, written during

a residence of between two and three years, in different parts of those countries, and addressed to a lady
in Virginia...Boston, Wells and Lilly, 1819. 2 v.
CtW; DLC; ICU; MBev; MC; MH; MNBedf; MWA; MW;
MeLewB; MoKU; NcD; OAU; RNR; ScU; Vi; ViU; WvW.
48433

Kippis, Andrew
A sermon on the Lord's supper...Boston, Wells
and Lilly, 1819. 36 p. CBPac; CSt; ICMe; MBC;
MMeT; MWA; MiD-B; NjPT; OClWHi; PPL; WHi. 48434

Knapp, Samuel Lorenzo, 1783-1838
Eulogy delivered in Christ-church, Boston, at the
request of Saint John's lodge, June 8, 1819, on the
character of their brother and past master, Shubael
Bell. Boston, Pr. by J. T. Buckingham, [1819] 19 p.
DLC; ICP; IaCrM; MB; MBr; MH; MMeT; MWA; MnHi;
NCH; PPFM; RPB. 48435

-- Sir, I have...been engaged...in collecting materials
for writing biographical sketches of several of the
most distinguished lawyers and statesmen who have
lived in New England...Sam. L. L. Knapp. December
28, 1819. DNA. Broadside. 48436

Kneeland, Abner
The Philadelphia hymn book; or, A selection of
sacred poetry. Philadelphia, Pr. by Clark & Raser,
1819. 634 p. MMeT; MWA; NCaS. 48437

-- Presbyterianism versus Presbyterianism; or, A
candid review of "An essay on the inability of sinners,
by a Presbyterian;"...Ed. 2. Philadelphia, Pr. by
Adam Waldie, for the author, 1819. 24 p. MWA; NNG;
NjPT. 48438

Knight, Daniel
An oration, pronounced at Charlton [Mass.] on the
forty-third anniversary of American independence...
Worcester, Mass., Pr. by William Manning, 1819.
20 p. CSt; MB; MDeeP; MHi; MWA; MWHi; MiD-B.
48439

Knoxville Intelligencer. Knoxville, Tenn., P. Carey,

Aug. 3, 1819, 1st issue.   Weekly newspaper. TKL.
                                                      48440
Kortz, John
    Interesting memoirs of four German gentlemen,
particularly distinguished by their advintures [!] among
the fair sex... New York, Pr. by S. Marks, 1819.
226 p. DLC; MWA; NN.   48441

Kotzebue, August Friedrich Ferdinand von, 1761-1819.
    Pizarro: a tragedy, in five acts... New-York,
Thomas Longworth, 1819. 68 p. DLC; MH; MWA.
                                                      48442
Krauss, Johann
    Oeconomisches Haus-und Kunst-Buch... Allentown,
Pa., Pr. by Henrich Ebner, 1819. 452 p. MWA; NN;
NjR; P; PDoBHi; PHi.   48443

[Kurz, Benjamin]
    Fragen eines Evangelischen Lehrers an seine
Gemien-Glieder. Hagerstown, Md., Gruber und May,
1819. 24 p. MdBE.   48444

Kurzen Entwurf der Christlichen Lehre.   Zum Unterricht bey der Confirmation. Zweyte Ausgabe. Reading,
Pa., Heinrich B. Sage, 1819. 29 p. P.   48445

Kurzer inbegriff der christlichen lehre, in fragen und
antworten, zum gebrauch bey dem unterricate der
jugend.   Philadelphia, Pr. by Conrad Zentler, 1819.
36 p. DLC.   48446.

                              L
Labaume, Eugene
    Circumstantial narrative of the campaign in Russia;
translated.   Hartford, 1819. 356 p. RNR.   48447

The ladies' and gentlemen's diary and almanac: with an
ephemeris, for the year of creation, according to sacred writ, 5782, and of the Christian era, 1820... By
Asa Houghton.   Bellows Falls, Vt., Bill Blake & Co.,
[1819] [48] p. MWA; MiD-B; Vt.   48448

The Ladies' and gentlemen's diary, or, United States almanac...No. 1. 1820. By M. Nash. New York, J. Seymour, 1819. 72 p. CtY; DLC; MHi; MWA; N; NCH; NHi; NUtHi; NjR; PU; MnU.   48449

Ladies' and gentlemen's weekly literary museum and musical magazine. Philadelphia, Jan. 1, 1819, 1st issue.   48450

Ladies' literary cabinet, ed. by Samuel Woodworth. New York, Woodworth & Huestis, 1819-20. Vol. 1, 15 nos. variously paged. NjR.   48451

La Pappe de Trevern, Jean François Marie
      An amicable discussion on the Church of England and on the reformation in general, dedicated to the clergy of every Protestant communion, and reduced into the form of letters, by the Right Rev. J. F. M. Trevern [sic] D. D. Bishop of Strasbourg (late of Aire) Translated by The Rev. William Richmond. Baltimore, Pr. by J. Robinson, for Fielding Lucas, Jr., [1819] 2 v. DGU; MWH.   48452

Last night but one of Mr. and Mrs. Bartley's appearance May 21st, 1819. Will be presented. Murphy's tragedy: Grecian daughter. folio. Broadside. (Charles F. Heartman. Auction no. 159. Sept. 1923. no. 155)   48453

Latin prosody; containing the rules of quantity and the principles of Latin versification. For the use of St. Mary's college. Baltimore, F. Lucas, Jr., 1819. 72 p. MWA; MdHi; MdW.   48454

The Latin tutor; or, An introduction to the making of Latin...Boston, Hilliard & Metcalf, 1819. 286 p. CtHT-W; ICHi; InGrD; KyBC; KyLxT; MH-AH; MBeHi; MMonsA; MWA; MeU; MiD-B; MoFloSS; PPL; ViU; RPB.   48455

La Tour, C. V. de
      Youth's French friend. Baltimore, Pr. by John D. Toy, for Harrod & Turner, 1819. 168 p. IU; MH; MWA; MdBE; MdBP; PWCHi.   48456

Latrobe, John Hazlehurst Boneval
    March of the Corps of Cadets from West Point,
to Hudson in August 1819. 13 p. NWM.   48457

Latta, John E.
    Sermon preached...at a meeting of a committee
of the Presbytery of New Castle...Wilmington, Del.,
Pr. by Porter, 1819. 23 p. PPPrHi.   48458

Law, Andrew, 1748-1821
    Harmonic companion, and guide to social worship
...Ed. 4. Philadelphia, Pr. by T.H. Palmer, for the
author, 1819. 120 p. CtY; MWA; NjR.   48459

-- Musical primer...Ed. 3. Philadelphia, Pr. by
Anderson & Meehan [1819] RPB.   48460

Law, William
    An humble, earnest and affectionate address to
the clergy...Philadelphia, Pr. by S. Probasco, for
William Marot, Emmor Matlack, 1819. 192 p. MWA;
OC.   48461

Leathley, Mrs.
    The story of Joseph and his Brethren, in three
parts, written for the benefit of youth, to which is
added, The History of Charles Jones. Wilmington,
Del., Pr. by R. Porter, 1819. [106] p. DeHi; DeWI;
MWA; N; PP; PRosC.   48462

Leavitt's genuine, improved New-England farmer's al-
manack and agricultural register for the year of our
Lord 1820 by Dudley Leavitt. Exeter, N.H., Pr. by
J.J. Williams, for Nath'l Boardman [1819] [24] p.
DLC; MWA; MPeHi; Nh-Hi.   48463

Lebanon Courier. Lebanon, Pa., George Hanke, 1819.
Weekly newspaper. P.   48464

Lee, Andrew, 1745-1832
    A half century sermon, preached at Hanover, the
North society in Lisborn, October 25, 1818...Windham,
Conn., Pr. by J. Byrne, 1819. 20 p. CSt; CtY; MWA;

NN.   48465

Lee, Joseph, 1742-1819
    A half-century discourse, delivered Monday, Oct.
19, 1818; being the fiftieth anniversary of his ordination...Worcester, Mass., Pr. by William Manning,
1819. 27 p. DLC; MBC; MH-AH; MBNEH; MWA;
MWHi; WHi.   48466

Lee, Richard Bland, 1761-1827
    An oration, delivered July 5, 1819, in the cham-
ber of the House of representatives... [Washington,
D.C., 1819] 15 p. DLC; MBAt.   48467

Legendre, Adrien Marie, 1752-1833
    Elements of geometry. Cambridge, N.E., Pr. by
Hilliard, & Metcalf, 1819. 208 p. MCM; MWA; MWiW;
ViU.   48468

Leggett & Shotwell
    Catalogue of British dry-goods, for sale at public
auction, by Leggett & Shotwell, on Saturday, April 24,
1819, at ten o'clock, at their auction room, corner of
Pine and Pearl-St. [New-York] Pr. by J. Seymour
[1819]   15 p. CtMMHi.   48469

Lemoine, Stephen P.
    Oration, delivered on the 17th of March, 1819, at
Washington hall, before the Shamrock friendly association...New-York, Pr. by Grattan and Banks, 1819.
27 p.   DLC; MWA; NN; NNC.   48470

Leonard, George
    A sermon delivered at Windsor, on Sunday, July 4,
1819...Windsor, Vt., Pr. by Ide & Aldrich, 1819. 21 p.
CtHT; MBAt; MWA; MiD-B; NjPT; PHi; RPB; Vt; VtU.
                                                        48471
Leonard, Seth
    The American grammar, to which is added elements
of reading and oratory, with a short explanation of the
seven liberal arts and sciences...New York, M'Duffee
& Tarrand, 1819. 144 p. MMeT; MWA; RPB.   48472

Le Prince de Beaumont, Marie
     The young misses' magazine... New York, Pr. by
J. & J. Harper, for Samuel Campbell and son... 1819.
2 v. in 1. CtY; MWA; MnU.   48473

A letter from Beelzebub, addressed to a Christian
church... 1st Amer. ed. Perth Amboy, N. J., J. T.
Murden & co., 1819. MWA.   48474

A letter, originally written to Mr. ...., and now
published by request, and addressed to whom it may
concern. "What is truth?" Pilate. Charleston, S. C.,
Pr. by T. B. Stephens, 1819. 8 p. MBC; MWA. 48475

A letter to "A Layman," in reply to his "Letter to
Rev. Mr. Channing." By Layman Junior. [1819]
MWA.   48476

A letter to Professor Stuart, in answer to his letters
to Rev. William E. Channing, and in vindication of a
large and respectable body of the New England and
other clergy, from the unfounded aspersions cast on
them in said letters... Boston, Pr. by Sylvester T.
Goss, 1819. 22 p. CSt; DLC; MBC; MWA; NjR;
PPAmP.   48477

A letter to Rev. Mr. Channing, in favor of the doctrine of the Trinity... [Boston, Pr. by Sylvester T.
Goss, 1819] 8 p. CSmH; MWA; MWiW.   48478

-- [Boston, Pr. by Sylvester T. Goss, 1819] (Pages
2-3 vary) MWA.   48479

Letter to the Edinburgh reviewers... [1819?] MWA.
                                              48480

A letter to the Rev. Harry Croswell... New Haven,
Pr. by S . Converse, 1819. 12 p. CSmH; CtHi; CtY;
MB; MWA; NjPT.   48481

Letters from Asia; written by a gentleman of Boston,
to his friend in that place. New-York, A. T. Goodrich
& Co., 1819. 60 p. DLC; N.   48482

The letters of Aegles, addressed to the Hon. John C.
Spencer, chairman of the bank committee, in which
are contained an examination of the report of that committee, and a complete refutation of every charge a-
gainst the directors of the bank, drawn from their own
documents. Originally published in the Federal Gazette. Baltimore, Pr. by John D. Toy, 1819. 64 p.
MdHi; MdTaH.   48483

Lever, Darcy, 1760?-1837
   ... The young sea officer's sheet anchor; or, A
key to the leading of rigging, and to practical seaman-
ship. Philadelphia, Carey, [1819] 120 p. CtHT;
MWA.   48484

Lewis, Isaac
   A sermon, delivered in West Greenwich, Connecti-
cut, at the installation of the Rev. Isaac Lewis... New
York, Pr. by J. Seymour, 1819. 32 p. CtY; MWA;
NHi; NjR.   48485

Lexington News-Letter. Lexington, Va., John N.
Snider, Feb. 13, 1819, 1st issue. Weekly newspaper.
ViLxW.   48486

L'Homond, A.
   De viris illustribus urbis Romae, new ed. New
York, F. Nichols, 1819. MWA.   48487

The life and death of Miss Abby Victoria Painter, who
died December 9, 1818, aged twenty-two years. Middlebury, Vt., Pr. by J.W. Copeland, 1819. 16 p.
NjPT; VtMiS.   48488

Life and dying confession of John Van Alstine... Schoharie, N.Y., Pr. [by Mathew M. Cole] at the office
of the Observer, 1819. MWA.   48489

The life of John Englebrecht... Hallowell, Me., Pr. by
E. Goodale, 1819. 108 p. CSmH; MWA; MeU. 48490

The life of Mary Mordant. ...By an American lady.
Philadelphia, Pr. by Clark & Raser, for the Sunday

and adult school union, 1819. 48 p. CSt; MWA. 48491

Life of William Kelley. (An authentic narrative.)
Andover, Mass., Pr. by Flagg & Gould, for the New
England Tract Society, 1819. 16 p. CtHi.   48492

Lillo, George
    George Barnwell. A tragedy, in five acts. New
York, David Longworth, 1819. 69 p. MBr; RPB. 48493

Lincoln, E.
    Scripture questions, or catechetical exercises.
Boston, Pr. by Lincoln and Edmands, 1819. 45 p.
MMhHi; MWA.   48494

-- -- Ed. 2, enl. Boston, E. & E. Hosford, 1819.
45 p. RPB.   48495

-- Ed. 2, enl. Boston, 1819. 45 p. MWA.   48496

-- -- Ed. 5. Boston, Pr. by Lincoln & Edmands,
1819. 72 p. PPAmS.   48497

Lincoln, Levi, 1782-1868
    Address, delivered before the Worcester agricul-
tural society, October 7, 1819, being their first anniversary cattle show and exhibition of manufactures.
Worcester, Mass., Pr. by Manning & Trumbull, 1819.
30 p. CSmH; DLC; MHi; MTemNHi; MW; MWA; MWHi;
MiD-B; MiHi; OClWHi; RPB.   48498

Litchfield Republican. Litchfield, Conn., I. Bruce,
May 12, 1819, 1st issue. Weekly newspaper. MWA.
                                                48499
Literary Cadet. Cincinnati, Ohio, Looker, Reynolds
& Co., Nov. 22, 1819, 1st issue. Weekly newspaper.
OC.   48500

Little, William
    The easy instructor; or, A new method of teaching
sacred harmony... Cincinnati, O., Pr. by J. Pace,
1819. 112 p. OC.   48501

Little poems for little readers. New-York, Samuel
Wood & sons; Baltimore, Samuel S. Wood & co., 1819.
28 p. MWA; MiU-C; RPB.   48502

The little spelling-book, or American primer. Philadelphia, 1819. (Private library of G. A. Plimpton.
Tingelstad 655)   48503

...Lives and confessions of John Williams, Francis
Frederick, John P. Rog, and Peter Peterson, who were
tried at the United States circuit court in Boston, for
murder and piracy; sentenced to be executed Jan. 21,
1819; and afterwards reprieved till Feb. 18, 1819...
[Ed. 2] Boston, Pr. by J. T. Buckingham [1819] 40 p.
DLC; MB; MBAt; MH; MHi; MWA; NBuG; NIC-L; NNC;
PHi; PP.   48504

Livingston, John H.
    An address to the Reformed German Churches in
the United States...New Brunswick, N. J., Pr. by Wm.
Myer, 1819. 36 p. KyDC; MH-AH; MHi; NNC. 48505

Locke, John
    Outlines of botany, taken chiefly from Smith's In-
troduction...Boston, Cummings and Hilliard, 1819.
161 p. KMK; MB; MBBCHS; MBHo; MH; MSa; MSaP;
MWA; MdBJ; OCHP.   48506

Logarithmic tables. Schenectady, N. Y., 1819. MWA.
                                            48507
Longley, John
    Observations on the trial by jury; particularly on
the unanimity required in the verdict...Charleston,
S. C., Pr. by A. E. Miller, for John Mill, 1819. 24 p.
MiD-B.   48508

[Longstreet, Augustus Baldwin]
    Patriotic effusions...New York, Pr. by J. & J.
Harper, for L. and F. Lockwood, 1819. 46 p. DLC;
MWA; NN; RPB.   48509

Longworth's American almanac, New York Register
City Directory. New York, 1819. Tuttle.   48510

Looking-glass for the mind; or, Intellectual mirror...
With...engr. on wood by Alex. Anderson. Philadelphia,
1819. CtHT-W.   48511

Loomis, Hubbel, 1775-1872
    Defence of letters on Christian baptism, against the
Strictures of Rev. Asa Wilcox of Saybrook...Hartford,
Pr. by P.B. Gleason & co., 1819. 52 p. Ct; CtHi;
CtHC; CtHT-W; CtSoP; MBC; MWA; NN; N; NRAB;
NjPT; NjR; PPPrHi.   48512

Lorain, John
    Hints to emigrants, or, A comparative estimate of
the advantages of Pennsylvania, and of the western territory...Philadelphia, Pr. by A. Waldie, for Littell &
Henry, 1819. 141 p. DLC; OClWHi.   48513

Louisiana (State)
    Acts passed at the 1st session of the 4th Legisla-
ture of the state of Louisiana, began...5th day of January...1819...New-Orleans, Pr. by J.C. de St.
Romes, 1819. 143 p. IU; LNH; LU; MH-L.   48514

-- Journal de la chambre des representans, durant la
premiere session de la quatrieme legislature...Nou-
velle-Orleans, imprimé par J.C. de St. Romes, 1819.
74 p. LU.   48515

-- Journal du senat durant la premiere session de la
quatrieme legislature...Nouvelle Orleans, J.C. de St.
Romes, 1819. 54 p. L.   48516

-- Journal of the House of Representatives during the
First session of the Fourth Legislature...New Orleans,
Pr. by J.C. de St. Romes, 1819. 72 p. IU; LNH;
LNT.   48517

-- Journal of the Senate during the first session of the
fourth legislature...New-Orleans, Pr. by J.C. de St.
Romes, 1819. 52 p. LNH; LU.   48518

Louisianian. St. Francisville, La., William M'Laran,
May 8, 1819, 1st issue. Weekly newspaper. DLC. 48519

Loveland, Samuel Chapman, 1787-1854
   Six lectures on Important subjects; delivered in
Bethel in the year 1819...Woodstock, Vt., Pr. by
David Watson, 1819. 162 p. MMeT-Hi.   48520

Lowndes, Thomas, 1765-1822
   Speech of Mr. Lowndes, delivered in the House of
representatives, Feb. 1819, on the Bank of the United
States. [Washington, D. C., 1819] 28 p. DLC; MiD-B;
NIC-A.   48521

Low's almanack, and agricultural kalendar for the year
1820...By Nathanael Low...Boston, Munroe & Francis
[1819] [22] p. MWA; NjR; RPB.   48522

Low's almanack, and astronomical and agricultural kal-
endar; for the year of our Lord and Saviour Jesus
Christ, 1820...Boston, Munroe & Francis [1819] [36] p.
ICMcHi; MBMu.   48523

Lucas, Fielding
   Mathematical tables. Baltimore, F. Lucas, jun.,
1819. MWiW.   48524

Luce, Mrs. Phebe
   Maternal admonition or the orphan's manual by Mrs.
Phebe Luce...Cooperstown, N. Y., Pr. by H. & E.
Phinney, 1819. 88 p. MH; RPB.   48525

Luther, Martin
   Der kleine Catechismus...Baltimore, Schaeffer und
Maund, 1819. 126 p. MWA; MdBE.   48526

-- -- Hagerstaun, Md., Gruber & May, 1819. PPPrHi.
                                             48527
Lutheran Synod. North Carolina.
   Minutes North Carolina Lutheran Synod, 1819.
PGL-Hi.   48528

Lyceum of Natural History of New York.
   Catalogue of plants, growing spontaneously within
thirty miles of the City of New-York...Albany, Pr. by
Websters and Skinners, 1819. 100 p. DLC; FDeS;

MSaP; NAL; NN; NNNBG; NSmB; NjN; NjR.   48529

Lyman, Joseph, 1749-1828
    A sermon, delivered at Northampton, Nov. 11,
1819, at the interment of the Hon. Caleb Strong...
Northampton, Mass., Pr. by Thomas W. Shepard and
Co., 1819.   23 p. CSmH; CtHC; MBAU; MNF; MWA;
MiD-B; WHi.   48530

-- A sermon, delivered March 11, 1819, at South Had-
ley, at the interment of Ruggles Woodbridge... Northampton, Mass., Pr. by Thomas W. Shepard and Co.,
1819. 17 p. CtHT-W; MH-AH; MNF; MWA; MWiW;
RBr.   48531

-- A sermon, preached at Boston, before the American
board of commissioners for foreign missions, at their
tenth annual meeting, Sept. 16, 1819...Boston, Pr. by
U. Crocker, for Samuel T. Armstrong, 1819. 19 p.
CSt; CtHC; KWiU; MBAt; MBC; MWA; MWiW; NCH;
NNUT; NcD; NjPT; NjR; OO; PHi; PPPrHi.   48532

Lyttelton, George Lyttelton, 1st baron.
    Observations on the conversion and apostleship of
St. Paul...Philadelphia, S. Potter & Co., 1819. 135 p.
CtHT; MNe; MWA; P.   48533

                           M

M., L.
    M's spelling book, imp. ed.   New York, D.D.
Smith, 1819.   MWA.   48534

McAfee, Robert Breckenridge
    Speech of Robert B. M'Afee on Education.   De-
livered in the Senate, on the Bill providing a literary
fund for the establishment and support of free schools,
as amended by attaching thereto appropriations for the
University, Centre and Southern Colleges.   [Frankfort?
Ky., 1819?] Broadside. DLC; ICU.   48535

M'Carty & Davis' Pennsylvania almanac, for the year
1820...By William Collom.   Philadelphia, M'Carty &

Davis [1819] [36] p. NjR.   48536

[McCoy, Joseph]
    The frontier maid; or, A tale of Wyoming, a poem,
in five cantos. Wilkesbarre, Pa., Pr. by Steuben
Butler & Samuel Maffet, 1819. 208 p. CSmH; DLC; ICU;
MWA; RPB.   48537

McDowell, John
    Questions on the Bible...Ed. 5. Elizabeth-Town,
N.J., Pr. by Joseph Justice, for Mervin Hale, 1819.
155 p. MWA.   48538

-- -- Ed. 5. Elizabethtown, N.J., Pr. by McDuffee
& Farrand for Mervin Hale, 1819. 155 p. NjR.   48539

M'Curdy, Dennis
    The Columbian tutors' assistant; or A full collec-
tion of rules and examples for the several calculations
of common, decimal and duodecimal arithmetic...
Washington City, Pr. by E. DeKrafft, 1819. 206 p.
OWo.   48540

MacGowan, John, 1726-1780
    The Arian's and Socinians' monitor; being a vision
that a young Socinian teacher lately had...1st Amer.,
from the 20th London ed., cor. Baltimore, H. Vicary
and O.B. Cornish, Philadelphia, 1819. 23 p. DLC;
ICMe; MBC; MH; MWA; MdBP; MiU; NNG; PPPrHi.
                                                   48541
-- Priestcraft defended: sermon occasioned by the ex-
pulsion of six young gentlemen, from Oxford University
for praying, reading, etc. 1st Amer. ed. Boston,
Thomas G. Bangs, 1819. 35 p. KyLx; MBNMHi. 48542

-- -- Stereotype ed. New York, T. Kinnersley, sold
also at his warehouses in Philadelphia and Baltimore,
1819. 33 p. KyLx.   48543

McGranaghan, William
    Proposals, for publishing in Clarksburgh, Virginia,
a weekly newspaper, to be entitled The Independent Virginian...[1819] Broadside. WvU.   48544

[M'Intyre, Archibald] 1772-1858
    A letter to His Excellency, Daniel D. Tompkins,
late governor of the state of New-York.   Albany, Pr.
by Jeremiah Tryon, 1819. 112 p.   CSmH; DLC; MBAt;
MWA; NN; NNC; NjR; WHi.   48545

McKenney, Frederic
    A complete key to the Teacher's assistant, or sys-
tem of practical arithmetic... Compiled by M'Kenney.
Ed. 2, rev.   Philadelphia, Pr. by Cusack & Franklin,
for B. Warner, 1819. 249 p.   CSmH; MWA; MsJM.
                                                  48546
MacKenzie, John
    A choice selection of psalms, hymns, and spiritual
songs... Woodstock, Vt., Pr. by David Watson, 1819.
600 p.   CSmH; CtHT-W; MWA; NBuG; VtU; VtWood.
                                                  48547
M'Kenzie, Lachlin
    Redemption... Pittsburgh, Pa., Pr. by Butler and
Lambdin, for George Baily, 1819. MWA.   48548

Macleay, Kenneth
    Historical memoirs of Rob Roy and the Clan Mac
Gregor... Philadelphia, David Hogan, 1819. 302 p.
MWA; NP; OMC.   48549

McMahon, Bernard
    The American gardener's calendar... Ed. 2, imp.
Philadelphia, Pr. by William Fry, for T. P. M'Mahon,
1819. 618 p.   CSt; InCW; MWA.   48550

McMurtrie, Henry, 1793-1865
    Sketches of Louisville and its environs; including...
a Florula louisvillensis... 1st ed.   Louisville [Ky.] Pr.
by S. Penn, Jun., 1819. 255 p.   C; C-S; DLC; ICJ;
ICU; KyHi; KyU; MBAt; MWA; NN; OCHP; PPiU; WHi.
                                                  48551
McNally, Edward A.
    The importance of education, particularly to fe-
males, with observations on the manner of conveying
instructions, and other useful remarks.   An address...
Baltimore, Pr. by R. J. Matchett, 1819. 64 p. MdBE;
MdBLC; MdBS; MdHi.   48552

McNemar, Richard, 1770-1839, comp.
The other side of the question. In three parts.
i. An explanation of the proceedings of Eunice Chapman
and the Legislature, against the United society...in the
state of New-York. ii. A refutation of the false statements of Mary Dyer against the said society, in the
state of New-Hampshire. iii. An account of the proceedings of Abram Van Vleet, esq., and his associates,
against the said United society at Union Village, Ohio.
Comprising a general vindication of the character of
Mother and the elders against the attacks of public
slander - the edicts of a prejudiced party - and the
misguided zeal of lawless mobs. Published by order of
the United society at Union Village, Ohio...Cincinnati,
O., Pr. by Looker, Reynolds & co., 1819. 168 p.
DLC; NHi; NN; OClWHi; WHi.   48553

Nacneven, William James, 1763-1841
Exposition of the atomic theory of chymistry; and
the doctrine of definite proportions...With an appendix
of chymical exercises, by the pupils of the laboratory,
&c. New York, Pr. by Grattan and Banks, 1819. 74 p.
DLC; KU; MA; MWA; NNNAM.   48554

Macomber, Job, d. 1810?
A poem, delivered in Bowdoinham, to a respectable
audience, on the fourth of July, 1806...Ed. 4. Exeter
[Me.] J. Richardson, 1819. 16 p. DLC; MWA. 48555

M'Pherson, John
An oration, delivered at Mr. Day's hotel, on Fri-
day, 16th April, 1819. On the rise and progress of
New-Orleans...1819. MWA.   48556

Madison, James, pres. U.S.
Religious freedom...Boston, Lincoln & Edmands,
1819. 12 p. CtHC; DLC; ICN; MB; MBAt; MH; MHi;
MWA; NN; OCHP; OMC.   48557

-- Report [on] the proceedings of the other states on
the Virginia resolutions, 1798, etc...Richmond, Va.,
1819. MBAt.   48558

Maine (District)

An address to the people of Maine, from the Convention of Delegates, assembled at Portland. Portland, Me., Pr. by F. Douglas, 1819. 7 p. MWA; MeHi; NN.   48559

No entry.   48560

-- An address to the people of Maine, on the question of separation. A review of the transactions in this District for thirty years past will show that the independence of Maine was early conceived and has never been abandoned...Portland, Me., July, 1819. Broadsheet. MeHi.   48561

-- The committee to whom was referred the subject of a constitution for Maine...[Portland, Pr. by F. Douglas, 1819] 8 p. MeHi.   48562

-- Constitution for the state of Maine: formed in convention, at Portland, 29th of October, A.D. 1819... and recommended to the people for their adoption in town meetings, on the sixth of December. Pub. by order of the Convention. Portland, Pr. by F. Douglas, 1819. 28 p. CSmH; CU-Law; DLC; MB; MeB; MeHi.   48563

-- -- Portland, Pr. by F. Douglas, 1819. 32 p. DLC; MBAt; MWA; MeB; NN.   48564

-- Constitution for the state of Maine...1819 and of the independence of the United States, the forty-third, and recommended to the people for their adoption in town meetings, on the sixth of December. Published by order of the Convention. Portland, Me., Pr. by Francis Douglas, 1819. 48 p. MeB.   48565

-- In committee, Portland, Oct. 18, 1819...[Portland, Me., Pr. by F. Douglas, 1819] 16 p. MB.   48566

-- Rules to be observed in the Proceedings of the Convention convened at Portland for the purpose of forming a constitution for the new State...Portland, Me., Pr.

by Francis Douglas, 1819. 17 p. MeHi.   48567

-- Separation. At a meeting held in Freeport, from
the counties of Cumberland, Lincoln and Kennebec...
the undersigned committee...beg leave respectfully to
address the people of Maine...[1819] Broadside. MWA.
48568
Maine farmer's almanack for 1820. By Moses Springer,
Jr. Hallowell, Me., E. Goodale [1819] [48] p. MWA;
MeHi.   48569

Maine Missionary Society
Sermons preached before the Maine missionary society at its annual meetings. 1819. 12 p. WHi. 48570

The Maine register and United States' calendar, for the
year of our Lord 1820...Portland, Me., F. Douglas
and A. Shirley [1819] 268 p. MBAt; MHi; MWA; MeB;
MeHi.   48571

Man and the snake. A new story for children. Hartford, Pr. by Roberts & Burr, for S. G. Goodrich,
1819. 16 p. CtHi.   48572

Manchester, Phebe
Reflections on the freedom of the will...Providence,
Pr. by H.H. Brown, 1819. MWA; RPB.   48573

Mangan, C.
Stenography, or the art of short hand. Ed. 5.
Boston, R.P. & C. Williams, 1819. MWA.   48574

Mann, Cyrus
A sermon, delivered at the ordination of the Rev.
Ebenezer Perkins...Worcester, Mass., Pr. by William
Manning, 1819. 22 p. CBPSR; CSt; MBC; MH-AH;
MWA; RPB.   48575

Mansfield, J.
Essays, mathematical and physical: containing new
theories and illustrations on some very important and
difficult subjects of the sciences...New-Haven, Pr. by
William W. Morse [1819?] 274 p. ViU.   48576

Manummission Intelligencer. Jonesborough, Tenn., J.
Howard, 1819, 1st issue. Weekly newspaper. T. 48577

A map of Massachusetts, Connecticut and Rhode Island.
Humbly submitted to the citizens thereof, by theirs re-
spectfully, E. Ruggles. Hartford, Engraved by M. M.
Peabody, for R. Hutchinson, 1819. 30 x 36 in. colors.
Tuttle NP 978. Map 800A.   48578

Marcet, Jane (Haldimand) 1769-1858
    Conversations on chemistry... New Haven, Sidney's
press, for Increase Cooke & Co., 1819. CSmH. 48579

Marcus, pseud.
    An examination of the expediency and constitution-
ality of prohibiting slavery in the state of Missouri.
New York, Pr. by J. Seymour, for C. Wiley & Co.,
1819. 22 p. MB.   48580

Maréchal, Ambrose, Archbp.
    [Directions to confessors regarding cases of resti-
tution.] Baltimore, April 15, 1819. Broadside. MdBS.
                                                      48581
-- Pastoral letter of the Archbishop of Baltimore, to
the Roman Catholics of Norfolk, Virginia. Baltimore,
Pr. by J. Robinson, Circulating Library, 1819. 58 p.
DGU; DLC; MdBS; MdW.   48582

Maria; or, The ever-blooming flower. (A tale for
young ladies) Adorned with cuts. New-Haven, Sidney's
press, for J. Babcock & son, 1819. 30 p. CSmH; CtHi;
CtY; MWA.   48583

Marine Bible society of Charleston, S. C.
    The first annual report... Charleston, S. C., Pr.
by W. P. Young, 1819. MH-AH; MWA.   48584

Marine Bible society of New York
    The third annual report... May 5, 1819... New
York, Pr. by J. Seymour, 1819. MWA; PPPrHi. 48585

Marine Society, Newport, R. I.
    Charter of the Fellowship Club, instituted at New-

port [R. I.] Dec. 5th, A. D. 1752, and incorporated June
15th, A. D. 1754 which charter was renewed and al-
tered, by the General Assembly, June 15th, A. D. 1785,
and incorporated by the name of the Marine Society.
Newport, R. I., Pr. by Wm. & J. H. Barber, for the
Society, 1819. 24 p.   CSmH; MH; MWA; PPL-R; RHi;
RNHi; RPB.   48586

Marshall, Mrs. Louisa A.
    A sketch of my friend's family, intended to sug-
gest some practical hints on religion and domestic
manners...Ed. 3.   Boston, Pr. [by Sylvester T. Goss]
for Charles Ewer, 1819. 164 p.   DLC; MB; MBC; MSwe;
MWA.   48587

Martin, David
    Trial of the Rev. Jacob Gruber, minister in the
Methodist Episcopal Church, at the March term, 1819,
in the Frederick county Court, for a misdemeanor, by
David Martin...Fredericktown, Md., Pr. by Geo. Kolb,
for David Martin, 1819. 111 p. DLC; MdHi; NN.48588

Martin, Wheeler
    The ultimatum, or the rejoinder...Providence,
Miller and Hutchens, 1819. MWA.   48589

Martinet, Jan Florens, 1735-1796
    The catechism of nature, for the use of children...
New York, Daniel D. Smith, 1819. 96 p. NjR.   48590

-- -- Woodstock, Vt., Pr. by David Watson, 1819.
68 p. MBedf-Hi; MDeeP.   48591

The Martling-man; or, Says I to myself - how is this?
From the New-York Columbian of March, 1819. New-
York, 1819. 23 p. NSmb.   48592

Maryland (State)
    An Act to establish pilots...[1819] DLC.   48593

-- The Acts of Assembly; together with the governor's
proclamation, and the Rules and regulations respecting
the penitentiary of Maryland.   Collected and published

by order of the board of inspectors. Baltimore, Pr.
by J. Robinson, 1819. 54 p. MdHi; NNS.   48594

-- Council Chambers, Jan. 20th, 1819. To the Honorable The President of the Senate, and The Honorable
The Speaker of the House of Delegates. [3 letters
from the agent of the state, and the Treasurer of the
Western Shore, respecting the claim of the state of
Maryland on the General Government, for militia expenditures during the late war.] [1819?] [4] p. MdHi.
                                                   48595

-- Executive communication to the general assembly of
Maryland, at December session, 1818, on the subject
of Turnpike roads, made in pursuance of a resolve of
December session, 1817, with the accompanying documents. Annapolis, Pr. by Jehu Chandler, January,
1819. 45 p. DLC; MWA; MdBE; MdBP; MdHi. 48596

-- Executive communication to the House of Delegates
relative to the collection of public arms, Feb. 5, 1819.
[Annapolis, 1819] 12 p. (Edward G. Howard, 1308
Bolton St., Baltimore)   48597

-- Executive communication to the House of Delegates,
relative to the State's claim against the general government for monies expended during the late war. February 1, 1819. [Annapolis, 1819] 55 p. MdHi. 48598

-- Laws made and passed by the General Assembly of
the state of Maryland, at a session begun and held at
the city of Annapolis, on Monday the seventh day of
December, eighteen hundred and eighteen. Annapolis,
Md., Pr. by Jonas Green, 1819. [159] p. DLC;
IaU-L; MiL; Mo; Nb; Nj; Nv; RPL; Wa-L.   48599

-- Laws...passed at a session of Assembly begun the
first Monday of December being the 7th day of said
month, 1818, ending the 19th of February, 1819. Annapolis, Md., Jonas Green, 1819. [159] p. MdBJ;
MdHi; RPL; TxU-L; W.   48600

-- Petition to th[e] general assembly of Maryland, by
citizens of the state, praying to be relieved from il-

legal exactions of toll, on the Turnpike roads; leading
to Baltimore. Baltimore, Pr. for the committee, 1819.
65 p. MdHi.   48601

-- Report of the Committee of Ways and Means on the
finances and resources of the state of Maryland. [An-
napolis?] January, 1819. 18 p. MdBE; MdHi.   48602

-- Sketch of proceedings in the Legislature of Maryland, December session, 1818, on what is commonly
called the Jew bill; containing the report of the Committee appointed by the House of Delegates. Baltimore,
Pr. by Joseph Robinson, 1819. 86 p. MdBD; MdBE;
MdHi; MdBP; Nh-Hi; PPDrop; PPl; PPPrHi.   48603

-- Votes and proceedings of the House of Delegates of
the state of Maryland, December session, 1818... Annapolis, Pr. by Jonas Green, 1819. 126 p. DLC; M;
MdBB; MdHi.   48604

-- Votes and proceedings of the Senate of Maryland.
December session, 1818... Annapolis, Pr. by Jonas
Green, 1819. 62 p. DLC; MdHi.   48605

Maryland; [map with inset plan "City of Baltimore"]
Scale of miles 1-30. Baltimore, F. Lucas, jr., 1819.
col. fold. map. MdBJ.   48606

The Maryland pocket companion, or Every man his own
lawyer... By a gentleman of the bar. Frederick-Town,
[Md.] M. Bartgis, 1819. 118 p. DLC; MWA; MdHi;
MoSHi; NIC-L.   48607

Mason, John
    A treatise on self knowledge... Boston, James Lor-
ing, 1819. 175 p. MB; MMeT; MWA; MdAN; MiToC;
MiU; NcD; PU; VtMiS; WWanHi.   48608

-- -- Montpelier, Vt., E. P. Walton, 1819.   177 p.
CSt; DLC; MMeT; MWA; N; VtHi; VtMiM; VtVe; VtU.
                                                   48609
Mason, William
    The believer's pocket companion... Brattleborough,

Vt., John Holbrook, 1819. 167 p. CtW; MWA; VtHi;
VtU.   48610

-- The pious parent's gift... New York, John C. Totten,
1819. 48 p. MHi; MWA.   48611

Massachusetts (State)
    ...Abstract of the certificates of corporations...
Boston, 1819. DLC; ICJ; MB.   48612

-- Abstract of the number of convicts... Boston, 1819.
PPL.   48613

-- ...An act for the encouragement of agriculture and
manufactures. [Boston, 1819] MWA.   48614

-- An act to incorporate the president, directors and
company of the Commercial bank. Salem, Mass., Pr.
by W. Palfray, Jr., 1819. 16 p. MSaE; MWA. 48615

-- Acts of the Legislature... for regulating the practice
of physick and surgery. With the regulations adopted
by the Massachusetts Medical Society for carrying these
acts into operation, and a list of the books required
and recommended by the Society. Boston, Wells &
Lilly, 1819. 21 p. DNLM; ICJ; MBM; MWA; NNNAM.
                                                  48616
-- Address to the people of the commonwealth of Massachusetts. [Massachusetts, 1819] 24 p. MiD-B.
                                                  48617
-- Committee on contested elections... report... [Bos-
ton, 1819] MWA.   48618

-- Committee to revise the criminal code. ...To the
Honorable the Senate, and the Honorable the House of
representatives, of the Commonwealth of Massachusetts. [Boston, 1819] 23 p. MB; MWA.   48619

-- Joint committee concerning the separation of the
District of Maine... The Committee of both Houses, to
whom were referred the petitions concerning the separation of the District of Maine... [Boston, 1819] MWA.
                                                  48620

-- Joint committee on petition of the trustees of the
Maine literary and theological institution. The committee of both Houses...beg leave to report...[Boston,
1819] MWA.   48621

-- Laws of the Commonwealth establishing and defining
the powers of the Charlestown Board of Health; with
the rules, order and regulation of said Board relative
to internal health, etc.   Charlestown, Mass., the
Board, 1819. 20 p. MB; MHi.   48622

-- Laws of the Commonwealth of Massachusetts, passed
by the General court, at their session, which commenced on Wednesday, January 13th and ended on Saturday, February 20th, 1819. Boston, Pr. by Russell
& Gardner, for Benjamin Russell, 1819. 204 p. Ia;
MH-L; MHa; MeU; Nb; Nj; RPL.   48623

-- Laws of the Commonwealth of Massachusetts, passed
by the General Court, at their session which commenced on Wednesday, the twenty-sixth day of May,
and ended on the nineteenth of June, one thousand eight
hundred and nineteen. Boston, Pr. by Russell & Gardner, for Benjamin Russell, 1819. 104 p. Ia; MdBB;
MeU; Nc-S; Nv.   48624

-- A proclamation, for a day of public Thanksgiving
and prayer to be observed December 2, 1819. Boston,
1819. Broadside. MBB.   48625

-- Resolves of the general court of the Commonwealth
of Massachusetts, passed at their session from May 31,
1815, to February 20, 1819. Vol. VII. Boston, Russell & Gardner, for Benjamin Russell, 1819. 654-
740 p.   CSfLaw; IaU-L; MeU; Mi-L; NNLI; RPL.48626

-- Resolves of the General court of the Commonwealth
of Massachusetts, passed at their sessions, which commenced on the twenty-sixth of May, and ended the nineteenth of June, one thousand eight hundred and nineteen.   Boston, Pr. by Russell & Gardner, for Benjamin Russell, 1819. 87 p. CSfLaw; MHi; MMeT; MWn;
MeHi; Nb; Nj.   48627

-- Rules and orders to be observed in the House of representatives, of the Commonwealth of Massachusetts... Pub. by order of the house.   Boston, 1819.
Ct.   48628

-- Statement of the bank corporations.   Boston, 1819.
PPL.   48629

-- Tax for the year 1819... [Boston, 1819] 28 p. DLC.
                                                      48630

-- To the honorable Senate and House of Representatives of the Commonwealth of Massachusetts... May,
1819.   Broadside. MB.   48631

-- To the Honorable the Senate and House of Representatives of the Commonwealth of Massachusetts, in
General Court assembled.   [Memorial against the removal of Williams College to Hampshire County]
[1819?] Broadside. MWiW.   48632

Massachusetts Ancient and Honourable Artillery Company.
    Rules and regulations of the ancient and honourable
artillery company; with the charter, To which is added
the names of the members, from its commencement to
the present time, with the dates of their admission,
titles, and commands sustained in the company. June 7,
1819.   Boston, Pr. by E. G. House, for the Company,
1819.   DLC; MBB; MH.   48633

Massachusetts General Hospital, Boston.
    Address [of the Trustees.] [Boston? 1819?] MWiW.
                                                      48634

Massachusetts Historical Society
    Collections of the Massachusetts Historical Society.
Vol. VIII of the second series.   Boston, Pr. by Sewell
Phelps, 1819.   332 p. KyLxT; MHa; MeBa; MeHi.
                                                      48635

Massachusetts medical society.
    Acts of the Legislature of Massachusetts for regulating the practice of physicks and surgery.   With the
regulations adopted by the Society... Boston, Pr. by
Wells and Lilly, 1819. 21 p. M; MH; MWA; MiD-M;

NNNAM.   48636

Massachusetts Missionary Society
    Constitution of the Massachusetts Missionary Soci-
ety, with list of officers and members.   Salem, Mass.,
Thomas C. Cushing, 1819. MSaE.   48637

Massachusetts Peace Society
    A catalogue of the officers... Cambridge, Hilliard
& Metcalf, 1819. 12 p. DLC; MB.   48638

-- Second annual report... Cambridge, Hilliard & Metcalf, 1819. 14 p. DLC.   48639

-- Third report made at the annual meeting in Boston,
Dec. 25, 1818 [1819] 12 p. Tuttle S 2986.   48640

The Massachusetts Register and United States calendar
...1820... Boston, James Loring; West, Richardson &
Lord... Cornhill [1819] 252 p. MBB; MHa; MMeT;
MS; MWHi; MWat; MeBa; MeBat.   48641

Massachusetts society for promoting Christian knowledge.
    An account of the transactions... from May 1817 to
May 1819. Cambridge, Pr. by Hilliard and Metcalf,
1819. 18 p. DLC; MWA.   48642

[Masson, Charles François Philibert]
    Maria, or the ever-blooming flower... New Haven,
Sidney's press, for J. Babcock & son, 1819. MWA.
                                                 48643
Mathematical tables: difference of latitude and departure; logarithms,... Baltimore, Pr. by T.H. Palmer,
for Fielding Lucas, Jun., 1819. 152 p. NNE.   48644

Maturin, C. Robert
    Fredolfo, a tragedy, in five acts.   Philadelphia,
M. Carey and Son, 1819. RNR.   48645

Mauger, John Jersey
    An oration, delivered in the French Calvinistic
Church, on the fifth of July, 1819; (the fourth being
Sunday) in commemoration of American independence...

Charleston, S. C., Pr. by W. P. Young & son, 1819.
19 p. DLC; MWA; NAuT; NN; PPM; ScC.   48646

Mavor, William Fordyce, 1758-1837
    Catechism of animated nature...New York, Samuel
Wood & Sons, and Samuel S. Wood & Co., Baltimore,
1819. 70 p. MWA; NNC; PHi; PP.   48647

-- The catechism of health; containing simple and easy
rules and directions for the management of children,
and observations on the conduct of health in general...
New-York, Samuel Wood & Sons, Samuel S. Wood &
co., Baltimore, 1819. 68 p. CSmH; DLC; MWA;
NNT-C.   48648

-- Catechism of universal history...New York, Samuel
Wood & Sons, and Samuel S. Wood & Co., Baltimore,
1819. 72 p. CSmH; DLC; MH; MWA; PHi.   48649

-- The elements of knowledge contained in catechisms
on general knowledge, universal history, geography,
animated nature, botany, health, and Bible, Mather's
catechism. New York, S. Wood and sons, 1819. 2 v.
MB; MWA; NH.   48650

Maxcy, Jonathan
    A discourse delivered in South-Carolina College,
July 4th, A. D. 1819, at request of the inhabitants of
Columbia. Ed. 2. Columbia, S. C., Pr. at the State
Gazette office, 1819. 28 p. KyLoS; PPL; ScCC. 48651

-- A funeral sermon, occasioned by the death of John
Sampson Bobo, a member of the junior class, in the
South-Carolina college. Delivered, Oct. 10, 1819.
Columbia, S. C., Pr. by D. Faust, for the students,
1819. 16 p. MB; MWA.   48652

Maxim, Abraham
    Northern harmony...Ed. 5. Hallowell, Me., 1819.
39 p. DLC.   48653

[Mayo, Robert]
    The mythology of the pagan world, illustrated by 52

plates engraved by Tanner, Vallance, Kearney & Co.
Philadelphia, Pr. by Cammeyer & Acock, for Geo.
May & Co., 1819. 12 p. CoDI; ViRVal.   48654

-- The rhyming spelling book... Baltimore, N. G. Maxwell, 1819. 147 p. MB; MWA; PU.   48655

Mead, Charles
   Mississippian scenery; a poem, descriptive of the
interior of North America by Charles Mead... Philadelphia, Pr. by W. Fry, for S. Potter & Co., 1819.
113 p. CSmH; MH; MWA; P; RPB.   48656

Mead, Matthew, 1630?-1699
   The almost Christian discovered; or, The false
professor tried and cast.   Being the substance of seven
sermons, preached at St. Sepulchre's, in London, 1661.
Middletown, [Conn.] Clark & Lyman, 1819. 216 p.
CtHC; MWA; ViU.   48657

-- -- Philadelphia, 1819. 192 p. NjP.   48658

-- -- 2d Amer. ed.   Winchester, Va., Pr. by J.
Foster, 1819. 220 p. CSt; MWA; ViRU.   48659

Mead, William
   Letter to the American Colonization Society.   Washington, D. C., 1819. 4 p. Sabin 47230.   48660

Mease, James
   A treatise on the causes, means of prevention, and
cure of the sick-headache... Philadelphia, Pr. by Wm.
Fry, for M. Carey and son, 1819. 48 p. MHi; NNNAM;
P.   48661

Mecklenburg county, North Carolina
   Declaration of independence by the citizens of Meck-
lenburg county, North Carolina... [Knoxville, Tenn.]
Pr. by Heiskel & Brown [1819] Broadside. MWA; TU.
                                              48662
Medford association for discountenancing intemperance,
and the kindred vices.
   Constitution... Salem, Mass., Pr. by Thomas C.

Cushing, 1819.   22 p.   MSaE;   MWA.   48663

Medical Society of the County of New York
   Statutes... New York, G. Forman, 1819. NNNAM.
                                               48664
Medical society of the state of New York
   Transactions... 1819... Albany, Pr. by E. and E.
Hosford, 1819. 36 p. CtHT-W; MWA; NNNAM.   48665

Meikle, James
   The select remains of Mr. James Meikle late sur-
geon in Carnwath; or extracts from manuscripts found
among his papers... Pittsburgh, Pa., Pr. by Butler &
Lambdin, for R. Patterson & Lambdin, 1819.   DLC;
MeBat; MSan; MWA; NN; TNP.   48666

-- Solitude sweetened... Ed. 3. New York, Pr. by Geo.
Long, for E. Duyckinck, 1819. 249 p. GAuY; PU.
                                               48667
Melish, John
   Information and advice to emigrants to the United
States... Philadelphia, John Melish, 1819. 144 p. IC;
MWA; WHi.   48668

-- The traveler's directory through the United States of
America; being a complete list of the direct and cross-
roads, together with the conveyance by water... compiled
by John Melish.   Philadelphia, J. Melish and S. Harrison, 1819.   102 p. MBeHi.   48669

-- -- Ed. 5.   Philadelphia, 1819. 134+ p. MHi;
OClWHi; NUt.   48670

Mellen, P.
   Letter to the governor (on the claim of Massachusetts against the United States, with report of a committee thereon) [Boston, 1819] MBAt.   48671

Memminger, Gustavus C.
   An eulogy on Dr. Edward D. Smith, late professor
of chemistry in the South Carolina College, delivered
before the Clariosophic Society, November 20th, 1819.
Columbia, S.C., Pr. by D. Faust, 1819. 8 p.

ScU.   48672

Memoir of Miriam Warner, who died at Northampton,
Mass., Feb. 21, 1819 in the 11th year of her age.
New York, The American Tract Society [1819?] 16 p.
MH; RPB.   48673

Memoirs of Isaac P. Anderson, A.B., who died at
Beverly, Mass., Dec. 16, 1818...Boston, Pr. by U.
Crocker, for Samuel T. Armstrong, 1819. 143 p.
MeB; MWA.   48674

Memoirs of Simeon Wilhelm, a native of the Susoo
country, West Africa; who died at the house of the
Church missionary society, London, Aug. 29, 1817;
aged 17 years...Published for the Yale college society
...respecting missions. New Haven, Pr. by S. Converse, 1819. 108 p. NN-Sc.   48675

Memoirs of the life and campaigns of the Hon. Nathanael Greene...1st ed.   Philadelphia, 1819. (No. 213.
Anderson Galleries sale no. 102. May 19, 1914) 48676

Memorial to Congress of Cadets at West Point.   West
Point, New York, 1819. 9 p. MWA.   48677

Merlin, Lewis
     The treasure of health, or, A wonderful collection
of the most valuable secrets in medicine...Philadelphia,
the society, 1819. 341 p.   DLC; IaDuMtC; InU-M;
NNNAM.   48678

Merrill, Daniel
     The gospel church, vindicated by the scriptures...
Concord, N.H., Pr. by Hill & Moore, 1819. 207 p.
CBB; MH-AH; MWA; Nh; Nh-Hi; OO; RPB.   48679

Merrill, Phinehas
     The scholar's guide to arithmetic...3d Dover ed.,
rev., cor., and improved.   Dover [N.H.] Pr. by J.J.
Williams, for Jesse Varney, 1819. 107 p. CSmH;
CtHT-W; MH; MWA.   48680

Merritt, Timothy, 1775-1845
    A short account of the Christian experience and
happy death of Emily Spare, an orphan.   Daughter of
the late James and Elizabeth Spare of Boston.   Who
died Jan. 21, 1819, in the 13th year of her age... Ed.
2.   Boston, N. Coverly, 1819. 28 p. DLC.   48681

Metcalfe, Bela
    An address delivered to the society of free and ac-
cepted masons, on the Feast of St. John the Baptist,
June 24th, 1818.   By Brother Bela Metcalfe. Natchez,
Miss., Pr. by Marschalk & Evens, 1819. 17 p. MsFM.
                                                   48682

Methodist Episcopal Church
    Minutes... for the year 1819.   New York, Pr. by
J. C. Totten, for Joshua Soule and Thomas Mason...
1819.   (Two varied issues) DLC; MWA; PPM; Wv.
                                                   48683

Methodist error; or, Friendly, Christian advice... Cincinnati, Pr. by Looker, Reynolds & Co., repub. by
Phillips and Speer, 1819. 59 p. ICU.   48684

-- Trenton, N.J., D. & E. Fenton, 1819. MWA.48685

The Methodist pocket hymn-book, revised and improved.
...Ed. 46.   New-York, Pr. by Abraham Paul, for J.
Soule and T. Mason... 1819. 293 p.   MWA.   48685

Miami University, Oxford, O.
    Communication, made to the committee appointed
to inspect the books and accounts of the Miami University [Hamilton? 1819] 5 p. NN; OClWHi; OOxM. 48686

-- Ordinanaces of 'the Miami university.' [Hamilton,
O., 1819] 9 p. MiU; NN.   48687

Middlebrook's almanack for 1820... New Haven, A.H.
Maltby & co. [1819] [24] p. CtY; MWA.   48688

Middlebury College. Middlebury, Vt.
    Middlebury College, November, 1819.   The follow-
ing statement is published, for the purpose of communicating information to the parents, guardians, and

instructors of youth, who are pursuing studies prepara-
tory for admission to this college.   Terms of admis-
sion... Course of instruction and study... Lectures...
Annual expences... [Middlebury, Vt., 1819] [2] p. MH.
                                                                48689
-- Philomathesian society.
    Catalogue of books... Middlebury, Vt., Pr. by
Francis Burnap, 1819. 13 p. MWA.   48690

Middlesex Massachusetts auxiliary society.
    Address to the clergy and the people of the county
of Middlesex... Cambridge, Pr. by Hilliard and Metcalf,
1819. 16 p. CtSoP; MWA.   48691

Miller, Andrew
    New states and territories, or The Ohio, Indiana,
Illinois, Michigan and North-western, Missouri, Louisiana, Mississippi and Alabama, in their character, in
1818... Printed for the benefit of emigrants and others,
intending to visit the western county. [Keene, N. H.]
1819. 96 p. DLC; Mi; OCHP.   48692

-- -- [Keene, N. H., 1819] 32 p. WHi.   48693

Miller, Jesse
    Strictures on Baldwin's letters.   Philadelphia,
1819. 24 p. MH-AH; NRAB.   48693a

Miller, Orren
    A funeral sermon, preached on the occasion of the
death of Mrs. Hannah Miller, September 14, 1819, at
Mount Morris, (Genesee Co., N. Y.). Moscow, N. Y.,
Pr. by H. Ripley, 1819. 20 p. NRU.   48694

Miller, Samuel
    Circular letter to Dr. Richards.   By S. Miller and
A. Alexander... Princeton, 1819. 3 p. NjP.   48695

Miller, Silvanus
    An address delivered in behalf of the New-York in-
stitution for the instruction of the deaf and dumb...
[New York] Pr. by E. Conrad, 1819. 15 p. MdBM;
NHi; NNNAM; NbU.   48696

Milligan, James
    A narrative of the late controversy between the As-
sociate and Reformed Presbyterians of Ryegate and
Barnet...Danville, Vt., Pr. by Ebenezer Eaton, 1819.
136 p. CSmH; MWA; MeBat; N; VtHi.   48697

Milman, Henry Hart
    Fazio, or the Italian wife, a tragedy. Philadel-
phia, Pr. by T. Town, for I. Riley, 1819. MWA.
                                              48698
Milner, Henry M.
    Barmecide; or, The fatal offspring. A dramatick
romance, in three acts...Baltimore, J. Robinson,
1819. 47 p. MB; MH; MWA; MdBJ; MdHi; NN. 48699

Milner, John
    The end of religious controversy in a friendly cor-
respondence, between Religious Society Protestants and
a Roman Catholic Divine...Baltimore, Fielding Lucas,
Jun'r, [1819] 338 p. DGU; Ia; MSNF; MSchU; MoWgT;
OMC; NSchU.   48700

Milnor, James
    The widow and her mites...New York, Pr. by T.
& J. Swords, 1819. 23 p. MWA; NNC; NNG; PHi.
                                              48701
Milton, John
    Adam and Eve...[Boston, Lincoln & Edmands,
1819] 72 p.   MWA.   48702

-- -- [Boston, Lincoln & Edmands, 1819] 70 p. MWA.
                                              48703
-- Paradise lost...Philadelphia, Pr. by Griggs & Co.,
1819. 356 p. CSt; MBridT; MWA; MdW; NLag; PPP.
                                              48704
-- The works of the British poets. With lives of the
authors. Philadelphia, Mitchell, Ames & White, 1819.
429 p. KyDC.   48705

Miner's agricultural almanac...1820. Doylestown, Pa.,
Pr. by Asher Miner, 1819. DLC.   48706

Ming's Hutchins' improved; being an almanac and

ephemeris...for...1820...New York, Alexander Ming, 1819. 36 p. DLC; MB; MWA; NHi; NN; NjR. 48707

No entry.
48708

Miniature almanack for 1820. Boston, Pr. by Sylvester T. Goss, for Charles Ewer [1819] MB; MH; MWA; OClWHi. 48709

-- Boston, Mass., Pr. by Sylvester T. Goss, for Charles Ewer [1819] (Varying ed.) MWA. 48710

Missionary & Bible Society of the Protestant Episcopal Church in America.
Address and constitution. New York, 1819. N.
48711
The Missionary. Mount Zion, Ga., J. P. Norton, May, 1819, 1st issue. Weekly newspaper. MWA. 48712

Missionary society of Connecticut.
Twentieth annual narrative of missionary labours...
for the year 1818...Hartford, Pr. by Peter B. Gleason & Co., 1819. MWA. 48713

Mississippi (State)
Acts passed at the first session of the second General Assembly of the state of Mississippi. Natchez, Miss., Pr. by Marschalk and Evens, 1819. 138 p. DLC; ICLaw; In-Sc; MH-L; MWA; MdBB; MiU-L; Ms; MsJS; NNB; O-SC; PU-L. 48714

The Mississippi almanac, for the year of our Lord 1820...Natchez [Miss.] Marschalk and Evens [1819] 48 p. ViU. 48715

Missouri (Ter.)
Acts passed by the General Assembly of the Territory of Missouri, in Oct., Nov. and Dec., 1818. St. Louis, Pr. by Joseph Charless, 1819. 163 p. DLC; MoHi; Mo; MoSHi; NNB. 48716

-- A digest of the General Assembly of Missouri in

January 1815.   St. Louis, Pr. at the office of the Enquirer, 1819.   23 p. Mo.   48717

Missouri Herald.   Jackson, Mo., T.E. Strange, June
25, 1819, 1st issue.   Weekly newspaper.   DLC.   48718

Missouri Intelligencer.   Franklin, Mo., Patten & Hol-
laday, Apr. 23, 1819, 1st issue.   Weekly newspaper.
MoHi.   48719

Mitchell, Thomas Daché
    Medical chemistry; or, a compendious view of the
various substances employed in the practice of medicine, that depend on chemical principles for their formation; designed for the use of medical students...
1819.   131 p.   CtY; DNLM; ICJ; MBM; IEN; MWA;
PPL; PU.   48720

Mobile, Ala.
    Report of the Committee appointed to investigate the
causes and extent of the late extraordinary sickness
and mortality in the town of Mobile.   [Mobile, Ala.]
Pr. at the office of the Mobile Gazette, 1819.   12 p.
MBM; MB; MWA.   48721

Modern characters.   Annapolis, Md., Pr. by J. Green,
1819.   170 p.   MWA; MdBP; MdHi.   48722

Monitor.   Huntingdon, Pa., 1819.   Newspaper.   Brigham,
p. 863.   48723

Monmouth Star.   Freehold, N.J., H. Jones, Nov. 2,
1819, 1st issue.   Weekly newspaper.   NjHi.   48724

Montgomery, James, 1771-1854
    Greenland, and other poems...New-York, Repr. for
Kirk & Mercein, C. Wiley & Co., ...1819.   207 p.
DLC; DeGE; MLy; MWA; NNUT.   48725

Montgomery Co., N.Y.   Court of Common Pleas.
    Rules of the Court of Common Pleas of Montgomery
County.   Adopted September term, 1819.   [Johnstown?
N.Y., 1819]   24 p.   CtY.   48726

[Montrose, James Graham, 1st Marquis of]
The power of faith; exemplified in the life and
writings of Mrs. Isabella Graham of New-York. Ed. 4.
New York, Pr. by W. A. Mercein, 1819. 334 p. MA.
                                              48727
A monument to the praise of the Lord's goodness, and
to the memory of Eliza Cunningham. [Philadelphia]
1819. MWA.   48728

[Moody, Eleazer]
The school of good manners.   Montpelier, Vt., E.
P. Walton, 1819. 64 p. MWA.   48729

Moody, Samuel
Sketch of a sermon, preached to some children...
Newburyport, Mass., 1819. MSaE; MWA.   48730

Moor, Jacobi
Elementa linguae Graecae;... Studio Jacobi Moor,
LL. D. ... Secunda editio Americana... Novi Eboraci:
impensis T. & J. Swords, 1819. 215 p. ICP; N; NNS.
                                              48731
[Moore, Frances] 1789 or 90-1881.
A year and a day.   A novel... By Madame Pa-
nache [pseud.] author of Manners... New-York, Pr. by
J. Seymour, for C. Wiley & Co., 1819. 267 p.
CtHT; DLC; IaFair.   48732

Moore, Henry
A letter to William Penn, Esq. concerning baptism and the Lord's Supper... First published in London, A. D. 1710.   Philadelphia, repub. by S. Potter &
co., 1819. 36 p. MWA; NjR; OClWHi.   48733

-- The life of Mrs. Mary Fletcher, consort and relict
of the Rev. John Fletcher, Vicar of Madely, Salop.
Compiled from her Journal, and other authentic documents... Philadelphia, Jonathan Pounder, 1819. 2 v.
NNS.   48734

Moore, Humphrey
A reply to A series of letters on the mode and
subjects of baptism... Amherst, N. H., Richard Boyls-

ton, 1819. 79 p. CSt; MWA; Nh.   48735

Moore, John Bayly
    A digested index to the Term reports; containing
all the points of law argued and determined in the
Kings Bench and Common Pleas from 1785, to 1818...
Philadelphia, Harrison Hall, 1819. 2 v. MWA; NNLI;
NUtSC; NjR; ViPet.   48736

Moore, Martin
    Death of the saints precious in God's sight. A
sermon, delivered in Natick, June 13, 1819, occasioned by the death of Mrs. Hannah Coolidge...Dedham,
Mass., Pr. by H. & W. H. Mann [1819] 15 p. MBAt;
MH; MSaE; MWA.   48737

Moore, Nathaniel Fish, 1782-1872
    Remarks on the pronunciation of the Greek lan-
guage... New York, Pr. by Clayton & Kingsland, for
James Eastburn and Co., 1819. 46 p. MWA; MWiW;
NNS; N; NjR.   48738

Moore, Richard Channing
    St. Paul's views on fidelity, as expressed in Ro-
mans, 10th chapter and 1st verse, a sermon delivered
...By the Rt. Rev'd Richard Channing Moore...Fay-
etteville, N. C., Pr. by Carney & Dismukes, at the Observer Press, 1819. 13 p. DLC; NNG; NcAS.   48739

Moore, Thomas
    Melodies, songs, sacred songs, and national airs...
New York, Pr. by J. Seymour, for A. T. Goodrich &
Co., 1819. 238 p. MEab; MWA.   48740

[--] Tom Crib's memorial to Congress.   London pr.
1819.   New-York, Pr. by William A. Mercein, for
Kirk & Mercein, C. Wiley and Co., ...1819. 120 p.
MB; MWiW; NN; OC.   48741

Moore, Zephaniah Swift
    The Sabbath a permanent and benevolent institution.
A sermon, preached at the annual election, May 27,
1818, before His Excellency John Brooks, Esq. Gover-

nor; his honor William Phillips, Esq. Lieutenant Governor; the Honorable council; and the Legislature of Massachusetts by Zephaniah Swift Moore... Boston, Pr. by Russell, Cutler and Co., for Benjamin Russell, 1819. DLC.   48742

Moral agency; or, natural ability consistent with moral inability: being remarks on "An essay on the inability of sinners, by a Presbyterian." By a Christian. Philadelphia, Pr. by Anderson & Meehan, for William Bradford, 1819. 36 p. MAnP; NjR. PPiW.   48743

Moravians
    The church litany of the United Brethren.   Philadelphia, Pr. by Conrad Zentler, 1819. MWA.   48744

-- A collection of hymns for the use of the Protestant Church of the United Brethren. New and revised ed. Philadelphia, Pr. by Conrad Zentler, 1819. 348 p. DLC; IaOskW; MWA; NjR; OClWHi.   48745

[More, Hannah] 1745-1833
    The happy waterman; or, Honesty the best policy. To which are added, The boy of Dundee. And The gardener and rose tree. Suitable for Sabbath-school readings. [Boston] Lincoln & Edmands, 1819. 24 p. DLC.   48746

-- Moral sketches of prevailing opinions and manners, foreign and domestic: with reflections on prayer... From the London ed. Boston, Wells and Lilly, 1819. 302 p. MB; MBC; MWiW; NCH; NcD; OMC.   48747

-- -- Boston, Wells & Lilly, 1819. 207 p. MWA; NNS; Nh; ScC.   48748

-- -- Boston, Wells and Lilly, 1819. 2 v. DGU; MB; MBL; MWA; NjR; PPLT; PU; ViRut.   48749

[--] Parley the porter. An allegory. Also an anecdote on card playing. Ed. 4. Andover, Mass., Flagg & Gould, 1819. MB.   48750

-- Reflections on prayer, and on the errors which may
prevent its efficacy. Philadelphia, Pr. by Wm. Fry,
for Anthony Finley, 1819. 207 p. DLC; NRAB; OO.
                                                    48751

[--] 'Tis all for the best... Philadelphia, William
Bradford, 1819. MWA.   48752

No entry   48753

Morey, Samuel, 177(?)-1843
    Copy of a letter...to William A. Dluer, Esq., Ox-
ford [N.H.] October 31, 1818. [Hartford, 1819] 6 p.
CtHT-W.   48754

Morgan, Asaph
    Thoughts on the Circular Letter issued by the Fair-
field Baptist Association holden at Enosburgh, August
1818. Burlington, Vt., Pr. by E. & T. Mills, 1819.
12 p. VtHi.   48755

Morgan, Sydney (Owenson) Lady, 1783?-1889
    Florence Macarthy; an Irish tale...In two volumes.
Baltimore, Pr. by J. Robinson, for Nathaniel G. Max-
well and M. Carey & son, Philadelphia, 1819. 2 v.
MdHi; ViU.   48756

-- -- New York, Pr. by C.S. Van Winkle, for W.B.
Gilley, 1819. 2 v. PMA.   48757

Morning Chronicle. Baltimore, Schaeffer and Maund,
April 8, 1819, 1st issue. Daily newspaper. MdHi.
                                                    48758
Morrell, Thomas
    The history of Rome, from its earliest records to
its decline: in a series of essays, accompanied with re-
flections...Philadelphia, Pr. by Griggs & Co., for
Benjamin Johnson, 1819. 412 p. NcU; NcWsS; PPP.
                                                    48759
-- Studies in history; containing the history of Greece,
from its earliest period, to its final subjugation by the

Romans; in a series of essays...Philadelphia, Pr. by
G. L. Austin, for Benjamin Johnson, 1819. 400 p.
MWA; NcWsS.   48760

Morril, David Lawrence
   A discourse, delivered at the funeral of Mr. Willi-
am Parker, merchant, of Piscataquog Village, Bed-
ford, N. H., who died July seventh 1819...Amherst,
N. H., Pr. by Richard Boylston [1819] 18 p. CSmH;
DLC; MWA; Nh; Nh-Hi; NhM.   48761

-- A discourse, delivered before the General assembly
of the Grand lodge of New-Hampshire...Concord, N. H.,
Pr. by Hill & Moore, 1819. 27 p. DLC; MWA; Nh;
Nh-Hi; PPFM.   48762

Morrison, William
   A sermon [on Job. v. 26] ...occasioned by the
death of J. Pinkerton, Esq. Concord, N. H., 1817.
BrMus.   48763

Morse, Jedidiah, 1761-1826
   The American universal geography...Ed. 7.
Charlestown, G. Clarke; Boston, Lincoln & Edmands,
...1819. 2 v. CSt; CoCsC; CoD; DLC; IP; In; KyLo;
LNH; MB; MH-AH; MSaP; MWA; MWak; MiD-B; MiU-C;
MsCliM; NPV; NbHi; NhD; NjP; NjR; OClWHi; OCY;
PAtM; ScC; TNP; WHi.   48764

-- Geography made easy: being an abridgement of the
American Universal Geography...Ed. 20. Utica, N. Y.,
William Williams, 1819. 364 p. CtHT-W; DLC; MShi;
MTaHi; MWA; MeHi; NN; NcU; WMOSC.   48765

Morton, Thomas, 1764-1838
   A Roland for an Oliver; a farce first performed
1819. New York, Longworth, 1819. 43 p. CtHT-W;
MBr; N; NN.   48766

Mott, James, 1788-1868
   Observations on the education of children and hints
to young people, on the duties of civil life. New York,
Woodbridge B. Smith, 1819. 74 p. NdU.   48767

Mott, Valentine, 1785-1865
    Reflections on securing in a ligature the arteria
innominata.   To which is added, a case in which this
artery was tied by a surgical operation.   [New York,
1819]   46 p.   DNLM; MBM; NNNAM; PPAmP; PU.
                                                        48768

Murphey, Archibald De Bow
    Memoir on the internal improvements contemplated
by the legislature of North-Carolina; and on the resources and finances of that state.   Raleigh, N. C.,
Pr. by J. Gales, 1819.   88 p.   CSmH; DLC; N; NcAS;
NcU; WHi.   48769

Murphy, John S., pub.
    Interesting documents... New-York, Pr. by South-
wick & Pelsue, for John S. Murphy, 1819.   128 p.   DLC;
DeGE; MWA; MiU-C; NvHi.   48770

Murray, John
    Memoir of M. by John Murray of New York.   New
York, 1819.   MBAt.   48771

Murray, Lindley
    Abridgement of Murray's English grammar... Al-
bany, E. & E. Hosford, 1819.   107 p.   CSfCW; MWeyHi.
                                                        48772
-- -- Andover, Mass., 1819.   96 p.   MWA; Nh-Hi.
                                                        48773
-- -- Baltimore, Joseph Robinson, 1819.   105 p.   MdHi.
                                                        48774
-- -- 12th Boston ed.   Boston, J. Loring, 1819.   MWA.
                                                        48775
-- -- Concord, N. H., 1819.   106 p.   MWA; Nh-Hi.
                                                        48776
-- -- Concord, N. H., Hill & Moore, 1819.   84 p.   MH;
MWA; Nh-Hi.   48777

-- -- 4th Hallowell ed., cor. and enl.   Hallowell,
Me., E. Goodale, 1819.   Tuttle C 6461-A.   48778

-- -- New York, Franklin Juvenile Book-Store, [1819]
108 p.   MH; MHi; ViRJ.   48779

-- -- From the latest English ed., cor. by the author.
Newbury, Vt., Pr. by C. Spear, for Ira White, 1819.
108 p. MH; MWA; VtHi.   48780

-- -- Philadelphia, Benjamin Warner, 1819. 107 p.
MWA; PReaHi.   48781

-- -- Pittsburgh, Pa., Cramer & Spear, 1819. 108 p.
PWCHi.   48782

-- -- From the 30th English ed., cor. by the author.
Utica, N.Y., William Williams, 1819. 107 p. MWA;
NUt.   48783

-- -- Ed. 2. Hartford, S.G. Goodrich, 1819. 144 p.
CtHT-W; CtHi; MWA; MiD-B; MiDSH; NNC; OClWHi.
                                                  48784
-- -- New Haven, A.H. Maltby & co., 1819. 126 p.
CtHT-W; CtY; NNC.   48785

-- -- Pittsburgh, Pa., Pr. by Eichbaum & Johnson,
for Randolph Barnes, 1819. 143 p. CtEhad; CtHT;
CtHT-W; IU; MH; MWA; NBuCC; OClWHi.   48786

-- English exercises adapted to Murray's English gram-
mar...9th Boston, from the 20th English ed. Boston,
James Loring, 1819. 213 p. CSt; MB; MH; MPeHi.
MWA; MeU.   48787

-- -- Stereotyped from the last English ed., by B. &
J. Collins, New-York. New York, Pr. by Collins &
co., 1819. 192 p. DLC; MLow; MWA.   48788

-- -- From the 7th English ed., with additions and improvements. Utica, N.Y., William Williams, 1819.
155 p. GDC; KyU; MWA; MdBLC; MiD-B; NSyHi; NUt;
NcG; OClWHi; P; TWcW; WU.   48789

-- English grammar, adapted to the different classes of
learners...Albany, Pr. by E. & E. Hosford, 1819.
312 p. MH; MWA; NPtjerHi; NJost; NRU-W; NSyHi;
OrBE; PLFM; VtMiS.   48790

-- -- From the 18th English ed., enl. and improved by the author. Brattleborough, Vt., John Holbrook, 1819. 312 p. ICU; MH; MWA; NN; VtHi; VtU-W. 48791

-- English grammar... 3d Hallowell from the 18th English ed. Hallowell, Me., E. Goodale and S. K. Gilman, 1819. 309 p. MAshlHi; MWA; MeBat; MeU; MiD; NcAS; TJoT. 48792

-- English grammar with an appendix. Hanover, N. H., Pr. by D. Watson, 1819. 312 p. MWHi. 48793

-- -- Hanover, N. H., J. Hinds, 1819. 312 p. MWA; NGH. 48794

-- An English grammar comprehending the principle rules of the language... 4th Amer. ed. from last English. New York, Collins & Co., 1819. 2 v. in 1. CSansS; CoGrS; MH; MWA; NNC. 48795

-- The English reader... Albany, E. & E. Hosford, 1819. 264 p. MChiA; MH; MWA; N. 48796

-- -- Albany, J. R. Shute & Co., 1819. 228 p. MWbor. 48797

-- -- Boston ed. Boston, Lincoln & Edmands, 1819. 264 p. ICU; MBC; MH; MWA; MWHi; RPB. 48798

-- -- Canandaigua, N. Y., Pr. by J. D. Bemis & Co., 1819. 272 p. CSmH; MWA; N; NBuG. 48799

-- -- Stereotyped by E. & H. Wallis. Concord, N. H., Horatio Hill & Co. [1819?] 261 p. NcGw. 48800

-- -- Fredericktown, Md., Pr. by George Kolb, for George Kolb, 1819. 252 p. DGU; DLC; MWA; MdHi; NN; PSC-Hi; TxU. 48801

-- -- Fredericktown, Md., Pr. by George Kolb, for M. Bartgis, 1819. 252 p. MdHi. 48802

-- -- ..Or, Pieces in prose and poetry, selected from the best writers... Stereotyped by B. & J. Collins,

from the last English ed. New-York, Collins & co.,
1819. 263 p. N. 48803

-- -- An improved ed. New York, Daniel D. Smith,
1819. CtHT-W; MWA. 48804

-- -- New York, Evert Duyckinck, 1819. MNF; MSaE;
MWA. 48805

-- -- New York, Joseph Desnoues, 1819. CtSoP; MWA.
48806
-- -- New-York, L. & F. Lockwood, 1819. 222 p.
MWA; MiD-B; MoU. 48807

-- -- From the last English ed. New York, S. Campbell & Son, 1819. MWA. 48808

-- -- Philadelphia, John Carson, 1819. 316 p. MWA.
(Forrest Bowe Coll. 110 Morningside Dr., NYC.)48809

-- -- Rutland, Vt., Fay and Burt, 1819. 266 p. CSt;
MH; MWA; VtHi. 48810

-- -- Utica, N.Y., William Williams, 1819. 263 p.
MWA; NNC-T. 48811

-- An epitome of the English language; or, A catechetical grammar...New-York, Pr. by S. Marks, for J.A.
Burtus...1819. 108 p. DLC. 48812

-- Introduction to the English reader: Or, a selection of
pieces, in prose and poetry...Stereotyped by B. & J.
Collins. Philadelphia, Benjamin Warner, 1819. 166 p.
ICU; KTW; MPeHi; MWA. 48813

-- Key to the Exercises adapted to Murray's English
grammar...2d Albany, from the 12th London ed. Albany, G.J. Loomis & Co., 1819. 151 p. MWA. 48814

-- -- Stereotyped from the last English ed., by B. &
J. Collins, New York. New York, Collins & Co., 1819.
168 p. DLC; NRom. 48815

-- -- 2d Albany, from the 12th London ed.   Utica,
N. Y., Pr. by G. J. Loomis & Co., for William Williams, 1819.   151 p.   NUtHi.   48816

-- Murray's spelling book, imp. ed.   New York, D. D.
Smith, 1819.   MWA.   48817

Musings at an evening club in Boston.   Somewhat like
a poem... Boston, Pr. by True & Weston, 1819.   53 p.
CSmH; MB; MH; PHi; RPB.   48818

My tippoo; a poem.   Illustrated with engravings.
[Philadelphia] Wm. Charles, 1819.   12 p.   NNC.   48819

                            N
Nashville Gazette.   Nashville, Tenn., G. Wilson, May
26, 1819, 1st issue.   Semi-weekly and weekly newspaper.   THi.   48820

A national calendar, for 1820... To which is added an
almanac for the current year... By Peter Force.
Washington, Davis & Force... [1819] 228 p. MdHi;
MeBat.   48821

National Recorder.   Philadelphia, July, 1819, 1st issue.   DLC; P; TxU.   48822

Nautical almanac for 1821.   New York, W. Hooker and
Edmund M. Blunt, 1819.   MWA.   48823

Neal, John, 1793-1876
    The battle of Niagara.   Ed. 2, enl.: with other po-
ems... Baltimore, Pr. by B. Edes, for N. G. Maxwell,
1819.   272 p.   DLC; MB; MdHi; RPB.   48824

-- Otho: a tragedy, in five acts... Boston, Pr. by
John H. A. Frost, for West, Richardson & Lord, 1819.
120 p.   DLC; ICU; MB; MBAt; MWA; NNC; NNP; PU;
RPB.   48825

Nelson, Robert
    Instructions necessary and useful for those who are

to be confirmed; in the way of question and answer:
with prayers suitable to the occasion...Baltimore, Pr.
by J. Robinson, 1819. 12 p. MWA; MdHi.   48826

Neue Americanische Landwirthschafts Calender, 1820.
Reading, Pa., Johann Ritter und comp. [1819] MWA;
P; PHi.   48827

Der neue Ohio Calender, auf das Jahr...1820...Lan-
caster, O., Johann Herman [1819] 34 p. OHi. 48828

A new and complete preceptor for the German flute.
Together with a choice collection of songs, duets,
marches, dances, &c. Rev. and enl. Utica, N.Y.,
William Williams, 1819. 47 p. MWA; NRU.   48829

A new and easy introduction to the art of penmanship,
on an improved plan of distance and proportion, made
easy and attainable to the capacities of youth of both
sexes. ...Philadelphia, Samuel Parmele & Co., 1819.
47 p. MWA; MiGr; PWCHi.   48830

New Castle Library Company
    Catalogue of the books belonging to the New Castle
Library Company 1819, to which are prefixed the act
of incorporation, and the by-laws of the company. Wilmington, Del., Porter, 1819. 67 p. DeWi.   48831

A new conductor generalis: being a summary of the
law relative to the duty and office of justices of the
peace...Albany, E.F. Backus, 1819. 482 p. IaU-L;
NNLI.   48832

New England almanack for 1820.   By Nathan Daboll.
New London, Conn., Samuel Green [1819] [32] p. CtHi;
MWA.   48833

New-England farmer's diary and almanac for 1820.
Weathersfield, 1819. NhHi.   48834

The New-England farmer's diary and almanac, from the
year of the creation, according to sacred writ, 5782;
and the Christian era, 1820...By Truman Abell, philom.

Windsor, Vt., Pr. by Ide & Aldrich, for Ebenezer
Hutchinson, Hartford, [1819] [48] p. MH; MWA; MeHi;
VtU-W.   48835

New England Guards
    Constitution of the New England Guards. Instituted
September 22d, 1812. Ed. 2. Boston, Pr. by T. Hudson, 1819. 46 p. MBB.   48836

The New-England missionary intelligencer, and general
repository... Concord, N.H., Pr. by Hill & Moore,
1819. 100 p. Vol. 1. MBC; MBradJ; Nh.   48837

The New England primer... Brattleborough, Vt., J.
Holbrook, 1819. 64 p. DLC; MB; MWA; NN; VtHi.
                                                   48838
The New-England primer, improved... To which is
added, The Assembly of Divines and Episcopal cate-
chisms. Bridgeport, Conn., Pr. by Nichols & Price,
for Josiah H. Baldwin, 1819. [72] p. CtHi; MB; MWA.
                                                   48839
-- Haverhill [Mass.] Nathan Burrill, 1819. 62 p.
MSaE; MWA.   48840

-- Newark [N.J.] William Tuttle, 1819. CtHT-W; NN.
                                                   48841
The New England primer improved, for the more easy
attaining the true reading of English. Albany, E. & E.
Hosford, 1819. 86 p. VtU.   48842

-- Rutland, Vt., Fay and Burt, 1819. [62] p. VtHi.
                                                   48843
New England Tract Society
    A word in season. No. 90. Andover, Mass.,
Flagg & Gould, 1819. CtHC.   48844

The new family receipt-book, containing eight hundred
truly valuable receipts in various branches of domestic
economy... New ed., cor. New-Haven, Pr. by Howe
& Spalding, and Samuel Wadsworth, 1819. 429 p. Ct;
CtHi; DLC; MW; MWA; MdBP; OO; ViU; WaSpHi-M.
                                                   48845
-- New ed. New Haven, A.H. Maltby & Co., 1819.

429 p. MBedf.   48846

The new freemason's monitor; or Masonic guide. Ed.
2. New York, George Longworth, 1819. 346 p. NIC.
                                      48847
New Hampshire (State)
    An Act for arranging and regulating the militia
within this state and for repealing all laws heretofore
made for that purpose. Approved July 1, 1819. Published by authority. Concord, N. H., 1819. 50 p.
CL; MH-L; Nh.   48848

-- Communication from His Excellency the Governor,
covering the report of the Justice of the Superior
Court (N. H.) on the questions of new trials. (Case of
Dorothy Merrill, adm. V Joseph Sherman, et al, Rock-
ingham 1818). New Hampshire 1819. (June 1819)
MBS; MH-L; MWA.   48849

-- (William Plumer). Governor's message. June 7,
1819. 8 p. MWA.   48850

-- Journal of the honorable Senate of the state of New
Hampshire, at their session, begun and holden at Con-
cord, on the first Wednesday of June, 1819. Concord,
N. H., Pr. by Hill & Moore, 1819. 312 p. DLC; IaHi;
Mi.   48851

-- Journal of the House of Representatives, of the
state of New-Hampshire at their session, begun and
holden at Concord, on the first Wednesday of June,
1819. Concord, N. H., Pr. by Hill & Moore, 1819.
383 p. DLC; Mi.   48852

-- Laws of the state of New-Hampshire. June session,
1819. [Concord, N. H., 1819] 254 p. DLC; Nb; R; T.
                                      48853
-- Report of the Committee, appointed to investigate
the affairs of the state prison, 1817. [Concord? 1819]
24 p. DLC.   48854

-- Reports of cases argued and determined in the Superior court of judicature for the state of New-Hamp-

shire, from September 1816, to February 1819. By
Nathaniel Adams.   Exeter, N.H., Pr. by J.J. Willi-
ams, for the proprietor, 1819. 288 p.   KU-L; MBS;
MHi; MLowM; NN; NdU-L; TxU-L; WaU.   48855

New Hampshire Baptist Domestick Mission Society.
    The constitution of the New Hampshire Baptist
Domestick Mission Society, adopted by the convention
at Concord, N.H., Wednesday June 2, 1819.   Concord,
N.H., Pr. by Hill & Moore, 1819. 8 p. DLC.   48856

New Hampshire Bible Society
    Eighth report of the New Hampshire Bible Society,
communicated at the annual meeting of the Society,
holden at Haverhill, September 22, 1819... Concord,
N.H., Pr. by George Hough, 1819. 45 p. DLC. 48857

New Hampshire Intelligencer.   Haverhill, N.H., Sylvester T. Goss, 1819. Newspaper. Brigham, p. 464.
                                                      48858
New Hampshire Medical Society
    Medical policy, of the N.H. medical society,
adopted, June 1819.   Concord, Pr. by George Hough,
1819. 8 p. DLC; RBR.   48859

New-Hampshire missionary society.
    Eighteenth annual report... September 23, 1819...
Concord, N.H., Pr. by George Hough, 1819. 24 p.
DLC; KWiU; MWA; MiD-B; WHi.   48860

-- The sixth report of the concerns of the New Hamp-
shire Cent. Institution, for September 1819.   By the
Committee of the Missionary Society.   Concord, N.H.,
Pr. by George Hough, 1819. 10 p. DLC.   48861

The New-Hampshire register, and United States' calen-
dar, for the year of Our Lord, 1820... Concord, N.H.,
Hill & Moore, 1819. 143 p. MHa; MWA; MiD-B;
Nh-Hi.   48862

New Jersey (State)
    Journal of the proceedings of the Legislative Coun-
cil of the state of New Jersey... Jan., 1819... 2d sitting

of the 43d session.   Newark [N.J.] Pr. by John Tuttle
& Co., 1819. [19]-85, 10 p. Nj; NjR.   48863

-- Journal of the proceedings of the Legislative Council of the state of New Jersey...Oct., 1919...1st sitting of the 44th session.   Newark, Pr. by John Tuttle
& Co., 1819. [86]-101 p. Nj; NjR.   48864

-- Private and temporary acts.   Acts of the 43d General Assembly of the state of New Jersey...Oct., 1818
...1st sitting.   Trenton, Pr. by Joseph Justice, 1819.
12 p.   DLC; NjR.   48865

-- -- Acts of the 43d General Assembly of the state
of New Jersey...Oct., 1818...2d sitting. Trenton, Pr.
by Joseph Justice, 1819. [13]-81 p. DLC; NjR. 48866

-- Public acts.   Acts of the 43d General Assembly of
the state of New Jersey...Oct., 1818.   Trenton, Pr.
by Joseph Justice, 1819. 36 p. DLC; NjR.   48867

-- A second supplement to an act, entitled "An act establishing a militia system," passed Feb. 18, 1815.
Trenton, N.J., Pr. by J. Justice, 1819. 4 p. NjR.
                                                48868
-- Votes and proceedings of the 43d General Assembly
of the state of New Jersey...Oct., 1818...1st sitting
+ [2d sitting] Trenton, Pr. by James J. Wilson, 1819.
156 p.   Nj; NjR.   48869

The New-Jersey and Pennsylvania almanac, for...1820.
By Joshua Sharp...Trenton, N.J., George Sherman
[1819] [36] p. DLC; MB; MWA; N; NjHi; NjR. 48870

New-Jersey Gazette.   Perth Amboy, N.J., J.T. Murden & Co., Feb. 4, 1819, 1st issue. Weekly newspaper. MWA.   48871

New-Jersey Mirror.   Mount Holly, N.J., Nathan
Palmer & Son, Sept. 15, 1819, 1st issue with this
title.   Weekly continuation of "The Burlington Mirror."
NjHi; NjR.   48872

New states and territories of the Ohio, Indiana, etc.
[Keene?] 1819. MB.   48873

New system of astronomy and geography.   Middletown
[Conn.] Clark & Lyman, 1819. MWA.   48874

New Year's gift.   New York, 1819. MWA.   48875

-- New York, 1819. 26 p. MWA.   48876

New York (City)
    Annual report of the Comptroller, with the ac-
counts of the corporation, for the year ending 10th day
of May, 1819...published by order of the Common
Council, May 10, 1819.   New York, Pr. by G. L.
Birch and Co., 1819.   17 p. MdBJ; NNS.   48877

-- The charter of the City of New-York.   Published
pursuant to an order of Common Council, passed June
14th, 1819.   New-York, Pr. by Grattan & Banks,
1819.   114 p. MH; MWA; NNC; NjR.   48878

-- Report of deaths in the city and county of New York,
for the year 1818... (annual report of the City inspector) New-York, Birch, 1819. 10 p. NN; NNC; NNNAM.
                                                     48879
-- Report of the committee on finance.   In common
council, December 27, 1819.   New-York, Pr. by L.
Birch & Co., 1819.   NNS.   48880

New York (County)
    Letter.   [Accompanied by report, respecting the
state of the register's office of the city and county of
New York] [New York, 1819] 11 p. DLC.   48881

New York (State)
    The act for the support of common schools.
Passed April 12, 1819.   Published in compliance with
a provision contained in its thirty-eighth section. Albany, Pr. by Websters and Skinners, 1819.   32 p. MH.
                                                     48882
-- -- Published in compliance with a provision contained in its thirty-eighth section.   Albany, Pr. by

Websters and Skinners, 1819. 15 p. ViRut.   48883

-- An act to abolish imprisonment for debt in certain
cases. Passed April 7, 1819. Albany, William Gould
& Co., 1819. 7 p. MWA.   48884

No entry.   48885

-- Acts of the Legislature of the State of New-York,
respecting navigable communications between the great
western and northern lakes and the Hudson river. Albany, Pr. by Websters and Skinners, 1819. 20 p.
DLC; DeGE; MBAt; N; NN.   48886

-- Annual report of the canal commissioners, communicated to the Legislature, Jan. 25, 1819. Albany, Pr.
by J. Buehl, 1819. 46 p. DLC; NCanHi; NRom; PPM.
                                                48887
-- Harbour regulations, relating to warden harbour
masters and pilots, conformable to an act of Assembly,
Feb. 19, 1819. New-York, Pr. by J. Seymour, for
Wm. Hooker, 1819. 23 p. MWA.   48888

-- No. 19. In Assembly, Jan. 23, 1819. (By Mr.
Huntington) An act to incorporate the Western Educa-
tion Society of the state of New-York. [Albany, 1819]
Broadsheet. NHi.   48889

-- In the Court for the trial of impeachments, and the
correction of errors. Jacob Rhinelander, appellant,
vs. John Barrow, Thomas Buckley...Case on the part
of the appellant. New York, Pr. by Grattan and Banks,
1819. 159 p. NjR.   48890

-- In the Court for the trial of impeachments and the
correction of errors between James I. Roosevelt and
Robert M. M'Menomy. Case on the part of the respond-
ents. New York, Clayton & Kingsland, 1819. ICLaw.
                                                48891

-- Instructions for the better government and organiza-
tion of common schools... Albany, Pr. by Websters &
Skinners, 1819. 16 p.   CtHT-W; DLC; MWA; NHuntHi;
NjR.   48892

-- Journal of the assembly of the state of New York:
at their forty-second session, begun and held at the
Capitol, in the city of Albany, the fifth day of January,
1819.   Albany, Pr. by J. Buel, 1819.   1091 p.   DLC;
NNLI.   48893

-- Journal of the Senate of the state of New-York: at
their forty-second session, begun and held at the capitol, in the city of Albany, the fifth day of January,
1819.   Albany, Pr. by J. Buel, 1819.   326 p.   ICU; N;
NNLI.   48894

-- Laws of the state of New-York, passed at the forty-
second session of the Legislature, begun and held at
the city of Albany, the fifth day of January, 1819.   Albany, Pr. by J. Buel, for Websters & Skinners, 1819.
339 p.   CU; In-SC; MdBB; N; NNLI; NNebgL; OCLaw;
OrPML; W.   48895

-- List of all the incorporations in the state of New-
York, except religious incorporations, with a recital of
all their important particulars and peculiarities.   Reported to the Assembly, pursuant to a resolution thereof.   Albany, Pr. by J. Buel, 1819.   106 p.   DLC;
DeGE; NIC; NNLI.   48896

-- List of lands to be sold in October, 1819, for ar-
rears of taxes.   Albany, Pr. by I. W. Clark, 1819.
170 p.   MHi; NN.   48897

-- Message to the Legislature of New York, Jan.,
1819.   Albany, Pr. at Register Office, 1819.   16 p.
DLC; PPi.   48898

-- Report of the joint committee of the Senate and Assembly, relative to the internal improvements of the
state; to whom was referred the annual report of the
Canal commissioners.   Albany, Pr. by J. Buel, 1819.

14 p. N. 48899

-- Report of the Select Committee, to whom was referred "that part of the speech of His Excellency the Governor, which relates to lotteries. Made in Assembly," April 6, 1819. Albany, Pr. by Jesse Buel, 1819. 39 p. NNC; NNS. 48900

-- Rules and orders of the Court of Common Pleas of Suffolk County, New York. Sag Harbor, N. Y., Pr. by Samuel Seabury, 1819. 16 p. NEh; NSmB. 48901

-- Speech of Governor Clincon, delivered this day to the Legislature of the state of New-York. [Albany, Albany register - Extra. Tuesday, January 5, 1819] 16 p. N. 48902

-- Speech of Governor Clinton, to the Legislature of the state of New-York, on the sixth day of January, 1819. Albany, Pr. at the Register office, 1819. 16 p. DLC; MBAt; MH-BA; MWA; NNS; NjPT. 48903

-- ...Statutes regulating the practice of physic and surgery in the state of New York...adopted July 6, 1819...New York, Pr. by George Forman, 1819. 38 p. NHi; NNC-M; NNNAM. 48904

New York and New Jersey almanack. By William Collom. New York, George Long, 1819. MWA. 48905

New York and New Jersey Calendar, or Beer's almanac. New York, P.V. Van Pelt, 1819. MWA. 48906

New-York corresponding association for the promotion of internal improvements.
An examination into the expediency of establishing a board of agriculture...Brooklyn, N. Y., Pr. by E. Worthington, 1819. 64 p. CSmH; DLC; ICMcHi; MWA. 48907

New York Evangelical Missionary Society
The Constitution, act of incorporation, and list of members and managers of the New-York Evangelical Missionary society. New York, J. C. Totten, 1819.

11 p. MBC.   48908

-- The third annual report... New York, Pr. by John
C. Totten, 1819. MWA.   48909

New York Farmer's almanack for 1820. By David
Young, [1819] MWA; NHi.   48910

New York Female Association
    Annual report of the Female Association in the
City of New-York. New York, Pr. by Samuel Wood
& Sons, 1819. 6 p. DLC.   48911

New York Female Union Society for the Promotion of
Sabbath schools.
    The third report of the New-York female union so-
ciety for the promotion of Sabbath schools read at
their annual meeting... To which is added an appendix.
New York, Pr. by J. Seymour, for the society, 1819.
39 p. MiD-B; NjR.   48912

New York free-school society.
    An address to the parents and guardians of the
children belonging to the schools under the care of the
New-York free-school society, by the trustees of the
institution. New York, Samuel Wood & sons, 1819.
14 p. OClWHi.   48913

-- By-laws of the Free school society, of New-York,
as revised and adopted by the Trustees, 12th month
(December) 1818. New York, Pr. by W. Treadwell,
1819. 24 p. NNFMH.   48914

New York institution for the instruction of the deaf
and dumb.
    An act to incorporate the members of the New-
York institution for the instruction of the deaf and dumb,
passed April 15, 1819. To which is added the by-
laws, and the names and residence of the officers and
directors, also the directors arranged into committees
and a list of the pupils. New York, Pr. by E. Conrad, 1819. 23 p. MBM; MH; MHi; MWA; N; NNNAM;
PPAmP.   48915

New-York Messenger. New York, J.W. Bell & M.Y.
Scott, Dec. 10, 1819, 1st issue. Semi-weekly newspaper. NHi.   48916

New York missionary society.
    The twenty-second annual report...New York, Pr.
by Abraham Paul, 1819. MWA.   48917

New York Orphan Asylum
    Annual report and account current of the Asylum
Society, in the City of New York, for 1819. With a
list of donations, subscribers, New-York, Pr. by
Samuel Wood & Sons, 1819. 19 p. DLC; N.   48918

The New York primer; or Second book. New York,
Samuel Wood & Sons, 1819. 32 p. MH; VtMiS. 48919

New York Protestant Episcopal missionary society.
    The third annual report...New York, Pr. by T. &
J. Swords, 1819. 7 p. MWA; NNG.   48920

New York Protestant Episcopal Sunday school society.
    Second annual report of the Board of managers of
the New York Protestant Episcopal Sunday school society. New York, 1819. 8 p. NNG.   48921

The New York reader, no. 1. New York, S. S. &
W. Wood, 1819. 3 v. DLC; LN; MMhHi; MWA; NhD;
RPB.   48922

New York Religious Tract Society
    Annual report of the New York tract society, with
extracts of correspondence and a list of subscribers.
New York, 1819. WHi.   48923

Newark Patriot. Newark, N.J., Pares & Son, Jan. 1,
1819, 1st issue. Weekly newspaper. NjPla.   48924

Newcomb, Ebenezer
    Letter on the subject of Episcopacy. Greenfield,
Mass., 1819. 35 p. MWA.   48925

-- A second letter to the Rev. Mr. S. on the subject

of Episcopacy...Greenfield, Mass., Pr. by Denio &
Phelps, 1819. MDeeP; MWA.   48926

-- Strictures on a pamphlet entitled "Candid examination of the Episcopal Church." Greenfield, Mass.,
1819. MDeeP.   48927

Newton, John
    An account of Eliza Cunningham. An abridgment.
Ed. 4. Andover, Mass., Pr. by Flagg and Gould, for
the New England Tract Society, 1819. 3 p. MDeeP;
MMeT.   48928

[--] A monument to the praise of the Lord's goodness
...[Philadelphia] 1819. MWA.   48929

-- The praying negro. Andover, Mass., Pr. by Flagg
& Gould, 1819. 8 p. MMeT.   48930

-- Olney hymns. In three books. By the Rev. John
Newton. New York, William and Whiting, 1819. 400 p.
MdBD.   48931

Nicholas, John
    Address, delivered before the Ontario agricultural
society...Oct. 13, 1819...Canandaigua, N.Y., Pr. by
J.D. Bemis & Co., [1819] MWA; NCanHi; NGH. 48932

Nichols, Ammi, 1781-1873
    A funeral sermon, occasioned by the death of a
young man of color, by the name of William More.
Delivered at Braintree, October 5, 1819. Montpelier,
Vt., Pr. by E.P. Walton, 1819. 12 p. ICN.   48933

Nichols, Andrew
    Address, delivered in the South meeting house, in
Danvers, before the society...for suppressing intem-
perance...Salem, Mass., Pr. by John D. Cushing, for
Cushing & Appleton, 1819. 24 p. MBAt; MH; MSaE;
MWA; NN; NNUT; NjR.   48934

Nicholson, John
    The farmer's assistant; being a digest of all that

relates to agriculture, and the conducting of rural affairs... Lancaster, Pa., Pr. by William Dickson, for
Benjamin Warner, Philadelphia and Richmond, 1819.
468 p. NjR.   48935

Nicholson, William, 1753-1815
    American edition of the British Encyclopedia or
Dictionary of Arts and Sciences... Philadelphia, Pr. by
W. Brown, for Mitchell, Ames and White, 1819. 12 v.
NPlaK; Nj.   48936

-- -- Philadelphia, Mitchell, Ames and White, 1819-
21. 12 v. Nj.   48937

-- -- 3d Amer. ed. Philadelphia, Mitchell, Ames and
White, 1819-21. 12 v. Nj.   48938

Nimmo, William R.
    My companion; or, A familiar elucidation of the
most interesting problems on the terrestrial and celes-
tial globes. Baltimore, 1819. 57 p. MH; MWA. 48939

Noah, Mordecai Manuel, 1785-1851
    She would be a soldier; or, The plains of Chip-
pewa; an historical drama, in three acts. New York,
Longworth's Dramatic Repository, 1819. 73 p. CSmH;
MH; MWA; NIC; NN; RPB.   48940

-- Travels in England, France, Spain, and the Barbary
States, in the years 1813-14 and 15. New-York, Kirk
& Mercein, 1819. 431 p. DLC; MFiHi; MH; MNBedf;
MdBE; N; NHi; NIC; NPtw; NcAS.   48941

Norfolk Provident Society
    Consitution of... [Norfolk, Va.] Pr. by O'Connor &
Broughton [1819] 7 p. Vi.   48942

North-American Calendar, or the Columbian almanac
for 1820. Wilmington, Del., Robert Porter [1819]
36 p. MWA; PHi.   48943

North Carolina (State)
    Journal of the Senate. At a General Assembly be-

gun and held in the city of Raleigh, on Monday the
sixteenth day of November, in the year of our Lord
one thousand eight hundred and eighteen...[Raleigh,
N. C. ? Thomas Henderson, 1819?] 130 p. Nc-SC.
48944

-- Journals of the Senate and House of Commons of
the General Assembly of North-Carolina. At its session in 1818...Raleigh, N. C., Pr. by Thomas Henderson, Jr., 1819. 239 p. NcU. 48945

-- The laws of the state of North Carolina, enacted in
the year 1818...Raleigh, N. C., Pr. by Thomas Henderson, 1819. 114 p. Ar-SC; MdBB; NNLI; Nc-SC;
NcU; T. 48946

-- Rules of decorum for the government of the Senate,
1819. Broadside. NcU. 48947

North Carolina University
    Catalogue of the faculty and students of the Uni-
versity of North-Carolina. October, 1819. Raleigh,
N. C., Pr. by J. Harvey [1819] Broadside. NcU.48948

Der Northampton Bauern calendar auf das Jahr 1820...
Easton, Pa., C. J. Huetter & son [1819] [40] p. MWA.
48949

Northampton Mechanic Association
    The constitution...January, 1819. Northampton,
Mass., Pr. by T. W. Shepard, 1819. 16 p. MNF.
48950

Northern association of Universalists
    Proceedings...1819. Woodstock, Vt., Pr. by
David Watson, 1819. MWA. 48951

Northern Missionary Society
    Report of the directors of the Northern Missionary
Society, at their annual meeting, in the City of Troy,
September 1st, 1819. Together with the treasurer's
account, &c. &c. Albany, Pr. by E. & E. Hosford,
1819. 14 p. DLC. 48952

North-Western Union Missionary Society
    The constitution...formed in September, 1819.

Cincinnati, O., Pr. by Looker, Reynolds and co.
[1819?] 8 p. OCHP.   48953

[Norton, Andrews]
    Review of "Letters to the Rev. Wm. E. Channing,
containing remarks on his sermon, recently preached
and published at Baltimore." Boston, Pr. by Wells
& Lilly, 1819. 20 p. M; MHi; MWA.   48954

[--] A statement of reasons for not believing the doc-
trines of Trinitarians respecting the nature of God,
and the person of Christ, occasioned by Professor
Stuart's letters to Mr. Channing...Boston, Pr. by
Wells and Lilly, 1819. 64 p. CBPSR; DLC; ICMe;
ICN; M; MBC; MNe; MWA; MdHi; NjR.   48955

Norton, Jacob
    "The awakener;" a sermon, delivered before the
First Religious Society in Weymouth...Boston, Parmenter & Balch, 1819. MB.   48956

-- An humble attempt to ascertain the scripture doc-
trine of the Father, Son, and Holy Spirit...Boston,
Pr. by Parmenter and Balch, 1819. 116 p. CBPac;
ICMe; MAnP; MB; MHi; MMeT; MSaE; MWA; MWey;
OO.   48957

Nott, Eliphalet
    Miscellaneous works by Eliphalet Nott, D.D.,
President of Union College. With an appendix. Schen-
ectady, N.Y., Pr. by Ryer Schermerhorn, for Wm. J.
McCartee, 1819. 240 p. CtHC; NSy.   48958

Nott, Samuel
    Nott's testimony in favour of Judson. A letter ad-
dressed to Rev. Enoch Pond, of Ward [Mass.] on the
insinuations and charges contained in his reply to Mr.
Judson's sermon on baptism...Boston, Lincoln & Edmands, 1819. 16 p. CBPSR; CSt; MB; MBC; MH-AH;
MHi; MWA; MiD-B; NNUT; ViU.   48959

O

Observations concerning the canal bridge. [Boston?
1819] MWA.   48960

Observations on Christian baptism and the Lord's supper, respectfully addressed to Jacob Rush...written in
the summer of 1818. By a Christian layman. Burlington [N.J.] Pr. by David Allinson, for the author,
1819. 23 p. MWA; PHC; PPL-R; PPPrHi.   48961

Observations on the Bank of the United States. Annapolis, Md., Pr. by J. Green [1819?] 21 p. DLC; IU.
                                                  48962
Observations on the pernicious practice of the law.
As published occasionally in the Independent Chronicle,
in the year 1786, and republished at the request of a
number of respectable citizens. Boston, Pr. by True
& Weston, 1819. 60 p. DLC; RPL.   48963

Ocane, Francis
    The government and laws of every country, are
the effect, not the cause of the condition of the people.
Charleston, S.C., Pr. by A.E. Miller, 1819. MWA;
PPL.   48964

[--] The government is an effect, not a cause, of the
situation of every country. Boston, Pr. for the author, 1819. 31 p. ICU; MHi; NNG.   48965

Occom, Samson
    A sermon, preached at the execution of Moses
Paul...Exeter, N.H., Josiah Richardson, 1819. MWA.
                                                  48966
O'Connor, T.
    The globe. Vol. I. New York, 1819. 384 p.
NjR.   48967

Ohio (State)
    Abstract of the annual return of the militia...1818.
Columbus, O., Monitor print [1819] Broadside. O-Ar.
                                                  48968
-- An act for disciplining the militia of the state of
Ohio, passed February 6, 1819...Columbus, O., Pr.

by P. H. Olmsted, at the office of the Columbus gazette, 1819. 79 p. DLC; MH-L; MiU-L; OClWHi;
O-SC; OClL.   48969

-- Acts passed at the first session of the seventeenth
General assembly, of the state of Ohio, begun and held
in the town of Columbus, December 7, 1818; and in
the seventeenth year of said state...Chillicothe, O.,
Geo. Nashee, 1819. 236 p. Ct; CtY; DLC; Ia; M;
NNC; NNB; Nj; OCHP; OCLaw; OClWHi.   48970

-- Communications from the auditor and treasurer of
Ohio, to both Houses of the Legislature, at the commencement of the first session of the eighteenth General assembly, December 8, 1819. Columbus, O.,
Pr. by P. H. Olmsted, at the office of the Columbus
gazette, 1819. 16 p. NN; NNC; OClWHi.   48971

-- Governor's message. To the Senate and House of
Representatives. [Columbus, O., 1819] Broadside.
O-Ar.   48972

-- Journal of the House of Representatives of the state
of Ohio, being the 17th General Assembly, begun...
7th of Dec., 1818...Columbus, David Smith, 1818!
[1819] 599 p. N; O; O-LR; OClWHi; OHi.   48973

-- Journal of the Senate of the state of Ohio, being the
17th General Assembly, begun...7th of December...
Columbus, David Smith [1819] 467 p. NHi; O; OCHP;
OClWHi; OHi; O-LR; OU.   48974

-- Message of the Governor to both houses of the
legislature, Dec. 7, 1819. Columbus, 1819. 8 p.
O-SC.   48975

-- Report of the audito re Ohio penitentiary. Dec. 7,
1819. Columbus, 1819. 7 p. O-SC.   48976

-- The standing committee of finance, to whom was re-
ferred so much of the message of His Excellency the
Governor, as relates to the public revenue. Report...
[Columbus, 1819?] 12 p. DLC; O-SC; WHi.   48977

The Ohio Register and Western Calendar, containing an almanac for the year...1820...By William Lusk... Columbus, O., Pr. by David Smith [1819] 84 p. CSmH; OClWHi.   48978

O'Keeffe, John
    Sprigs of laurel, a comic opera...Ed. 2.   New York, David Longworth, 1819. MB; MH; MWA.   48979

Old colony musical society, ed.
    Old colony collection of anthems, selected and pub-lished under the particular patronage and direction of the Old colony musical association in Plymouth county and the Handel and Haydn Society in Boston.   Vol. II. Ed. 2.   Boston, J. Loring, 1819.   MBNEC.   48980

Olive Branch.   Ebensburg, Pa., Thomas Foley, Feb., 1819, 1st issue.   Weekly newspaper. DLC.   48981

[Olmsted, Denison]
    Outlines of the lectures on chemistry, mineralogy, and geology, delivered at the University of North Caro-lina; for the use of the students. Raleigh, N.C., Pr. by J. Gales, 1819.   44 p.   NcD; NcU; NcWfC.   48982

On self-examination...New York, Pr. by Day & Turner, 1819.   MWA.   48983

On the general resurrection...[Philadelphia]   Wm. Bradford, 1819.   MWA.   48984

On Unitarian controversy.   Ed. 2.   Boston, Pr. by Nathaniel Willis ...1819.   600 p.   MNe.   48985

O'Neill, John, d. 1808?
    A new and easy system of geography and popular astronomy; together with the use of the globes...Ed. 5, rev. and cor.   Baltimore, Pr. by J. Robinson, for Fielding Lucas, Jun., 1819. 386 p.   DLC; MdBS; MdHi; MdW.   48986

Onion, Stephen B.
    Narrative of the mutiny on board the Schooner

Plattsburg, William Hackett, master, in consequence of
which John Williams, Francis Frederick, Nils Peterson and John P. Rog suffered death on the 18th March,
1819...Boston, Pr. by Sylvester T. Goss, 1819. 13 p.
DLC; MBAt; MH; MWA; PHi.   48987

Order of exercises at the ordination of Mr. John Pier-
pont, as Pastor of the church and society in Hollis-
Street, Boston, April 14, 1819. Broadside. MBr; MHi.
                                             48988
Order of performance at the ordination of Mr. Jared
Sparks, to the pastoral care of the First Independent
Church of Baltimore, on Wednesday, May 5, 1819...
[Baltimore] Pr. by Schaeffer & Maund, [1819] Broad-
side. MdHi.   48989

O'Reilly, Francis S.
    The evidence in the case of Commonwealth against
Francis S. O'Reilly, for stabbing James Madison
Pleasants, on the 31st October, 1818. Richmond, Pr.
by W.W. Gray, at the Franklin press, [1819] 8 p. Vi.
                                             48990
Orfila, Matthieu Joseph Bonaventure, 1787-1853
    Directions for the treatment of persons who have
taken poison, and those in a state of apparent death...
1st Amer. ed. Baltimore, Pr. by J. Robinson, for
Nathaniel G. Maxwell, 1819. 240 p. DLC; MBM;
MWA; RPB; RPM.   48991

Osbourn, James
    Good things aimed at; or, Divine truths touched on.
...Baltimore, W. Warner, 1819. 2 v. in 1. MH-AH;
MWA; MeLewB; TxU.   48992

Oscar Fitz-James, a drama in three acts. Written by
a native of Virginia, a youth in the eighteenth year of
his age. Richmond, Va., William A. Bartow, 1819.
36 p. ICU; RPB.   48993

Osgood, David
    A sermon at the ordination of the Reverend Con-
vers Francis...Cambridge, Pr. by Hilliard and Metcalf, 1819. MWA.   48994

Osgood, John B.
     Quarantine law published by Salem Board of Health,
June 8, 1819.   Salem, Mass., 1819.   Broadside.   MSaE.
                                                          48995
Oswego Palladium.   Oswego, N. Y., John Haines Lord,
Jun., Oct. 7, 1819, 1st issue.   Weekly newspaper.
Oswego City Library.   48996

Otis, Harrison Gray
     Letter to His Excellency the Governor [John
Brooks, respecting the claim of the Commonwealth a-
gainst the United States, together with the report of
the committee of the House thereon.]   [Boston, 1819]
MB; MBAt.   48997

-- Mr. Otis's speech in Congress, on the sedition
law...[Boston, Pr. by Hews & Goss, 1819] MWA.
                                                          48998
Outline of a plan for establishing a Baptist Literary
and Theological Institution in a central situation in New
England.   By a friend to an able ministry.   Worcester,
Mass., Pr. by William Manning, 1819.   16 p.   MWA;
MWHi.   48999

Outline of the method of teaching the mathematical sciences in the Asbury College in the department of Professor Blackburn.   Baltimore, Pr. by Richard J.
Matchett, 1819.   24 p.   (J.W. Garrett Library) 49000

Overton, John, 1766-1833
     A vindication of the measures of the president
and his commanding generals, in the commencement
and termination of the Seminole war...Nashville, Tenn.,
Pr. by Tunstall & Norvell [1819] 119 p.   ICN; MB.
                                                          49001
[--] -- Washington, D.C., Pr. by Gales & Seaton,
1819.   133 p.   DLC; FSaHi; ICN; MB; MH-AH; MWA;
NN; NNS; NcD; Nh; OkU; TxU; WHi.   49002

                             P
A pack of cards changed into a complete almanac, and
prayer book.   Adapted to the entertainment of the hu-

mourous, as well as to the satisfaction of the grave, learned and ingenious. [Boston?] Pr. for the purchasers, 1819. 10 p. MnU.   49003

Packard, Theophilus
    The evil of slander... Exeter, N.H., Josiah Richardson, 1819. MWA.   49004

[Paine, Robert Treat]
    The invention of letters: a poem... Ed. 3. Boston, Pr. by Henry Bowen, 1819. MWA; RPB.   49005

Paley, William, 1743-1805
    Natural theology: or evidences of the existence and attributes of the deity... Hallowell, Me., E. Goodale, 1819. 292 p. CSt; MWA; MeU; MiD-B; OkEnP; RP.   49006

-- The young Christian instructed in reading and in the principles of religion... Andover, Mass., Pr. by Flagg & Gould, 1819. 72 p. MB; MWA; MSaE; NjR.   49007

Paley, William, barrister-at-law.
    A treatise on the law of principal and agent, chiefly with reference to mercantile transactions... 2d Amer. ed., with further extensive additions. By John A.Dunlap. Albany, Banks, Gould & co., 1819. CSt.   49008

Palmer, Benjamin Morgan
    A sermon, delivered at the anniversary of the Sabbath school association... Charleston, S.C., Pr. by J. Hoff, for the Association, 1819. 18 p. ICU; MH; MWA.
                                                    49009
Papers relative to the restriction of slavery. Philadelphia, Hall & Atkinson, 1819. 35 p. DLC; MWA; MWiW; P; WHi.   49010

Parker, Daniel
    Proscription delineated; or A development of facts appertaining to the arbitrary and oppressive proceedings of the North Association of Litchfield County, in relation to the author. Hudson, N.Y., Stone and Corss, 1819. 290 p. MMeT; MWA; NSyU.   49011

Parker, Edward Lutwyche, 1785-1850
A century sermon, delivered in the East-parish
meeting house, Londonderry, New Hampshire, April
22, 1819... Concord, N. H., Pr. by G. Hough, 1819.
44 p. DLC; MA; MBC; MC; MH; MHi; MiD-B; MiGr;
Nh; Nh-Hi; NjR; OO.   49012

Parker, Nathan
A sermon, preached at Concord, before His Ex-
cellency William Plumer, Governor, the Honourable
Council, and the two houses composing the legislature
of the state of New-Hampshire, June 3, 1819.   Being
the anniversary election.   Concord, N. H., Pr. by Hill
& Moore, 1819.   26 p.   CtHT-W; DLC; ICMe; MB;
MBAU; MBC; MH; MHi; MW; MeBat; MiD-B; Nh-Hi;
NjR.   49013

Parkes, Samuel
A letter to the farmers and graziers of Great
Britain... Philadelphia, M. Carey and son, 1819. MWA;
NHi; NjR; PP.   49014

[Parmele, Henry]
Key to the first chart of the Masonic mirror...
Philadelphia, Pr. by J. Maxwell, for H. Parmele,
1819.   MWA.   49015

Parmele, Philander
A sermon delivered at the funeral of Oliver Webster, April 20, 1818... Hartford, Pr. by G. Goodwin
& sons, 1819.   14 p.   Ct; CtHi; ICN; MWA; NAuT;
NcD; PPPrHi.   49016

Parmly, Levi Spear
A practical guide to the management of the teeth...
Philadelphia, Pr. by J.R.A. Skerrett, for Collins &
Croft, 1819. 198 p. DLC; MWA; MdUD; NNNAM; OU.
                                                       49017

Parr, Bartholomew
The London medical dictionary... Philadelphia, Pr.
by William Brown, for Mitchell, Ames, and White,
1819.   2 v.   MWA; NIC; NNNAM; NjP.   49018

Parsons, Levi, 1792-1822
   The dereliction and restoration of the Jews. A
sermon, preached in Park-street church, Boston, Sab-
bath, Oct. 31, 1819, just before the departure of the
Palestine mission...Boston, Pr. by U. Crocker, for
Samuel T. Armstrong, 1819. 52 p. CSansS; CSmH;
CtHT-W; ICP; IEG; MBAt; MH-AH; MSaE; MWA; MWiW;
MeB; MeBat; MeLewB; MiD-B; NjR; PLT; RBr; RPB;
VtMiS; WHi.   49019

[Pascalis-Ouvière, Felix]
   A statement of the occurrences during a malig-
nant yellow fever, in the city of New York, in 1819.
New York, Pr. by W.A. Mercein, 1819. 52 p. MB;
MWA; NNNAM; NjR; PHi.   49020

Patterson, Robert
   A treatise of practical arithmetic, intended for the
use of schools...Pittsburgh, Pa., Pr. by F.H. Palmer,
for R. Patterson and Lambdin, 1819. 156 p. MWA;
PPL-R; PPiU.   49021

Patterson's Pittsburgh, town & country almanac, for
1820...John Armstrong, teacher of mathematics, calcu-
lator. Pittsburgh, Pa., R. Patterson & Lambdin,
1819. [34] p. MWA; WHi.   49022

Pattison, Granville Sharp, 1791-1851
   Syllabus of a popular course of lectures on general
anatomy and physiology, as illustrative of the natural
history of man. Philadelphia, 1819. 13 p. PPC;
PPAmP.   49023

Paul, Mrs. Almira, b. 1790.
   The surprising adventures of Almira Paul, a young
woman, who, garbed as a male, has for three of the
last preceding years, actually served as a common
sailor on board of English and American armed vessels,
without a discovery of her sex being made...Boston,
M. Brewster, 1819. 24 p. DLC.   49024

Paulding, James Kirke
   The merry tales of the three wise men of Gotham.

New York, Pr. by G. C. Carver, 1819. 324 p. MMeT.
49025

[--] Salmagundi. Second series... Philadelphia, Pr.
by J. Maxwell, for M. Thomas and J. Haly and C.
Thomas, New York, 1819-20. 3 v. in 2. DLC; MB;
MWA; MH; NN. 49026

[--] -- Second series. Nos. 3-5. Philadelphia, Pr. by
J. Maxwell, for M. Thomas and J. Haly and C. Thomas, New York, 1819. MWA. 49027

Payne, John Howard, 1792-1852
Brutus; or, The fall of Tarquin. An historical
tragedy, in five acts... Baltimore, J. Robinson, 1819.
65 p. DLC; MH; RPB. 49028

-- -- New York, D. Longworth, 1819. 54 p. CSmH;
MH; MWA; NcU; RPB. 49029

Payson, Seth
The death of the godly a call to prayer. A sermon, preached at the funeral of the Rev. Levi Pils-
berry, late pastor of the Congregational church in Win-
chendon, April 8, 1819... Worcester, Mass., Pr. by
William Manning, 1819. 19 p. CSt; MWA; MWHi; NjR.
49030

Pazos Kanki, Vicente, 1780 (ca.)-1851?
Letters on the United Provinces of South America,
addressed to the Hon. Henry Clay, speaker of the
House of representatives of the United States... Translated from the Spanish by Platt H. Crosby, esq. New-
York, Pr. by J. Seymour; London, by J. Miller, 1819.
259 p. DLC; MB; NBu; NIC; NSchU; NjN. 49031

[Peacock, Thomas Love]
Nightmare Abbey... Philadelphia, M. Carey and
son, 1819. 222 p. DeGE; MWA. 49032

Pearsall, Richard
Two pious letters, written after a dangerous sick-
ness, Ed. 2. Andover, Mass., 1819. (Caption title:
N.E. Tract Soc. Tract no. 91) MSaE. 49033

Pease, John Chauncey, 1782-1859
A gazetteer of the states of Connecticut and Rhode-Island...Hartford, William S. Marsh, 1819. 391 p.
CSf; CSt; Ct; CtB; CtHi; I; ICN; ICU; IP; IU; IaHa; KHi;
M; MB; MBAt; MBC; MH; MHi; MNBedf; MWiW; MdHi;
MeHi; MiU; NN; NNC; NNS; NSy; OClWHi; OMC; RPA;
WHi.   49034

Pell, Ferris
A review of the administration and civil police of
the state of New York, from the year 1807, to the
year 1819...New-York, Pr. by E. Conrad, 1819. 184 p.
DLC; NIC.   49035

Penitent Female's Refuge, Boston.
Constitution of the society and directors of the
penitent females refuge...with an address to the pious
and benevolent. Boston, Pr. by True & Weston, 1819.
16 p.   MWA; NjR.   49036

Penington, Isaac
Brief extracts from the works of Isaac Penington.
Philadelphia, Pr. by Joseph Rakestraw, 1819. 62 p.
NcGW; PReaHi; PSC-Hi.   49037

Pennsylvania (State)
An act of incorporation, for that part of the Northern Liberties, lying between the middle of Sixth Street
and the River Delaware, and between Vine Street and
Cohocksink Creek. ...Philadelphia, Pr. by S. Probasco, 1819. 106 p.   Sabin 59791.   49038

-- Acts of the General Assembly of the Commonwealth
of Pennsylvania, passed at a session which was begun
and held at the Borough of Harrisburg on Tuesday, the
first day of December, in the year of Our Lord, one
thousand eight hundred and eighteen...Harrisburg, Pa.,
Pr. by C. Gleim, 1819. 302 p.   DLC; IaU-L; In-SC;
MdBB; Mi-L; Mo; Ms; NNLI; Nb; Nc-SC; Nj; Nv; P;
PAtM; PLL; PScrLL; R; RPL.   49039

-- Bills of the Senate members which they proposed and
read before the Senate.   Harrisburg, Pr. by John Wyeth,

1819-20.   P.   49040

-- The commissioners for erecting a state capitol on
the public grounds at Harrisburg, invite architects to
exhibit to them plans and elevations... Harrisburg,
Jan., 1819. Broadside. DLC.   49041

-- First annual report of the controllers of the public
schools of the First school district of the state of
Pennsylvania; with their accounts. Also an abstract of
the law of March 6th, 1818, providing for public education, and a list of the controllers and directors con-
stituted under the act, &c., &c. Philadelphia, Pr. by
order of the Board of control, 1819. CSt; DLC; MWA.
                                                     49042

-- Impeachment of Gov. William Findlay, ... The pa-
role and documentary evidence, delivered before a
committee of the house of Representatives, appointed
to inquire into the conduct of the Governor of the Commonwealth of Pennsylvania, 1819. [Harrisburg] Pr.
by J. Wyeth, 1819. 275 p. Ia.   49043

-- Journal of the Senate of the Commonwealth of Pennsylvania, which commenced... first day of December...
1818... Vol. XXVIV. Harrisburg, Pr. by Christian
Gleim, 1818[!] [1819] 574 p. CSmH; DLC; PWaybuGHi.
                                                     49044

-- Journal of the 29th House of Representatives of the
Commonwealth of Pennsylvania. Commenced... 1st day
of December... 1818... Harrisburg, Pr. by James Peacock, 1818-19.   833 p. DLC; P; PWaybuGHi; WHi.
                                                     49045

-- Journal of the 30th House of Representatives of the
Commonwealth of Pennsylvania, commenced... 7th of
December... 1819... Harrisburg, Pr. by James Peacock,
1819-20. 1206 p.   DLC; PWaybuGHi.   49046

-- Receipts and payments at the treasury of Pennsylvania, from the ninth day of December, 1817, to the
thirtieth day of November, 1818... Harrisburg, Pr. by
James Peacock, 1818[!] [1819] 226 p. DLC.   49047

-- Receipts and payments at the treasury of Pennsyl-

vania, from the first day of December, 1818, to the
thirtieth day of November, 1819...Harrisburg, Pr. by
J. Peacock, 1819. 356 p. DLC; P.   49048

-- Report, etc., House of Representatives of the Commonwealth of Pennsylvania, December 10, 1819. 23 p.
[Caption title; imprint, p. 23] Pr. by James Peacock,
1819? P; PHi.   49049

-- Report of the Committee of Inquiry of the House of
Representatives of Pennsylvania, appointed to investigate the official conduct of Thomas Sergeant, 1819.
[Harrisburg, Pa., 1819] 26 p. OCLaw; PHi; PPAmP.
                                                    49050
-- Report of the committee of Senate, appointed to en-
quire into the extent and causes of the present general
distress; December 8, 1819. 16 p. PHi.   49051

-- Report of the finances of the Commonwealth of
Pennsylvania, for the year 1818...Haarisburg[!] Pr.
by James Peacock, 1818[!] [1819] 28 p. DLC. 49052

-- Report of the finances of the Commonwealth of
Pennsylvania, for the year 1819...Harrisburg, Pa.,
Pr. by James Peacock, 1819. 22 p. DLC; MWA.
                                                    49053
-- Report of the joint committee appointed by the Sen-
ate and House...for the purpose of examining the
works erected by the former Schuylkill & Susquehanna
canal company, &c. Harrisburg, Pa., 1812. 12 p.
PPAmP.   49054

-- Reports from the Pennsylvania, Philadelphia and
farmers and mechanics' banks. Read in Senate, January 18, 1819. 8 p. PHi.   49055

-- Resolutions relative to preventing the introduction of
slavery into new states. [Harrisburg, Pa., 1819] 4 p.
MiU-C.   49056

-- Rules for regulating the practice of several of the
Courts in Pennsylvania. Collected by a member of the
profession, and revised by the Judges. Philadelphia,

1819. 113 p. MH-L. 49057

-- Rules regulating the practice of the courts in the
11th Judicial District of Pennsylvania, adopted at the
August term, 1819. Wilkes-Barre, Pa., Pr. by Samuel Maffet, 1819. 22 p. PWbWHi. 49058

-- Tagebuch des dreissigsten Heuses der Representan-
ten der Republik Pennsylvanien. Libanon, Pa., Pr.
by Jacob Stoever, 1819. Seidensticker p. 208. 49059

-- Tagebuch des Senats der Republik Pennsylvanien.
1818-19. Libanon, Pr. by Jacob Stoever, 1819.
Seidensticker p. 208. 49060

The Pennsylvania and New Jersey almanac for 1820...
carefully calculated by William Collom. Doylestown,
Pa., Pr. by Asher Miner [1819] [40] p. MWA; NjR.
49061
-- Philadelphia, Griggs & co., J.C. Griggs, New
Brunswick, N.J., [1819] [36] p. NjR. 49062

Pennsylvania society for promoting the abolition of
slavery.
    An address from the Pennsylvania society for pro-
moting the abolition of slavery, for the relief of free
negroes unlawfully held in bondage, and for improving
the condition of the African race; on the origin, purposes and utility of their institution. Philadelphia, Pr.
by Hall & Atkinson, for the society, 1819. 6 p. DLC;
MWA; MB; OO. 49063

Perkins, Nathan
    Sabbath school catechism; containing all the chief
doctrines of religion...Hartford, Oliver D. Cooke,
1819. 72 p. CSmH; Ct; CtHC; CtHT-W; CtHi; CtSoP;
DLC; MB; MBC; MH; MNF; MWA; NcD; OCHP; PPPrHi.
49064
Perkins, Thomas S.
    An address delivered before the New-London county
agricultural society...New London, Conn., Pr. by
Clapp & Francis, 1819. CtNl; MWA. 49065

Perrin, Jean Baptiste, b. 1779
    The elements of French and English conversation;
...Rev. and cor. by C. Preudhomme. New York, E.
Duyckinck, 1819. 216 p. MNe; MWA; NN.   49066

-- Fables amusantes...Baltimore, Pr. by John D.
Toy, for A. Neal, 1819. 180 p. InGrD; MB; MH;
MWA.   49067

Perrin, Jean Baptiste, fl. 1786
    A grammar of the French tongue; grounded upon
the decisions of the French academy...New-York, Pr.
by G. Long, for Evert Duyckinck, 1819. 346 p. DLC;
KyHi; MWA.   49068

Perry, Gardner Braman
    Submission to the will of God. A sermon preached
in Newbury, Mass., Feb. 4th, 1819. Occasioned by
the death of Rev. John Kirby.   Newburyport, Mass.,
Pr. by Ephraim W. Allen, 1819. 28 p. MH; MSaE;
MWA.   49069

Perry, William
    Only sure guide to English tongue. New improved
ed., Thomas's 1st ed.   Boston, I. Thomas, Jun.,
1819. MWA.   49070

-- -- With an appendix...2d Brookfield ed. Brookfield, Mass., Pr. by E. Merriam & co., 1819. 168 p.
MBAt; MH; MWA; NNC.   49071

Pester, Lester [pseud.]
    A dandy's history...Boston, N. Coverly, 1819.
MB; MWA.   49072

[Peyre-Ferry, Alexandre Rene François]
    La Napoleonide, poeme en douze chants, avec des
notes historiques. Tome premier. New-York: J.
Desnouses, 1819. 87 p.   N; NN; TxU. 49073

Philadelphia (City)
    Accounts for 1818.   Robert Cochran, Philadelphia.
1819? MWA.   49074

-- Additional report on water power. Philadelphia,
Wm. Fry, 1819. 15 p. P.   49075

-- Report of the Watering Committee of the agreements
with the Schuylkill Navigation Company and White and
Gillingham, relating to the water power of the river
Schuylkill. Published by order of Councils. Philadelphia, Pr. by W. Fry, 1819. 23 p. DeGE; MWA. 49076

-- Rules and regulations made by the Controllers of
the Public schools...1819. Philadelphia, 1819. 2 p.
MHi.   49077

Philadelphia. Asylum company.
    Catalogue of the lands and stock offered for sale
at the Merchants' coffee-house. Philadelphia, 1819.
17 p. NNC.   49078

The Philadelphia directory. John Adams Paxton, ed.
Philadelphia, pub. by Editor, 1819. [450] p. MBNEH;
MWA; P; PHi.   49079

Philadelphia. Methodist Episcopal union church.
    Constitution...[Philadelphia] Pr. by T.S. Manning,
1819. MWA.   49080

Philadelphia Missionary Society
    First annual report of the managers, May 10,
1819. Philadelphia [1819?] 8 p. MH-AH.   49081

Philadelphia Register and National Recorder. Philadelphia, Jan., 1819, 1st issue. ICU; NjR; TxU. 49082

Philadelphia society for promoting agriculture.
    The society was incorporated in the year one thou-
sand eight hundred and nine, for the term of ten years;
at the expiration of which the following charter was
granted:- An act to incorporate the Philadelphia society

for promoting agriculture. [Philadelphia, 1819] 16 p.
CSmH.   49083

Philadelphia Society for the Promotion of National In-
dustry.
    Address... No. 1-8. [Philadelphia, 1819] NjR.
                                                          49084
-- Address... No. 9. [Philadelphia, 1819] MWA.
                                                          49085
-- Address... No. 10. [Philadelphia, 1819] MWA.
                                                          49086
-- Address... No. 11. [Philadelphia, 1819] MWA.
                                                          49087
-- Address... No. 11. Ed. 2. Philadelphia [1819]
MWA.   49088
-- Address... No. 12. [Philadelphia, 1819] MWA.
                                                          49089
-- Address... No. 13. [Philadelphia, 1819] MWA.
                                                          49090
-- Address... New series No. I. [Philadelphia, 1819]
MWA.   49091

-- Address... New series No. I. Ed. 2. [Philadelphia,
1819] MWA.   49092

-- Address... New series No. II. [Philadelphia, 1819]
MWA.   49093

-- Addresses... Philadelphia, M. Carey & son, pr. on
J. & T. Gilpin's machine paper, 1819. 280 p. ICU;
MWA; MdHi; NcAS.   49094

-- Addresses... Ed. 4. Philadelphia, Pr. by G. L.
Austin, for M. Carey and son, 1819. 248 p. MWA;
MiDSH.   49095

Philadelphia society for the promotion of domestic in-
dustry.
    National interests and domestic manufactures...
Boston, Pr. by William W. Clapp, 1819. 116 p. MHi;
MWA; NHi; NN; P; PHi; PPAmP; PPL; PU; PV.
                                                          49096
Philadelphia spelling book. Ed. 5. Philadelphia,

1819. MWA.   49097

Philadelphia Sunday and Adult School Union
    The second report of the Philadelphia Sunday and
Adult School Union; read at their annual meeting, held
in St. Paul's Church, May 25, 1819. Philadelphia, Pr.
by Clark & Raser, for the Sunday and Adult School
Union, 1819. CSmH; DLC.   49098

[Phillips, Sir Richard]
    The first catechism for children... Loring's 10th
Boston ed. Boston, James Loring's Sabbath School
Book-store, [1819] 72 p. MH; MPiB; MSaE; NNC-T.
                                                49099
[--] A grammar of chemistry... and a glossary of
terms in common use. By the Rev. D. Blair (pseud.)
...cor. and rev. by Benjamin Tucker... Ed. 3. Phila-
delphia, David Hogan, 1819. 184 p. MNe; MWA; MeHi;
NNC.   49100

[--] Reading exercises... Ed. 4. Philadelphia, E. and
R. Parker, 1819. CtHT-W.   49101

[--] The Universal preceptor: being a general grammar
of arts, sciences and useful knowledge. By the Rev.
David Blair (pseud.) 3d Amer. ed. Philadelphia,
Edwards & Richard Parker, 1819. 316 p. MB; MWA;
MoKU.   49102

Phillips Academy, Andover.
    Catalogue of the trustees, instructors, and stu-
dents of Phillips Academy, Andover, August, 1819.
[Andover, Mass. ? 1819?] MAnP.   49103

Phinney's calendar; or, western almanac, for the year
of our Lord 1820... By Andrew Beers, philom. Cooperstown, N. Y., Pr. by H. & E. Phinney [1819] [36] p.
DLC; ICN; MWA; NCH; NN; NNHiST; NPalk; NRAB;
NUtHi.   49104

Pickering, David
    A sermon, delivered in the city of Schenectady,
November 8, 1818... Hudson, N. Y., Pr. by Ashbel

Stoddard, 1819. 24 p. MMeT-Hi; MSaE; MWA; N.
                                                        49105
Pickering, Timothy
    A letter from Colonel Pickering, containing a nar-
rative of the outrage committed on him at Wyoming...
[Salem, Mass., Pr. by T. C. Cushing, 1819] 38 p.
MHi; MSaE; MWA; MiD-B; NN; Nh-Hi.   49106

Picket, Albert
    Pickets' American school class books... New York,
Pr. for the authors, 1819. MWA.   49107

Picket, Albert
    The juvenile expositor, or American school class-
book, no. 4, improved and enl... New-York, American
school class-book warehouse, 1819. 381 p. DLC.
                                                        49108
-- Juvenile spelling book.   Stereo. ed.   Exeter, N. H.,
C. Norris, 1819. MWA.   49109

-- -- New York, American School class-book warehouse, 1819. MWA.   49110

-- -- ...Being an easy introduction to the English
language... improved and stereotyped, 11th stereotype
ed.   New York, stereotyped by E. and J. White, for
Daniel D. Smith, 1819. 246 p. NHem; NN.   49111

Picton, Thomas
    On some of the duties of congregations towards
their pastors.   A farewell sermon: delivered at West-
field (New-Jersey) Sept. 13th, 1818... Elizabeth-Town,
N. J., Pr. by Peter Chatterton, 1819. 16 p. NjR.
                                                        49112
Pierce, G. W.
    The life-romance of an algebraist.   Boston [1819]
MB.   49113

Pike, Albert
    Prose sketches and poems, written in the Western
Country.   Boston, Light & Horton, 1819. 200 p.
MMeT.   49114

Pike, James
    The Columbian orthographer... For the use of
schools.   Stereotyped by E. & J. White, New-York.
Boston, R. P. & C. Williams, 1819. 168 p. MWA;
NNC.   49115

Pike, S.
    Key to Teacher's assistant.   Ed. 2.   Philadelphia,
Cusack & Frankish, B. Warner [1819] MWA.   49116

Pilsbury, Amos
    The sacred songster; or, A collection of hymns
and spiritual songs, for the use of religious assemblies... Ed. 4.   New York, Pr. by Abraham Paul, pub.
and sold by Duke Goodman, for the benefit of the wid-
ow and children of the author, 1819. 252 p.   IEC;
TCooP.   49117

The pious instructor, being a selection in prose and
verse, from various authors eminent for virtue and piety on moral and religious subjects... Hallowell, Me.,
William F. Laine, 1819. 214 p.   ICT; MBC.   49118

The pirates.   A brief account of the horrid massacre
of the captain, mate and supercargo of the schooner
Plattsburg, of Baltimore, on the high seas, in July
1816, by a part of the crew of said vessel... Ed. 3.
Boston, Pr. by H. Trumbull, 1819. 24 p.   DLC;
MSaP; MWA; NIC-L.   49119

-- A brief account of the horrid murder of the captain
and mate of a Buenos Ayrean prize schooner, on the
high seas, in July 1818, by William Holmes, Thomas
Warrington and Edward Rosewaine, comprising a part
of the crew of said vessel.   To which is added, a
brief sketch of the important trial of said prisoners,
at the Circuit court of the United States, in January
1819.   Boston, Pr. by H. Trumbull [1819?] 24 p.
DLC; RPB.   49120

Pittsburgh University
    General catalogue of the Western University of
Pennsylvania.   [Pittsburgh, Pa.] 1819-86. MH.   49121

Plain questions to Calvinists... 1819. MWA.   49122

Plan of the city of Philadelphia and environs. In-
scribed to William Sansom.   Philadelphia, 1819. 1 p.
PHi.   49123

The planters' and merchants' city almanac... 1820...
[1819?] MWA.   49124

A platform of church discipline.   Boston, 1819. MB.
                                                   49125
-- Gathered out of the word of God, and agreed upon
by the Elders and Messengers of the churches assembled in the Synod, at Cambridge, in New-England...
Reading [Mass.] J. Watson, 1819.   Sabin 63343. 49126

Plattsburgh Sunday School Societies
     The first semi-annual report of the Committee of
the ...read ... on the 31st of January, 1819. Pub.
by request of the Societies.   Plattsburgh, N.Y., Pr.
by A. C. Flagg, 1819.   24 p.   ScCoB.   49127

Playfair, John
     Dissertation second: exhibiting a general view of
the progress of mathematical and physical science,
since the revival of letters in Europe... [Boston, Wells
& Lilly, 1819?] 2 v.   ViU.   49128

A plea for the Baptist petition; signed by Rev. Asa
Wilcox, and others, which was heard before the Hon.
General Assembly, May, 1818 and continued to the next
October session.   The profits to be appropriated for
the benefit of foreign missions.   Hartford, F.D. Bolles
& Co., 1819.   16 p.   Ct; DLC.   49129

A pleasing toy.   New York, Samuel Wood & sons...
and Samuel S. Wood & Co., Baltimore, 1819. 27 p.
MWA; RPB.   49130

Pleasing traits in the characters of children.   Boston,
Lincoln & Edmands, 1819. 16 p. MWA.   49131

-- Boston, Lincoln & Edmands, 1819. 16 p. (Varying

cover.) MWA.   49132

The pleasures of piety in youth exemplified... Boston,
Lincoln & Edmands, 1819. MWA.   49133

-- Extracted from unquestionable authorities.   Boston,
Lincoln & Edmands, 1819. 70 p. MBNMHi.   49134

-- -- Boston, Lincoln & Edmands, 1819. 76 p. NN.
                                                     49135
-- -- Boston, Lincoln and Edmands, 1819. 71 p.
MBedf-Hi.   49136

Ploetz, C.
   Easy... French grammar. Boston, 1819. MB.
                                                     49137
Plough Boy.   Albany, John O. Cole, June 5, 1819, 1st
issue. Weekly newspaper. MWA; NIC-L.   49138

The pocket companion: or, Every man his own lawyer;
by a gentleman of the bar... Ed. 3.   Philadelphia,
M'Carty, 1819. 106 p. MWA; NNC; ScSp.   49139

-- Ed. 4.   Philadelphia, M'Carty & Davis, 1819.
MWA.   49140

-- Ed. 7.   Philadelphia, S. Parmele, 1819. MWA.
                                                     49141
Poems for children.   New York, Samuel Wood & sons,
and Samuel S. Wood & Co., Baltimore, 1819. MWA.
                                                     49142
Poems for little children... Boston, Lincoln & Edmands,
1819. MWA.   49143

A poetic selection for Sabbath schools.   Boston, Lincoln & Edmands, 1819. 16 p. MWA; RPB.   49144

A poetical description of a Methodist camp-meeting.
Philadelphia, 1819. 24 p. MB.   49145

Poetry for children... New Haven, Sidney's press, for
J. Babcock & son, 1819. 30 p. CtHi; MWA.   49146

[Pond, Enoch] 1791-1882
  The eternity of the future punishment of the wicked
illustrated and proved, in a letter to a friend. By a
clergyman of Massachusetts...Worcester, Mass., Wm.
Manning, 1819. 12 p. CSt; MBC; MWA; MWHi;
VtMiM.   49147

-- "Nott's testimony in favor of Judson" examined...
Boston, Pr. by U. Crocker, for Samuel T. Armstrong,
1819. 12 p. CBPSR; ICN; MBC; MH; MWA; MeBat.
                                                   49148
-- A treatise on the mode and subjects of Christian
baptism. In two parts. Designed as a reply to the
statements and reasonings of the Rev. Adoniram Judson, Jun. ...Worcester, Mass., Pr. by William Manning, 1819. MWA; MWHi.   49149

-- -- Ed. 2. Worcester, Mass., Pr. by William
Manning, 1819. 151 p. MBC; MMeT-Hi; MWA; MWHi;
MWiW; MoSpD; NCH; NRAB; NSyU; RPB.   49150

Poor Joseph...New York, Religious tract society,
1819. PPPrHi.   49151

Poor Will's almanac, for the year 1820...By William
Collom. Philadelphia, Joseph Rakestraw [1819] 36 p.
NjR.   49152

Pope, Alexander, 1688-1744
  An essay on man...Bellows Falls, Vt., Bill Blake
& Co., 1819. 64 p. MH; MHi; MWA; RPB; VtMiS; Vt.
                                                   49153
-- -- Brattleborough, Vt., John Holbrook, 1819. 52 p.
DLC; GMW; MWA.   49154

-- -- Hallowell, Me., S.K. Gilman, 1819. 47 p. MH;
MWA; MeHi; NHi.   49155

-- -- New York, George Long, 1819. MWA.   49156

-- The poetical works of Alexander Pope, esq. To
which is prefixed the life of the author. New York,
Pr. by G. Long, for E. Duyckinck, 1819. 2 v. MWA;

N; OCl; ViU.   49157

-- -- New York, G. Long, 1819. 2 v. MWA.   49158

-- -- Philadelphia, Pr. by William Fry, for Samuel
A. Bascom, 1819. 3 v. CtHC; InCW; MWA; MWiW;
MtBiP; NcD.   49159

Porter, Anna Maria, 1780-1832
     The fast of St. Magdalen...Boston, Wells and
Lilly, 1819. 2 v. CStclU; MB; MWA; MWiW; OUrC.
                                               49160
-- -- New York, Pr. by A. Paul, for C. Wiley &
Co., and W.B. Gilley, 1819. 2 v. MWA.   49161

-- -- New-York, W.B. Gilley and C. Wiley & co.,
1819. 2 v. MWA; NcU; TxU.   49162

Porter, Ebenezer
     A sermon preached Feb. 18, 1818, at the installa-
tion of the Rev. David Oliphant...Andover, Mass.,
Flagg and Gould, 1819. 24 p. MWA; OO.   49163

-- A sermon preached Sept. 29, 1819, at the ordination of the Rev. Thomas J. Murdock...Andover, Mass.,
Flagg and Gould, 1819. 24 p. MWA.   49164

-- -- Andover, Mass., Flagg and Gould, 1819. 31 p.
MWA; MeBat.   49165

-- The young preacher's manual...Boston, Pr. by
Flagg and Gould, for Charles Ewer, 1819. 428 p.
CBPSR; CSansS; CU; GDC; ICP; ICT; KTW; KyBC;
KyLoS; MBAt; MBC; MBD; MH-AH; MMCA; MMonsA;
MWA; MeBat; MeLewB; NNUT; NSyU; NbCrD; NcCJ;
NjR; OSW; PLT; ScCliP.   49166

Porter, James
     A sermon, delivered at Pomfret, July 18, 1819,
at the funeral of Deacon Simeon Cotton...Providence,
Pr. by Miller and Hutchens, 1819. MWA.   49167

Porter, Jane
    The Scottish chiefs...New York, Pr. [by John C.
Totten] for Evert Duyckinck, 1819. 5 v. in 2. MWA;
ViRVal.   49168

Porteus, Bielby, bp., 1731-1808
    A summary of the principal evidence for the truth
and divine origin of the Christian revelation...Haver-
hill [Mass.] P. N. Green, 1819. 148 p. CSmH; CSt;
MCET; MHa; MWA.   49169

Post-Boy. Chester, Pa., Butler & Worthington, 1819,
1st issue. Weekly newspaper. MWA.   49170

Potomack Register. Shepherdstown, Va., Robinson
& Harper, Apr. 15, 1819, 1st issue. Weekly newspaper. Brigham, p. 1174.   49171

Pott, Percivall
    The chirurgical works of Percivall Pott...1st Amer.
ed. Philadelphia, Pr. by William Brown, for James
Webster, 1819. 2 v. DNLM; GEU-M; MWA; MWiW;
NNNAM; OCGHM; TNV.   49172

Pottstown Times. Pottstown, Pa., John Royer, July
1, 1819, 1st issue. Weekly newspaper. MWA. 49173

Pounder's Wesleyan almanac, for 1818. Philadelphia,
Jonathan Pounder, 1819. MWA.   49174

The practical American gardener; exhibiting the time
for every kind of work in the kitchen garden, fruit
garden, orchard, nursery...Baltimore, F. Lucas, jr.,
1819. 424 p. DA; MWA; MdHi.   49175

Prayer Book and homily Society of Maryland.
    First annual report of the prayer book and homily
society of Maryland. 1819. With the constitution, and
a list of subscribers and benefactors...Baltimore, Pr.
by William Warner, for the society, [1819?] 16 p.
MdHi.   49176

A premium for Sabbath schools. Children's hymn book;

being a selection of hymns, from various authors.
Newark, N.J., William Tuttle, 1819. 35 p. MWA.
                                              49177

[Prentiss, Charles]
    The trial: Calvin and Hopkins versus the Bible
and common sense. By a lover of the truth. [Boston]
pub. for the author [1819] 39 p. CSt; MWA; N; O;
RHi; WHi.   49178

[--] -- Ed. 2, enl. Boston, 1819. 39 p. CBPac;
CtHT-W; DLC; ICT; MB; MH; MMeT; MNe; MSaE;
MWA; MeLewB; MiD-B; NN; NjR; RHi.   49179

Presbyterian Church in the U.S.A.
    The address of the Board of education, established
by the General assembly of the Presbyterian church in
the United States of America, to the presbyteries, ministers, churches and people under the care of the Assembly. Philadelphia, Pr. by J.W. Scott, 1819. 20 p.
CSt; NCH.   49180

-- A circular on the subject of the Education society of
the Presbyterian church in the United States. [Newark,
N.J., 1819] 12 p. NNUT.   49181

-- Extracts from the minutes of the General Assembly
of the Presbyterian church in the United States of
America. Philadelphia, Pr. by Thomas & William
Bradford, 1819. 294 p. MiD-B; WHi.   49182

-- First annual report of the Education Society of the
Presbyterian Church... under the care of the General
Assembly... Philadelphia, Pr. by Jacob Frick and Co.,
1819. NCH; PWCHi.   49183

-- A narrative of the state of religion... [Philadelphia,
1819] MWA.   49184

-- Report of a committee of the General assembly, appointed for revising the form of government... Philadelphia, Pr. by Thomas and William Bradford, 1819. 37 p.
MWA; NjR.   49185

-- Presbytery of Albany.
An act concerning ministerial libraries, passed by
the Presbytery of Albany, in session at Ballston
Springs, August 17, 1819.   Albany, Pr. by Websters
& Skinners, 1819. 4 p. N.   49186

-- Presbytery of Oneida, N. Y.
Extracts from the minutes... at their session...
February, 1819.   Utica, N. Y., Pr. by William Willi-
ams, 1819. 8 p.   MBC; MWA; NUtHi; NjR.   49187

A present for Sabbath school children... Boston, Lincoln & Edmands, 1819. MWA.   49188

Prince, John
A sermon, preached before the North Church and
Society in Salem, October 16, 1814, on the death of
their pastor, the Rev. Thomas Barnard, D. D. who
died October 1, 1814, in the sixty-seventh year of his
age. Ed. 2.   Salem, 1819. 24 p. N.   49189

Princeton University
The charter of the trustees of the College of New-
Jersey.   Trenton, N. J., Pr. by George Sherman,
1819. MWA.   49190

-- Laws of the College of New-Jersey; revised, a-
mended and adopted by the Board of trustees, April
14th, 1819.   Trenton, N. J., Pr. by George Sherman,
1819. 28 p. CSmH; DLC; GDC; ICN; MB; Nj; NjR;
PHi; PPAmP; PPiXT; TU.   49191

-- A report of a committee of the Board of trustees of
the College of New-Jersey, relative to measures for
extending and improving the college establishment.
Read before the Board, April 14, 1819, and ordered to
be printed. 15 p. TNP.   49192

The prodigal daughter... Philadelphia, D. Dickinson
[1819?] MWA.   49193

The progress of the dairy... New York, Samuel Wood &
sons, and Samuel S. Wood & Co., Baltimore, 1819.

25 p. MWA.   49194

A proposed memorial to the Congress of the United
States. [1819] MWA.   49195

Protestant Episcopal Church in the U.S.A.
    The Book of Common Prayer, and administration
of the Sacraments and other rites and ceremonies of
the Church...together with The Psalter, or Psalms of
David. Baltimore, F. Lucas, Jr., 1819. 465 p.
MWA.   49196

-- -- Baltimore, Joseph Robinson, 1819. 465 p. MWA;
MdBD; MdBS.   49197

-- -- New York, Bartow, 1819. MCE.   49198

-- -- Stereotyped by D. & G. Bruce, New-York. New
York, Pr.[by J. & J. Harper] for Henry I. Megarey,
1819. 752 p. CtW; MMeT; MWA; RPB.   49199

-- -- New York, T. & J. Swords, 1819. MdBD. 49200

-- -- New York, Stereotyped by E. & J. White, for
W.B. Gilley, 1819. 224 p. CL; Ky; N.   49201

-- -- New York, W.B. Gilley, 1819. 524 p. (verso
of t.p. Van Riper, print. - Greenwich) MWA; NPStA.
                                               49202
-- A familiar exposition of Catechism, adapted to the
use of the Protestant Episcopal church in the United
States of America. From Bishop Mann, and others.
Recommended...by the bishop and clergy of...South
Carolina. Charleston, P.E. society for the advance-
ment of Christianity in South Carolina, 1819. 82 p.
MWA; NNG.   49203

-- A set of chants adapted to the hymns in the morning
and evening prayer, and to the communion service of
the Protestant Episcopal Church in the United States of
America. Boston, Pr. by Thomas Badger, Jun., 1819.
49 p. CtHT-W; MBDiL; MWA.   49204

-- Delaware (Diocese)
Journal of the proceedings of a convention of the
Protestant Episcopal Church in the state of Delaware,
held at Dover, June 5, 1819.   Dover, Del., Pr. by J.
Robertson [1819?] 27 p. DeWi; MBD; PHi.   49205

-- Maryland (Diocese)
Journal of a convention of the Protestant Episcopal
Church, in Maryland, held in St. Paul's Church, Balti-
more, June 9th, 10th and 11th, 1819.   Annapolis, Md.,
Pr. by Jonas Green, 1819. 22 p. CSmH; MBD; MHi;
MWA; MdBD; NN; WHi.   49206

-- New Jersey (Diocese)
Journal of the proceedings of the 36th annual con-
vention...18th and 19th days of August, 1819.   New
Brunswick, N.J., Pr. by William Meyer, 1819. 24 p.
NjR.   49207

-- New York (Diocese)
...A catechism designed as an explanation and en-
largement of the church catechism...with some additions by James Morss...Newburyport, Mass., W.B.
Allen & co., 1819. 36 p. NNG.   49208

-- -- Journal of the proceedings of the annual conven-
tion of the Protestant Episcopal Church, in the state of
New-York: held in St. Peter's Church, in the City of
Albany, on Tuesday, October 19th, and Wednesday, Oc-
tober 20th, A.D. 1819... New York, Pr. by T. and J.
Swords, 1819. 48 p. MBD; MWA; NGH; NNG; NNS.
                                               49209
-- North Carolina (Diocese)
Journal of the proceedings of the annual convention
of the Protestant Episcopal Church, in the state of
North Carolina.   Held in St. James Church, in the
town of Wilmington, on Thursday, April 22, and con-
tinued by adjournments. A.D. 1819.   Fayetteville,
N.C., Pr. by Carney & Dismukes, 1819. 15 p. CSmH;
ICU; NBuDD.   49210

-- Ohio (Diocese)
Journal of the proceedings of the second annual

convention of the Protestant Episcopal church in the
state of Ohio; held at Worthington, June 2d, 3d and
4th, 1819. Columbus, Pr. by P. H. Olmsted, at the
Columbus gazette office, [1819?] 30 p. CtY; NHi; NN;
OClWHi. 49211

-- Pennsylvania (Diocese)
Journal of the thirty-fifth convention of the Protestant Episcopal Church in the state of Pennsylvania,
held in St. James's Church in the City of Philadelphia,
on Tuesday and Wednesday, the fourth and fifth of May,
1819. Philadelphia, Pr. by William Fry, for S. Potter & Co., 1819. DLC; MHi; MWA. 49212

-- South Carolina (Diocese)
Journal of the proceedings of the annual convention of the Protestant Episcopal Church, in the state
of South-Carolina; held in St. Michael's Church,
Charleston, from February 16th, to February 19th,
1819. Both days inclusive. Charleston, S. C., Pr. by
J. Hoff, 1819. 32 p. NN. 49213

-- Virginia (Diocese)
Journals of convention... 1819-1820, 1826-1835.
Richmond, Va., 1819- CtHT. 49214

Protestant Episcopal society for the advancement of
Christianity in South-Carolina.
The ninth report... Charleston, S. C., Pr. by A. E.
Miller, 1819. 24 p. MWA; PPAmP; ScCC. 49215

Protestant Episcopal tract society.
The ninth annual report... New York, Pr. by T.
and J. Swords, 1819. 12 p. MHi; MWA. 49216

Providence institution for savings, Providence, R. I.
Charter... Providence, Pr. by Miller & Hutchens,
1819. MWA. 49217

Pryor, Abraham
An interesting description of British America...
A new and last ed. Providence, Pr. by Miller and
Hutchens, 1819. MWA. 49218

-- -- ... From personal knowledge and observation;
containing many and various communications never before made public.   Troy, N. Y.,   Pr. by F. Adancourt
for the author, 1819. (Am. Art - Anderson 4353.
Dec. 1937 (Shea) No. 520)   49219

Publicola [pseud.]
    New vade mecum; or, Pocket companion for law-
yers, deputy sheriffs and constables, suggesting many
grievous abuses and alarming evils which attend the
present mode of administering the laws of New Hampshire with means of redressing them.   Boston, Hews
& Goss, 1819. 155 p. MH-L; MWA.   49220

Purves, James
    An humble attempt to investigate and defend the
scripture doctrine, concerning the Father, the Son,
and the Holy Spirit: with an appendix...by James
Purvis... Philadelphia, John Gillespie, 1819. 312 p.
IaDa; MMeT-Hi; OSW.   49221

Putnam, D.
    A collection of favorite hymns: designed for the
use of private churches, and conference meetings. By
D. Putnam, pastor of the Baptist church in Richfield,
N. Y. and A. Smith, pastor of Baptist church in Schuy-
ler, N. Y. ...Morris' Flats, N. Y., Pr. by J. B. Johnson & son, 1819. 102 p. (Collection of Henry F.
Kieser, Bellevue Blvd., Omaha, Nebr.)   49222

                           Q
The quarter-master; or, The second part of the boat-
swain's mate... Cincinnati, O., Pr. by Mason and
Palmer, for the Western Navigation Bible and Tract
Society, 1819. 23 p. ICN.   49223

Queens County Society for the Promotion of Agriculture and Domestic Manufactures.
    Constitution.   New York, 1819. 8 p. NBLiHi.
                                                49224
Questions adapted to Blair's rhetoric abridged.   By an
experienced teacher of youth.   For the use of schools

and academies. Northampton, Mass., Pr. by J. Metcalf, for Simeon Butler, 1819. 36 p. MNF; NNU. 49225

-- Ed. 3. Salem, Mass., Pr. by Thomas Cushing, 1819. 36 p. MWfo.   49226

Questions adapted to Mason's self knowledge... Boston, James Loring, 1819. MWA.   49227

Questions and counsel addressed to young persons. New York, Religious tract, 1819. PPPrHi.   49228

Quincy, Josiah
    An address delivered before the Massachusetts Agricultural Society, at the Brighton Cattle Show, October 12th, 1819. 15 p. M; MNBedf; MWA; MiHi; NjR.
                                                     49229

R

Raffles, Thomas
    The Sunday school teacher's monitor... Boston, Lincoln & Edmands, 1819. 36 p. MBAt; MWA; WHi.
                                                     49230

Ragland, Thomas
    Defence before a general court-martial, held at West Point in the state of New-York, in the month of May, eighteen hundred and nineteen. By Thomas Ragland, cadet. Newburgh, N.Y., Uriah C. Lewis, 1819. 29 p. MWA; N.   49231

Rambach, Johann Jacob
    Meditations on the sufferings of... Jesus Christ... an abridgment of the work as first translated. Ed. 2. New York, Pr. by T. Wilson & Sons, for J. Wolstenholme, 1819. 564 p. ICP.   49232

Ramsay, Alexander
    Address and anatomical prospectus by Alexander Ramsay, M.D. ...to patriots of every denomination, to medical gentlemen, and medical students in America. Concord, N.H., Hill and Moose, 1819. 24 p. MBAt; MH-AH; MHi; MWA; NNC; NNNAM.   49233

Ramsay, David
    Universal history Americanised... Philadelphia, Pr.
by M. Carey & son, 1819. 12 v. DLC; KyDC; KyLx;
MWA; MtBip; NcWfC.   49234

Ramsay, James
    Memorial address in honor of the late Dr. James
Edwards Burr Finley, A.M., delivered before the Med-
ical Association of South Carolina. 1819. 9 p. ScCC.
                                                 49235
Rand, B.H.
    Rand's system of penmanship. Philadelphia, J.
Perkins, 1819. MWA.   49236

Rankin, Adam
    Dialogues, pleasant and interesting... Lexington,
Ky., Pr. for the author, 1819. 350 p. ICU; KyHi;
KyLx; MWA; NNUT; NcMHi; PPM; PPPrHi.   49237

Rational Brethren of the West.
    The belief of the Rational brethren of the West.
Cincinnati, O., Pr. for the society, 1819. 128 p. O;
OClWHi; PLT.   49238

Rawle, William
    An address delivered before the Philadelphia so-
ciety... Philadelphia, by order of the Society, 1819.
35 p. MH.   49239

Raymond, Daniel, 1786-1849
    The Missouri question... Baltimore, Pr. by Schaef-
fer & Maund, 1819. 39 p. CSmH; DLC; ICU; MB;
MWA; MdHi; MoSM; NcU; PHi; PPAmP; RHi; RP; RPB.
                                                 49240
[Raymond, Mrs. Jane (Osborn)]
    Early piety exemplified in Elizabeth Osborn... Bos-
ton, Lincoln & Edmands, 1819. MWA.   49241

Rayner, Menzies
    Examination of Mr. Tylers second pamphlet en-
titled "The doctrine of the Saints' perseverance"... New
Haven, J. Babcock & Son and Flagg & Gray, 1819.
74 p. CtHC; CtHT; CtY; MB; MWA.   49242

The Red book...[v. 1] Oct. 23, 1819- Baltimore, J.
Robinson [1819] (Issued irregularly) DLC; MBAt;
MdBJ; MdBP; MdHi; PPL-R.   49243

[Redfield, Lewis H.]
    Genealogy of the Redfields. Onondaga, N.Y., Pr.
by Lewis H. Redfield, 1819. Broadside. Sabin 68506.
                                                49244
Redford, John C.
    The student's library; an entertaining and useful
work; original and selected by John C. Redford. Petersburg [Va.] 1819. DLC.   49245

Reese, David Meredith, 1800-1861
    Observations on the epidemic of 1819, as it pre-
vailed in a part of the city of Baltimore...Baltimore,
Pr. by John D. Toy, for the author, 1819. 114 p.
CSmH; DLC; MWA; NNC; NNNAM; PPM.   49246

[Reeve, Mark]
    Some account of Ann Reeve, daughter of Mark and
Hannah Reeve, of Lower Greenwich, state of New Jersey, who departed this life...1778, aged fourteen years
...Philadelphia, Pr. for the Female Tract Association
of Friends, 1819.   8 p. NjR.   49247

Reformed Church in North America
    The acts and proceedings of the General Synod of
the Reformed Dutch Church in North America, at Albany, June, 1819. New York, Pr. by Abraham Paul,
1819.   80 p. IaPeC; MB; MiD-B; NPtjerHi; NSchHi.
                                                49248
-- The psalms and hymns, with the catechism, confession of faith, and liturgy of the Reformed Dutch church
in North America...by John H. Livingston... New York,
W.B. Gilley, 1819. 520 p. NNG.   49249

-- The constitution of the Reformed Dutch Church in
America.   New York, Board of Publication, 1819. 138 p.
ViRut.   49250

Reformed Church in the U.S.
    Verhandlungen der Synode der Hoch-Deutschen Refor-

mirten Kirche in den vereinigten Staaten von Nord-Ameri-
ka, gehalten zu Lancaster, Pa., Sept. 1819. Hagers-Stadt,
Md., Johann Gruber & Daniel May, 1819. 33 p. DLC;
MdBSHG; PHi; PLFM.   49251

-- Verrichtungen des Synodes der Hochdeutschen Reformir-
ten Kirche in den Vereinigten Staaten von Nord Amerika;
gehalten zu Carlisle, Pennsylvanien, im Sept. 1818. Hä-
gers Taun, Md., Pr. by J. Gruber & D. May, 1819. 28 p.
MdBSHG; PLERCHi; PLFM; PReaHi;   49252

-- Rules of the Classis of New York, as amended
April, 1819. 19 p. New York, 1819. N.   49253

Reinke, Abraham
    Einige Worte oder Wohlgemeinter Rath an Johannes
Herr. Ed. 2. Lancaster, Pa., Johann Bar, 1819.
Seidensticker p. 208.   49254

Religious Tract Society of Baltimore
    ...Address to parents from persons who support
Sunday School. Baltimore, Pr. by J. Robinson, for
the Religious Tract Society of Baltimore, 1819. 4 p.
MdHi.   49255

-- ...Advice to youth. Baltimore, Pr. by J. Robinson,
for the Religious Tract Society of Baltimore, 1819. 4 p.
MdHi.   49256

-- ...The narrative of Francis Newport, shewing the
horrors of infidelity, as manifested on the death-bed of
this modern free-thinker. Baltimore, Pr. by J. Robinson, for the Religious Tract Society of Baltimore,
1819. 12 p. MdHi.   49257

-- ...Short sermons, designed for the use of those who
have little time to read longer discourses. Baltimore,
Pr. by J. Robinson, for the Religious Tract Society of
Baltimore, 1819. 24 p. MdHi.   49258

-- ...Two dialogues between a corporal and a private
soldier, written by Lieutenant Colonel of the Army.
Baltimore, Pr. by J. Robinson, for the Religious Tract

Society of Baltimore, 1819. 12 p. MdHi.   49259

-- The third annual report of the Religious tract society of Baltimore, 1819. With the constitution, an appendix, and a list of subscribers. Baltimore, Pr. by
William Warner, for Cushing & Jewett, 1819. 23 p.
MdHi.   49260

Remarks on a pamphlet, entitled "An enquiry respecting the capture of Washington by British, on 24th of
August, 1814, etc." By spectator. Baltimore, 1819.
(Anderson Galleries Cat. Sale, no. 170, Jan. 1923.
no. 886)   49261

Remarks on children's play. New-York, Samuel Wood
& Sons, and Samuel S. Wood & Co., Baltimore [1819?]
44 p. MWA.   49262

Remarks on the Bankrupt law; to which are added, the
proposed amendments of Hopkinson and Webster. By
Civis... New-York, Pr. by C.S. Van Winkle, for Haly
and Thomas, 1819. 71 p. CSt; MB; MWA.   49263

A reply to Mr. Colden's vindication of the steam-boat
monopoly, with an appendix, containing copies of the
most important documents referred to in the argument.
Albany, 1819. 184 p. NIC.   49264

A reply to the "Strictures" of Ebenezer Newcomb...
Greenfield, Mass., Denio & Phelps, 1819. MWA.49265

Report of the trial of Jacob Cochrane on sundry charges
of adultery, and lewd and lascivious conduct, before
the Supreme Judicial Court, begun and holden at York,
within and for the county of York, in the Commonwealth
of Massachusetts, on the third Tuesday of May 1819.
By Gamaliel E. Smith, Esq. Kennebunk, Me., Pr. by
James K. Remick, 1819. 40 p. DLC; MB; MBAt; NN;
RPL.   49266

Report of the trials of the murderers of Richard Jennings, at a Special Court of Oyer and Terminer for the
county of Orange, held at the court house in the village

of Goshen, on Tuesday, February 23rd 1819. With
arguments of counsel. Newburgh, N.Y., Pr. by Benjamin F. Lewis & Co., 1819. 132 p. MH-L.   49267

Republican institution, Boston, Mass.
   Republican institution. [Boston? 1819?] MWA.
                                              49268
Review of a pamphlet, entitled "Moral agency..." by a
Presbyterian. Philadelphia, Pr. by A. Waldie, 1819.
50 p.   MWA; NNG; NjR.   49269

Review of "Letters to the Rev. Wm. E. Channing, containing remarks on his sermon, recently preached and
published at Baltimore. By Moses Stuart, associate
professor of Sacred literature in the Theological Seminary, Andover." Boston, Pr. by Wells and Lilly,
1819. 20 p. CBPSR; CSmH; MWA; NNUT; NjR;
PPAmP.   49270

The reviewer reviewed; or strictures on Dr. Ezra
Stiles Ely's Review of the work entitled "Methodist Error," by a Wesleyan Methodist. Philadelphia, Jonathan Pounder, 1819. 12 p. PMA.   49271

The reward of integrity, or the history of Martin and
James. New York, John C. Totten, 1819. MWA.
                                               49272
Rhode Island (State)
   At the General Assembly of the state of Rhode-Is-
land...by adjournment...third Monday of February,
1819. [Providence, 1819] 48 p. DLC; In-SC.   49273

-- At the General Assembly of the state of Rhode-Island...begun...first Wednesday of May, 1819. [Provi-
dence, 1819] 50 p. DLC; In-SC.   49274

-- At the General Assembly of the State of Rhode-Island...by adjournment...third Monday of June, 1819.
[Providence, 1819] 48 p. DLC; In-SC.   49275

-- At the General Assembly of the state of Rhode-Island...begun...last Monday in October, 1819. [Provi-
dence, 1819] 48 p. DLC.   49276

-- Public laws of the state of Rhode-Island...passed
since the session of the General Assembly, in Feb.,
1817. [Providence, 1819] 239-276 p. DLC.   49277

The Rhode-Island almanack for 1820.   By Isaac Bicker-
staff.   Providence, Hugh H. Brown [1819] 28 p. MWA;
NjR; RHi; RPB.   49278

The Rhode-Island register and United States Calendar
for 1820.   Providence, H. H. Brown [1819] 108 p.
MWA; RHi.   49279

Ricardo, David, 1772-1823
    On the principles of political economy...1st Amer.
ed.   Georgetown, D. C., J. Milligan; Washington City,
J. Gideon, jr., printer, 1819. 448 p. CtHT; DLC;
MWA; MeBat; OPosm; RBR.   49280

Rice, John Holt, 1777-1831
    The instrumentality of man...Richmond, Va., Pr.
by W. W. Gray, 1819. 21 p. CSansS; CSmH; DLC;
MH-AH; MWA; MnHi; NAuT; OClWHi; PHi; PPPrHi;
PPiXT; Vi; ViU.   49281

-- A sermon to young women, republished from the
Virginia Evangelical and Literary magazine.   Richmond,
Va., Franklin Press, 1819. 19 p. MBC; MH-AH;
MiU; MWA; NN; Vi; ViU.   49282

[--] The pamphletteer No. 1.   Essay on baptism.
Richmond, Va., Franklin press, 1819. 400 p. CSmH;
KyLoP; MB; MH-AH; MWA; N; NNG; NNUT; NcD; NjR;
OO; PPPrHi; ViU.   49283

[--] -- No. I - II. Richmond, Pr. by W. W. Gray,
from the Franklin press, 1819-20. 2 v. in 1. Paged
continuously.   Imprint varies slightly. CSmH; MH-AH;
MWA; PPPrHi; ViRut.   49284

Rich man's meditation and poor man's appeal for the
benefit of the community at large.   By the author, a
resident of Henrico County, Virginia. 1819. 21 p.
(James Lewis Hook cat. no. 29 Spring 1940 no. 498) 49285

Richard, Louis Claude Marie
    A botanical dictionary... Ed. 2.   New Haven, Pr.
by Clark & Lyman, for Howe & Spalding, 1819. 191 p.
CLSU; CtHT; CtY; DA; IU; MB; MBHo; MH; MNan;
MWA; MiGr; MiU; MoSB; NCH; NNC; NNNBG; NNC;
NR; NSyU; PPA; PPHor; PPi; VtU.   49286

Richards, George Hallam
    An oration, delivered before Union lodge... New
York, Pr. by James Oram, 1819. 26 p.   CtHT-W;
CtNl; IaCrM; MBFM; MH; MWA; NjR.   49287

Richards, James, 1767-1843
    A sermon, preached May 12, 1819, in the Cedar
street church, New-York, before the Education society
of the Presbyterian church in the United States of
America... Newark [N.J.] Pr. by John Tuttle & Co.,
1819. 25 p. CSmH; MB; MBC; MH-AH; MWA; MWiW.
                                                  49288
Richmond, Edward
    A sermon, delivered at Lexington, April 28, 1819,
at the ordination of the Reverend Charles Briggs...
Boston, Pr. by Munroe & Francis, 1819. 24 p. CtSoP;
ICMe; MBC; MH; MHi; MLex; MPiB; MSaE; MWA;
MiD-B; NN; RPB.   49289

[Richmond, Legh]
    The dairy man's daughter.   To which is added, an
interesting account of a child.   Ed. 5.   Andover,
Mass., 1819. 24 p. MB.   49290

Richmond, Va. Young Men's Missionary Society.
    Extracts from the minutes... Constitution and annu-
al report... with an address ... Richmond, Va., Franklin press, 1819. PPPrHi; ViHi.   49291

The Richmond directory, register and almanac for the
year 1819.   Richmond, John Maddox, 1819. 76 p.
CSmH; DLC; ViRVal.   49292

The riddle-book for the entertainment of young children... New Haven, Sidney's press, for J. Babcock &
son, 1819. MWA.   49293

Rinck, Johann Christian Heinrich, 1770-1846
    The first three months at the organ...Boston,
Reed [1819]   34 p.   MB.   49294

Ripley, Dorothy
    An account of Rose Butler, aged nineteen years,
whose execution I attended in the Potter's Field...for
setting fire to her mistress dwelling house.   New York,
J. C. Totten Co., 1819.   35 p.   ICN; MWA; PPM. 49295

-- The bank of faith and works united...Philadelphia,
Pr. by J. H. Cunningham, for the authoress, 1819.
204 p.   CtHC; MWA; NcD.   49296

Ripley, Ezra
    A sermon at the installation of the Rev. William
Frothingham...Cambridge, Pr. by Hilliard and Metcalf,
1819.   MWA.   49297

Rippon, John
    A selection of hymns, from the best authors.   4th
Amer., from 15th London ed., together with appendix.
Philadelphia, Pr. by W. Hill Woodward, for W. W.
Woodward, 1819. 670 hymns.   MWA. 49298

Ritchie, Andrew, 1782-1862
    Address delivered to the Massachusetts peace so-
ciety at their third anniversary December 25, 1818...
Boston, Pr. by Wells and Lilly, 1819.   16 p.   CSt;
DLC; ICMe; MBAt; MB; MH; MMeT; MWA; PPF; RPB.
                                                49299

[Roane, Spencer] 1762-1822, comp.
    Exposition of the federal constitution.   Contained in
the report of the Committee of Virginia House of delegates; Richmond, Pr. by Thomas Ritchie, 1819. 27 p.
Sabin 100463   49300

Roanoke Sentinel.   Danville, Va., James Lanier, Aug.
7, 1819, 1st issue.   Weekly newspaper. MBAt. 49301

Robbins, Archibald
    A journal comprising an account of the loss of the
brig Commerce, of Hartford, upon the western coast of

Africa, August 28th, 1815...Ed. 2. Hartford, S. Andrus, 1819. 275 p. CtHi; DLC; MH; MiD-B; NjP; ViU. 49302

Robbins, Thomas
Continuation of Tytler's elements of general history from the close of the 17th century to the general peace in Europe, A.D. 1815. New York, 1819. MBC. 49303

Roberts, Sylvester
Roberts's second edition of The Secret "Customs" and Revenue of the sheriff's office. Philadelphia, 1819. 29 p. MWA; PHi; PPAmP. 49304

Roberts, Thomas
The resurrection: A sermon delivered at the Baptist Meeting-House, in the Great Valley, Pennsylvania, December, 1818...Philadelphia, Pr. by Anderson and Meehan, for the author, 1819. 20 p. NRAB. 49305

The robin's nest...New Haven, Sidney's press, for J. Babcock & son, 1819. 35 p. CtHi; MWA. 49306

Robinson, Daniel A.
An inaugural essay on the treatment of wounds of the femoral vein...Geneva, N.Y., Pr. by J. Bogert, 1819. 30 p. NBMS; NNNAM. 49307

Robinson, John
An easy grammar of history, ancient and modern ...4th Amer. ed. Philadelphia, Pr. by Griggs & Co., for Bennett & Walton, 1819. 180 p. MWA; NcWsS; PReaHi. 49308

Robinson, Robert
A plea for the divinity of the Lord Jesus Christ... Philadelphia, Pr. by J.H. Cunningham, 1819. 144 p. MWA; ViRut. 49309

Robinson's Circulating Library, Baltimore.
Third supplement, for 1819, to the catalogue of Robinson's Circulating Library, established at No. 96, Baltimore-street corner of Belvidere-street. Baltimore,

Pr. by J. Robinson, Circulating Library, 1819. 12 p.
MdHi.   49310

Rochester encyclopaedian society library, N. Y.
    Bye-laws... Kingston, N. Y., Pr. by John Tappen,
1819. MWA.   49311

Rockingham Charitable Society, New Hampshire.
    Second report of the Rockingham Charitable So-
ciety, in New Hampshire... holden at Portsmouth, Apr.
21, 1819... Concord, N. H., Pr. by George Hough,
1819. 29 p. MiD-B; NN; WHi.   49312

Rockville Courier. Rockville, Md., Andrew Kennedy,
Sept. 6, 1819, 1st issue. Weekly newspaper. DLC.
                                                        49313

Rockwood, Elisha
    A century sermon, delivered in Westborough...
December 3, 1818... Boston, Pr. by Parmenter and
Balch, 1819. 22 p. DLC; ICMe; M; MBC; MHi; MWA;
MiD-B; NN; RPB.   49314

Rogers, Daniel
    The New York City Hall recorder for the year
1819, containing reports of the most interesting trials
and decisions which have arisen in the various courts
of judicature for the trial of jury causes in the hall
during that year, particularly in the court of sessions
with notes and remarks, critical and explanatory, by
Daniel Rogers... New York, Pr. by Clayton & Kingsland, 1819. 192 p. Ms; Nc-SC; RPL.   49315

Rogers, John K. & Co., Boston.
    Specimen sheets from the letter foundry of John K.
Rogers & Co. Known as the Boston Type Foundry,
commenced A. D. 1819. No. 6 Spring Lane, Boston.
...1819. NNC-Atf.   49316

Rogers, Samuel
    Human life, a poem. By Samuel Rogers. Phila-
delphia, Pr. by J. Maxwell, for M. Thomas, 1819.
62 p. DLC; MH; MWA; NjP.   49317

Romaine, William
    A treatise upon the life of faith... Hagers-Town,
Md., W.D. Bell, 1819. 159 p. MWA; MdBE; MdHi;
PPLT.   49318

Romeyn, John Brodhead
    A sermon, delivered in the Middle Dutch Church,
on the evening of the Lord's Day, March 21, 1819, for
the benefit of the New York Marine Missionary Society.
New York, J. Seymour, 1819. 24 p. MB; MBC; MWA;
OC; PMA.   49319

Rood, Zebulon
    An oration delivered at the celebration of the anni-
versary of St. John the Baptist... at Granville, Ohio
...Delaware, O., Pr. by J.S. Linn [1819] 15 p.
MBFM.   49320

Rordansz, C.W.
    European commerce; or, Complete mercantile
guide to the continent of Europe... Boston, Cummings
& Hilliard, 1819. 595 p. Ct Y-L; ICU; MH-BA; MMeT;
MNe; MSaE; MWA; MdBJ; MoSpD; NNLI; NPtjerHi;
PPA; PPL-R; PPWa; PU; VtU.   49321

[Rose, Robert Hutchinson] 1776-1842
    Letters from the British settlement in Pennsyl-
vania.   To which are added, the constitutions of the
United States and of Pennsylvania;... By C.B. Johnson,
M.D. [pseud.] Philadelphia, H. Hall...1819. 192 p.
CSmH; DLC.   49322

[Ross, Mrs.]
    Hesitation... v. 1.   New York, Pr. by Clayton &
Kingsland, for W.B. Gilley, 1819. MWA.   49323

[--] -- v. 2.   New York, Pr. by C.S. Van Winkle,
for W.B. Gilley, 1819. MWA.   49324

The Round table. Nos. 1-3.   ...by George Bickers-
taffe, and others. Hartford, 1819-20. Nos. 1-3 in 1
v.   (Knights of the Round Table. Hartford, Conn.)
CtHi; DLC; PHi.   49325

272   Rowan

Rowan, Stephen N.
Review of the reply to his sermon of the 9th of
August 1818: including a summary of the evidence on
the minutes of the classis of New-York and their de-
cision in his case.   New-York, Pr. by Abraham Paul,
1819.   87 p.   MBC; N; NjR.   49326

Rowson Susanna (Haswell)
Charlotte Temple, a tale of truth.   Baltimore, W.
Warner, 1819.   MH.   49327

-- -- 12th Amer. ed.   Poughkeepsie, N. Y., P. Potter, 1819.   2 v. in 1.   DLC; MWA.   49328

Roxbury, Brookline & Brighton Society for the Purpose
of Apprehending Horse Thieves.
Constitution.   Boston, 1819.   12 p. WHi.   49329

Roxbury, Mass. Library
Catalogue of the books.   Boston, 1819.   10 p. PHi.
                                                       49330
Rudd, John Churchill
Compendium of geography.   Ed. 2.   Trenton,
N. J., D. & E. Fenton, 1819. MWA; NjR.   49331

Rules and regulations for the pilots of Sandy-Hook.
New York, Pr. by Chambers & Co., 1819. Broadside.
DNA.   49332

[Rundell, Maria Eliza (Ketelby)]
American domestic cookery, formed on principles
of economy, for the use of private families.   By an experienced housekeeper.   Baltimore, Pr. by R. J. Matchett, for Fielding Lucas, Jun., 1819.   347 p. DLC;
KyLxT; PPFHi; RPB; WGr.   49333

The rural magazine and farmer's monthly museum, de-
voted to history, biography, agriculture, manufacture,
miscellany, poetry, and foreign and domestic intelli-
gence... Ed. by S. Putnam Waldo... v. 1, no. 1-6;
Feb. to July 1819.   Hartford, J. & W. Russell, 1819.
208 p. (No more published) CtHi; DLC; MH; MiD-B;
N; OClWHi; PPL.   49334

Rush, Benjamin
    An inquiry into the effects of ardent spirits...
Ed. 8, with additions.   Exeter, N.H., Josiah Richardson, 1819. 36 p. DNLM; MWA.   49335

-- Medical inquiries and observations...4 v. in 2.
Philadelphia, Anthony Finley, 1819. 2 v. DNLM;
IU-M; MdU-D; NNC; NNNAM; TU-M.   49336

Rush, Jacob
    An inquiry into the doctrine of Christian baptism
with a view to unite Christians of every denomination
at the Lord's Supper...Philadelphia, Pr. for the author, 1819. 58 p. MWA; RPB.   49337

                         S
S., J.
    The divinity of Christ, vindicated...Philadelphia,
Pr. by Anderson & Meehan, for Thomas and William
Bradford, 1819. IC; MWA.   49338

Sabbatarians
    Minutes of the Seventh-Day Baptist General Confer-
ence, held at Brookfield, Madison Co., N.Y. September 23-27, 1819, with their circular letter, to which
are added, The constitution of the Central Missionary
Society; the Transactions of the Board, and a Summary
of Brother Amos R. Wells' Journal while on a missionary tour in the summer of 1819.   Schenectady,
N.Y., Pr. by Isaac Riggs, 1819. 12 p. MWA; NAlf.
                                                     49339
Sabine, James
    Glorying in the cross; a sermon delivered before
the Associated Congregational ministers of Salem and
vicinity, at Malden, Mass., on Tuesday, Sept. 3, 1818.
...Ed. 2.   Charlestown, Mass., G. Clark, 1819. 32 p.
CBPSR; DLC; MB; MBAt; MH; MHaHi; MSaE; MWA;
NN; PHi; RPB.   49340

-- A sermon, delivered December 15, 1819, on the
dedication of the house recently erected for public worship...Essex-street...Boston... Boston, Pr. by True

& Weston, for G. Clarke & Co., Charlestown; S. T.
Armstrong and Lincoln & Edmands, Boston, 1819.
29 p. DLC; MB; MBAt; MH; MHi; MWA; MWiW;
MiD-B; PPPrHi; RPB.   49341

Sacket, Augustus
    For Sale, 400,000 acres of land, in the counties
of Rutherford, Mecklenburgh and Buncomb in... North
Carolina... [Sacket's Harbor, N.Y. ? 1819?] Broadside.
NN.   49342

Sacred harmony: being a selection of tunes of approved
excellence. Suited to the various subjects and metres
of the psalms and hymns of Dr. Watts, and also to the
supplement attached to them, by the Rev. Mr. Winchell.
Boston, James Loring, 1819. 7 p. 120 tunes. MBC;
MWA.   49343

Sailors' Snug harbour, New York.
    Act of incorporation, and by-laws, of the trustees
of the Sailors' Snug harbour... New-York, Pr. by Wm.
A. Mercein, 1819. 16 p. NNG; NjR.   49344

St. John's college, Annapolis
    The memorial of the visitors and governors of St.
John's college, to the General assembly of Maryland.
Annapolis, Md., Pr. by J. Green, 1819. 14 p. MdAS;
MdBP; MdHi.   49345

Salem, Mass. (Town)
    Abstract of the Bill of Mortality, for the town of
Salem, 1818. Salem, Mass., Jan. 1, 1819. Broadside. MSaE.   49346

-- Expences of the Town of Salem for the year ending
March, 1819... John Saunders, Town Clerk. Salem,
Mass., 1819. Broadside. MSaE.   49347

Salem Gazette. January 1, 1820. To the patrons of
the Salem Gazette, the carriers wish a happy new year.
[Salem, Mass., 1819] Broadside. MeHi.   49348

Salem Messenger. Salem, N.J., Elijah Brooks, Sept.

18, 1819, 1st issue. Weekly newspaper. NjHi. 49349

Salem, Mass. Active Fire Club
Active Fire Club. Annual meeting and list of
members. Salem, Mass., 1819. Broadside. MSaE.
49350
-- Commercial bank.
An act to incorporate the president, directors and
company of the Commercial Bank. Salem, Mass., Pr.
by W. Palfray, Jr., 1819. 16 p. M; MBeHi; MWA.
49351
-- North Meeting House.
Commemoration of Washington, February 22d,
1819. Order of performances at the North Meeting-
House. [Salem, Mass., 1819] Broadside. MSaE.
49352
Sampson, Ezra
Beauties of the Bible...Stereotyped by D. & G.
Bruce, New-York. Hudson, N. Y., William E. Nor-
man, 1819. 282 p. MBC; MWA; NNG; OCo.   49353

Sampson, William
Catholic question in America. New York, 1819.
OCMtSM.   49354

-- Is a whale a fish? An accurate report of the case
of James Maurice against Samuel Judd, tried in the
Mayor's Court of the city of New York, on the 30th
and 31st of December, 1818. Wherein the above prob-
lem is discussed theologically, scholastically and his-
torically...New York, C. S. Van Winkle, 1819. 83 p.
MWiW; NIC-A; NjR; OCLaw; PPAmP.   49355

Sanderson, Joseph M.
Proposals for publishing by subscription a biography of the signers to the Declaration of Independence,
accompanied with plates, and the Declaration itself
with facsimile engravings of the signatures...Philadel-
phia, 1819. 7 p. MWA; PPAmP.   49356

Sanford, Ezekiel
A history of the Unites States before the Revolution...Philadelphia, Pr. by William Brown, for Anthony

Finley, 1819. 342 p. DLC; DeGE; ICU; MWA; MdBD;
MeBa; NIC; NjR; RP; RPB. 49357

Sanger, Ralph
A sermon, occasioned by the death of Capt. Lewis
Smith...Dedham, Mass., Pr. by H. & W.H. Mann,
1819. 15 p. MBAt; MBNEH; MH; MSaE; MWA; MW;
RPB. 49358

Sangmeister, Ezechiel
Mystische Theologie. Ephrata, Pa., 1819. DLC;
MWA; PHi; PLT; RPB. 49359

Saratoga Sentinel. Saratoga Springs, N.Y., Gideon M.
Davison, May 26, 1819, 1st issue. Weekly newspaper.
49360
[Sargent, Charles Lenox]
The life of Alexander Smith, captain of the island
of Pitcairn; one of the mutineers on board His Majes-
ty's ship Bounty; commanded by Lieut. Wm. Bligh.
Written by Smith himself, on the above island, and
bringing the accounts from Pitcairn, down to the year
1815. Boston, Pr. by S.T. Goss, 1819. 240 p. DLC;
ICN; MB; MH; MBAt; MBL; MBNEH; MSaE; MW; NhD.
49361
[Sargent, Winthrop]
Detail of the rise and fall of the Mississippi River
at Natchez Landing, for more than 20 years...[Natchez,
Miss., 1819] Broadside. MWA. 49362

[--] From the meteorological observations at Gloster
Place, two miles south of Natchez. Lat. of Natchez
31 deg. 33 m. 46 s. N Long 6 Hr 6 m w Mean temper-
ature of each and every month in the year, and of every year from 1810 to 1818, inclusive...Natchez, 1819.
Broadside. MHi; MWA. 49363

[Satchel, John]
Thornton Abbey...Philadelphia, Pr. by S. Probas-
co, for Jones & Probasco, 1819. 2 v. in 1. MWA;
NbBla. 49364

The Saturday magazine: being in great part a compila-

tion from the British reviews, magazines, and scientific journals. v. 1-5, Jan. 2, 1819-June 20, 1821 [new ser.] v. 1-2, July 7, 1821-June 29, 1822. Philadelphia, Littell & Henry... 1819-22. 7 v. DLC; TxU.
49365

[Savage & Company]
Louisville, Ky. (Falls of Ohio,) June 1, 1819. Permit me to refer you to the circulars of my late firm of Savage & Lewis; and that of mine of April last, which announced the intended dissolution of that concern, which occurs on this first of June, and of my continuing the Commission Business under the firm of Savage & Co. in which I renew a tender of services. Louisville, Ky., 1819. Broadside. MHi; WHi.   49366

Scenes in China, exhibiting the manners, customs, diversions and singular peculiarities of the Chinese... New York, Samuel Wood & Sons, and Samuel S. Wood & Co., Baltimore, 1819. 188 p. CoPu; MWA; RPB.
49367

Schaeffer, Frederick Christian
Der Deutsche Freund. 1B. 1st. New York, 1819. MH-AH.   49368

Schaeffer und Maund's Amerikanischer Stadt- und Land Calender auf das Jahr, 1820... Baltimore, Schaeffer und Maund [1819] 36 p. DLC; MWA; MdBE; NN; PHi.
49369

Schoell, Fred
Recueil de Pieces Officielles... New York, 1819. NIC.   49370

Schoharie Republican. Schoharie, N.Y., Derick Van Veghten, Dec., 1819, 1st issue. Weekly newspaper. Brigham, p. 740.   49371

Schoolcraft, Henry Rowe, 1793-1864
A view of the lead mines of Missouri; including some observations on the mineralogy, geology, geography, antiquities, soil, climate, population, and productions of Missouri and Arkansaw... New-York, Pr. by J. Seymour, for Charles Wiley & Co., 1819. 299 p.

DLC; FTaB; DeGE; InI; InThR; MA; MFiHi; MSaP;
MWA; MWiW; MiDSH; MnHi; NWM; NcD.   49372

Schröckh, Johann Matthias
    Kurzer Begriff der Biblischen Geschichte... Easton,
Pa., Pr. by Christ. J. Hutter & son, 1819. 116 p.
MWA; PE.   49373

Schwenkfelder, Caspar
    Einige christliche und lehrreiche Send-Briefe...
Allentown, Pa., Pr. by Heinrich Ebner, 1819. 100 p.
DLC; MH; MWA; P; PHi; PPL.   49374

Scott, Job
    The baptism of Christ.   A Gospel ordinance...
Baltimore, Joseph James, 1819. 200 p. NBF.   49375

Scott, Moses Y.
    The deaf and dumb; a poem... Written and pub-
lished for the benefit of "The New-York institution for
the instruction of the deaf and dumb." New York, Pr.
by J. Seymour, for Elam Bliss, 1819. 23 p. MH;
MWA; N; NNC; NNNAM; RPB.   49376

-- Fatal jest, a tale: and other poems... New-York,
Pr. by J. Seymour, for Elam Bliss, 1819. 142 p.
DLC; MB; MWA; NNC; RPB.   49377

Scott, Thomas
    The force of truth... Brattleborough, Vt., John
Holbrook, 1819. 164 p. CtHT-W; CoD; DGU; MDeeP;
MWA; VtBrt; VtHi; VtU.   49378

-- Treatises on various theological subjects... 2d Middletown ed.   Middletown, Conn., Clark & Lyman, 1819.
v. 6.   MWA.   49379

Scott, Sir Walter
    Tales of my landlord: third series.   New York,
Pr. by Clayton & Kingsland, for Charles Wiley & Co.,
W.B. Gilley... 1819. 297 p. KyBC; MPlyP; NN. 49380

-- Waverley; or 'Tis sixty years since... New York,

Pr. by G. Long, for James Eastburn & Co., 1819.
2 v.   NN; OClStM.   49381

Scott, William
     Lessons in elocution.   Boston ed.   Boston, Lin-
coln & Edmands, 1819.   MWA.   49382

-- -- Greenfield, Pr. by A. J. Newcomb, for Clark &
Hunt, 1819.   428 p.   MH; MHi; MNS; MWA; VtWinds.
                                                       49383
Scriptural and experimental songs, for those who wish
to praise God... Windham, Conn., F. Plummer, 1819.
RPB.   49384

Scripture catechism for children... Boston, Cummings
& Hilliard, 1819.   11 p.   MWA; NN.   49385

Scripture history, abridged.   In which it is designed to
give children such a taste of the writings of the in-
spired penmen... Boston, Lincoln & Edmands, 1819.
70 p.   DLC; MWA; MiD-B.   49386

-- Boston, Lincoln & Edmands, 1819.   70, [2] p.
MBMu; MWA; NjR.   49387

Scudamore, Sir Charles
     A treatise on the nature and cure of gout and
rheumatism... 1st Amer. ed.   Philadelphia, Pr. by
William Brown, for Edward Earle, 1819.   335 p.
ICU-R; IU-M; MWA; NClsM; NIC; NNNAM.   49388

The seaman's spy-glass... [Philadelphia] Wm. Bradford,
agent, 1819.   MWA.   49389

Sears, Reuben
     A poem on the mineral waters of Ballston and
Saratoga... Ballston Spa, N. Y., Pr. by J. Comstock,
1819.   108 p.   CSmH; DLC; MB; MBAt; MH; MWA; NN;
NNC; RPB.   49390

Seats near Natchez for sale.   Notice is hereby given
that on Tuesday the 28th instant, at the store of Messrs.
H. Postlethwaite & Co. in Natchez, will be sold at pub-

lic sale the real estate of Col. John Steele, deceased
...[Natchez, Miss., 1819] Broadside. Ms-Ar.   49391

Secker, William, d. 1681?
    The nonsuch professor in his meridian splendor;
or The singular actions of sanctified Christians... New
York, [Pr. by Largin & Thompson] George Lindsay,
1819. 284 p. CSt.   49392

A selection of hymns for the use of Sunday schools.
New-York, Pr. by J. Seymour, for P. W. Gallaudet...
1819. 88 p. MWA.   49393

A selection of hymns from various authors, designed
as a supplement to the Methodist Pocket Hymn Book
...Ed. 12.   New York, Pr. by Abraham Paul, for J.
Soule, 1819. 282 p. (Bound with "The Methodist Pocket
Hymn Book, 46th ed.   New-York, 1819. A. Paul, Pr.)
MWA.   49394

The self-taught conveyancer... York, Pa., P. Hardt,
and Shaeffer & Maund, Baltimore, 1819. 91 p. DLC;
MWA.   49395

Sergeant, John, 1779-1852
    Speech of Mr. Sergeant, delivered in the House of
representatives, Feb. 22, on the Bank of the United
States...[Washington? 1819] 68 p. CtW; DLC; LU;
MWA; PHi.   49396

A series of essays on agriculture and rural affairs.
Raleigh, N.C., J. Gales, 1819. NcAS.   49397

Serious soliloquies... Boston, Pr. by Sewell Phelps,
1819. MWA.   49398

A sermon, delivered in the East, North, and South,
and published for their benefit, as well as for the West;
and all inclined to Unitarian sentiments; upon the bad
effects of Secret assemblies and party designs in Church
and State... Salem, Pr. for the author, 1819. 12 p.
MWA.   49399

A sermon to young women...Richmond, Va., Pr. by
W.W. Gray, from the Franklin press, 1819. MWA.
49400

A set of flowers, alphabetically arranged, for little
children. New York, Samuel Wood and sons, 1819.
[24] p. MWA; PP.   49401

Seven wonders of the world; and other magnificent
buildings. New York, Samuel Wood & sons, 1819.
42 p. MWA.   49402

Shakers
The memorial of the society of people of Canter-
bury, in the County of Rockingham, and Enfield, in the
County of Grafton, commonly called Shakers.   13 p.
(Though credited by N. Y. P. L. cataloguer to Enfield
N. H. , 1818, it was likely printed at Andover, N. H. , in
1819) NN.   49403

[Sharman, Edward]
The Christian world unmasked...Watertown, N. Y.,
Pr. for the author, 1819. 72 p. CSmH; MH; MWA;
NjR.   49404

Shaw, Oliver
Melodia   Sacra: or Providence selection of sacred
musick... Providence, Miller & Hutchens, 1819. 151 p.
MWA.   49405

Shecut, John Linnaeus Edward Whitridge
Shecut's medical and philosophical essays...
Charleston, S. C. , Pr. by A. E. Miller, for the author,
1819. 260 p. DLC; MB; NNNAM; PPC; RPM; TxU.
49406

Shedden, Mrs. Cecilia
Abridgment of the logographic emblematical French
spelling book... New York, Pr. by Southwick & Pelsue,
1819. 100 p. DLC; MWA; NN; PPM.   49407

Sheil, Richard Lalor
The apostate; a tragedy in five acts... New York,
1819. 64 p. MB; NN; NjP.   49408

-- Evadne; or, The statue; a tragedy in five acts...
(From the 1st London ed. of 1819) New York, Thomas Longworth, 1819. 83 p. MWA; NjP; PPL-R; RNR.
49409

[Sherman, ... (of Fairfield, Conn.)]
Letter to the Secretary of the Treasury, on the commerce and currency of the United States; by Aristides. New York, 1819. 39 p. MH-L.   49410

Sherwood, Mrs. Mary Martha (Butt)
History of Emily and her brothers... Philadelphia, Pr. by Clark & Raser, 1819. MWA.   49411

[--] The history of little Henry and his bearer. New York, J. C. Totten, 1819. MWA.   49412

[--] -- Newburyport, Mass., Pr. by W. & J. Gilman, 1819. MWA.   49413

Shore, Thomas
The merchants and traveller's companion; ...
Petersburg, Va., Republican press, for Thomas Shore, 1819. 258 p. DLC; NcD; OClWHi; OOC; Vi.   49414

Short, Bob
Patriotic effusions, by Bob Short. New-York, Pr. by J. & J. Harper, for L. and F. Lockwood, 1819. 47 p. N.   49415

Siffer, Edward D.
The extent of the atonement... New York, Stephen Dodge, 1819. TxAuPT.   49416

[Simmons, Amelia]
American cookery; or the art of dressing viands, fish, poultry and vegetables... Brattleborough, Vt., John Holbrook, 1819. 48 p. McCorison List.   49417

[Simmons, James Wright]
The exile's return: a tale; in three cantos: with other pieces. By a South-Carolinian. Charleston, S. C., Pr. by A. E. Miller, for the author, 1819. 131 p. MH; PPAmP; ScC.   49418

Simpson, David
    An extract from a celebrated modern English pub-
lication... Providence, Pr. by H. H. Brown, 1819.
MWA.   49419

Sinclair, Hannah
    A letter on the principles of the Christian faith.
1st Amer. from the 2d London ed.   Philadelphia, 1819.
32 p.   N; NjR; P.   49420

-- -- 1st Amer. ed.   Richmond, Va. , Pr. by W. W.
Gray, from the Franklin press, 1819.   56 p. MWA; Vi.
                                                49421
-- -- ...Who died May 22, 1818.   2d Amer., from
2d London ed.   Washington, Pr. by Davis and Force,
1819.   DLC; NjR.   49422

The sisters; and The rose, or History of Ellen Selwyn
...New-Haven, Sidney's press, for J. Babcock and son,
1819. 36 p.   CtHi; DLC; MWA; NN.   49423

Sketch of the life and character of the Rev. John
Emery Abbott...[Boston? 1819?]   16 p. DLC; MH.
                                                49424
...Sketch of the religious experience of Mahala Holcomb...Middlebury, Vt., Pr. [by Francis Burnap] at
the Messenger office, 1819. MWA.   49425

[Skinner, Thomas Harvey]
    Another voice from the grave...Boston, Pr. by U.
Crocker, for Samuel T. Armstrong, 1819. 24 p. DLC;
MBAt; MWA; NN.   49426

[--] -- Philadelphia, William Bradford, agent, 1819.
MWA.   49427

Slocumb, Jesse
    To the electors of the counties of Johnston, Wayne,
Greene, Lenoir, Jones, Craven and Carteret.   Fellow-
Citizens: At the general election in August, you will be
called on to select some individual to represent you in
the next Congress of the United States...Jesse Slocumb.
Wayne County [N. C.] June 10, 1819. Broadside.

NcD.   49428

Smelt, Caroline E.
    Extracts from the memoirs of Caroline E. Smelt.
Philadelphia, Benjamin & Thomas Kite and W. Conrad,
1819. 16 p. InRchE; MWA; NcD.   49429

Smith, Daniel
    The believer's rest. Poughkeepsie, N. Y., Charles
P. Barnum, 1819. 15 p. NP.   49430

-- Biography of St. John the Evangelist. Discourse
before the Masonick Lodges--of Natchez. December
27, 1818. Natchez (Miss.) Peter Isler, 1819. 18 p.
MBFM.   49431

Smith, David
    A sermon, delivered at Durham, April 4, 1819...
death of Deacon John Tibbals...Middletown, Conn., Pr.
by Clark & Lyman, 1819. 15 p. CtHi; CtHT-W; MWA;
OO.   49432

Smith, Elias
    The herald of life and immortality. Boston,
Henry Bowen, 1819. 288 p. MBAt; MMeT-Hi; NCaS.
                                                       49433
-- The judgement of this world cast out; and all men
drawn to Christ. A sermon...Boston, 1819. 13 p.
MMeT-Hi.   49434

Smith, Ethan
    The blessing of Abraham come on the gentiles...
Ballston Spa, N. Y., Pr. by James Comstock, 1819.
MWA.   49435

-- Ministers of Christ, made instruments of man's
salvation. A sermon...at the installation of Rev.
Stephen Martindale...Rutland, Vt., Pr. by Fay & Burt,
1819. 26 p. MBC; MWA; N; NcMHi; NhHi; RPB. 49436

Smith, James S.
    To the Freemen of Orange, Wake and Person coun-
ties. Fellow-Citizens, After tendering to you my most

sincere acknowledgments for the liberal support that I
had the honor to receive from you at the last election,
I again tender you my services and am a candidate to
represent you in the 16th Congress... Hillsboro, July
3rd, 1819. [1819?] Broadside. NcD.   49437

Smith, John
     The true travels, adventures and observations of
Captain John Smith... Richmond, Va., Pr. by William
W. Gray, repub. at the Franklin press, 1819. 2 v.
CSmH; CtB; CtHC; CtHWatk; CtMW; CtWat; DeWI; FSa;
GEU; GU; I; Ia; ICHi; ICNC; ICU; IHi; KSalW; KyLoF;
KyLx; L; LN; LNT; M; MA; MB; MBeHi; MBL; MC;
MWA; Md; MdAN; MdBE; MdHi; MdBJ; MdBS; Me;
MeHi; Mi; MiD-B; MiU; MiU-C; MH; MH-Z; MLoW;
MnDu; MNe; MNF; MnHi; MnM; MoK; MoSHi; MoSM;
MStow; NWC; NBi; NBu; NcH; NGH; NNUT; NNC;
NNHuC; NNP; NNS; NPV; NR; NT; NcAS; NcD; NcMHi;
NcU; Nh; NjP; NjT; O; OClWHi; OFH; OMC; OO; P;
PHi; PPL-R; PPFr; PLFM; PMA; PPD; PPiU;   PU;
RNR; RPJCB; RBA; ScCC; TSewU; TxAuPi; TxU; Vi;
ViAl; ViFre; ViHi; ViL; ViLRM; ViPet; ViRU; ViVal;
ViRVU; ViSwc; ViU; ViW; ViWRP; WHi; WM.   49438

Smith, Randolph Wellford
     The Sober world. Boston, 1819. 291 p. Tuttle EC961.
                                                  49439
Smith, Thomas
     A few remarks on the reports of the committees
on the currency.   1819.   MH-BA.   49440

[Smollett, Tobias George]
     The adventures of Roderick Random... New York,
Pr. by S. Marks, for Scott and Seguine, 1819. CSmH;
MWA.   49441

Smyth, Alexander, 1765-1830
     Speech of the Hon. Alexander Smyth, in the House
of Representatives, on the Seminole War.   House of
Representatives.   January 21 [1819] [Washington?
1819] 36 p.   CtHT-W; GU-De; MWA.   49442

Snowden, Richard
    The history of North and South America... Phila-
delphia, Pr. by William Greer, for Benjamin Warner,
1819. 2 v. in 1. DLC; MWA; MeHi; NCH; NPalk;
NWatt; OCHP; TNP; Vi; ViW.   49443

Soane, George, 1790-1860
    The dwarf of Naples. A tragi-comedy, in five
acts... Baltimore, J. Robinson, 1819. 66 p. DLC;
MBr.   49444

A sober appeal to the Christian public. New-Haven,
Flagg & Gray and J. Babcock & Son, Church-street,
1819. 23 p. MiD-B.   49445

Social and camp meeting songs for the pious. Baltimore, 1819. 216 p. MWA.   49446

Society for propagating the gospel among the Indians
and others in North America.
    Report of the select committee... Cambridge, Pr.
by Hilliard and Metcalf, 1819. 28 p. MWA; WHi. 49447

Society for the prevention of pauperism in the city of
New York.
    Documents relative to savings banks, intemperance,
and lotteries.   Pub. by order of the Society for the pre-
vention of pauperism, in the city of New York. [New
York] Pr. by E. Conrad, 1819. 26 p. DLC; MH;
MiD-B; NbU.   49448

-- Report to the managers... New York, Pr. by Clayton & Kingsland, 1819. 13 p. MB; MH; MWA; N.
                                                49449
Society for the relief of worthy aged colored persons.
    New York, 1819. MB.   49450

Society for the relief of the widows and orphans of the
clergy of Protestant Episcopal Church.
    Rules of the Society for the relief of the widows
and orphans of the clergy of the Protestant Episcopal
Church, in the state of South Carolina; adopted the 21st
day of October, 1818, being the fifty-sixth anniversary

of the society.   To which is prefixed an historical account of the society.   Charleston [S.C.] Pr. by A.E.
Miller, for the society, 1819.   53 p. ScHi.   49451

Society for Worcester county and vicinity, auxiliary to
the Baptist board for foreign missions.
      Constitution...Worcester, Mass., Pr. by Manning
& Trumbull, 1819. MWA.   49452

Society of New-Castle County
      ...Report of the Committee appointed...[18 May
1819] to prepare a plan for an association to promote
the industry and domestic economy of the state...[Wil-
mington, Del. ? 1819] 19 p. DeGE.   49453

Society of the Protestant Episcopal church for the advancement of Christianity in Pennsylvania.
      Seventh annual report...Philadelphia, Pr. by Jesper
Harding, 1819.   24 p. DLC; MWA.   49454

Some particulars of the life of Thomas H. Daniels,
alias Daniel H. Thomas.   Annexed is a serious address to the public on the Pernicious effects of vice
and immorality.   Boston, 1819. 24 p. RHi.   49455

Song, for the anniversary of American independence,
1819.   Tune - "Ye Mariners of England."   Newburyport, Mass., Pr. by E.W. Allen, [1819] Broadside.
MWA.   49456

Songs for the nursery.   Hudson, N.Y., 1819. MB.
                                                     49457
The songster's pocket companion, or Gentlemen and
ladies' vocal museum...New Haven, A.H. Maltby &
co., 1819.   96 p. DLC; NN; RPB.   49458

Sopater, of Berea, pseud.
      A letter addressed to the Right Rev. Father in God,
Ricardus, D.D. by divine permission bishop of the
diocese of Virginia[!]...[Richmond? Va.] America, Pr.
by Elias & Thomas, 1819. 11 p. CSmH.   49459

Sorrows of Yamba; or the negro woman's lamentation.

Boston, Lincoln & Edmands, 1819. MWA; NcD; RPB.
49460

South Carolina (State)
    Acts and resolutions of the General Assembly of
the state of South -Carolina. Passed in Dec., 1818.
Columbia, Pr. by D. Faust, 1819. iii [4] p. DLC; Ia;
MdBB.   49461

-- The constitution of the United States, and of the
state of South Carolina, with the amendments... Columbia, Pr. at the Telescope press, 1819. 27 p. NN.
49462

-- Report of the civil and military engineer of the
state of South-Carolina, for the year 1818. [Columbia,
Pr. by D. Faust, 1819] 23 p. N.   49463

-- Reports of judicial decisions in the Constitutional
Court of South Carolina, held at Charleston and Columbia in 1817, 1818. Collected and published by virtue
of the act of Assembly of the said state, and under the
sanction of the judges of the said court... Charleston,
J. Mill, 1819. 2 v. CSfBar; MTaB; NN.   49464

South Carolina College Library
    Catalogue of books in the South-Carolina College
Library, September 1, 1819. Columbia, S. C., Pr. by
Daniel Faust, 1819. 54 p. ScU.   49465

Southern Evangelical Intelligencer. Charleston, S. C.,
W. P. Young, March 27, 1819, 1st issue. Weekly
newspaper. NHi.   49466

Southern Gazette. Bowling Green, Ky., Thomas Green,
Mar. 20, 1819, 1st issue. Brigham, p. 148.   49467

Southwick, Solomon, 1773-1839
    S. Southwick's address: To the Republican elec-
tors of the Middle District. February, 1819. [Albany?
1819] 14 p. N; NN; NbU.   49468

-- Two letters: by Solomon Southwick, anti-caucus
candidate for Senator for the Middle district, at the
ensuing election. Albany, Feb. 22d, 1819. Albany,

Pr. by E. & E. Hosford, 1819. 16 p. CSmH; N.
49469

Spalding, Joshua
The felicities of the Church of God...Newburgh,
N. Y., Ward M. Gazlay, 1819. 19 p. PPiXT.   49470

Spalding, Lyman
A history of the introduction and use of Scutellaria
lateri-flora (skullcap) as a remedy for preventing and
curing hydrophobia, occasioned by the bite of rabid
animals, with cases. New York, 1819. 30 p. DNLM;
MBM; NNNAM; PPAN.   49471

-- Reflections of yellow fever period; or, A particular
investigation of the long contested question, whether the
yellow fever can originate amongst us...New-York, C.
Turner & co., 1819. 23 p. DNLM; MB; MWA;
NNNAM.   49472

Spaulding, Jonah
A summary history of persecution, from the cruci-
fixion of our Saviour to the present time...Hallowell,
Me., Pr. by S. K. Gilman, 1819. 182 p. DLC; MWA;
MeLewB.   49473

The Spectator. By Addison, Steele, Parnell, Hughes,
Parker, Tickell, Budgell, Grove, Byron, Henley and
others. Philadelphia, Edward Earle, 1819. 12 v.
MChiL.   49474

-- -- Philadelphia, Robert Desilver, 1819. 12 v. CU;
MHa.   49475

-- -- Philadelphia, Thomas Desilver, 1819. 12 v. CSt;
MWA; NcD.   49476

Speech...New York, Pr. by E. Conrad, 1819. 20 p.
RP.   47477

Spencer, Walter G.
Outlines of practical surgery. New York, William
Wood & Co., 1819. 694 p. ViRMC.   49478

Sperry, Ebenezer Peck
    A summary history of the Church of Christ in
Dunstable, N.H. ...Amherst, N.H., [Pr. by Richard
Boylston] 1819. MWA.   49479

Spirit of the Times. Batavia, N.Y., O. Follett, Feb.,
1819, 1st issue. Weekly newspaper. MWA.   49480

The spiritual songster: containing a variety of camp-
meeting, and other hymns...1st ed. Frederick-town,
Md., George Kolb, 1819. 174 p. MWA; RPB.   49481

Sprague, Charles
    Ode. [Boston, Pr. by Munroe & Francis, 1819]
MWA.   49482

-- Eulogy, delivered in the chapel of Brown university,
on Mr. Isaac Fuller...Providence, R.I., Pr. [by Wm.
G. Goddard] at the office of the American, 1819. MWA.
                                                49483
Spring, Gardiner
    Essays on the distinguishing traits of Christian
character...Boston, Samuel T. Armstrong; John Sayre,
New York; W.W. Woodward, Philadelphia; and S.C.
& I. Schenk, Savannah, Ga., 1819. 184 p. MBAt;
MSwe; MWA; MiD-B; PPPrHi; TWcW.   49484

Spring, Samuel
    Three sermons to little children...Newark, N.J.,
Repub. by William Tuttle, 1819. 70 p. MBC; MWA.
                                                49485
Springer, Moses, 1796-1870?
    Songs of Zion: Being a collection of hymns, for
the use of the pious of all denominations...Ed. 3.,
improved. Hallowell, Me., E. Goodale, 1819. 160 p.
CtHT-W; MWA; RPB.   49486

Springfield bridge lottery.
    Managers' list of prizes, in the 7th class, Spring-
field bridge lottery...Boston, Pr. by Sylvester T. Goss,
1819. MWA.   49487

Sproat, Mrs. Nancy
Family lectures... Boston, Pr. by Samuel T. Armstrong, 1819. 202 p. MB; MNBedf; MPem; MWA; NNMer; RPB. 49488

[--] Poetic tales for children... New York, Samuel Wood & Sons and Samuel S. Wood & Co., Baltimore, 1819. MWA; RPB. 49489

[--] Stories for children; in familiar verse... Boston, Munroe & Francis, 1819. RPB. 49490

The square table. Hartford, Pr. by P. B. Gleason & co., for Samuel G. Goodrich, 1819. Nos. 1-2. 24 p. CtHi; MWA; RPB. 49491

Stanford, John
An authentic statement of the case and conduct of Rose Butler; who was tried, convicted, and executed for the crime of arson. Revised and approved by the ... Chaplain to the public institutions. New-York, Broderick and Ritter, 1819. 15 p. NHi. 49492

-- A catechism for the use of the schools in the Alms House, and the penitentiary, New York. New York, 1819. NHi. 49493

-- A discourse on the duty and advantages of improving our baptism. New York, Pr. by J. Gray and Co., 1819. 24 p. MWA; NN; NNG; TSewU; TxDaM. 49494

Stanley, William
Religious tracts. Vol. I. -- No. 2. The faith and practice of a churchman; extracted from the works of the Rev. William Stanley, Dean of St. Asaph. Charleston, S. C., Pr. by A. E. Miller, for the Protestant Episcopal Society for the advancement of Christianity in South Carolina, 1819. 56 p. MWA. 49495

The Star. Flemingsburg, Ky., Peter Akers, 1819, 1st issue. Newspaper. OHi. 49496

Star in the West. New York, Thomas W. Cummings,

Mar. 6, 1819, 1st issue.   Weekly newspaper. NjHi.
49497

State papers and publick documents of the United
States, from the accession of George Washington to the
presidency, exhibiting a complete view of our foreign
relations since that time... Ed. 3.   Pub. under the
patronage of Congress.   Including confidential documents, first published in the second edition of this
work.   Boston, Thomas B. Wait, 1819.   12 v. AzU;
CLSU; CSmH; DLC; IGK; IaDuC; IaU; InGrD; MB; MH;
MNBedf; MWA; MdBLC; MiD-B; MoSHi; NIC; NN; NNF;
NcAS; NcU; PU; RPA; TN; TNJ; USlC.   49498

A statement for the theological seminary of the Protestant Episcopal church made... February 1819, in the
convention... of South-Carolina... Charleston, S. C., Pr.
by J. Hoff, 1819. 14 p.   CSmH; MB; NNG.   49499

Statement of reasons for not believing the doctrines of
Trinitarians respecting the nature of God, and the person of Christ.   Occasioned by Prof. Stuart's letters to
Mr. Channing.   Boston, Wells, 1819.   64 p. PPPrHi.
49500

Statement of the committee appointed at a general
meeting of the citizens of the city of New York... on
the subject of colonizing the free people of color of the
United States.   New York, Pr. by Grattan & Banks,
1819.   8 p. NjR.   49501

A statement of the occurrences during a malignant
yellow fever in the city of New York... and of the check
given to its progress, by the measures adopted by the
Board of Health... New York, Pr. by William A. Mercein, 1819.   52 p. NNNAM.   49502

Steel, John Honeywood
    An analysis of the mineral waters of Saratoga and
Ballston... Ed. 2.   Albany, Pr. by Packard & Van
Benthuysen, for D. Steele, 1819.   118 p. CSdNHM;
DLC; MBAt; MH; MWA; NBMS; NN; NNNAM; NNS; NT;
ScCC.   49503

Stephens, Edward
    A plan for renovating the Navy. Newport, R. I.,
[1819] 33 p. MWA.   49504

Stevens, Ezra A.
    Geographical keys, containing a brief explanation
of the terms used in geography; questions on the map
of the world, North America, the United States, New-
England, South America, Europe, the British Isles,
Asia and Africa... Portsmouth, N. H., Pr. by S. Whidden, 1819. 52 p. MWA; NN.   49505

[Stevens, Robert, Jr.]
    An account of Odessa... Newport, R. I., Pr. by
William Simons, 1819. 18 p. DLC; MB; MBAt; MWA;
PPAmP; RHi.   49506

Stevens, Henry & Co., pub.
    Logarithmic tables. Table 1. Logarithms of
numbers from 1 to 10,000. Logarithms, sines, tangents, and secants, calculated for every degree and
minute of the quadrant. Table 3, A traverse table,
calculated for every degree of the compass. With directions for using. Schenectady, N. Y., Stevens, 1819.
108 p. CtHT-W; IaU; RPB.   49507

Stevenson, John
    On the morbid sensibility of the eye, commonly
called weakness of sight. Hartford, 1819. 99 p. RPM.
                                                       49508
Stewart, James
    Washington, Feb. 25th, 1819. Sir: The greatest
part of this session of Congress was spent in settling
the unfinished business of the last... The term for
which I was elected as your Representative in Congress, expires at the end of this session. I feel a
just sense of the very great obligation I am under for
the honor done me by the people of the District of Fayetteville, and I embrace this opportunity of making
them a tender of my most unfeigned thanks. I am,
Sir, with great respect, Your Obedient Servant, James
Stewart. [1819?] Broadside.   49509

[Stinchfield, Ephraim] 1761-1837
    Cochranism delineated: or, A description of, and
specific for a religious hydrophobia, which has spread,
and is still spreading, in a number of towns in the
counties of York and Cumberland, District of Maine.
By a watchman...Boston, N. Coverly, 1819. 22 p.
DLC; MH; MHi; MWA; Me; Nh-Hi.   49510

-- Some memoirs of the life, experience, and travels
of Elder Ephraim Stinchfield...Portland, Me., Pr. by
F. Douglas, at the Argus office, 1819. 105 p. MH;
MWA; Me;NHi.   49511

Stockton, Joseph
    The Western spelling book, containing a general
collection of tables and rules, for dividing, spelling,
and accenting almost all the words in the English language...Pittsburgh, Pa., Eichbaum, 1819. 156 p.
OClW; PSeU.   49512

Stoddard's diary, or Columbia almanack, for ...1820
...By Andrew Beers...Hudson, N. Y., Pr. by Ashbel
Stoddard [1819] [36] p.   MWA; NN.   49513

Storrs, Henry Randolph, 1787-1837
    Speech of the Hon. Mr. Storrs, in the House of
representatives, on the Seminole war...January 23
[1819] [Washington? 1819?]   18 p. DLC; MWA; WHi.
                                                  49514

The story of Joseph and his brethren...Wilmington,
Del., Pr. by R. Porter, 1819. MWA.   49515

Streeter, Sebastian
    A discourse, delivered at Portsmouth, N.H., Nov.
4th, A.L. 5809, at the consecration of Pythagoras
lodge...Portsmouth, N.H., Pr. [by Beck & Foster] at
the Gazette office, 1819. 16 p. MBFM; MWA.   49516

-- A sermon, delivered on Christmas morning, Dec.
25th, A.D. 1819. Portsmouth, N.H., Pr. [by Gideon
Beck and David C. Foster] at the Gazette office, 1819.
MWA.   49517

Strictures on Ezra Stiles Ely's review of "Methodist
Errour" &c. By a Wesleyan Methodist. Philadelphia,
1819. 12 p. PHi. 49518

Strictures on Mr. Lacock's report, in the Senate of the
U.S. on the Seminole war. [Washington, D.C.? 1819?]
21 p. MB; MH; MWA; OClWHi. 49519

Strobel, Martin
    A report of the trial of Michael and Martin Toohey,
on an indictment for the murder of James W. Gadsden,
esq. before the Honorable, Abraham Nott...at the
Court of sessions, held in Charleston, for January
term, 1819...By Martin Strobel...Charleston, S.C.,
Pr. by A.E. Miller, 1819. 162 p. MHL; ScU. 49520

Strong, T.
    The common reader...Ed. 2, cor. and imp. and
enl. Greenfield, Mass., Denio & Phelps, 1819. 228 p.
CtY; MDeeP; MH; MWA. 49521

[Strong, Titus] 1787-1855
    Candid examination of the Episcopal church, in
two letters to a friend. Norwalk, Conn., Pr. by
Nichols & Price, 1819. 24 p. CtHi. 49522

[--] A reply to the "Strictures" of Ebenezer Newcomb,
on a pamphlet entitled Candid examination of the Episcopal church. Greenfield, Mass., Denio & Phelps,
1819. 24 p. CSmH; CtHT; MBDiL. 49523

-- A sermon, delivered in Claremont, N.H. at the in-
stitution of the Rev. James B. Howe...Windsor, Vt.,
Pr. by Ide & Aldrich, 1819. 22 p. CSmH; MH; MWA;
Nh; VtHi; VtU; WHi. 49524

Strong, William Lightbourn
    The Israelite indeed. A sermon delivered at
Somers, January 12, 1819, at the funeral of Deacon
Joseph Sexton...Hartford, G. Goodwin & sons, 1819.
23 p. CtHi; Ct; MBC; MWA; NAuT; PPPrHi; RPB.
49525

Stuart, Moses, 1780-1852
A letter to Rev. Mr. Channing in favor of the doctrine of the Trinity, and in opposition to the sentiments contained in his Baltimore sermon. [Baltimore] Pr. by Sylvester T. Goss, 1819. 8 p. DLC; M. 49526

-- Letters to the Rev. Wm. E. Channing, containing remarks on his sermon, recently preached and published at Baltimore... Andover, Mass., Flagg & Gould, 1819. 167 p. CSt; MBAU; MWA; MWiW. 49527

-- Letters to the Rev. Wm. E. Channing... Ed. 2. Andover, Mass., Flagg and Gould, 1819. DLC; MH; MWA; ICMe. 49528

-- -- Ed. 3, cor. and enl. from the 2d. Andover, Mass., Flagg and Gould, 1819. 156 p. CtHT-W; MA; ICN; MCNC; MWA; NNUT; NjR. 49529

-- A sermon preached in the Tabernacle Church, Salem, November 5, 1818, at the ordination of the Rev. Messrs. Pliny Fisk, Levi Spaulding, Miron Winslow, and Henry Woodard... Andover, Mass., Flagg & Gould, 1819. 44 p. MWA; MeB; NjR. 49530

Stuart, Thomas Middleton
An inaugural essay on genius and its diseases; submitted to the examination... and publicly defended for the degree of Doctor of medicine, April 6, 1819... New-York, Pr. by Collins & co., 1819. 46 p. MBAt; MWA; NNC-M; NNNAM; OCHP. 49531

Suffolk, Co., Mass.
Rules of the bar of the County of Suffolk, June 1819. Boston, Pr. by Sewell Phelps, 1819. 23 p. CSt; MH-L; MWA; MiD-B; WHi. 49532

Sullivan, Richard, 1779-1861
Address delivered before the governour and council, members of the legislature and other patrons of the Massachusetts general hospital. At King's chapel, Boston, June 3, 1819... Boston, Pr. by Wells and Lilly, 1819. 32 p. CSt; CtY; DLC; DNLM; MB; MBAt; MBM;

MH; MHi; MWA;   NHi; NN; NNC; NNNAM; NjR;
OClWHi; PHi.   49533

Sumner, Joseph
    A sermon delivered at Shrewsbury, June 23d,
1812, the day which completed fifty years from the
time of his induction into the pastoral office over the
church and people in that place. Ed. 2. Worcester,
Mass., William Manning, 1819. 26 p. M; MBev; MH;
MSaE; MWA; MeBat; Nh-Hi.   49534

Sunday and adult school union, Philadelphia.
    The second report... Philadelphia, Pr. by Clark &
Raser, 1819. MWA.   49535

Sunday Morning's Messenger. Baltimore, 1819. A
newspaper. Brigham, p. 249.   49536

Sunday School Tracts... No. 6. Sketch of the Religious
Experience of Mahala Holcomb, who was killed by light-
ning, at Ticonderoga, N. Y. August 7, 1819, aged 12
years. Middlebury, Vt., Pr. at the Messenger office,
1819. 12 p. MWA.   49537

Swain, Joseph, 1761-1796
    Redemption, a poem in five books... Charleston,
S. C., Pr. by J. Hoff, for Robert Missildine, 1819.
114 p. DLC; MWA; PU; ScC; ScCC.   49538

Swan, James
    An address to the President, Senate and House of
Representatives, of the United States, on the means of
creating a national paper by loan offices, which shall
replace that of the discredited banks, and supercede the
use of gold and silver coin. Boston, Pr. by William
W. Clapp, from the Intelligencer press, 1819. 24 p.
DLC; IU; MWA; NCH; PHi; WHi.   49539

Sword's pocket almanack... for 1820. By Joel Sanford. New York, T. & J. Swords [1819] CtHT; MWA;
NHi; NNG; PHi; PU.   49540

Symmes, Thomas
     Historical memoirs of the late fight at Piggwacket
...Boston, N. Coverly, 1819. 24 p. MWA.   49541

                              T

Taggart, Samuel
     Christ Jesus the Lord, the great subject of gospel
preaching... Brattleborough, Vt., Pr. by John Holbrook,
1819.   21 p. CSmH; MBC; MH-AH; MWA; NNUT; RPB;
VtMiM.   49542

-- A farewell sermon, preached in Colrain, January
31, 1819... Greenfield, Mass., Pr. by Denio & Phelps,
1819.   34 p. CSmH; DLC; MA; MAnP; MBC; MH-AH;
MDeeP; MWA; RPB; VtMiM.   49543

Tallmadge, James, 1778-1853
     Speech... in the House of representatives of the
U.S. on slavery, to which is added the Proceedings of
the Manumission Society of the city of New York...
New York, Conrad, 1819. 20 p. MB; NjP.   49544

-- Speech of the Hon. James Tallmadge, Jun. in the
House of Representatives of the United States, on the
bill for authorizing the people of the Territory of Missouri to form a constitution and state government, and
for the admission of the same into the Union. February 16, 1819. 8 p. MoSHi; PHi; PPAmP.   49545

-- Speech in the House of Representatives of the U-
nited States, on the Seminole war. New York, E. Conrad, 1819. 31 p. ICN.   49546

-- -- Jan. 22, 1819. [Washington, D.C. 1819] 34 p.
CtHT-W; MWA; WHi.   49547

-- -- [1819?]   MWA.   49548

No entry   49549

Tammany Society or Columbian Order. New York.
     Address of the Society of Tammany, or Columbian
order, to its absent members, and the members of its

several branches throughout the United States. New-
York, Pr. by George L. Birch & Co., 1819. 39 p.
MB; MH; MWA; NN; PPM.   49550

-- Ohio.
    Address...to its absent members...Cincinnati, O.,
Pr. by Morgan, Lodge & co., 1819. 33 p. OCHP.
                                                49551
Tannahill, Robert
    Poems and songs, chiefly in the Scottish dialect.
By Robert Tannahill. A notice respecting the life and
writings of the author, is prefixed. New York, Pr.
by Broderick & Ritter, for John Caine, 1819. 228 p.
NNC; NjR.   49552

Tanner, Henry Schench
    The travellers guide through the state of New York,
showing all the important roads, post-towns, &c.
Philadelphia [1819] 52 x 65 cm. ICN.   49553

Tappan, Benjamin
    A sermon, delivered at the interment of the Rev-
erend Jesse Appleton...Hallowell, Me., Pr. by E.
Goodale, 1819. 39 p. CSmH; CtHT; CtY; DLC; MA;
MB; MBAt; MH; MNe; MWA; MeB; NN.   49554

Tappan, William Bingham
    New England, and other poems...Philadelphia, Pr.
by J.H. Cunningham, 1819. CSmH; IaU; MWA; PPL-R;
RPB.   49555

Tariff of duties on importations into the United States,
compiled for P. P. F. Degrand's Boston Weekly Report
of public sales and of arrivals...and revised and corrected by the Hon. The Sec. of the Treasury. Boston,
Elisha Bellamy, 1819. MiD-B.   49556

Taylor, Mrs. Ann (Martin)
    Reciprocal duties of parents and children...Phila-
delphia, Pr. by J. Maxwell, for Moses Thomas (Johnson's Head.), 1819. MWA.   49557

Taylor, Jeremy
    The life of our blessed Saviour Jesus Christ...
Philadelphia, D. Dickinson, 1819. MWA.   49558

Taylor, John
    A lecture on witchcraft; in which the whole secrets
thereof are disclosed.   Pittsburgh [Pa.] Pr. by Eichbaum and Johnston, 1819. 35 p. CSmH; MWA.   49559

[Taylor, Samuel] fl. 1786
    Stenography, or The art of short hand perfected
...Ed. 5, enl., cor. and imp. with an additional plate.
By C. Mangan.   Boston, R. P. & C. Williams, 1819.
16 p.   DLC; MB; MHi; MWA; NN; PHi; PPL-R; PU.
                                                49560
[Taylor, Vermilye]
    The banker, or Things as they have been! a farce,
in three acts.   By A. Tyro.   New York, 1819. 16 p.
MH; MWA.   49561

-- False appearances, or A hit on the dandies. A
farce in 3 acts, by Who do you think? New York, Atkinson, 1819. 16 p. ICU.   49562

[--] Things as they will be, or, All barkers are not
biters; a farce, in three acts.   By who d'ye think?
Ed. 2.   New-York, M'Duffee & Farrand, 1819. 17 p.
MH; RPB.   49563

Taylor, Waller
    Remarks of Mr. Taylor...on the bill to authorize
the people of Missouri to form a constitution...[1819]
MWA.   49564

Taylor, William
    The Christian's monitor, or Practical guide to fu-
ture happiness; A new Roman Catholic prayer book...
1st ed.   New York, W.H. Creagh, 1819. 385 p. DGU;
DLC; MWA; MdW; NNG.   49565

-- A sermon, on the festival of St. Patrick...New
York, Pr. by McDuffee & Farrand, 1819. MBAt; MWA.
                                                49566

Taylor, William, 1763-1838
    Mill dam survey. Map. [Boston, 1819] Size: 52 x
75 in. Scale: 20 rods to 1 in. MB.   49567

-- Plan of the aqueduct from Jamaica Pond to William's
store. [Boston, 1819] Size: 52 x 75 in. Scale: 20 rods
to 1 inch. MB.   49568

Teale, Thomas Pridgin
    A treatise on neuralgic diseases, dependent upon
irritation of the spinal marrow and ganglia of the sym-
pathetic nerve. Concord, N.H., Pr. by Hill and Barton, for Horatio Hill & Co., 1819. 120 p. MeB; RPM.
                                                  49569
Ten Eick, Coanrod
    A defence, delivered before the Classis of Mont-
gomery, October 29, 1819. By the Rev. Coanrod Ten
Eick. Auburn, N.Y., Pr. by David Rumsey, 1819.
27 p. CSmH; MWA; MnHi; NAuT; NjR.   49570

Tennessee (State)
    An act to revise and amend the militia laws of the
state of Tennessee, passed at Murfreesborough on the
19th of November, 1819...Nashville, Pr. by George
Wilson for G.A. & A.C. Sublett [1819] 31 p. CSmH;
MH-L; TKL.   49571

-- Acts of a local or private nature, passed at the 1st
session of the 13th General Assembly of the state of
Tennessee...Sept., 1819...Nashville, Pr. by George
Wilson, for G.A. & A.C. Sublett [1819] 220 p. DLC;
IU; In-SC; Ky; MH-L; MdBB; Ms; NNB; Nb; Nv; RPL;
T; TKL; WaU.   49572

-- Acts of a public or general nature, passed at the
1st session of the 13th General Assembly of the state
of Tennessee...Sept., 1819...Nashville, Pr. by Geo.
Wilson, for G.A. & A.C. Sublett [1819] 150 p. DLC;
IU; In-SC; Ky; MH-L; MdBB; Mi-L; Ms; NNB; Nb; Nj;
Nv; Or-SC; RPL; T; TKL.   49573

-- ...In General Assembly...29th November, 1819.
[Nashville? 1819] Broadsheet. O-Ar.   49574

-- Journal of the House of Representatives at the 1st
session of the 13th General Assembly...Murfrees-
borough, Pr. by G. A. & A. C. Sublett, 1819. 301 p.
CtY-L; DLC; MWA; T; TKL-Mc; TNJ; TU.   49575

-- Journal of the Senate at the 1st session of the 13th
General Assembly...Murfreesborough, Pr. by G. A. &
A. C. Sublett, 1819. 333 p. DLC; MWA; NN; T; TKL;
TNJ; TU.   49576

Tennessee Weekly Chronicle. Clarksville, Tenn., B.
H. Peeples, Jan. 27, 1819, 1st issue with this title.
A weekly continuation of "The Weekly Chronicle." DLC.
                                              49577

Tersteegen, Gerhard, 1697-1769
    Geistliche und erbauliche briefe über das inwendige
leben und wahre wesen des Christenthums...Erste
Americanische auflage...Libanon, Pa., Pr. by Joseph
Hartman, 1819. 2 v. in 1. CSmH; MH; MWA; MiU-C.
                                              49578

Texas Republican. Nacogdoches, Tex., Eli Harris,
Aug. 14, 1819, 1st issue. Newspaper. Brigham, p.
1069.   49579

Thalhimer, B.
    The annual register and military roster...Albany,
1819. 52 p. RPB.   49580

Thaxter, Joseph
    A scripture catechism. Boston, 1819. 30 p. MB.
                                              49581

Thayer, Caroline Matilda
    Religion recommended to youth, in a series of let-
ters addressed to a young lady...New York, Pr. by A.
Paul, for J. Soule and T. Mason and the Methodist
Episcopal church in the United States, 1819. 220 p.
MWA; Nh; RPB; TNT.   49582

Theatre. Last night but one, of Mr. & Mrs. Bartley's
appearance...May 21st, 1819...[Petersburg, Va.]
Whitworth & Yancey [1819] Broadside. Vi.   49583

The Theological repertory, and churchman's guide.

v. 1- Aug. 1819.   Washington City, J. C. Dunn...1819.
DLC; ICU.   49584

Thomas, David
    Travels through the western country in the summer
of 1816...Auburn, N. Y., Pr. by David Rumsey, 1819.
320 p.   CSmH; CtY; DLC; IC; ICHi; ICU; In; InU;
InRch; MB; MWA; MiD-B; NAuHi; NBuG; NCH; NIC;
NN; NRU; OCHP; OClWHi; OCU; PPiU; PU; WHi. 49585

Thomas, Joseph
    The trump of Christian union, containing a collec-
tion of hymns...Winchester, Va., Pr. by J. Foster,
1819.   401 p. Vi.   49586

Thomson, James
    The poetical works of James Thomson...Philadel-
phia, Pr. by G. L. Austin, for Benjamin Johnson, 1819.
MWA.   49587

Thomson, James
    The Seasons, by James Thomson, to which is pre-
fixed The life of the author, by P. Murdoch...New
York, Pr. by J. Gray & Co., for R. & W. A. Barton
and W. A. Barton, Richmond, Va., 1819. 220 p.
MWA; MiD-B; NRSB; NjP.   49588

-- ...The Seasons; with the Castle of indolence...New-
York, Pr. by Clayton & Kingsland, for W. B. Gilley,
1819.   237 p. GHi; LNX; MB; N; RNHi.   49589

Thomson, Samuel, 1769-1843
    Family botanic medicine with the preparation and
system of practice, under the nature and operation of
the four elements.   Boston, the author, 1819. 16 p.
MB; MBM.   49590

-- The secrets of that noted empyric Samuel Thompson, comprehending his theory of disease and mode of
practice. 1819. 8 p. MBM.   49591

Thurston, David
    Causes of an unsuccessful ministry. A sermon,

preached at the installation of the Rev. Henry Sewall
...Jan. 20, 1819. Hallowell, Me., Pr. by E. Goodale, 1819. 23 p. MBC; MWA; RPB.   49592

-- A sermon preached at the ordination of the Rev.
Samuel Johnson...in Alna, Nov. 25, 1818. By David
Thurston,...Hallowell, Me., Pr. by E. Goodale, 1819.
22 p. MeBat.   49593

-- Sermon, before the Somerset Association for the
reformation of morals, at their annual meeting in Nor-
ridgewock, February 17, 1819. Hallowell, Me., Pr.
by C. Govdale, 1819. 15 p. MWA; MeHi; RPB. 49594

Tibbits, George
     Address, delivered before the Rensselaer agricul-
tural society, at their first anniversary meeting, October 13, 1819...Troy, N.Y., Pr. by Wm. S. Parker,
1819. 16 p. NN; NT.   49595

Tinsley, James
     A new theory of yellow fever...Charleston, S.C.,
Pr. by W.P. Young and son, 1819. 55 p. DNLM; MWA;
ScC.   49596

To the aged.   New York, Religious Tract Society, 1819.
PPPrHi.   49597

To the Citizens of Portland.   You are this day asked
to decide...whether you will continue your ...with the
state of Massachusetts...or...take upon you this burden
of supporting a separate Government...And let us re-
member...to defeat this daring attempt to wrest from us
our excellent Constitution...July 26, 1819. Broadside.
                                                     49598
To the electors of the County of Morris.   The time has
now arrived...[Morristown? 1819] Broadside. NjHi.
                                                     49599
To the free Electors of the Fourth Eastern District.
Gentlemen: We take the liberty once more to address
you on the subject of the approaching election of a Federal Representative...being the same time of the meeting on the very interesting question of the separation of

the District of Maine... Bangor, Me., June 28, 1819.
Broadside. MeHi.   49600

To the freemen of Frederick County. In the last Herald,
a most grave and weighty charge was made against
Samuel Barnes... He was charged with being one of the
editors of the Whig, in 1812, when the mob took place
in Baltimore... [Frederick-Town, Md., 1819] Handbill.
MdHi.   49601

To the gallant defenders of Baltimore. Read the following certificate of Doctor Belt Brashear... and then
say what you think of Captain William's patriotism...
Belt Brashear. Oct. 1st, 1819. [Frederick Town, Md.
1819] Handbill. MdHi.   49602

To the people of Maine. Fellow Citizens! It is a
principle, resulting from the free spirit of our Constitution, that men in power should account to the people
for their official conduct... Boston, June 18, 1819.
Broadside. MHi.   49603

To the Polls: Freemen of Frederick County, the approaching election is an important one to you... [Fred-
erick Town, Md., 1819] Handbill. MdHi.   49604

To the votaries of pleasure. Written on New-Year's
eve 1819. New York, Methodist Tracts no. 37, 1819.
IEG.   49605

To the voters of Frederick County. Fellow citizens,
you have long known it to be the practice of the Federal Party to clandestinely circulate, a few days previ-
ous to every election, the most false and slanderous
publications... 30 Sept., 1819. [Frederick-Town, Md.,
1819] Handbill. MdHi.   49606

Todd, Charles Burr
     Life of Colonel Aaron Burr. New York, Green,
1819. PPiU.   49607

[Tompkins, Daniel D.] 1774-1825
     A letter to Archibald M'Intyre, esq., comptroller

of the state of New-York. [New York? 1819] 64 p.
DLC; MH; MWA; NNC.   49608

-- A letter to Archibald M'Intyre, esq., comptroller
of the state of New York. [New York? 1819] 16 p.
NjR.   49609

[--] -- Ed. 2. New York, Pr. by George L. Birch &
Co., 1819. 64 p. MWA; NIC; TxU.   49610

Tompkins, Isaac
    A sermon delivered in Amesbury, West parish,
July 7, 1819, at the ordination of the Rev. Moses
Welch...Newburyport, Mass., Pr. by W. and J. Gil-
man, for Charles Whipple, 1819. 23 p. MBC; MWA;
NN; RPB.   49611

Tone, William Theobald Wolfe, 1791-1828
    Essay on the necessity of improving our national
forces...New York, Kirk and Mercein, 1819. 112 p.
DLC; LNH; MWA; Nh-Hi; NjR; ScU.   49612

Torrey, Jesse, fl. 1787-1834
    The moral instructor and guide to virtue and happi-
ness. In five parts...With an appendix containing a
constitution and form of subscription for the institution
of free public libraries, etc...Ballston Spa, N.Y., Pr.
by U.F. Doubleday, for the author, 1819. 228 p.
CSmH; Ct; DLC; MWA; MiU; NNC; NT; OC; RP. 49613

-- -- Ed. 2, rev. Albany, Pr. by E. & E. Hosford,
sold by them and L. and B. Todd, Otsego, 1819. 228 p.
CSmH; MH; MWA; NNC; NjP; NjR; TWcW.   49614

-- A portraiture of domestic slavery in the United
States...Ballston Spa, N.Y., the author, 1819. (Anderson auction catal. 2016 (1925), item 293) 49615

Tour to Cowneck and North-Hempstead, in Queens Coun-
ty. In the form of a letter of a gentleman on Long-
Island, to his friend in the City of New-York. New-
York, Pr. by G.L. Birch & Co., 1819. Ct; NSmB.
                                             49616

Tourtelle, Étienne, 1756-1801
    The principles of health, (elements of hygiene;) or,
A treatise on the influence of physical and moral
causes on man, and on the means of preserving health.
From the 2d French ed., cor. and augm... Baltimore,
Pr. by J. D. Toy, 1819. 2 v. DLC; MdBM; MdBP;
NNNAM.   49617

Town and country almanack for 1820. Calculated by
John Sharp. Alexandria, D. C., John A. Stewart [1819]
MWA.   49618

-- Baltimore, Cushing and Jewett [1819] MWA. 49619

The town and country almanac, for the year of our
Lord, 1820... Calculated... by John Sharp... Baltimore,
J. Robinson [1819] [35] p. MWA; NNA.   49620

Town Gazette. Clarksville, Tenn., Thomas H. M'Keen,
July 5, 1819, 1st issue. Weekly newspaper. DLC.
                                                49621
Tract Association, Philadelphia.
    Christianity and infidelity contrasted. Philadelphia,
1819. (Tract no. 22) PSC-Hi.   49622

Transactions of a convention of delegates from several
moral societies... Albany, Pr. by E. and E. Hosford,
1819. 16 p. MWA; NHi; NjR.   49623

Treadwell, John, 1745-1823
    The inaugural address... (delivered at the inaugura-
tion of the Rev. Herman Daggett, as principal of the
Foreign mission school in Cornwall, Conn., May 6,
1818) [New Haven? 1819?] 6 p. CU-B; Ct; MSwe.
                                                49624
A treatise on agriculture; comprising a concise history
of its origin and progress, the present condition of the
art, abroad and at home, and the theory and practice
of husbandry, which have arisen out of the present state
of philosophical attainments in Europe. By a practical
farmer. Albany, Pr. by J. Buel [1819?] 168 p.
N Geno.   49625

A treatise upon the Sabbath... Schenectady, N. Y., Pr.
by Isaac Riggs, 1819. 32 p. MWA; NAlf.   49626

Tresize, Thomas
    The Christian's guide... Zanesville, O., 1819.
216 p. CSmH; IaDmD; MWA; NRAB; OClWHi; OHi;
PPPrHi.   49627

The trial in full, of Edward Arrowsmith for slandering
the character of the Rev. Alexander Cumming... New
York, Pr. by S. Walker [1819] 52 p. MoU; NjR. 49628

Trial of Holmes, Thomas Warrington and Edward Rose-
wain, for murder, Circuit Court of the United States,
Massachusetts, 1819. Boston, 1819. 20 p. MH-L.
                                                 49629
The trial of John Williams, Francis Frederick, John P.
Rog, Nils Peterson, and Nathaniel White, on an indictment for murder on the high seas; before the Circuit court of the United States; holden for the district
of Massachusetts, at Boston, on the 28th of December,
1818. Boston, Pr. by Russell & Gardiner, 1819. 92 p.
CSmH; MBeHi; MBS; MH; MMeT; MWeA; MdBP; MeP;
MnU; NIC-L; NN; NTSC; Nh; R; RPL; Vi; W.   49630

Trial of Samuel Davies, for the murder of Henry
Pendleton Smith, at a court held in Harrodsburg, Sept.
term, 1818... Frankfort [Ky.] Pr. by Kendall & Rus-
sels, 1819. 104 p. ICU; OCHP.   49631

Trial of Stephen and Jesse Boorn, for the murder of
Russel Colvin, with the subsequent wonderful discovery
of Colvin alive and an account of his return to Man-
chester, where the murder was alleged to have been
committed... Ed. 2. Rutland, Vt., Fay & Burt, [1819]
36 p. Ct; IcLaw; MH-L; MB-B; NN; NNS; Vt; VtHi.
                                                 49632
Trial of the Rev. Jacob Gruber, minister in the M. E.
Church for inciting slaves to rebel. Fredericktown,
Md., Pr. by Geo. Kolb, for David Martin, 1819. 111 p.
DLC; MdH; PPL-R.   49633

The tricks of the times, or, The world of quacks; a

farce, of domestic origin. In two acts. New-York, 1819. 24 p. DLC; MWA. 49634

Trimmer, Mrs.
Concise history of England. Boston, Munroe & Francis, 1819. MWA. 49635

The Trotter, Choker & Company exhibited. By a visitor...Columbia, Pa., pr. by Wm. Greer, for the publisher, 1819. 22 p. NN. 49636

True and surprising account of the appearance of the Devil! to a company of card players, in Manchester (Penn.) In letter from a gentleman in that town to his friend in New York. 1819. 12 p. MB. 49637

The true Briton (weekly). June 9, 1819 - Dec. 8, 1819. Boston, 1819. v. 1, nos. 1-27. IU. 49638

True stories related. By a friend to little children. New York, Samuel Wood & sons, 1819. 43 p. MWA. 49639

Trumbull, Benjamin, 1735-1820
A complete history of Connecticut...New Haven, Maltby, Goldsmith & Co., 1819. 2 v. MdBE. 49640

-- "What therefore God hath joined together, let not man put asunder."...Ed. 2 abridged. New Haven, Pr. by S. Converse, 1819. 40 p. CtHi; CtSoP; CtY; MB; MWA; MHi; PPPrHi. 49641

Trumbull, Henry
History of the discovery of America, of the landing of our forefathers, at Plymouth, and of their most remarkable engagements with the Indians, in New-England, from their first landing in 1620, until the final subjugation of the natives in 1679. To which is annexed, the particulars of almost every important engagement with the savages, at the westward, to the present day, including the defeat of Generals Braddock, Harmer and St. Clair, by the Indians at the westward, the Creek and Siminole[!] war, &c. By Henry Trumbull ...Boston, Pr. by S. Sewell, for the author, 1819.

256 p.   CSmH; CtHi; DLC; IC; ICN; MB; MBAt; MBr;
MH; MHingHi; MMeT; MSaE; MWeyHi; MWA; MWat;
MWiW; MeBa; MiU-C; MoSHi; MtBilP; NN; OClWHi;
RNR.   49642

Trumbull, pseud.
     The mischiefs of legislative caucuses, exposed in
an address to the people of Connecticut.   By Trumbull.
Hartford, Pr. by G. Goodwin & sons, 1819. 15 p.
C-S; CSmH; Ct; CtHi; CtHT-W; CtSoP; DLC; Ia-E; MH;
MWA; NHi; NN; NNC; NjN; PPL; RPB.   49643

Tuckerman, Joseph
     A sermon, delivered at the ordination of the Rev.
Samuel Gilman...Dec. 1st, 1819...Charleston, S. C.,
Pr. by A. E. Miller [1819?] 46 p. ICMe; MWA;
MdBD.   49644

-- -- Charleston, S. C., Pr. by A. E. Miller [1819?]
60 p. MWA.   49645

Tudor, William
     Memoirs of Hon. William Tudor.   By William Tu-
dor, Jr.   (Repr. from Coll. Massachusetts Historical
Society. 2d s. viii 285-325) [Boston, 1819] 41 p.
MHi; MSaE; RPB.   49646

Tuke, Henry, 1755-1814
     The principles of religion, as professed by the so-
ciety of Christians, called Friends...New-York, Samuel Wood & sons, 1819. 138 p. CSt; DLC; MBAt; MWA;
MdToH; PSC-Hi.   49647

Turner, Edward
     A discourse delivered at the Universalist meeting
house in Boston, August 19, 1819, at the installation of
the Rev. Paul Dean...Boston, J. T. Buckingham, 1819.
30 p. OClWHi.   49648

-- A series of lectures and occasional discourses...
Charlestown, Mass., Pr. by Bellamy and Green,
[1819] 13 p. CSmH; MWA.   49649

Turner, Jesse H.
     True heroism, an essential trait in the character
of a minister... Fayetteville, N.C., Pr. by D. Black,
1819. MWA. P.   49650

Turnpike Company
     Report of the Turnpike company, 1819. Harris-
burg, Pa., 1819. 17 p.   49651

Tuscaloosa Republican. Tuscaloosa, Ala., Thomas M.
Davenport, 1819, 1st issue. Brigham, p. 8.   49652

Tuscarawas Chronicle. New Philadelphia, Ohio, James
Patrick, Aug. 24, 1819, 1st issue. Weekly newspaper.
Brigham, p. 812.   49653

Two apple-trees and the two boys... New Haven, Sidney's press, J. Babcock & sons, 1819. 30 p. CtHi;
MWA.   49654

The two doves, and the owl... Hartford, Pr. by Roberts & Burr, for S.G. Goodrich, 1819. 14 p. CtHi;
MWA.   49655

[Tyler, Bennet]
     A serious call to those who are without the pale of
the Episcopal Church. By a consistent churchman. To
which is added, an appendix containing animadversions
upon the conduct of inconsistent churchmen. [New
Haven, 1819] 24 p. CtHi; DLC; MB; MWA; MBAt; MH;
NN; NNG.   49656

[Tyler, John]
     Universal damnation and salvation... Buffalo, N.Y.,
H.A. Salisbury, 1819. MWA.   49657

                         U

Union bank of Maryland
     An act to incorporate the stockholders in the
Union bank of Maryland. Passed at Nov. session, 1804,
chap. 48, together with the several supplements, and
the by-laws of said institution. Baltimore, Pr. by J.

D. Toy, 1819. 44 p. DLC; MdHi.   49658

Union Canal Company of Pennsylvania
    Accounts, (Oct. 11, 1812, to Dec. 8, 1818) [Har-
risburg, Pa., 1819] 8 p. PHi; PPHi.   49659

-- Report... Philadelphia, Pr. by John Bioren, 1819.
MWA.   49660

Union College, Schenectady, N.Y.
    Catalogus Senatus Academici, et eorum qui munera
et officia Academica Gesserunt, quique aliquovis gradu
exornati fuerunt in Collegio Concordiae, Schenectadiae,
in Republica Novi Eboraci, Schenectadiae: Excudebat
Isaacus Riggs. [1819] 16 p. CtHT; DLC; MB; MBC;
MH; N; NN; NSchU; OCHP; TNP; RNR; VtMiM. 49661

Union Sunday School Society abstract of Report of managers. Windsor, 1819. OCHP.   49662

United Brethren in Christ
    Doctrine and discipline of the United Brethren in
Christ.   Hagers-town, Md., Pr. by Gruber & May,
1819. 77 p. DLC; MWA; MdBE; MiDSH; ODaB. 49663

United Foreign Missionary Society
    The second annual report of the United Foreign
Missionary Society, presented at the annual meeting,
held in the City of New York, on Wednesday, May 12,
1819.   New York, Pr. by J. Seymour, 1819. 27 p.
NjR; PHi; PLT.   49664

United Society of Plymouth County and Vicinities
    Annual report of the United Society of Plymouth
county and vicinities (Mass.) Auxiliary to the Baptist
Board of Foreign Missions for the United States [1819?]
4 p. NRAB.   49665

United States
    An account of the receipts and expenditures of the
United States for the year 1818...Washington, D.C.,
Pr. by E. deKrafft, 1819. [173] p. MWA.   49666

-- An act making further provision for the sale of public lands. In the House of Representatives, Feb. 19, 1819. [Washington, D.C., 1819] (S. 76) DLC. 49667

-- An act providing for the better organization of the Treasury Department. In the House of Representatives. Feb. 25, 1819. [Washington, D.C., 1819] (S. 56) DLC. 49668

-- An act to protect the commerce of the United States, and punish the crime of piracy... Approved March 3rd, 1819. Broadside. DNA. 49669

-- Acts passed at the second session of the fifteenth Congress of the United States. [Washington, D.C., 1819] 116 p. CU; DLC; MDi; MWA; MsJS; PLL; R; RPB; Vi. 49670

-- Acts of the Parliament of Great Britain. January 27, 1819. Pr. by order of the Senate of the United States. Washington, D.C., Pr. by E. deKrafft, 1819. 12 p. DLC; G; NjP; PPiU; TxH. 49671

-- ... Additional regulations for the Medical Department of September 1818. Washington, D.C., 1819. 4 p. DNLM. 49672

-- Annual report of the Commissioners of the sinking fund. Feb. 5, 1819... Washington, D.C., Pr. by E. DeKrafft, 1819. 43 p. DLC; NjP; R. 49673

-- Annual report of the Secretary of the treasury, on the state of the finances. December 13, 1819. Read, and ordered to lie upon the table. Washington, Pr. by Gales & Seaton, 1819. 31 p. 4 broadsides. DLC; G; NjP; O; PPAmP; R. 49674

-- A bill augthorizing [!] an equitable settlement of the accounts of the late captain James M'Donald, of the Fourteenth Regiment United States Infantry. Jan. 18, 1819. [Washington, D.C., 1819] (H.R. 282) DLC.
49675
-- A bill authorizing the payment of a sum of money to

Thomas Shields. January 4, 1819. [Washington, D.C., 1819] (H.R. 258) DLC.   49676

-- A bill authorizing the purchase of live oak timber for building small vessels of war. January 4, 1819. [Washington, D.C., 1819] (H.R. 259) DLC.   49677

-- A bill concerning invalid pensions. February 5, 1819. [Washington, D.C., 1819] (H.R. 308) DLC.
49678
-- A bill concerning Navy agents. January 5, 1819. [Washington, D.C., 1819] (H.R. 263) DLC.   49679

-- A bill for establishing an additional Military Academy, and a Military School of Application. February 15, 1819. [Washington, D.C., 1819] (H.R. 321) DLC.
49680
-- A bill for the admission of the state of Maine into the Union, and to extend the laws of the United States to said state. December 21, 1819. [Washington, D.C., 1819] (H.R. 17.) DLC.   49681

-- A bill for the benefit of Thomas Carr and others. December 14, 1819. [Washington, D.C., 1819] (H.R. 5) DLC.   49682

-- A bill for the relief of Ambrose Vasse. February 3, 1819. [Washington, D.C., 1819] (H.R. 305) DLC.
49683
-- A bill for the relief of Beck and Harvey. December 16, 1819. [Washington, D.C., 1819] (H.R. 10) DLC.   49684

-- A bill for the relief of Clement B. Penrose. December 27, 1819. [Washington, D.C., 1819] (H.R. 24) DLC.   49685

-- A bill for the relief of Denton, Little, and Co., and of Harman Hendrick, of New York. December 18, 1819. [Washington, D.C., 1819] (H.R. 3.) DLC.
49686
-- A bill for the relief of Ether Shipley, administrator of Thomas Buckminster, late lieutenant in the thirty-

third regiment of United States' infantry. December
28, 1819. [Washington, D. C., 1819] (H. R. 25) DLC.
49687

-- A bill for the relief of Gad Worthington. December
13, 1819. [Washington, D. C., 1819] (H. R. No. 2)
DLC.   49688

-- A bill for the relief of James Hughes, of the state
of Illinois. February 3, 1819. [Washington, D. C.,
1819] (H. R. 306.) DLC.   49689

-- A bill for the relief of James Hughes. December
16, 1819. [Washington, D. C., 1819] (H. R. 11.) DLC.
49690

-- A bill for the relief of James Mackay, of the Missouri Territory. January 18, 1819. [Washington,
D. C., 1819] (H. R. 285) DLC.   49691

-- A bill for the relief of John B. C. Lucas. December 27, 1819. [Washington, D. C., 1819] (H. R. 23)
DLC.   49692

-- A bill for the relief of John Gooding and James
Williams. January 5, 1819. [Washington, D. C., 1819]
(H. R. 261) DLC.   49693

-- A bill for the relief of John Gooding and James Williams. December 13, 1819. [Washington, D. C.,
1819] (H. R. 4.) DLC.   49694

-- A bill for the relief of Louis Joseph De Beaulieu.
December 14, 1819. [Washington, D. C., 1819] (H. R.
6) DLC.   49695

-- A bill for the relief of Malcomb Bennett. January
4, 1819. [Washington, D. C., 1819] (H. R. 260) DLC.
49696

-- A bill for the relief of persons holding confirmed
unlocated claims for lands in the state of Illinois. December 31, 1819. [Washington, D. C., 1819] (H. R. 30)
DLC.   49697

-- A bill for the relief of the heirs of Anthony Burk.

December 28, 1819. [Washington, D.C., 1819] (H.R.
19) DLC.   49698

-- A bill for the relief of the legal representative of
Col. Daniel Appling and others. December 27, 1819.
[Washington, D.C., 1819] (H.R. 21) DLC.   49699

-- A bill for the relief of the legal representative of
Philip Barbour, deceased. December 16, 1819. [Wash-
ington, D.C., 1819] (H.R. 12) DLC.   49700

-- A bill for the relief of the surviving officers of the
army of the Revolution. December 14, 1819. [Wash-
ington, D.C., 1819] (H.R. 14) DLC.   49701

-- A bill for the relief of William M'Donald, Administrator of James M'Donald, deceased, late Captain in
the Army of the United States. December 14, 1819.
[Washington, D.C., 1819] (H.R. 7.) DLC.   49702

-- A bill for the relief of William Coffin, and others.
December 29, 1819. [Washington, D.C., 1819] (H.R.
27) DLC.   49703

-- A bill freeing from postage, letters and packets to
and from certain officers of agricultural societies.
February 12, 1819. [Washington, D.C., 1819] (H.R.
318) DLC.   49704

-- A bill further to establish the compensation of the
officers employed in the collection of the duties on imports and tonnage, and for other purposes. February
5, 1819. [Washington, D.C., 1819] (H.R. 310) DLC.
                                                            49705
-- A bill further to extend the Judicial system of the
United States. In the House of Representatives, January 27, 1819. [Washington, D.C., 1819] (S. 4) DLC.
                                                            49706
-- A bill in addition to the "Act making appropriations
for the support of the Navy of the United States, for
the year one thousand eight hundred and nineteen. December 20, 1819. [Washington, D.C., 1819] (H.R. 13)
DLC.   49707

-- A bill in addition to the acts prohibiting the slave
trade.   January 13, 1819.   [Washington, D. C., 1819]
(H. R.   272)   DLC.   49708

-- A bill in behalf of the Connecticut Asylum for teaching the deaf and dumb.   February 22, 1819.   [Washing-
ton, D. C., 1819]   (H. R.   327)   DLC.   49709

-- A bill in behalf of the New York Institution for the
instruction of the deaf and dumb.   December 28, 1819.
[Washington, D. C., 1819]   (H. R.   26)   DLC.   49710

-- A bill in relation to the Banks in the District of
Columbia.   February 12, 1819.   [Washington, D. C.,
1819]   (H. R.   320)   DLC.   49711

-- A bill making a partial appropriation for the military service of the United States for the year one
thousand eight hundred and twenty.   December 20,
1819.   [Washington, D. C., 1819]   (H. R.   15)   DLC.
                                                        49712
-- A bill making an appropriation for carrying into effect the provisions of an act, passed on the first day
of March, eighteen hundred and seventeen, entitled "An
act making reservation of certain public lands, to supply timber for naval purposes."   February 15, 1819.
[Washington, D. C., 1819]   (H. R.   322)   DLC.   49713

-- A bill making appropriations for the Public Buildings, for the purchase of a lot of land, and furnishing
a supply of water for the use of certain public buildings.   January 7, 1819.   [Washington, D. C., 1819]
(H. R.   265)   DLC.   49714

-- A bill making appropriations for the support of government for the year one thousand eight hundred and
nineteen.   January 26, 1819.   [Washington, D. C., 1819]
(H. R.   294)   DLC.   49715

-- A bill providing for the abolition of the existing Indian trading establishments of the United States, and providing for the opening of the trade with the Indians to
individuals.   January 15, 1819.   [Washington, D. C.,

1819]   (H. R.)   DLC.   49716

-- A bill providing for the payment for horses and
other property lost, captured, or destroyed, in the
Seminole War.   December 15, 1819.   [Washington,
D. C., 1819]   (H. R.   8)   DLC.   49717

-- A bill relative to the direct tax and internal duties.
January 18, 1819.   [Washington, D. C., 1819]   (H. R.
284)   DLC.   49718

-- A bill supplementary to "An act to provide for certain persons engaged in the land and naval service of
the United States, in the revolutionary war. " February
18, 1819.   [Washington, D. C., 1819]   (H. R. 323) DLC.
                                                     49719
-- A bill supplementary to, and to amend, the act, entitled "An act to continue in force an act further to
provide for the collection of duties on imports and tonnage, and for other purposes;" passed the third day of
March, one thousand eight hundred and seventeen. January 14, 1819.   [Washington, D. C., 1819]   (H. R. 273)
DLC.   49720

-- A bill supplementary to the act, entitled "An act for
the relief of Benjamin Wells. "   January 27, 1819.
[Washington, D. C., 1819]   (H. R.   295) DLC.   49721

-- A bill supplementary to the act, entitled "An act to
provide for the prompt settlement of public accounts. "
January 18, 1819.   [Washington, D. C., 1819]   (H. R.
283)   DLC.   49722

-- A bill supplementary to the Act establishing a mint.
January 26, 1819.   [Washington, D. C., 1819]   (H. R.
292)   DLC.   49723

-- A bill to alter and establish certain Post roads.
Feb. 10, 1819.   [Washington, D. C., 1819]   (H. R. 316)
DLC.   49724

-- A bill to amend an act, entitled "An act regulating
the Post Office establishment, " passed thirtieth April,

one thousand eight hundred and ten.   February 20,
1819.   [Washington, D. C., 1819] (H. R. 325) DLC.
49725

-- A bill to authorize certain insane persons to be
placed on the pension list, and for guardians to receive
pensions.   December 30, 1819.   [Washington, D. C.,
1819] (H. R. 28) DLC.   49726

-- A bill to authorize the Commissioner of the General
Land Office to remit the instalments due on certain lots
in Shawaneetown, in the State of Illinois.   December
23, 1819.   [Washington, D. C., 1819] (H. R. 18) DLC.
49727

-- A bill to authorize the people of the Missouri Territory to form a Constitution and state government, and
for the admission of such state into the Union on an
equal footing with the original states.   December 9th,
1819.   [Washington, D. C., 1819] (H. R. no. 1) DLC.
49728

-- A bill to authorize the President of the United
States, to select such tribes of Indians as he may think
best prepared for the change, and to adopt such means
as he may judge expedient, in order to civilize the
same.   January 15, 1819.   [Washington, D. C., 1819]
(H. R. 278) DLC.   49729

-- A bill to authorize the President of the United States
to take possession of East and West Florida, and establish a temporary government therein.   February 27,
1819.   [Washington, D. C., 1819] (H. R. 330) DLC.
49730

-- A bill to authorize the prosecution of suits, in the
nature of petitions of right, and informations of intru-
sion in cases in which the United States are concerned.
January 5, 1819.   [Washington, D. C., 1819] (H. R.
262) DLC.   49731

-- A bill to enforce those provisions of the act, entitled "An act to incorporate the subscribers to the
Bank of the United States, " which relate to the right of
voting for Directors.   January 16, 1819.   [Washington,
D. C., 1819] (H. R. 281) DLC.   49732

-- A bill to enforce those provisions of the act, entitled "An act to incorporate the subscribers to the Bank of the United States," which relate to the right of voting for directors. As amended in committee of the whole, on the state of the Union, and reported to the House on the 24th February, 1819. [Washington, D. C., 1819] (H. R. 281) DLC.   49733

-- A bill to establish an uniform system of Bankruptcy throughout the United States. December 16, 1819. [Washington, D. C., 1819] (H. R. 9) DLC.   49734

-- A bill to incorporate the inhabitants of the City of Washington, and to repeal all acts heretofore passed for that purpose. December 31, 1819. [Washington, D. C., 1819] (H. R. 29) DLC.   49735

-- A bill to increase the duties on certain manufactured articles imported into the United States. January 30, 1819. [Washington, D. C., 1819] (H. R. 299) DLC.   49736

-- A bill to increase the salaries of the Assistant Postmasters General. January 7, 1819. [Washington, D. C., 1819] (H. R. 266) DLC.   49737

-- A bill to provide for delivering up persons held to labor or service in any of the states or territories, who shall escape into any other state or territory. January 16, 1819. [Washington, D. C., 1819] (H. R. 280) DLC.   49738

-- A bill to provide for taking the fourth Census, or enumeration of the inhabitants of the United States. December 27, 1819. [Washington, D. C., 1819] (H. R. 22) DLC.   49739

-- A bill to provide for the more convenient organization of the courts of the United States, and the appointment of circuit judges. Printed by order of the House of Representatives. [Washington, D. C., 1819] (S. 3.) DLC.   49740

-- A bill to provide for the payment of the pensions of

persons under guardianship, to their guardians. January 13, 1819. Read and ordered to lie upon the table.
[Washington, D. C., 1819] (H. R. 271) DLC.   49741

-- Case of Thaddeus Mayhew. Jan. 6, 1819...Report
of the commissioners appointed to examine and assess
the damages occasioned by the troops of the United
States, in the neighborhood of the City of New Orleans.
[Washington, D. C., 1819] 19 p. DLC; G; NN; RPB.
49742
-- A charge delivered to the grand juries of the Circuit court, at October term, 1819, in Boston, and at
November term, 1819, in Providence, and published at
their unanimous request. By the Hon. Joseph Story.
[Boston? 1819] 8 p. DLC.   49743

-- Commercial regulations of the foreign countries with
which the United States have commercial intercourse,
collected, digested and printed, under the direction of
the President of the United States, conformably to a
resolution of the Senate, of the third of March, 1817.
Washington, D. C., Pr. by Gales & Seaton, 1819. 528 p.
CtHT; DLC; GEU; IaU-L; LNH; MH; MiDSH; MiU; MoU;
NIC; NNU; NcU; Nh; OO; OSW; PPAmP; PPL-R; PLFM;
USlC; ViU; WBeloC.   49744

-- Congressional directory, for the first session of the
sixteenth Congress of the United States. Washington,
D. C., Pr. by Daniel Rapine, 1819. 40 p. DLC; ViU.
49745
-- ...Constitution of the state of Alabama. December
6, 1819. Pr. by order of the House of representatives.
Washington, D. C., Pr. by Gales & Seaton, 1819. 24 p.
CtY; DLC; G; NjP; O; OCLaw; RPB.   49746

-- Constitution of the United States of America, as proposed by the convention held at Philadelphia, September
17, 1787, and since ratified by the several states: with
the amendments thereto. Published by order of the
House of representatives. Washington, D. C., Pr. by
Gales & Seaton, 1819. 44 p. DLC; NNC; NcG; PPL.
49747
-- Debate, in the House of representatives...on the

Seminole war, in January and February, 1819. Washington, D. C., Pr. at the office of the National intelligencer, 1819.   591 p. AZ; CSfU; CSmH; InRch;
KSalW; MB; MH; MHi; MSaE; MWA; MoSW; NNC; NcD;
NcU; Nh; NjP; OClWHi; OCY; OkU; P; RP; WHi.   49748

-- Documents presented by the Committee on Finance,
in relation to sundry estimates of money requested for
the expenses of the War Department, and military service of the United States, for the year 1819, January
22, 1819. Pr. by order of the Senate of the United
States. Washington, D. C., Pr. by E. DeKrafft, 1819.
85 p. DLC; G; NjP; O.   49749

-- Extract from act of Congress...protection of American seamen...1819. Broadside. RPJCB.   49750

-- ... Extracts from documents in the departments of
state, of the treasury, and of the navy, in relation to
the illicit introduction of slaves into the United States.
January 19, 1819. Washington, D. C., E. DeKrafft,
1819. 14 p. CtSoP; DLC; NcWfC; NN; O; OClWHi; R;
RP.   49751

-- In Senate of the United States, January 4, 1819.
The Committee of Commerce and Manufactures, have
considered the memorial of Nicholas Brown and Thomas
P. Ives, of Providence, in the state of Rhode Island,
which was referred to them by the Senate; and they submit the following report...[Washington, D. C., 1819]
4 p. DLC.   49752

-- In Senate of the United States, January 7, 1819.
The committee, to whom was referred the petition of
Charles Higgins, report...[Washington, D. C., 1819]
4 p. DLC.   49753

-- In Senate of the United States, January 11, 1819.
Mr. Sanford submitted the following motion for consideration: Resolved...[Washington, D. C., 1819] 1 p.
(The Senate requested accurate lists of all causes pend-
ing in United States Courts.) DLC.   49754

-- In Senate of the United States, Jan. 12, 1819. Mr. Roberts, from the committee of Claims, to whom was referred the petition of John Clark, report...[Washington, D. C., 1819] 2 p. DLC.   49755

-- In Senate of the United States, Jan. 14, 1819. Mr. Forsyth submitted the following motion for consideration: Resolved...[Washington, D. C., 1819] 1 p. (Inquiry regarding the mode of quartering soldiers.) DLC. 49756

-- In Senate of the United States, Jan. 20, 1819. Read, and ordered to be printed. The Committee, to whom was referred the petition of Alexander M'Cormick, repetition of Alexander M'Cormick, report...[Washington, D. C., 1819] 1 p. DLC.   49757

-- In Senate of the United States, Jan. 20, 1819. Read, and ordered to be printed. The Committee, to whom was referred the petition of B. & P. Jourdan, report...[Washington, D. C., 1819] 1 p. DLC.   49758

-- In Senate of the United States, Jan. 20, 1819. Read, and ordered to be printed. The Committee, to whom was referred the petition of Jacob Purkill, report...[Washington, D. C., 1819] 1 p. DLC.   49759

-- In Senate of the United States, Jan. 21, 1819. Mr. Williams, of Tennessee, from the committee on military affairs, submitted the following Estimate, with a Bill for the better organization of the Military Academy; which was read and ordered to be printed for the use of the Senate. [Washington, D. C., 1819] 1 p. DLC.
49760
-- In Senate of the United States, Jan. 22, 1819. The Committee of claims, to whom was referred the petition of Thomas J. Ogden, report...[Washington, D. C., 1819] 1 p. DLC; NjP.   49761

-- In Senate of the United States, Jan. 25, 1819. The Committee on Finance, to whom was referred a resolution to inquire into the expediency of prohibiting by law, the exportation of the gold, silver, and copper coins, of the United States, report...[Washington, D. C., 1819]

7 p. DLC; NjP.   49762

-- In Senate of the United States, Jan. 25, 1819. The
Committee, to whom was referred the petition of Ro-
bert Sewall, report... [Washington, D. C., 1819] 1 p.
DLC; NjP.   49763

-- In Senate of the United States, Jan. 26, 1819. The
Committee of Claims, to whom was referred the petition of Rees Hill, report... [Washington, D. C., 1819]
1 p. DLC; NjP.   49764

-- In Senate of the United States, Jan. 26, 1819. The
Committee on the Public Lands, to whom was re-
ferred the petition of Wm. Bell, report... [Washington,
D. C., 1819] 1 p. DLC; NjP.   49765

-- In Senate of the United States, Jan. 26, 1819. The
Committee on the Public Lands, to whom was referred the petition of Wm. N. Perry, and Mark Barnett, report... [Washington, D. C., 1819] 1 p. DLC;
NjP.   49766

-- In Senate of the United States, Jan. 28, 1819. The
Committee of Claims, to whom was referred the peti-
tion of Cornelia Schoonmaker... report... [Washington,
D. C., 1819] 1 p. DLC; NjP.   49767

-- In Senate of the United States, Jan. 28, 1819. The
Committee of Claims, to whom was referred the petition of David Henley, report... [Washington, D. C.,
1819] 1 p. DLC; NjP.   49768

-- In Senate of the United States, Jan. 28, 1819. The
Committee of Claims, to whom was referred the petition of Eli Hart, report... [Washington, D. C., 1819]
2 p. DLC; NjP.   49769

-- In Senate of the United States, Jan. 28, 1819. The
Committee of Claims, to whom was referred the peti-
tion of Gabriel Godfroy, of Michigan Territory, report
... [Washington, D. C., 1819] 1 p. DLC; NjP.   49770

-- In Senate of the United States, Jan. 29, 1819. The
Committee on Pensions, on the petition of Otho Ste-
phens, report...[Washington, D.C., 1819] 1 p. DLC;
NjP.   49771

-- In Senate of the United States, Jan. 29, 1819. The
Committee on Pensions, on the petition of Rachel Stur-
gis, report...[Washington, D.C., 1819] 1 p. DLC;
NjP.   49772

-- In Senate of the United States, Jan. 29, 1819. The
Committee on Pensions, on the petition of William
M'Farland, report...[Washington, D.C., 1819] 1 p.
DLC; NjP.   49773

-- In Senate of the United States, Jan. 29, 1819. The
Committee on Pensions, to whom was referred the
case of Peter Francisco, report...[Washington, D.C.,
1819] 1 p. DLC; NjP.   49774

-- In Senate of the United States, Feb. 1, 1819. Mr.
Barbour submitted the following resolution, which was
read, and passed to a second reading: Resolved...
[Washington, D.C., 1819] 1 p. (On the employment of
a skillful artist to ascertain the latitude of thirty-six
degrees thirty minutes north, on the west bank of Tennessee River.) DLC; NjP.   49775

-- In Senate of the United States, Feb. 2, 1819. The
Committee to whom was referred the petition of Benja-
min Putny, report...[Washington, D.C., 1819] 1 p.
DLC; NjP.   49776

-- In Senate of the United States, Feb. 2, 1819. The
Committee, to whom was referred the petition of Pierre
Lacoste, report...[Washington, D.C., 1819] 1 p. DLC;
NjP.   49777

-- In Senate of the United States, Feb. 3, 1819. The
Committee of Claims, to whom was referred the peti-
tion of Joseph Dozet and Antoine Bourgoud, report...
[Washington, D.C., 1819] 1 p. DLC; NjP.   49778

-- In Senate of the United States, Feb. 3, 1819. The Committee, to whom was referred the petition of Christopher Fowler, report...[Washington, D.C., 1819] 1 p. DLC; NjP.   49779

-- In Senate of the United States, Feb. 9, 1819. The Committee on Military Affairs, to whom was referred the petition of Harbaugh and Potter, report...[Washington, D.C., 1819] 1 p. DLC; NjP.   49780

-- In Senate of the United States, Feb. 9, 1819. The Committee on the public lands being instructed "to inquire into the expediency of so altering the laws respecting the sale of the public lands, that from and after the .....day of ..... next, credit shall not be given on such sales," report...[Washington, D.C., 1819] 5 p. DLC; NjP.   49781

-- In Senate of the United States, Feb. 9, 1819. The Committee, to whom was referred the petition of Joseph Lefebre, report...[Washington, D.C., 1819] 1 p. DLC; NjP.   49782

-- In Senate of the United States, Feb. 10, 1819. Mr. Burrill...To whom was referred the memorial of William Thornton, reported the following bill...A bill relative to the patent office, and to the salary of the Superintendent thereof. 1 p. DNA.   49783

-- In Senate of the United States, Feb. 15, 1819. The Committee of Claims, to whom was referred the memorial of Vincent Grant, of Buffalo, in the state of New York, report...[Washington, D.C., 1819] 1 p. DLC; NjP.   49784

-- In Senate of the United States, Feb. 16, 1819. The Committee on post offices and post roads, to whom was referred a resolution of the Senate of the 4th inst. instructing them to "inquire into the expediency of authorizing the Postmaster General to employ an armed guard for the protection of the mails...", Resolved... [Washington, D.C., 1819] 1 p. DLC; NjP.   49785

-- In Senate of the United States, Feb. 16, 1819.
Statements respecting the sale of the public lands.
[Washington, D. C., 1819] 3 p. DLC; NjP.   49786

-- In Senate of the United States, Feb. 19, 1819. The
Committee on military affairs, to whom was referred
the petition of Captain Biggars' company, report...
[Washington, D. C., 1819] 1 p. DLC; NjP.   49787

-- In Senate of the United States, Feb. 19, 1819. The
Joint Committee, on the subject of the Public Printing,
report...[Washington, D. C., 1819] 3 p. DLC; NjP.
                                                  49788
-- In Senate of the United States, Feb. 24, 1819. Mr.
Lacock, from the committee appointed in pursuance of
the resolution of the Senate, of the 18th of December
last, "That the message of the President, and documents, relative to the Seminole war, be referred to a
select committee...", report...[Washington, D. C.,
1819] 50 p. DLC; NjP.   49789

-- In Senate of the United States, Mar. 3, 1819. Mr.
Lacock, from the committee appointed in pursuance of
the resolution of the Senate of the 18th of December,
1818, on the subject of the Seminole war, communicated the following additional testimony, which was
read; and, ordered to be printed for the use of the Senate. [Washington, D. C., 1819.] 5 p. DLC; NjP. 49790

-- In Senate...Dec. 14, 1819. Agreeably to notice
given, Mr. Dickerson asked and obtained leave to in-
troduce the following resolution...A resolution proposing an amendment to the Constitution of the U. S., as it
respects the choice of electors of the President and
Vice President...[Washington, D. C., 1819] 1 p. DLC;
NjP.   49791

-- In Senate...Dec. 15, 1819. Ordered that the resolution proposing an amendment to the Constitution...be
referred to Mr. Dickerson, Mr. Trimble, Mr. Brown,
Mr. Elliott, Mr. Logan...[Washington, D. C., 1819]
1 p. DLC; NjP.   49792

-- In Senate...Dec. 20, 1819. Mr. Roberts, from the
Committee appointed on the 16th instant, who were directed to ascertain whether convenient apartments could
be had in the North Wing of the Capitol, for the accommodation of the committees and officers of the Senate, reports...[Washington, D.C., 1819] 2 p. DLC;
NjP.   49793

-- In Senate...Dec. 20, 1819. Mr. Sanford, from the
Committee of Commerce and Manufactures, made the
following report... The exports and imports of the U-
nited States...[Washington, D.C., 1819] 34 p. DLC;
NjP.   49794

-- In Senate...Dec. 27, 1819. Mr. Burrill, from the
committee appointed to arrange and report the rules
for conducting business in the Senate...report...[Wash-
ington, D.C., 1819] 8 p. DLC; NjP.   49795

-- In Senate...Dec. 28, 1819. Mr. Logan submitted
the following motion for consideration, which was read,
and ordered printed...[Washington, D.C., 1819] 1 p.
(Concerning branches of the Bank of the United States)
DLC; NjP.   49796

-- In Senate...Dec. 28, 1819. Mr. Lowndes' motion. Ordered to lie on the table, and be pr. [Washington, D.C.,
1819] 1 p. (Concerning unexpended balances of the War
and Navy departments.) DLC.   49797

-- In Senate...Dec. 28, 1819. Read, and ordered
printed. Mr. Roberts, from the committee of claims
to whom was referred the petition of Benjamin Putney,
submit the following report...[Washington, D.C., 1819]
1 p. DLC; NjP.   49798

-- In Senate...Dec. 28, 1819. Read, and ordered to
be printed...Mr. Roberts, from the committee of
claims, to whom was referred the petition of Jasper
Parrish, submit the following report...[Washington,
D.C., 1819] 1 p. DLC; NjP.   49799

-- In Senate...Dec. 29, 1819. Mr. Roberts, from the

committee of claims, to whom was referred the petition of Noah Brown, for himself and others, submit the
following report...[Washington, D.C., 1819] 2 p. DLC;
NjP.   49800

-- In Senate...Dec. 29, 1819.   Mr. Roberts, from the
committee of claims, to whom was referred the petition of Rebecca Hodgson, submit the following report
...[Washington, D.C., 1819] 1 p. DLC; NjP.   49801

-- Journal, acts and proceedings of the convention, as-
sembled at Philadelphia, Monday, May 14, and dis-
solved Monday, September 17, 1787, which formed the
Constitution of the United States...Boston, Thomas B.
Wait, 1819. 510 p. CLSU; CSmH; CSfLaw; DGU; DLC;
GEU; ICN; IaGG; MB; MH; MWA; MWiW; MdBE;
MdBS; MiD; Mi-L; NB; NGcA; NIC; NN; NNLI; NbO;
Nh; Nh-Hi; NjR; OAU; OCHP; PHi; PPAmP; PP;
PPL-R; PMA; PPiAL; PU; RNR; RPA; ScCC; ScU;
TChU; TJoT; WHi; WU.   49802

-- A journal of a march performed by the Corps of
Cadets of the United States Military Academy in the
year eighteen hundred and nineteen.   Newburgh, N.Y.,
Pr. by Uriah C. Lewis, 1819. 44 p. NWM.   49803

-- Journal of the House of Representatives of the U-
nited States, at the second session of the fifteenth Congress...Washington, D.C., Pr. by E. DeKraft,
1818! [1819] 433 p. CoFcS; G; MiD-B; NNLI; NUtHi;
Nj; O; PPAmP; PU; TU.   49804

-- Journal of the Senate of the United States of America, being the second session of the fifteenth Congress
...Washington, Pr. by E. DeKrafft, 1818! [1819] 435
p. NNU; NUtHi; NjP; O; PPAmP; PMA; PScr; PU;
TU.   49805

-- Letter from the Comptroller of the Treasury, transmitting a list made out by the Register of the Treasury,
of those persons who have rendered their accounts for
settlement within the year, January 5, 1819. Washington, Pr. by E. DeKrafft, 1819. 5 p. DLC; G; NN;

O; R.   49806

-- Letter from the Comptroller of the Treasury, transmitting a list of balances, on the books of the Register,
which appear to have been due more than three years
prior to the thirtieth of September last, or to have remained unsettled on that day.   February 24, 1819.
Washington, D. C., Pr. by E. DeKrafft, 1819. 1 p. +
19 Broadsides.   DLC; KyDC; NjP; O.   49807

-- Letter from the Comptroller of the Treasury, transmitting a report of the fourth auditor of the balances on
his books, which appear to have been due more than
three years prior to the thirtieth September last, or to
have remained unsettled on that day.   February 10,
1819.   Washington, D. C., Pr. by E. DeKrafft, 1819.
3 p.   DLC; NjP; R.   49808

-- Letter from the Comptroller of the Treasury, transmitting an abstract of monies advanced prior to March
3, 1809, and which remain to be accounted for on the
books of the third auditor of the treasury... February
18, 1819.   Washington, D. C., Pr. by E. DeKrafft,
1819.   DLC; KyDC; MoU; NjP; O; R.   49809

-- Letter from the Postmaster General to the Chairman of the Committee on the Post Office and Post
Roads, as to the expediency of authorizing the Post-
master General to employ an armed guard for the protection of the mails of the United States, on such mail
routes as he may deem necessary, Feb. 16, 1819.
Washington, D. C., Pr. by E. DeKrafft, 1819. 4 p.
DLC; G; NjP; O.   49810

-- Letter from the Postmaster General, transmitting a
list of names of the clerks employed in his office during the year 1818, and the compensation received by
each.   February 9, 1819... Washington, D. C., Pr. by
E. DeKrafft, 1819. 6 p. DLC; NjP; R.   49811

-- Letter from the Secretary of State, transmitting a
list of the names of persons to whom patents have been
granted, for any useful invention, from the first of Jan-

uary, 1818, to first of January, 1819. Washington,
D. C., Pr. by E. DeKrafft, 1819. 13 p. DLC; G; NN;
PPAmP; R.   49812

-- Letter from the Secretary of the Navy to the Chairman of the Committee of Ways and Means, explanatory
of the Expenditures of Appropriations for the Naval Service, during the year 1819. December 20, 1819.
Washington, D. C., Pr. by Gales & Seaton, 1819. 7 p.
DLC; G; O; NjP; R.   49813

-- Letter from the Secretary of the Navy, transmitting
a statement of the contracts made by the Navy Commissioners during the year 1818. January 11, 1819...
Washington, D. C., Pr. by E. DeKrafft, 1819. 12 p.
DLC; G; NN; O; R.   49814

-- Letter from the Secretary of the Navy, transmitting
copies of the instructions, which have been issued to
Naval Commanders, upon the subject of the importation
of slaves, made in pursuance of a resolution of the
House of Representatives, of the fourth January, inst.
January 12, 1819. Washington, D. C., Pr. by E. De-
Krafft, 1819. DLC; G; NN; O; R; RP.   49815

-- Letter from the Secretary of the Navy, transmitting
in obedience to a Resolution of the House of Representatives of the twenty-sixth ultimo, sundry documents
relating to the destruction of the Negro Fort in East
Florida, in the month of July, 1816. February, 1819,
...Washington, D. C., Pr. by E. DeKrafft, 1819. 21 p.
DLC; NN; Nh-Hi; O; R.   49816

-- Letter from the Secretary of the Navy, transmitting
lists of the clerks employed in the Navy Department
and the office of the Commissioners of the Navy during
the year 1818 and the salaries paid to each. January
11, 1819, read and ordered to lie upon the table.
Washington, D. C., Pr. by E. DeKrafft, 1819. 6 p.
DLC; G; NN; O; R.   49817

-- Letter from the Secretary of the Navy, transmitting
statements in relation to the Navy Pension Fund. Janu-

ary 12, 1819. Washington, D.C., Pr. by E. DeKrafft, 1819. 38 p. DLC; G; NN; O; R.   49818

-- Letter from the Secretary of the Navy transmitting statements of the expenditure and application of moneys drawn from the treasury on account of the navy for one year, preceeding the 30th September 1818 and the unexpended balances of former appropriations, January 11, 1819. Washington, D.C., Pr. by E. DeKrafft, 1819. 4 p. DLC; G; NN; O; R.   49819

-- Letter from the Secretary of the Navy, transmitting sundry statement[!] and papers, showing the provisions which have been made for the accommodation of seamen; the number of persons accommodated, and the expense attending the same. Prepared in obedience to a Resolution of the House of Representatives, of April 17, 1818. January 14, 1819. Washington, D.C., Pr. by E. DeKrafft, 1819. 35 p. DLC; NN; O; R.   49820

-- ... Letter from the Secretary of the Navy, transmitting sundry statements, in relation to the expenditure of appropriations, to reward the officers and crews of certain vessels for captures made during the late war with Great Britain... Dec. 17, 1818. Washington city, Pr. by E. DeKrafft, 1819. 87 p. CSmH; DLC; G; NjP; R; RPB.   49821

-- ... Letter from the Secretary of the Treasury, communicating information, in obedience to a resolution of the House of representatives, of the 22d instant, in relation to balances transferred from the Treasury to the United States bank, under... agreement with the receiving banks, of 31st January, 1817. February 25, 1819. Washington, D.C., Pr. by E. DeKrafft, 1819. 3 p. DLC; NjP; O; OO; RPB.   49822

-- Letter from the Secretary of the Treasury, in obedience to a resolution of the Senate, to inquire into the expediency of continuing in force the Act of the 29th of April, 1816, regulating the currency of certain foreign coins, within the United States, Jan. 25, 1819. Pr. by order of the Senate of the United States. Washing-

ington, D. C., Pr. by E. DeKrafft, 1819. 11 p. DLC;
G; NjP; O; WHi.   49823

-- ... Letter from the Secretary of the Treasury, communicating information pursuant to a resolution of the
House of representatives, of the 22d instant, in relation to the balances due by the state banks to the Bank
of the United States.   February 25, 1819...Washington,
D. C., Pr. by E. DeKrafft, 1819.   3 p. DLC; KyDC;
NjP; O; R.   49824

-- Letter from the Secretary of the Treasury, in obedience to a resolution of the 24th ultimo, directing the
Secretary of the treasury to lay before the Senate, information relative to the effect of "An act to suspend,
for a limited time, the sale or forfeiture of lands" of
the 18th of April last, upon the receipts into the treasury...Jan. 6, 1819.   Pr. by order of the Senate of the
United States.   Washington, D. C., Pr. by E. DeKrafft,
1819.   5 p. DLC; G; O.   49825

-- Letter from the Secretary of the Treasury, in reply
to one from the Chairman of the committee of finance
respecting the coasting trade.   February 5, 1819.
Printed by order of the Senate of the United States.
Washington, D. C., Pr. by E. DeKrafft, 1819. 4 p.
DLC; G; NjP; O; RP.   49826

-- Letter from the Secretary of the Treasury, submit-
ting to the Committee of finance, an official statement
of the gross amount of duties upon merchandise and
tonnage, which accrued during the two first quarters of
the year 1817, and a like statement for the same quarters of the year 1818.   February 3, 1819.   Pr. by order of the Senate of the United States.   Washington,
D. C., Pr. by E. DeKrafft, 1819. 4 p. DLC; NjP; O.
                                                   49827
-- Letter from the Secretary of the Treasury, to the
Chairman of the Committee of Ways and Means, transmitting a statement of the gross amount of duties of
merchandise and tonnage, for the two first quarters of
the year 1817.   Feb. 5, 1819.   Washington, D. C., Pr.
by E. DeKrafft, 1819. 4 p. CoU; DLC; MoU; NjP;

R.   49828

-- Letter from the Secretary of the Treasury, to the
Chairman of the Committee on Naval Affairs, transmitting the names of such persons, as have settled
their accounts at the Treasury since the report of the
eighteenth ultimo of Naval Agents whose accounts then
remained unsettled.   February 2, 1819.   Washington,
D. C., Pr. by E. DeKrafft, 1819. 4 p. DLC; NN; O;
R.   49829

-- Letter from the Secretary of the Treasury to the
Committee of Ways and Means, in relation to moneys
drawn from the Treasury for the War and Navy Departments, and of re-payments of money drawn for those
departments.   December 28, 1819... Washington, D. C.,
Pr. by Gales & Seaton, 1819. 6 p. DLC; NjP; O; R.
                                                      49830
-- Letter from the Secretary of the Treasury, transmitting a list of the clerks employed in the Treasury
Department during the year 1818, and the compensation
allowed to each.   January 19, 1819... Washington, D. C.,
Pr. by E. De Krafft, 1819. 22 p. DLC; NN; O; R.
                                                      49831
-- Letter from the Secretary of the Treasury, transmitting a report in obedience to a resolution of the
second instant, in relation to the memorial of the Gov-
ernors of New York Hospital.   January 5, 1819.   Pr.
by order of the Senate of the United States.   Washington, D. C., Pr. by E. DeKrafft, 1819. 6 p. DLC; G;
NNNAM; O.   49832

-- Letter from the Secretary of the Treasury, trans-
mitting a statement of the exports from the United
States during one year, ending on the thirtieth of Sep-
tember, 1819.   December 17, 1819.   Washington, D. C.,
Pr. by Gales & Seaton, 1819. 28 p. DLC; G; NjP; O;
R.   49833

-- Letter from the Secretary of the Treasury, transmitting an abstract of the official emoluments, &c of the
officers of the customs, for the year 1818, so far as
they have rendered the statements required of them by

law.   Feb. 24, 1819.   Washington, D. C., Pr. by E.
DeKrafft, 1819. 1 p. + 6 broadsides.   DLC; NjP; O.
                                              49834
-- Letter from the Secretary of the Treasury, trans-
mitting an estimate of the appropriations proposed for
the year 1820. December 27, 1819. Referred to the
Committee of Ways and Means. Washington, Pr. by
Gales & Seaton, 1819. 72 p. DLC; NjP; O; R.   49835

-- ... Letter from the Secretary of the Treasury, transmitting an estimate of the appropriations for the year
1820... Washington, D. C., Pr. by Gales & Seaton, 1819.
51 p. ([U. S. 16th Cong., 1st sess., 1819-1820. House.
Doc.] 13) DeGE.   49836

-- Letter from the Secretary of the Treasury, trans-
mitting information of the sums of money paid to the
Attorney General for extra services. March 3, 1819.
Washington, D. C., Pr. by E. DeKrafft, 1819. 6 p.
DLC; KyDC; NjP; R; O.   49837

-- Letter from the Secretary of the Treasury, transmitting pursuant to a resolution of the House of Representatives, of the twentieth April last, a statement, calculated to show the effect of changing the charges of specific duties on certain imported articles, to duties ad
valorem, etc.   February 8, 1819... Washington, D. C.,
Pr. by E. DeKrafft, 1819. 3 p. DLC; NjP; R. 49838

-- Letter from the Secretary of the Treasury, transmitting statements of payments made according to law,
at the Treasury during the year 1818.   January 18,
1819. Washington, D. C., Pr. by E. DeKrafft, 1819.
13 p. DLC; NN; O; PScr; R.   49839

-- Letter from the Secretary of the Treasury, transmitting statements of the debts, credits, and funds of
the Banks of the District of Columbia, incorporated by
the Act, third March, 1818.   January 12, 1819, read
and ordered to lie on the table. Washington, D. C., Pr.
by E. DeKrafft, 1819. 10 p. G; O; PPiU.   49840

-- Letter from the Secretary of the Treasury, transmitting statements of the exports of the United States during the year ending thirtieth, September, 1818. January 4, 1819, read and ordered to lie upon the table. Washington, D. C., Pr. by E. DeKrafft, 1819. 31 p. DLC; NN; O; R.   49841

-- Letter from the Secretary of the Treasury, transmitting statements of the debts, credits, and funds of all the Banks in the District of Columbia, not embraced in the terms of the resolution of the House of Representatives of the 7th of January, instant, January 20, 1819...Washington, D. C., Pr. by E. DeKrafft, 1819. 10 p. DLC; NN; R.   49842

-- Letter from the Secretary of the Treasury, transmitting statements of the importations of goods, wares, and merchandise, in American and foreign vessels; and an aggregate view of both, from first October, 1816, to thirtieth September, 1817. Feb. 10, 1819...Washington, D. C., Pr. by E. DeKrafft, 1819. 262 p. DLC; NjP; R.   49843

-- Letter from the Secretary of the Treasury, transmitting statements relative to the internal duties and direct tax. Dec. 18, 1818...Washington, D. C., Pr. by E. DeKrafft, 1819. 33 p., 40 broadsides. CoU; DLC; In; NjP; O; R.   49844

-- Letter from the Secretary of the Treasury, transmitting sundry statements from the Bank of the United States, of its concerns and transactions, in obedience to a resolution of the Senate of the 15th April last. Philadelphia, Pr. by W. Fry, 1819. 24 p. DeGE.
49845

-- Letter from the Secretary of the Treasury, transmitting sundry statements, in relation to the mint of the United States. February 25, 1819...Washington, D. C., Pr. by E. DeKrafft, 1819. 4 p. + 3 broadsides. DLC; NjP; O; R.   49846

-- Letter from the Secretary of the Treasury, transmitting sundry statements relative to the internal duties and direct taxes. Dec. 17, 1819. ...Washington, D. C.,

Pr. by Gales & Seaton, 1819. 30 p., 28 broadsides.
DLC; NjP. 49847

-- Letter from the Secretary of the Treasury transmitting the Annual Statement of the district tonnage of the United States, on the thirty-first December, 1817...
January 14, 1819. Washington, D. C., Pr. by E. DeKrafft, 1819. 6 p., 5 broadsides. DLC; DeGE; NN; R.
49848

-- Letter from the Secretary of the Treasury, transmitting the information called for, by the resolution of the House of Representatives, of the 4th instant, in relation to ships engaged in the slave trade, which have been seized and condemned, and the disposition which has been made of the Negroes, by the several state governments. Under whose jurisdiction they have fallen. Jan. 21, 1819... Washington, D. C., Pr. by E. DeKrafft, 1819. 9 p. DLC; NN; R. 49849

-- Letter from the Secretary of War, to the Chairman of Committee of Ways and Means, explanatory of sundry items in the estimate of appropriations for the military service for the year 1819. January 6, 1819...
Washington, D. C., Pr. by E. DeKrafft, 1819. 4 p.
DLC; G; NN; PPAmP; O; R. 49850

-- Letter from the Secretary of War, to the chairman of the Military Committee upon the subject of an additional Military Academy, and a school of practice. January 29, 1819. Washington, D. C., Pr. by E. De Krafft, 1819. 11 p., 1 broadside. DLC; NN; R.
49851

-- Letter from the Secretary of War, transmitting a draft of a bill making appropriations to carry into effect treaties concluded with the several Indian tribes therein mentioned, Feb. 3, 1819. Pr. by order of the Senate of the United States. Washington, D. C., Pr. by E. DeKrafft, 1818! [1819] 3 p. DLC; G; NjP; O.
49852

-- Letter from the Secretary of War, transmitting a statement of moneys, transferred during the recess of Congress, from sundry specific appropriations, to other specific appropriations, by authority of the President

of the United States, during the year 1818. And the
application of the same, February 5, 1819. Washington, D. C., Pr. by E. DeKrafft, 1819. DLC; NjP; R.
49853

-- Letter from the Secretary of War, transmitting a
statement of payments made for labor upon roads, and
other objects of fatigue duty, to the soldiers of the
United States' Army from first October, 1817, to first
October, 1818. January 15, 1819... Washington, D. C.,
Pr. by E. DeKrafft, 1819. 4 p., 1 broadside. DLC;
NN; O; TxU.   49854

-- Letter from the Secretary of War, transmitting a
statement of the expenditure and application of such
sums as have been drawn from the Treasury from the
first, October, 1817, to the thirtieth September, 1818.
January 14, 1819... Washington, D. C., Pr. by E. De
Krafft, 1819. 3 p. DLC; NN; O; R.   49855

-- Letter from the Secretary of War, transmitting a
statement showing the expenditure of moneys appropriated for the contingent expenses of the military establishment of the United States for the year 1818. January 19, 1819... Washington, D. C., Pr. by E. DeKrafft,
1819. 12 p. DLC; NN; O; R.   49856

-- Letter from the Secretary of War, transmitting information in relation to the destruction of the Negro
fort in East Florida, in July, 1816. Washington, D. C.,
1819. 26 p. ([U. S. 15th congress, 2d session, House
doc.] 122) Nh-Hi; WHi.   49857

-- Letter from the Secretary of War, transmitting information respecting the adjustment and payment of the
claims of the friendly Creek Indians, under the treaty
of the 9th August, 1814. January 18, 1819. Washington, Pr. by E. DeKrafft, 1819. 8 p. ([15th Cong., 2d
sess. House Doc. no. 98]) CtHT-W; DLC; NN; O;
OO; R; RPB.   49858

-- Letter from the Secretary of War, transmitting lists
of the names of the clerks employed in the War Department, in the last year and the compensation allowed to

each.   January 20, 1819...Washington, Pr. by E. De
Krafft, 1819. 7 p. DLC; NN; O; R.   49859

-- Letter from the Secretary of War, transmitting,
pursuant to a resolution of the House of Representatives, of the 26th ult., information in relation to the
destruction of the Negro fort, in East Florida, in the
month of July, 1816, etc., etc. February 2, 1819.
Read and committed to the Committee of the whole on
the state of the Union. Washington, D.C., Pr. by E.
DeKrafft, 1819. 26 p. DLC; NN; R.   49860

-- Letter from the Secretary of War, transmitting
statements of contracts made by the Commissary General of Subsistence, the Ordinance department, the Commissary General of purchases, and the engineer department, in the year 1818. February 25, 1819. Washington, Pr. by E. DeKrafft, 1819. 40 p. DLC; NjP; O;
R.   49861

-- Letter from the Secretary of the Treasury, transmitting sundry statements relative to the internal duties
and direct taxes. December 17, 1819. Washington,
Pr. by Gales & Seaton, 1819. 23 p. G; O; R.   49862

-- Letter from the Secretary of War, transmitting topo-
graphical reports, made with a view to ascertain the
practicability of uniting the waters of Illinois River, with
those of Lake Michigan. December 28, 1819. Washington, D.C., Pr. by Gales & Seaton, 1819. 10 p.
DLC; MH-BA; Nh-Hi; NjP; O; R.   49863

-- Memorial and resolutions of the legislature of the
Missouri Territory and a copy of the census of the
fall of 1817; amounting to 19, 218 males. December 8,
1819. Referred to a select committee. Washington,
D.C., Pr. by Gales & Seaton, 1819. 6 p. DLC; G;
MoU; NjP; O; R.   49864

-- Memorial of a convention of the Friends of National
Industry, assembled in the city of New York, to take
into consideration the prostrate situation of our manufactures, and to petition Congress for their relief and

protection; composed of delegates from Massachusetts, Rhode Island, Connecticut, New York, New Jersey, Pennsylvania, Maryland, Delaware, and Ohio. December 20, 1819. Referred to the Committee on Manufactures. Washington, D.C., Pr. by Gales & Seaton, 1819. 10 p. DLC; DeGE; G; MH; NjP; O; R.   49865

-- Memorial of Benjamin H. Latrobe, late surveyor of the public buildings, in the city of Washington, in vindication of his professional skill. January 5, 1819. Pr. by order of the Senate of the United States. Washington, D.C., Pr. by E. DeKrafft, 1819. 8 p. DLC; G; O.   49866

-- ...Memorial of George Williams... Feb. 15, 1819 ...Washington, D.C., Pr. by E. DeKrafft, 1819. 5 p. DLC; NjP.   49867

-- ... Memorial...of Nathaniel Hall Loring, and others, late cadets at the Military academy, West Point. December 27, 1819. Read, and referred to the Committee on military affairs. Washington, D.C., Pr. by Gales & Seaton, 1819. 72 p. DLC; NjP; R.   49868

-- Memorial of Noah Brown, and others, in behalf of the owners of the private armed brig, Warrior, praying... February 3, 1819. Pr. by order of the Senate of the United States. Washington, D.C., Pr. by E. De Krafft, 1818! [1819] 5 p. DLC; G; NjP; O.   49869

-- Memorial of sundry manufacturers residing in the state of Maryland, Dec. 22, 1819, referred to the Committee on manufactures. Washington, D.C., Gales & Seaton, 1819. 5 p. DLC; MH; MdBE; Nh-Hi; NjP; O; R.   49870

-- ... Memorial of sundry persons, residing in the town of Boston, and its vicinity, stockholders in the Bank of the United States. Feb. 9, 1819. Washington city, Pr. by E. DeKrafft, 1819. 6 p. DLC; KyDC; MH-L; NjP; O.   49871

-- Memorial of the Chamber of Commerce of the City

of New York.   December 27, 1819.   Referred to the
Committee on Commerce.   Washington, D. C., Pr. by
Gales & Seaton, 1819. 8 p. DLC; NjP; O; R.   49872

-- Memorial of the Trustees of Hancock College by
their Committee, A. R. Ellery and E. W. Ripley, January 20, 1819. Washington, D. C., Pr. by E. DeKrafft,
1819. 16 p. CtY; DLC; NN; Nh-Hi; O; R.   49873

-- ...Memorial of William Jones, late president of the
Bank of the United States... Feb. 8, 1819... Washington,
D. C., Pr. by E. DeKrafft, 1819. 11 p. ([15th Cong.,
2d sess. House. Ex. doc.] 130) DLC; NjP; PHi.
                                                 49874
-- Message from the President of the United States,
stating the interpretation which has been given to the
Act entitled "An act in addition to the acts prohibiting
the slave trade." Dec. 20, 1819. Washington, D. C.,
Pr. by Gales & Seaton, 1819. 4 p. DLC; NjP; O; R.
                                                 49875
-- Message from the President of the United States, to
the two Houses of Congress, at the commencement of
the first session of the sixteenth Congress; December
7, 1819.   Pr. by order of the Senate of the United
States. Washington, D. C., Pr. by Gales and Seaton,
1819. 96 p. CoU; DLC; G; NjP; O; P.   49876

-- Message from the President of the United States, to
the two Houses of Congress, at the commencement of
the first session of the sixteenth Congress. Dec. 7,
1819.   Read, and committed to a Committee of the
whole House on the state of the Union. Washington,
D. C., Pr. by Gales & Seaton, 1819. 96 p. DLC; G;
NjP; R.   49877

-- Message from the President of the United States,
transmitting a convention, signed at London, on the
twentieth of October last, between the United States and
Great Britain, together with the documents, showing
the course and progress of the negotiation. December
30, 1819. Washington, D. C., Pr. by E. DeKrafft,
1819. DLC.   49878

-- Message from the President of the United States, transmitting a letter from Governor Bibb to General Jackson, connected with the late military operations in Florida. February 6, 1819. Washington, D. C., Pr. by E. DeKrafft, 1819. 6 p. DLC; NjP; R.   49879

-- Message from the President of the United States, transmitting a proclamation of a Convention, between the United States and Spain, together with the translation of a letter from the Minister of Spain to the Secretary of State. Jan. 5, 1819, read and ordered to lie upon the table. Washington, D. C., Pr. by E. De Krafft, 1819. 16 p. DLC; G; MH; NN; Nh-Hi; O; R.
                                                                49880
-- Message from the President of the United States, transmitting a report from the Secretary of State, accompanied with a copy of a letter from Governor Rabun, which was not communicated on a former occasion, from that Department. January 4, 1819. Pr. by order of the Senate of the United States. Washington, D. C., Pr. by E. DeKrafft, 1819. 7 p. DLC; G; GU-De; O.   49881

-- Message from the President of the United States, transmitting a report from the Secretary of the Treasury in compliance with a Resolution of the Senate, of the 13th of last month... Feb. 2, 1819. Pr. by order of the Senate of the United States. Washington, D. C., Pr. by E. DeKrafft, 1819. 22 p. DLC; G; NjP; O.
                                                                49882
-- Message from the President of the United States, transmitting a report from the Secretary of War, in compliance with a resolution of the Senate of the 5th instant, requesting him to "cause to be laid before it, a statement of the effective force, now comprising the military establishment of the United States..." January 12, 1819. Pr. by order of the Senate of the United States. Washington, D. C., Pr. by E. DeKrafft, 1819. 8 p. DLC.   49883

-- Message from the President of the United States, transmitting a report from the Secretary of War, in compliance with a resolution of the Senate of the 25th of January last requesting him "to cause to be laid before it a copy of the rules and regulations...at West Point...Feb. 5, 1819. Washington, D.C., Pr. by E. DeKrafft, 1819. 13 p. DLC; G; NjP; O. 49884

-- Message from the President of the United States, transmitting a report of the Commissioner of the Public Buildings. December 28, 1819. Read and referred to the Committee on the Public Buildings. Washington, D.C., Pr. by Gales & Seaton, 1819. 4 p. DLC; NjP; O; R. 49885

-- Message from the President of the United States, transmitting a report of the Secretary of State, of applications by certain of the independent governments of South America, to have a Minister accredited by the United States, and the answers of the government of the United States, to such applications. January 30, 1819 ...Washington, D.C., Pr. by E. DeKrafft, 1819. 24 p. DLC; NN; O; R. 49886

-- Message from the President of the United States, transmitting a report from the Secretary of the Treasury in compliance with a resolution of the Senate...requesting him "to cause to be laid before it a statement showing the measures that have been taken to collect the balances stated to be due from the several supervisors, and collectors of the old direct tax...also... from the officers of the old internal revenue..." Washington, D.C., Pr. by E. DeKrafft, 1819. 7 p. DeGE. ([15th Con., 2d sess., 1818-1819. Senate Doc.] 101) 49887

-- Message from the President of the United States, transmitting applications from the Resident Minister of Prussia, and the Senates of the Hanseatic Cities of Hamburg and Bremen, to have extended to Prussia, Hamburg and Bremen the advantages secured by the act of Congress of the twentieth April last to the Netherlands. Feb. 8, 1819...Washington, D.C., Pr. by E. DeKrafft, 1819. 13 p. DLC; NjP; R. 49888

-- Message from the President of the United States, transmitting copies of applications by the British Minis-

ter, in behalf of certain subjects of Great Britain,
who have suffered in their property, by proceedings,
to which the United States, by their military and judicial officers, have been parties. Feb. 5, 1819. Washington, D. C., Pr. by E. DeKrafft, 1819. 26 p. DLC;
Nh-Hi; NjP; R.   49889

-- ... Message from the President... transmitting
copies of the remainder of the documents referred to
in his message of the seventeenth ult.   December 15,
1818.   Read and ordered to lie upon the table.   February 2, 1819.   Repr. by order of the House of representatives.   Washington, D. C., Pr. by E. deKrafft,
1819.   147 p.   DLC; MdHi; PWcHi; RPB; ScC; ScU.
                                                        49890
-- Message from the President of the United States,
transmitting documents in pursuance of the Resolution
of the Senate, of the seventeenth instant, December 28,
1818.   Pr. by order of the Senate of the United States.
Washington, Pr. by E. DeKrafft, 1819. 16 p. DLC; G;
NjP; O.   49891

-- ... Message from the President of the United States,
transmitting, in pursuance of a resolution of the House
of representatives, such further information, in relation to our affairs with Spain, as, in his opinion, is
not inconsistent with the public interest to divulge...
Dec. 28, 1818.   Washington, D. C., Pr. by E. De
Krafft, 1819. 215 p.   DLC; FSa; FTaSC; G; MH-L;
MdBJ; MoU; NN; Nh-Hi; O; P; PPL-R; RPA; RPB;
ScU; ViU; WHi.   49892

-- Message from the President of the United States,
transmitting information required by a Resolution of
the House of Representatives, of December 24, 1818,
of certain correspondence between the Department of
War, and the Governor of Georgia and of the said Department with General Andrew Jackson.   January 4,
1819... Washington, D. C., Pr. by E. DeKrafft, 1819.
7 p.   DLC; NN; O; R.   49893

-- Message from the President of the United States,
transmitting, pursuant to a Resolution of the House of

Representatives, of the eighteenth instant, information relative to the occupancy of Amelia Island, St. Marks and Pensacola, &c, &c. Jan. 30, 1819...Washington, D.C., Pr. by E. DeKrafft, 1819. 17 p. DLC; LNH; NN; Nh-Hi; O; R.   49894

-- Message from the President of the United States, transmitting (pursuant to a resolution of the House of Representatives of twenty-fourth, February, last) A report of the Secretary of State in relation to the causes of the inprisonment of William White, an American citizen, at Buenos Ayres. Dec. 15, 1819...Washington, D.C., Pr. by Gales & Seaton, 1819. 12 p. DLC; G; Nh-Hi; NjP; NjR; O; R.   49895

-- Message from the President of the United States, transmitting reports of the proceedings which have been had under the "Act for the gradual increase of the Navy" prepared in pursuance of a resolution of the House of Representatives of the seventh, December, 1818. January 4, 1819...Washington, D.C., Pr. by E. DeKrafft, 1819. 29 p. DLC; G; NN; O; R.   49896

-- ...Mr. Lacock, from the committee appointed in pursuance of the resolution of the Senate, of the 18th of December last, "That the message of the President, and documents, relative to the Seminole war, be referred to a select committee"...[Washington, D.C., 1819] 50 p. DLC; GU-De; NWM; RPB; WHi.   49897

-- Mr. Spencer's resolutions. Feb. 1, 1819...[Washington, D.C., 1819] 2 p. (On public deposits in the Bank of the United States) DLC; NN.   49898

-- Official army register for 1819. Adjutant and inspector general's office, January 1, 1819. [Washington, D.C.] Pr. by E. deKrafft, 1819. 22 p. MWA; MdHi.   49899

-- Official Congressional directory. Washington, D.C., 1819. RPA; RPE.   49899a

-- Official register of the officers and cadets of the

U. S. Military academy. West Point, N. Y., June 1819.
[West Point, N. Y., 1819] ICN; MiD-B. 49899b

-- ... Petition of a convention of the people of the district of Maine, praying to be admitted into the Union
as a separate and independent state, accompanied with
a constitution for said state. December 8, 1819.
Read, and referred to a select committee. Washington, D. C., Pr. by Gales & Seaton, 1819. 35 p. DLC;
G; MoU; Nh-Hi; NjP; O; OCLaw; OO; RPB. 49899c

-- A Register of officers and agents civil, military, and
naval, in the service of the United States on the 30th
of September 1818; prepared at the Department of
State. Washington, D. C., Pr. by Davis & Force,
1819. 235 p. MsJS. 49899d

-- Register of the commissioned and warrant officers
of the Navy of the United States; including officers of
the Marine Corps, &c. &c. Pr. by order of the secretary of the Navy, conformably to a resolution of the
Hon. Senate of the United States. Washington, D. C.,
Pr. by Wade & Company, 1819. 34 p. MdHi; RP;
RPA; RPB. 49899e

-- Report, in part, of the Committee on Revolutionary
pensions, upon the subject of the manner in which the
act of the 18th March, 1818, has been executed, &c,
&c. Dec. 28, 1819... [Washington, D. C., 1819] 6 p.
DLC; NjP; TxFwTCU. 49899f

-- Report in the case of Capt. Louis Joseph Beaulieu,
accompanied with a bill for his relief, Dec. 14, 1819.
[Washington, D. C., 1819] 1 p. DLC; NjP. 49899g

-- Report of a select committee, upon the subject of
fixing standards of weights and measures, Jan. 25,
1819... [Washington, D. C., 1819] 12 p. DLC; NN.
49899h

-- Report of the Committee, appointed on the 10th day
of April last, to inquire into the official conduct of
William P. Van Ness, Judge of the Southern, and Matthias B. Tallmadge, Judge of the Northern District of

New York, and of William Stephens, Judge of the District of Georgia. Feb. 17, 1819...[Washington, D.C., 1819] 5 p. DLC; NjP. 49899i

-- Report of the Committee, appointed on the 27th, November last, to inquire into the expediency of amending the laws which regulate the coins of the United States, and foreign coins; accompanied with, "A bill supplementary to the act establishing a mint," and, "A bill continuing for a limited time, the currency of the crowns and five franc pieces of France. January 26, 1819...Washington, D.C., Pr. by E. DeKrafft, 1819. 10 p. DLC; NN; R. 49900

-- Report of the committee appointed on the 30th of November, 1818, to inspect the books and examine into the proceedings of the Bank of the United States... January 16, 1819. [Washington, D.C., E. DeKrafft, 1819] 493 p. CSmH; DLC; In; MH-BA; MoK; MoU; NjP; R. 49901

-- Report of the Committee of claims, in the case of Alexander Worster. December 29, 1819...[Washington, D.C., 1819] 1 p. DLC; G; NjP. 49902

-- Report of the Committee of claims in the case of John J. Johnson, Samuel Plumb, Ralph Patcher, Samuel Benton, Hannah Debois, and Margaretta Duffield. January 5, 1819. [Washington, D.C., 1819] 4 p. DLC; G; NN. 49903

-- Report of the Committee of claims in the case of William Henderson. December 29, 1819...[Washington, D.C., 1819] 18 p. DLC; NjP; G; TxFwTCU. 49904

-- Report of the Committee of claims, on the case of Samuel Hughes. December 15, 1819. [Washington, D.C., 1819] 7 p. DLC; NjP; TxFwTCU. 49905

-- Report of the Committees of claims on the petition of Ether Shipley...Dec. 28, 1819. [Washington, D.C., 1819] 2 p. DLC; G; NjP; TxFwTCU. 49906

-- Report of the Committee of Claims, on the petition
of John M'Causland, accompanied with a bill for his
relief.   Feb. 2, 1819...[Washington, D.C., 1819] 2 p.
DLC; NN.   49907

-- Report of the Committee of Claims, on the petition
of William M'Donald...Jan. 18, 1819...[Washington,
D.C., 1819] 1 p. DLC; NN.   49908

-- Report of the Committee of Claims on the petition
of William M'Donald, administrator of James, accompanying a bill...Dec. 14, 1819...[Washington, D.C.,
1819] 1 p. DLC; NjP.   49909

-- ...Report of the Committee of Claims, to whom
was recommitted the bill for the relief of Thadeus Mayhew, of the state of Louisiana. December 28, 1818.
[Washington, D.C., 1819] 11 p. DLC; OClWHi. 49910

-- Report of the Committee of revisal and unfinished
business. December 31, 1819. [Washington, D.C.,
1819] 6 p. DLC; G; NjP; TxFwTCU.   49911

-- Report of the Committee of ways and means, on the
petition of Hugh M'Cullough. December 27, 1819.
[Washington, D.C., 1819] 1 p. DLC; NjP; TxFwTCU.
                                                            49912
-- Report of the Committee of ways and means on the
petition of John Gooding and James Williams, accompanied with a bill for their relief, Jan. 5, 1819...
[Washington, D.C., 1819] 5 p. DLC; NN.   49913

-- Report of the Committee of ways and means, on the
petition of John Gooding and James Williams...Jan. 5,
1819,...Dec. 13, 1819. Repr. by order of the House
of Representatives...[Washington, D.C., 1819] 5 p.
DLC; G; NjP; TxFwTCU.   49914

-- Report of the Committee of ways and means, on
the petition of William Coffin and others...Dec. 29,
1819. [Washington, D.C., 1819] 2 p. DLC; NjP;
TxFwTCU.   49915

-- Report of the Committee on military affairs, on the petition of Jasper Bennett, accompanied with a bill for the relief of Malcomb Bennett. Jan. 4, 1819...[Washington, D. C., 1819] 2 p. DLC; G; NN. 49916

-- Report of the Committee on military affairs, on the petition of Rebecca C. Appling...Dec. 27, 1819. [Washington, D. C., 1819] 1 p. DLC; NjP; TxFwTCU. 49917

-- Report of the Committee on military affairs, to whom was referred so much of the President's message, of 17th November last, as relates to the proceeding of the court martial, in the trial of Arbuthnott and Armbrister, and the conduct of the Seminole war. January 12, 1819...[Washington, D. C., 1819] 4 p. DLC; G; NN. 49918

-- Report of the Committee on naval affairs, on the memorial of Thomas Shields, accompanied with a bill, authorizing the payment of a sum of money to Thomas Shields. January 4, 1819...[Washington, D. C., 1819] 2 p. DLC; G; NN. 49919

-- Report of the Committee on naval affairs, on the resolution concerning navy agents, accompanying "A bill concerning navy agents." Jan. 5, 1819. [Washington, D. C., 1819] 4 p. DLC; G; NN. 49920

-- Report of the Committee on naval affairs, to whom was referred the report of the Commissioners of the Navy pension fund. Mar. 2, 1819...[Washington, D. C., 1819] 2 p. DLC; NjP. 49921

-- Report of the Committee on private land claims, on the petition of Philip C. S. Barbour...Dec. 16, 1819. [Washington, D. C., 1819] 6 p. DLC; NjP; TxFwTCU. 49922

-- Report of the Committee on private land claims, on the petition of Spiller Fillmore...December 23, 1819. [Washington, D. C., 1819] 2 p. DLC; NjP; TxFwTCU. 49923

-- ... Report of the Committee on private land claims, to whom was referred the report of the recorder of

land titles of the territory of Missouri, in obedience to
the act of Congress, of 20th April, 1818, for the relief of James Mackay...accompanied with a bill for his
relief. Jan. 18, 1819...[Washington, D.C., 1819] 6 p.
DLC; MoSHi; NN; OO; RPB.   49924

-- Report of the Committee on so much of the public
accounts and expenditurs[!], as relate to the Post Office, accompanied with a "Bill to amend an act entitled
an act regulating the Post Office establishment," passed
the 30th of April, 1810. Feb. 10, 1819...[Washington,
D.C., 1819] 35 p. DLC; NjP.   49925

-- Report of the Committee on the improvement and
organization of the militia, Jan. 22, 1819...[Washing-
ton, D.C., 1819] 31 p. DLC; NN.   49926

-- Report of the Committee on the memorial of the New
York institution for the instruction of the deaf and dumb
...December 28, 1819. [Washington, D.C., 1819] 1 p.
DLC; NjP; TxFwTCU.   49927

-- Report of the Committee on private land claims, on
the petition of James Hughes, accompanied with a Bill
for his relief. Feb. 3, 1819...[Washington, D.C.,
1819] 2 p. DLC; NN.   49928

-- Report of the Committee on private land claims on
the petition of Josiah H. M'Comas. Jan. 18, 1819...
[Washington, D.C., 1819] 4 p. DLC; NN.   49929

-- Report of the Committee on the public buildings, accompanying "A bill making appropriations for the public
buildings, for the purchase of a lot of land, and furnishing a supply of water for the use of certain public
buildings." Jan. 7, 1819...[Washington, D.C., 1819]
9 p. DLC; G; NN.   49930

-- Report of the Committee on the public lands, on the
petition of Clement B. Penrose...Dec. 27, 1819. [Wash-
ington, D.C., 1819] 1 p. DLC; G; NjP; TxFwTCU.
                                                   49931
-- Report of the Committee on the public lands, on the

petition of James Hughes, December 16, 1819. [Washington, D. C., 1819] 2 p. DLC; NjP; TxFwTCU. 49932

-- Report of the Committee on the public lands, on the petition of John B. C. Lucas...December 27, 1819. [Washington, D. C., 1819] 1 p. DLC; NjP; TxFwTCU.
49933

-- A report of the Committee on the public lands, upon the subject of granting to each state one hundred thousand acres of land, for the endowment of a university therein. Jan. 18, 1819...[Washington, D. C., 1819] 2 p. DLC; NN. 49934

-- Report of the Committee, to which was referred the petition of the Connecticut Asylum for the Education and instruction of deaf and dumb persons. Feb. 22, 1819...[Washington, D. C., 1819] 2 p. DLC; NjP.
49935

-- Report of the Committee, to whom was referred so much of the President's message as relates to the civilization of the Indian tribes. Jan. 15, 1819...[Washington, D. C., 1819] 3 p. DLC; NN. 49936

-- Report of the Joint Committee of the two houses of Congress, appointed to inquire and report what business it will be necessary to act upon during the present session of Congress. Feb. 22, 1819...[Washington, D. C., 1819] 5 p. DLC; NjP. 49937

-- Report of the Joint Committee on the subject of the public printing. Feb. 19, 1819...[Washington, D. C., 1819] 3 p. DLC; NjP. 49938

-- Report of the Secretary of State, of the names of the clerks employed in the Department of State, during the year 1818, and the compensation allowed to each. January 29, 1819...Washington, D. C., Pr. by E. De Krafft, 1819. 4 p. DLC; NN; R. 49939

-- Report of the Secretary of War, relative to roads and canals, in pursuance of a resolution of the House of Representatives of the 4th April last. January 14, 1819...Washington, D. C., Pr. by E. DeKrafft, 1819.

13 p. DLC; NN; O; OO; R; RPB; WHi.   49940

-- Report of the Select Committee, on the bill for the relief of Ebenezer Stevens and others. Jan. 20, 1819 ...[Washington, D.C., 1819] 6 p. DLC; NN.   49941

-- Report of the Select Committee, on the petition of Benjamin Wells, accompanied with "A supplement to the Act entitled an act for the relief of Benjamin Wells." Jan. 27, 1819...[Washington, D.C., 1819] 2 p. DLC; NN.   49942

-- Report of the select committee, to whom was referred, on the 10th instant, the memorial of the officers of the Revolutionary Army, accompanying a bill for their relief. Dec. 20, 1819. [Washington, D.C., 1819] 7 p. DLC; NjP.   49943

-- Report upon the claims of Thomas Carr, Andrew Jackson, and others accompanied with a "bill for the benefit of Thomas Carr, and others." December 14, 1819. Read, and with the bill, committed to a Committee of the whole House to-morrow. [Washington, D.C., 1819] 6 p. DLC; G; GU-De; NjP.   49944

-- Reports of cases argued and determined in the Circuit court of the United States, for the First circuit ...containing the cases determined in the districts of New Hampshire, Massachusetts, [Maine] and Rhode Island, in the years 1816[-1830]...By William P. Mason ...Boston, Wells and Lilly, 1819-[31] 5 v. CSt; DLC; LNBA; MB; MNBedf; Nc-SC; OCLaw; RPL; U.   49945

-- Reports of cases argued and determined in the Circuit court of the United States, for the third circuit. Containing cases determined in the district of New Jersey, from the year 1803 to 1818; and the district of Pennsylvania, in the years 1815, 1816, 1817, 1818. By Richard Peters, Jun. Counsellor at law. Philadelphia, Pr. by Wm. Fry, 1819. 581 p. F-SC; In-SC; MWA; NIC; OClW; OrSC; OCLaw; PLL; ViU.   49946

-- Resolutions of the Legislature of the Territory of

Missouri, securing to claimants of land, &c.   February
14, 1816.   Referred to the Committee on the public
lands March 23, 1816.   Bill reported - No. 148.   December 23, 1816.   Referred to the Committee on the
public lands.   Dec. 18, 1817.   Referred to the Committee on public lands.   December 28, 1819.   Referred to
the Committee on private lands claims.   Washington,
D. C. ,   Pr. by Gales & Seaton, 1819. 9 p. DLC; NjP;
O.   49947

-- Resolutions submitted by Mr. Johnson, of Kentucky,
January 29, 1819.   Read and ordered to lie on the
table. [Washington, D. C. , Pr. by E. DeKrafft, 1819]
1 p.   DLC; NN; R.   49948

-- A statement of the amount of duties...during the
years 1813, 1814 and 1815...Washington, D. C. , Pr.
by Jacob Gideon, Junr. , 1819.   4 p. MWA; NNS. 49949

-- A statement of the amount of duties...during the
years 1814, 1815, and 1816...Washington, D. C. , Pr.
by E. DeKrafft, 1819. MWA.   49950

-- -- ...During the years 1815, 1816, and 1817...
Washington, D. C. , Pr. by E. DeKrafft, 1819. MWA.
                                                        49951
-- Statements, in detail, of the revenues from merchandise...which accrued in the years 1815, 1816 and
1817...Washington, D. C. , Pr. by Jacob Gideon, Junr. ,
1819.   MWA.   49952

-- Statements exhibiting the revenue accruing from duties...during the year ending on the thirty-first December, 1816.   Washington, D. C. , Pr. by E. DeKrafft,
1819.   MWA.   49953

-- Statements exhibiting the revenue accruing from duties...during the year ending on the thirty-first December, 1817.   Washington, D. C. , Pr. by E. DeKrafft,
1819.   MWA.   49954

-- Table of post offices in the United States, with the
names of the Post-masters, the counties and states in

which they are situated; and the distances from the
City of Washington, and the distances from the capitals
of respective states.   By direction of the Post-master
General, Washington City, 1819. 86 p.   DLC; MWA;
PHi; PPAmP.   49955

-- To the Honorable the Senate, and the Honorable the
House of representatives of the United States, in Congress assembled, The memorial of the subscriber, so-
licitor on behalf of the surviving officers of the Revolutionary army of the United States.   [1819?] 4 p.
MiU-C.   49956

-- To the Senate and House of Representatives of the
United States, in Congress assembled.   The memorial
of the subscribers, respectfully sheweth:...[Washington
City, 1819] [4] p.   MWA.   49957

-- 21 Resolutions on the legislature of the territory of
Missouri, securing to claimants of land &c...Washing-
ton, D. C., Pr. by Gales & Seaton, 1819. 9 p. NjR.
                                                     49958
-- Views of the minority of the Committee on military
affairs, on the subject of the Seminole war, and the
trial and execution of Arbuthnott[!] and Armbrister[!]
Jan. 12, 1819. [Washington, D. C., 1819] 12 p. DLC;
MoU; NN; RPB; WHi.   49959

The United States almanac for...1820. By David
Young...Elizabeth-Town, N. J., P. Chatterton [1819]
[36] p.   DLC; MWA; NN; NjHi; NjR.   49960

Universal Book Store, Philadelphia.
    Universal Book-Store, No. 118, Chestnut-street,
corner of Carpenter's court, leading to the Bank of the
United States; Philadelphia...Catalogue for 1819, of a
very extensive collection of new and second hand,
scarce and valuable books, (ancient and modern authors)
in arts, sciences, and literature.   In about thirty different languages...Philadelphia, 1819. 195 p. MWA.
                                                     49961
Universalist Church in the U. S. A.
    Minutes and proceedings of the Genese branch of

the Western association of Universalists...
Greenville in Henrietta, L. Knap, 1819. MWA.   49962

-- Proceedings of the General convention...the 14th of
Sept. A.D. 1819...[1819] MWA.   49963

-- Northern Association.
    Proceedings of the Northern Association of Univer-
salists, Anno Domini Christi 1819. Woodstock, Vt.,
Pr. by David Watson, 1819. 12 p. MWA.   49964

Universalist Magazine. Boston, July 3, 1819. 1st issue. MH.   49965

Upham, Thomas Cogswell, 1799-1872
    American sketches...New-York, David Longworth,
1819. 120 p. DLC; MH; MWA; MeHi; RPB.   49966

-- Elements of intellectual philosophy. Portland, Me.,
Pr. by Shirley & Hyde, 1819. 576 p. MMeT.   49967

                          V
The vagabond. A new story for children. Hartford,
Pr. by Roberts & Burr, for S.G. Goodrich, 1819.
16 p. CSmH; CtHi; DLC.   49968

Validity of Presbyterian ordination, asserted in a letter to the author of a pamphlet, entitled "Presbyterian
ordination doubtful." New-Haven, Pr. by A.H. Maltby
& Co., 1819. 18 p.   CtHi; CtY; MBC; NNUT; NcMHi.
                                               49969
Valpy, Edward, 1764-1832
    Elegantiae latinae; or, Rules and exercises illus-
trative of elegant Latin styles. From the 5th English
ed., by Edward Valpy. New Haven, Pr. by S. Converse, for Howe & Spalding, 1819. 256 p. CtY; ICU;
InCW; MB; MH; MMeT; MWA; NN; NNC; NP; NcD;
NjP; PPM; PU; ScCC.   49970

[Valpy, Richard] 1754-1836
    Delectus sententiarum et historiarum, ad usum
tironum accommodatus...Bostoniae: Wells et Lilly...

1819. 108 p. DLC; MH. 49971

Van Alstine, John, 1779-1819
Life and dying confession of John Van Alstine,
executed March 19, 1819, for the murder of William
Huddleston... Cooperstown, N. Y., Pr. by H. & E.
Phinney, 1819. 24 p. DLC; MH. 49972

[Van Buren, Martin] President, U. S.
Considerations in favour of the appointment of Rufus King to the Senate of the U. S. submitted to the republican members of the legislature of the state of New
York by one of their colleagues. New York [1819]
32 p. DLC; IU. 49973

Vanderbilt, John, Jun.
Oration, 28th December, 5807, before Trinity and
Benevolent Lodges of New York and Fortitude Lodge...
of Brooklyn. To which is added: An address from
Trinity Lodge, New York, January 11, 1808, before
the Grand Lodge. By Wm. Burrill. New York,
Southwick and Pelsue, [1819] 31 p. MBFM. 49974

Vanderlyn, John
Description of the panoramic view of... Versailles
... New-York, Pr. by E. Conrad, 1819. NN. 49975

Van der Sloot, Frederick William
... Gott geheiligte gesange... Philadelphia, Zentler,
1819. PLFM. 49976

Van Heythuysen, F. M.
The equity draftsman... 1st Amer. ed. New York,
Pr. by Grattan & Banks, for Gould and Banks and
William Gould & Co., Albany, 1819. 658 p. CLSU;
MWA; MdBB; NjP; NjR. 49977

[Van Ness, William Peter]
A letter to the Secretary of the Treasury, on the
commerce and currency of the United States. By
Aristides [pseud.] New York, Pr. by C. S. Van Winkle,
1819. 39 p. IU; MH-BA; MWA; PPAmP. 49978

Ventum, Mrs. Harriet
    The holiday reward...New York, W. B. Gilley,
1819.   RPB; RPL.   49979

Vermont (State)
    An act regulating and governing the militia of Ver-
mont...Middlebury, Vt., Pr. by J. W. Copeland, 1819.
63 p.   DLC; MH-L; MWA; NN; NjR; Vt; VtHi; VtU.
                                                 49980
-- By His Excellency Jonas Galusha, Esquire, Govern-
or, Captain General, and Commander in Chief, in and
over the state of Vermont.   A proclamation...Shafts-
bury, this twenty-fourth day of February, in the year
of our Lord Christ, one thousand eight hundred and
nineteen...[1819]   Broadside. MB; VtHi.   49981

-- Journals of the General Assembly of the state of
Vermont at their session begun and held at Montpelier,
in the county of Washington, on Thursday, the 14th of
October, 1819.   William Haswell, Bennington [1819?]
270 p.   CSmH; DLC; MWA; Mi; NB; Vt; VtHi; VtU;
VtMiS.   49982

-- Laws passed by the Legislature of the state of Vermont...1819.   Rutland, Vt., Fay & Burt [1819] 207 p.
DLC.   49983

No. II. The Vermont almanac and farmer's calendar,
for the year of our Lord 1820...By Zadock Thompson.
...Woodstock, Vt., Pr. by David Watson [1819] [48] p.
MWA; VtU-W.   49984

The Vermont almanack, for the year of our Lord 1820
...By Andrew Beers, philom...Burlington, Vt., Pr.
by E. and T. Mills [1819] [48] p. MWA; VtU-W.49985

Vermont Bible Society
    Seventh report...October 20, 1819.   Montpelier,
Vt., Pr. by E. P. Walton, 1819.   31 p. CSt; GDC; IEG;
MWA; Vt; VtHi.   49986

Vermont University
    Order of exercises for the commencement of the

University of Vermont, August 11th, 1819...[Burling-
ton, Vt., 1819] Broadside. VtU-W.   49987

[Verplanck, Gulian Crommelin] 1786-1870
    Dick Shift or, The state triumvirate: a political
tale in imitation of Swift.   New York, 1819. RPB.
                                                     49988
[--] The state triumvirate, a political tale: and the
epistles of Brevet Major Pindar Puff [pseud.] ...New
York, Pr. by J. Seymour, for the author and W.B.
Gilley, 1819.   215 p.   DLC; DeGE; MB; MWA;
MiMarqN; MnU; NBu; NIC; NSyHi; NjP; PHi; RPB;
ScC.   49989

A very general misunderstanding amongst ship masters
and merchants respecting the law relating to ship letters...Joseph E. Sprague, Post-master, Salem.
Salem, Mass., 1819.   Broadside. MSaE.   49990

The vicar's garden...Philadelphia, Pr. by Clark &
Raser, 1819.   MWA.   49991

The vicar's garden, or the Greek medal.   By an American lady.   Philadelphia, Sunday and Adult School Union,
1819. MWA.   49992

The Village harmony: or, New-England repository of
sacred musick...Ed. 16, rev. and improved.   Exeter,
N.H., Pr. by J.J. Williams, for the proprietor, 1819.
347 p. MWA; Nh-Hi; RPB.   49993

Virginia (State)
    An act incorporating the Bank of Virginia, passed
the 30th of January, 1804; and an act extending the
charter of the bank of Virginia, passed January 24th,
1814.   With the rules and regulations for the government of the bank.   Richmond, Va., Pr. by John Warrock, 1819.   44 p.   CSmH; DLC.   49994

-- Acts passed at a General Assembly of the Common-
wealth of Virginia, begun...7th day of December, 1818
...Richmond, Pr. by Thomas Ritchie, 1819. 224 p.
DLC.   49995

-- Journal of the House of Delegates of the Commonwealth of Virginia, begun... 7th day of December, 1818.
Richmond, Pr. by Thomas Ritchie 1818[!] [1819]
235 p. DLC.   49996

-- Journal of the Senate of the Commonwealth of Virginia, Dec., 1818. Richmond, Pr. by John Warrock,
1818[!] [1819] 208 p. NN.   49997

-- The revised code of the laws of Virginia. Richmond [Va.] Pr. by Thos. Ritchie, 1819. 2 v. Ia.
                                                    49998
-- The statutes at large, being a collection of all the
laws of Virginia from the first session of the Legislature in the year 1619. Published pursuant to an act of
the general assembly of Virginia passed February 5,
1808. New York, Pr. by R. & W. & G. Bartow, for
the editor, 1819 [-23] 13 v. KyU-L.   49999

Virginia Reformer. Winchester, Va., Klipstine & Russell, Apr. 24, 1819, 1st issue. Weekly newspaper.
MWA.   50000

A visit to the bazaar. New Haven, Pr. [by A. H.
Maltby & Co.] for A. B. Goldsmith and N. & S. S.
Jocelyn, 1819. 22 p. CtHi; MWA.   50001

A voice from the grave; or, a letter from the dead to
the living, to which is added the Christian Drummer.
Philadelphia, 1819. MWA.   50002

Der Volksfreund und Baltimore calender. Auf das jahr
1820. Baltimore, Pr. by Schaeffer und Maund [1819]
[36] p. DLC; MWA; MdBE; NN; PHi.   50003

Der Volksfreund und Hagerstauner Calender, 1820.
Hagerstaun, Md., Gruber und May [1819] DLC; MWA;
MdBE; PHi; PPeSchw.   50004

                        W
Waddell, John H.
    The theatre. [New York, 1819] MBAt.   50005

-- Waddell to Coleman, facts and fancy - as you like
it - go on, or stop.   New York, 1819.   8 p. CSmH;
RPB.   50006

[Waddel, Moses]
   Extracts from the Memoirs of Caroline E. Smelt
...Philadelphia, Pr. [by J.R.A. Skerrett] for Benjamin
& Thomas Kite and Solomon W. Conrad, ...1819.
MWA.   50007

-- Memoirs of the life of Miss Caroline E. Smelt...
Ed. 2.   New York, D. Fanshaw, 1819.   180 p. GU-De;
MWA; NhFr; RHi; ViU.   50008

White, Eliza
   Life and writings of Miss Eliza Waite, who died at
Freeport (Me.) Jan. 13, 1819...Hallowell, Me., Pr.
by E. Goodale, 1819.   256 p.   MH; MWA; MeHi; NHi.
                                                       50009
Wakefield, Mrs. Priscilla (Bell)
   Mental improvements...4th Amer. ed.   Philadel-
phia, Pr. by Griggs & Co., for Benjamin Johnson,
1819.   MB; MWA.   50010

Waldo, Samuel Putnam, 1780-1826
   Memoirs of Andrew Jackson, major-general in the
army of the United States; and commander in chief of
the Division of the South...Ed. 3.   Hartford, S. Andrus, 1819.   312 p. DLC; LU; MBC; MNBedf; MnU;
NG; NGH; NN; NSyU; Nc; NcD; NcU; OClWHi; ScU; T;
TN; TNP; TxU; WHi.   50011

-- -- Hartford, Pr. [by S.L. Loomis] for S. Andrus,
1819.   316 p. Ct; CtHi; DLC; FJ; ICN; Ia; MBrigStJ;
MDeeP; MH; MSaE; MWA; MiD-B; NR; NcU; PHatU;
RPB; TCh; WHi.   50012

-- -- Ed. 5, improved.   Hartford, J. & W. Russell,
1819.   336 p. CSmH; CSt; Ct; CtHi; CtHT; IRo; InLog;
InNd; KyBgW; KyBgW-K; LNH; MHatf; MLaw; MSwe;
MWA; MdAN; MdBD; MdToN; Mi; MiD; MiD-B; MiMarq;
MiU; MnDu; NN; OClWHi; P; RPB; ViU.   50013

-- The tour of James Monroe, president of the United States, through the northern and eastern states, in 1817; his tour in the year 1818; together with a sketch of his life...Hartford, S. Andrus, 1819. 348 p. CSf; CSfCW; Ct; CtSoP; IP; MC; MMeT; MNe; MPiB; MoSW; NBLiHi; NNUT; NR; Nh; NhD; Nn-Hi; OCl; OMC; OO; RPB; RWe; TSewU; ViU; VtWood.   50014

Walker, John, 1732-1807
...A critical pronouncing dictionary, and expositor of the English language...New-York, Collins and Hannay, 1819. 773 p. DLC; LU; MH; NIC; NN.   50015

-- Walker's critical pronouncing dictionary, abr. by Thomas Smith. Cincinnati, O., E. Morgan & co., 1819. MWA.   50016

[Walker, Patrick]
The life and prophecies of Alexander Peden...
Pr. for the publisher, 1819. MWA.   50017

... Wall-street; or, Ten minutes before three; a farce, in three acts...New-York, 1819. 34 p. DLC; MB; MH; MWA; PU; RPB.   50018

-- Ed. 2. New York, 1819. 35 p. RPB.   50019

-- Ed. 3. ...New York, 1819. RPB.   50020

[Walls, John]
To the public. [1819?] MWA.   50021

[Waln, Robert, jr.]
The Hermit in America on a visit to Philadelphia: some account of the beaux and belles, dandies and coquettes...of that famous city...edited by Peter Atall, Esq. [pseud.] Philadelphia, M. Thomas, 1819. 215 p. DLC; IUC; MH; MWA; NNS; PPL; PU.   50022

[--] -- Ed. 2. Philadelphia, M. Thomas, 1819. 246 p. MWA; NjR.   50023

Walsh, Robert, 1784-1859
An appeal from the judgments of Great Britain respecting the United States of America. Part first,
containing an historical outline of their merits and
wrongs as colonies; and strictures upon the calumnies
of the British writers... Philadelphia, Pr. by William
Brown, for Mitchell, Ames & White, 1819. 512 p.
CSmH; IaU; KyU; MWA; NIC; NSherb; NWM; RPB.
50024

-- -- Ed. 2. Philadelphia, Pr. by William Brown,
for Mitchell, Ames and White, 1819. 512 p. MWA;
MWiW; NjR.   50025

[--] Free remarks on the spirit of the Federal Constitution, the practice of the Federal Government, and
the obligations of the Union, respecting the exclusion
of slavery from the territories and new states. Boston,
1819. MB.   50026

-- The works of the British poets, with lives of the authors. Edited by Robert Walsh, jr. ... Philadelphia,
Pr. by William Brown, for Mitchell, Ames, and White,
1819. CSmH; NT; RPB.   50027

[Walter, William Bicker]
A letter to Professor Stuart, in answer to his letters to Rev. William E. Channing, and in vindication of
a large and respectable body of the New England and
other clergy. Boston, Pr. by S. T. Goss, 1819. 28 p.
MH-AH; MWA.   50028

Walton's Vermont register and farmer's almanack, for
the year of our Lord 1820... Montpelier, Vt., E. P.
Walton, [1819] 119 p. DLC; MWA; NHi; Nh-Hi; OCHP;
Vt; VtHi.   50029

Wanostrocht, Nicolas, 1745-1812
A grammar of the French language, with practical
exercises... 1st Amer., from 14th London ed. Boston,
J. H. A. Frost, 1819. 480 p. MHi; TxU-T.   50030

-- -- 5th Amer. from 14th London ed... Boston, Pr.
by J. H. A. Frost, for West, Richardson and Lord, 1819.

480 p. MB; MH; MWA; NWM; OSW; OrSaW; PP; ScSpW. 50031

-- Receuil choisi de traits historique et de contes maraux: avec la signification des mots en anglais au bas de chaque page. A L'usage des jeunes gens... Troisiéme edition Americaine de la derniere anglaise; revue, corrigée et augmentée. Baltimore, Samuel Jeffries, 1819. 288 p. MdBLC. 50032

Ward, Francis
The substance of a sermon, preached in the school-house at the Goodrich Hollow in the town of Sharon, on Saturday evening, the twelfth of April, 1806... New York, Pr. by James & John Harper, for Mrs. H. Ward, 1819. 50 p. MiD-B; NN. 50033

Warden, David Baillie, 1778-1845
A statistical, political and historical account of the United States... Philadelphia, T. Wardle, 1819. 3 v. NjR. 50034

[Ware, Henry]
An essay on the use and meaning of the phrase "Holy Spirit." Boston, Wells & Lilly, for the Christian Disciple Soc. No. 1, 1819. 21 p. MBC; MH; MSaE. 50035

-- A sermon, delivered in Boston, April 14, 1819, at the ordination of the Reverend John Pierpont... Cambridge, Pr. by Hilliard and Metcalf, 1819. MWA. 50036
-- -- Ed. 2. Cambridge, Pr. by Hilliard and Metcalf, 1819. 24 p. MWA; NjR. 50037

[--] The trial. Calvin and Hopkins versus the Bible and common sense. By a lover of the truth. Ed. 2, enl. To which are added some remarks on the Andover Institution. Boston, 1819. 39 p. ICMe; ICT; LNH; NjR. 50038

Warner, William
Primer; or, First book for children. Baltimore,

Pr. by William Warner, 1819. 35 p. MdHi. 50039

Warner's almanac, for 1820. Calculated by Joshua
Sharp. Philadelphia, Benjamin Warner [1819] MWA.
50040

Warren Phalanx, Charlestown, Mass.
Rules and regulations... Charlestown, Mass., Pr.
by S. Etheridge, 1819. MWA. 50041

Washington, D. C. (City)
Acts of the corporation of the City of Washington,
passed by the sixteenth council. Pr. by order of the
council. City of Washington, Pr. by Jacob Gideon,
Jr., 1819. DLC. 50042

-- Laws passed by the sixteenth Council of the City of
Washington, 1818-19. 48 p. MdBB. 50043

Washington academy, Salem, N. Y. Theological Seminary.
Plan of the Theological seminary, established in
the Washington academy, and located in the village of
Salem, May 13, 1819. Salem, N. Y., Pr. by James
B. Gibson, 1819. 15 p. CSmH; N; NNUT. 50044

Washington Agricultural Society.
The constitution and by-laws... together with an address, delivered before the Society, at Argyle, February 11, 1819... By Zebulon R. Shipard, Esq. ... Sandy
Hill, N. Y., Pr. by E. G. Storer, for the society, 1819.
16 p. N. 50045

Washington almanac, for... 1820... By Joshua Sharp.
Philadelphia, D. Dickinson [1819] [40] p. NjR. 50046

Washington botanical society.
Florula Columbiensis... Washington, D. C., Pr. by
Jacob Gideon, jr., 1819. RPB. 50047

Washington County Bible Society, N. Y.
Seventh annual report... Salem, N. Y., Pr. by Dodd
& Stevenson, 1819. 16 p. NN. 50048

The Washington Theological Repertory, conducted by

clergymen of The Protestant Episcopal Church, for the
year commencing Aug. 1819. Vol. I. Washington
City, Pr. by Davis and Force, 1819. 392 p. CtHT;
MBD; MdBD; NcU; PLT. 50049

Waterman, Jotham
Fraternal affection and neighbourly kindness. A
discourse delivered at Plymouth, (North Carolina) Feb.
1818, and also at Ipswich, (Mass.) Feb. 1819, G.
Washington's birthday... Boston, Pr. by Elisha Bellamy, 1819. 18 p. CSmH; DLC; MB; MBFM; MSaE;
MWA; NjR; OClWHi; PHi. 50050

[--] A sermon, delivered in the East, North and
South... Salem, Mass., Pr. for the author, 1819.
MWA. 50051

[--] The wren and eagle in contest; or, A short method
with the Unitarian nobility. By Aquae homo. Boston,
author, 1819. 15 p. CBPac; CtSoP; MB; MBAt; MSaE;
MWA. 50052

Watkins, Lucy
Sophy; or the punishment of idleness... a moral
tale. Philadelphia, M'Carty & Davis, 1819. MWA.
50053

Watson, Elkanah
History of the rise, progress and existing state of
the Berkshire agricultural society in Massachusetts. Albany, E. & E. Hosford, 1819. 80 p. NN; NNNBG;
NcAS; Nj; NjR; WHi. 50054

Watson, Richard
An apology for the Bible... Dayton, O., Pr. by
R.J. Skinner, 1819. 190 p. CSmH; MWA; OClWHi;
ODa. 50055

[Watts, Isaac] 1674-1748
[Divine and moral songs for children. Ed. 5. Andover, Mass., Pr. by Flagg & Gould, for the New England tract society, 1819] 20 p. CtHi. 50056

-- Divine songs, attempted in easy language, for the

use of children...Boston, Pr. by U. Crocker, for
Samuel T. Armstrong, 1819. 36 p. MWA. 50057

-- -- ...To which is added Dr. Watts' Plain and easy
catechism: together with a collection of prayers, &c.
Designed and arranged for Sunday schools. New Haven,
A.H. Maltby & co., 1819. 72 p. CtHi; DLC; MLex;
MWA; MiD-B; NN; NNC; PHi; PP. 50058

-- Dr. Watts' Divine songs, suited to capacities of
children...Pittsburgh, Pa., Pr. by Butler and Lambdin, for the Sabbath Schools of the Western Country...
1819. 32 p. MWA. 50059

-- Songs. Divine and moral. For children...Albany,
G.J. Loomis & Co., 1819. 48 p. MB; MWA. 50060

-- -- New York, Samuel Wood & sons and Samuel S.
Wood & Co., Baltimore, 1819. 45 p. MWA; PCC.
50061

-- A historical catechism, for children and youth.
From Dr. I. Watts' second set of catechisms...2d Albany ed. Albany, Pr. by I. Loomis and Co., for the
Albany Union Sunday School Society for the promotion
of Sunday schools, 1819. MWA. 50062

-- Hymns and spiritual songs, in three books...Care-
fully revised. With directions for musical expression.
Boston, Pr. by U. Crocker, for Samuel T. Armstrong,
1819. 460 p. MB; MWA; VtMiS. 50063

-- -- Stereotyped by B. & J. Collins. Exeter, N.H.,
John I. Williams, 1819. 282 p. MH-AH; MWA. 50064

-- -- Geneva, N.Y., James Bogert, 1819. 279 p.
MWA. 50065

-- -- Philadelphia, Pr. by W. Hill Woodward, for W.
W. Woodward, 1819. 274 p. MWA; PPPrHi. 50066

-- -- Pittsburgh, Pa., Pr. by Butler & Lambdin, for
Patterson & Lambdin, 1819. 274 p. MWA. 50067

-- The improvement of the mind... New York, Pr. [by
James & John Harper] for Evert Duyckinck, 1819.
425 p. KyHop; MWA; MWiW; RP.   50068

-- Logic; or, The right use of reason, in the inquiry
after truth... 6th Amer. ed.   Boston, Pr. by E. P.
Walton, for West, Richardson & Lord, 1819. 288 p.
DLC; GDC; MBNMHi; MH; MS; MWA; MiDSH; NR;
PLT; ScC; ScCC; VtHi.   50069

-- Plain and easy catechisms for children, to which is
added a preservative from the sins and follies of
childhood and youth.   Fredericksburg, Va., Wm. F.
Gray, 1819.   64 p.   NRMA.   50070

-- A preservative from the sins and follies of childhood and youth... Fredericksburg, Va., Wm. F. Gray,
1819. MWA.   50071

-- Psalms, hymns and spiritual songs.   Boston, 1819.
585 p. MWA.   50072

-- A short view of the whole scripture history... 1st
Amer. ed.   Boston, Pr. by Sewell Phelps, for Charles
Ewer, 1819.   292 p.   CBPSR; CSt; CU; ICP; MBNMHi;
MS; MWA; MWiW; Mi; NNUT; NjR; RP.   50073

-- -- ... Represented in a way of question and answer
... From the 15th London ed., ed. 2.   Philadelphia,
1819.   465 p.   PHi; PLP; PRM.   50074

-- -- 3d Amer. ed.   Philadelphia, Rufus Little, John
P. Thomson... 1819.   MWA.   50075

Webb, Jonathan
     Particular directions for a family medicine chest
... Salem, Mass., Pr. by Warwick Palfray, Jr., 1819.
MWA.   50076

Webster, Josiah
     Christ, on his way to enlarge his kingdom...
Exeter, N.H., Pr. by J.J. Williams, 1819. 22 p.
MH-AH; MWA.   50077

Webster, Noah, 1758-1843
   The American spelling book; containing the rudi-
ments of the English language... The revised impression with the latest corrections.   Boston, Pr. by J.
H. A. Frost, 1819. 168 p. MeHi; MeU.   50078

-- -- Boston, West, Richardson & Lord, 1819. MWA.
                                                50079
-- -- Brattleborough, Vt., Pr. by John Holbrook, for
Abijah Burbank, on paper of his own manufacture, by
special contract, 1819. 168 p. NjR.   50080

-- -- Brattleborough, Vt., John Holbrook, 1819. 168 p.
CtHT-W; CtY; DLC; MH; MB; MWA; MiDenEd; NN;
NRU; OClWHi; OMC; VtU.   50081

-- -- Hartford, Pr. by Hudson & Co., 1819. 168 p. Ct;
MAtt; NBi; NNC.   50082

[--] A letter to the secretary of the Treasury, on the
commerce and currency of the United States. By
Aristides [pseud.] New-York, Pr. by C. S. Van Winkle,
1819. 39 p. DLC; ICJ; ICU; NN; RPB.   50083

Webster's calendar, or the Albany almanack for 1820.
By Andrew Beers.   Albany, Websters and Skinners
[1819] [36] p. MBNEH; MWA; NCH; N; NN; NHi;
NBLiHi; NjR; OClWHi; PHi.   50084

Weeks, William Raymond
   The doctrine of the universal decrees and agency of
God... Ed. 2.   Providence, Miller & Hutchens, 1819.
203 p. MHans; MWA.   50085

Weems, Mason Locke
   The life of George Washington... Ed. 22. Philadel-
phia, Pr. by M. Carey & son, 1819. 228 p. CSmH;
DLC; MWA; MdBJ.   50086

Weisse, John A.
   Origin progress and destiny of the English language
and literature.   New York, 1819. Tuttle   50087

Wells, Samuel Adams
    An oration, pronounced July 5, 1819, at the re-
quest of the Republicans of the town of Boston, in commemoration of the anniversary of American independence. Boston, T. Badger, Jr., 1819. 28 p. CSmH;
CSt; CtW; DLC; M; MB; MBAt; MH; MHi; MMeT; MWA;
MiU-C; NjR; RPB.   50088

Wescott, Stephen K.
    Selections of songs and hymns. Amherst [N. H.]
Pr. by Elijah Mansur, 1819. 36 p. MiD-B; Nh-Hi;
RPB.   50089

Wesley, John, 1703-1791
    Interesting extracts, from the journals of the Rev.
John Wesley, A. M., with a synopsis of his life and
death. Boston, Pr. by William S. Spear, 1819. 300 p.
MB; MMeT; MoSC; NHem; NTaHi; RPB; ViFTBE. 50090

Wesleyan Methodist Missionary society, 1819.
    Extract from the society, 1819, to which is added
an Extract from W. Brown's and A. Clarke's History
of Missions among the heathen since the reformation
...Wilmington, Del., Porter, 1819. 60 p. DeWi.
                                                   50091

West-Chester library company, Pa.
    Articles of association...Westchester, Pa., Charles
Miner, 1819. MWA; PWcT.   50092

Westchester Town, N. Y.
    Charter...New York, 1819. 16 p. (Hufeland's
check list of Westchester, 1929, p. 254)   50093

Western Education Society. N. Y.
    Report of the directors of the Western Education
Society of the state of New-York, to the first annual
meeting, which was held at Utica, December 30, 1818.
Utica, N. Y., Pr. by William Williams, for the Soci-
ety, 1819. 44 p. MBC; MH-AH; MWA; N; NAuT;
NGeno; NUtHi; NjR; WHi.   50094

Western Republican. Bath, N. Y., Erastus Shepard,
Oct. 6, 1819, 1st issue. Weekly newspaper. NNS. 50095

Western Review and Miscellaneous Magazine.   Lexington, Ky., William Gibbes Hunt, August, 1819, 1st issue.   Monthly periodical.   50096

Der Westliche Calender.   Für die Westlichen Staaten
neugerichtet.   Auf das Jahr... 1820.   Zum zweytenmal
herausgegeben.   Baltimore, Pr. by Schaeffer u. Maund
[1819] [36] p.   MWA; PHi.   50097

Weymouth, Mass. --Second Congregational Church.
     Report of the committee of inquiry... [1819] MWA.
                                                        50098
Whipple, Edwards
     A sermon, preached at Deerfield, Second parish,
February 10, 1819, at the installation of Rev. Benja-
min Rice... Deerfield, Mass., Pr. by C. J. Newcomb,
1819.   14 p.   CSmH; MA; MBAt; MHi; MWA; NN;
RPB.   50099

Whipple, William Jennison
     A masonic address, delivered before Corinthian
lodge at Concord... Concord, Mass., Pr. by Caleb
Cushing, 1819.   19 p.   ICP; IaCrM; MBAt; MBFM; MH;
RPB.   50100

White, John Blake, 1781-1859
     The triumph of liberty, or, Louisiana preserved.
A national drama... Charleston, S. C., J. Hoff, 1819.
52 p.   PPL-R.   50101

White, John J.
     Arithmetic simplified, being a plain, practical sys-
tem, adapted to the capacity of youth, and designed for
the use of schools, in the United States.   In two parts.
By John J. White.   Ed. 2.   Hartford, Pr. by Geo.
Goodwin and sons, 1819.   332 p.   CtHi; DLC; MDeeP;
MH; MHi; MLow; MWA; MeHi; MiU; MiU-C; NNC;
OMC; RNR.   50102

White, N.
     An easy guide to the art of spelling.   1st ed.   En-
field, Mass., Pr. by John Howe, for the author, 1819.
84 p.   MA; MWA.   50103

White, William, bp.
Of the Gospel, as the power of God unto salvation: a sermon, delivered in Trinity church, New-Haven, on Wednesday, Oct. 27, 1819, at the consecration of the Right Rev. Thomas C. Brownell...New-Haven, Pr. by A. H. Maltby & co., 1819. 36 p. CSmH; Ct; CtHC; CtHT; CtHi; MWA; NBuDD; NNG; NjR; RPB; TJaU.
50104

[Whiting, Henry]
The emigrant, a poem...Detroit, Mich., Pr. by Sheldon & Reed, 1819. 27 p. MWA; MiD-B.   50105

Whitman, Samuel
Christ, the son of God before he was made flesh ...Goshen, Mass., Pr. by Adam H. Hamilton, from the author's press, 1819. MWA.   50106

Whitney, Andrew G.
A Masonic address, delivered at Detroit, Dec. 28, A. L. 5818, before Zion Lodge No. 62...Detroit, Mich., Pr. by Sheldon & Reed, 1819. 26 p. DSC; IaCrM; MBFM; N.   50107

Whitney, Peter
A sermon on the Lord's day succeeding the interment of Madam Abigail Adams, consort of the Hon. John Adams, late President of the United States...Boston, Pr. by Hews & Goss, 1819. 24 p. ICMe; MB; MBAt; MH; MHi; MPlyP; MQ; NN; PHi; RPB; WHi.
50108
The whole duty of woman. A new edition, with considerable improvements, to which is added, Edwin and Angelina, a tale. Rochester, N. Y., E. Peck & Co., 1819. 118 p. MWA; NRU; NRHi.   50109

Wiestling, John S.
Der vollstandige Bienen-Wärter...Harrisburg, Pa., Pr. by John S. Wiestling, 1819. MWA.   50110

Wiggins, R.
North American spelling book. New York, S. Wood & Sons [1819] MWA.   50111

-- -- New York, S. Wood & sons, 1819. MWA. 50112

[Wilcocks, Thomas]
A choice drop of honey from the rock Christ...
Exeter, N.H., Josiah Richardson, 1819. MWA. 50113

Wilcox, Asa
Strictures on a pamphlet containing three letters on
infant baptism... New London, Conn., Pr. by Clapp &
Francis, 1819. CtNl; MDeeP; MWA. 50114

Willard, Emma (Hart) 1787-1870
An address to the public; (particularly) to the members of the Legislature of New-York, proposing a plan
for improving female education. Albany, Pr. by I.W.
Clark, 1819. 35 p. MB; MBAt; N. 50115

-- -- Ed. 2. Middlebury, Vt., Pr. by J.W. Copeland,
1819. 60 p. CSmH; CU; Ct; DLC; IU; MBAt; MH; M;
MWA; MdBP; NN; NNC; NCH; NE; NcGw; NjR; PU; N;
RPB; RPAC; TxU; VtHi; VtMiM; VtMiS; VtU. 50116

Willetts, Jacob, 1785-1860
A compendious system of geography... Poughkeepsie, [N.Y.] P. Potter and S. Potter & Co., 1819.
466 p. CSmH; MWA; InVi; NcGvE. 50117

-- An easy grammar of geography. Poughkeepsie,
N.Y., P. Potter, 1819. 215 p. MWA; NcAS. 50118

-- Scholar's arithmetic. Poughkeepsie, N.Y., P. Potter for S. Potter, 1819. MWA. 50119

William Penn, and other poetic effusions. Philadelphia,
Pr. by George Goodman, 1819. RPB. 50120

Williams, Amos A.
Correspondence (on the branch bank at Baltimore.
Baltimore, 1819.) 18 p. MBAt; MdHi. 50121

Williams, John
Dr. John Williams's last legacy... Boston, Pr. by
Nathaniel Coverly, 1819. 20 p. MWA. 50122

Williams, Nathaniel West, 1784-1853
To the Baltimore bar (on his removal from the office of counsel to the Baltimore branch of the Bank of
the U.S.   Baltimore, 1819)   MBAt; MdHi.   50123

Williams, R. P. & C.
Catalogue of medical, botanical, and chemical
books, for sale by R. P. & C. Williams, Conrhill-
square, Boston, July, 1819.   [1819]   4 p. MBM; MWA.
                                                  50124

Williams, Roger
Letter to Gov. Bradstreet, 1682.   Boston, 1819.
MSaE.   50125

Williams, William, 1787-1850
New and complete preceptor for the fiff [sic] together with a choice collection of songs, duets,
marches, dances, etc.   Utica, N. Y., Williams, 1819.
47 p.   NUt.   50126

Williams College
Catalogue of the faculty and students.   Albany,
Websters & Skinners [1819]   MWiW.   50127

Willis, William
An address, delivered before the New-Bedford Aux-
iliary Society for the Suppression of Intemperance...
New Bedford, Mass., Pr. by Benjamin Lindsey, 1819.
DLC; MBAt; MBC; MWA; MNBedf; RPB.   50128

Williston, Seth
Sermon to point out ways for females to lend their
aid in advancing the Kingdom of Christ.   Catskill, N. Y.,
1819.   14 p.   RPB.   50129

[Wilson, James Patriot]
Moral agency; or, natural ability consistent with
moral inability: answer to Janeway.   By a Christian.
Philadelphia, Thomas and William Bradford, 1819. 36 p.
MBC; MWA.   50130

Wilson, James
A sermon, delivered at Mendon, June 12, 1818, at

the interment of Mrs. Patience George, who died June 10, 1818...Worcester, Mass., Pr. by William Manning, Apr. 1819. 14 p. RHi; RPB. 50131

Wilson, Samuel
A sketch of the character, of the late Alexander Baron, M.D. Delivered before the Medical Society, of Charleston, South-Carolina...Charleston, S.C., Pr. by W.P. Young, 1819. 16 p. DLC; MWA; NNNAM; RPB; ScU. 50132

-- A scripture manual: or, a plain representation of the ordinance of baptism designed for the use of all who would answer a good conscience toward God; and give a reason of their faith and practice with meekness and fear...Philadelphia, Anderson and Meehan, 1819. 19 p. MH-AH; OMC. 50133

Wilson, Thomas, 1768-1828?
The biography of the principal American military and naval heroes; comprehending details of their a-chievements during the revolutionary and late wars... New York, J. Low, 1819. 2 v. DLC; FTU; MWA; NN; THi; ViU. 50134

Wilson, Thomas, bp.
Sacra Privata. The private meditations and prayers of the Right Rev. Thomas Wilson, D.D. Bishop of Soder and Man, accommodated to general use. And-over, Mass., Flagg and Gould, 1819. 130 p. MWA. 50135
-- -- New York, T. & J. Swords, 1819. 110 p. MDeeP; NBuG; Nh; PMA. 50136

-- -- A new ed. Philadelphia, S. Potter & Co., 1819. 170 p. GHi; KWiU; MB. 50137

Winchell, James Manning
Jubilee sermons, two discourses, exhibiting an his-torical sketch of the First Baptist Church in Boston. Boston, Pr. by True & Weston, 1819. 47 p. CBPSR; CSt; ICN; MB; MBB; MBD; MBAt; MH-AH; MWA; MeB; PHi; RPB; WHi. 50138

-- A selection of more than three hundred hymns, from the most approved authors...among which are all the hymns of Dr. Watts...Boston, James Loring and Lincoln & Edmands, 1819. 372 hymns. MB; MH-AH; MWA; RPB.   50139

Winchester, Elhanan
    The universal restoration...Bellows Falls, Vt., Pr. by Bill Blake & Co., 1819. 239 p. CSmH; CLSU; LNB; MB; MH; MMeT; MWA; MiD-B; NCaS; NNUT; NhNeP; VtHi; TxU.   50140

Windham county agricultural society, Connecticut.
    Constitution...Worcester, Mass., Pr. by Wm. Manning, 1819. MWA.   50141

Windsor, Vt. Bank.
    By-laws and rules of the Bank of Windsor. Pr. by W. Spooner [1819?] 13 p. McCorison List.   50142

Winslow, Miron, 1789-1864
    A sermon delivered at the Old South church, Boston, June 7, 1819...Andover, Mass., Pr. by Flagg & Gould, 1819. 23 p. MA; MH-AH; MNe; MWA; MWiW; NjR.   50143

-- Sketch of missions; or, History of the principal attempts to propagate Christianity among the heathen. Andover, Mass., Flagg & Gould, 1819. 432 p. GDC; IN; MSaE; MWA; MWiW; NCH; NcAS.   50144

Winstanley, Calvin
    A vindication of certain passages in the common English version of the New Testament...Cambridge, Hilliard and Metcalf, University press, 1819. MWA.
                                                   50145
Witherell, George
    A sermon, delivered at the installation of the Mountain lodge, of Free and accepted masons, in the town of Colrain...Greenfield, Mass., Pr. by Denio & Phelps, [1819] 12 p. MWA.   50146

Wood, Jacob
Remarks on a pamphlet, entitled The eternity of
the future punishment...Worcester, Mass., Pr. by
Manning & Trumbull, 1819. 40 p. MWA; MeP. 50147

Wood, Jethro
Specification of letters patent for an improvement
in a plow. New York, 1819. MSaE. 50148

Woodbury, Fanny
Writings of Miss Fanny Woodbury...Ed. 4. Boston,
Pr. by U. Crocker, for Samuel T. Armstrong; John
Sayre, New York...1819. 250 p. CL; MA; MBAt;
MH; MSaE; MWA; NBuG; NjR; ViRut. 50149

Woodhouselee, Alexander Fraser Tytler, lord.
Elements of general history. From the 7th British ed. New York, E. Duyckinck [etc.] 1819. 448 p.
CSt; CtHT-W; MB; MSaE; MWA; MoRH; MoSpD; N; NjP.
50150

Woodruff, Hezekiah North
A sermon delivered at the funeral of Daniel Morse
...June 4, 1819...Herkimer, N.Y., Pr. by Edward P.
Seymour, 1819. MWA. 50151

Woods, Leonard
The usefulness of the sacred office...A sermon de-
livered March 9, 1819, at the funeral of the Rev. Sam-
uel Spring...Newburyport, Mass., Pr. by Flagg and
Gould, for Charles Whipple, 1819. 39 p. ICT; MBNEH;
MNe; MSaE; MWA; Nh; Nh-Hi; NjR. 50152

Wood's almanac for the year 1820. Calculated by
Joshua Sharp. [Baltimore] Samuel S. Wood & Co.,
1819. MWA; MdHi. 50153

-- By Joshua Sharp. New York, Samuel Wood & Sons
[1819] MWA; N. 50154

Woodward, Augustus Elias Brevoort
To the electors of the Territory of Michigan.
Fellow citizens...[Detroit, Mich., 1819] Broadside.
MiD-B. 50155

Woodward, Thomas
    The Columbian Plutarch...Philadelphia, Pr. by
Clark & Raser, for the author, 1819. MBAt; MWA;
ViU.   50156

[Woodworth, John]
    An address to youth...Montpelier, Vt., 1819. 10 p.
MWA.   50157

[--] The battle of Plattsburgh, a poem...Montpelier,
Vt., Pr. by E. P. Walton, 1819. 46 p. CSmH; CtY;
DLC; ICN; MB; MWA; NBuG; OClWHi; RPB; VtHi;
VtMiS.   50158

Woodworth, Joseph
    The dyer's assistant. 1st ed. Copy right se-
cured. Middlebury, Vt., Pr. by J. W. Copeland, 1819.
14 p. MWA.   50159

Woodworth, Samuel
    The champions of freedom, or the mysterious
thief. A romance of the nineteenth century, founded on
the events of the war between the United States and
Great Britain, which terminated in March, 1815...New
York, Charles N. Baldwin, 1819. 2 v. MBrigStJ; WU.
                                              50160

Worcester, Joseph Emerson, 1784-1865
    Elements of geography, ancient and modern. With
an atlas. By J. E. Worcester. Boston, T. Swan,
1819. 322 p. CtHT-W; DLC; F; IHi; MBAt; MDedHi;
MH; MHad; MFiHi; MWA; MWHi; MWiW; MiDSH; NNC;
OHi; PMA; TxU-T; WBeloC.   50161

[Worcester, Noah] 1758-1837
    The friend of peace: by Philo Pacificus [pseud.]...
v. 1-4; [1815-1827] Boston, J. T. Buckingham [1819?]
4 v. CBPac; CtHC; DLC; MA; MB; MBr; MWA;
NBLiHi; NN; OClWHi; RNR.   50162

Worcester, Samuel
    Christian psalmody, in four parts: comprising Dr.
Watt's psalms abridged, Dr. Watt's hymns abridged;
select hymns from other authors and select harmony;

together with directions for musical expression. Ed. 3.
Boston, Pr. by U. Crocker, for Samuel T. Armstrong,
1819. 522 p. MSaE; MWA.   50163

-- The psalms, hymns and spiritual songs, of the Rev.
Isaac Watts. To which are added, selected hymns
from other authors; and directions for musical expressions. By Samuel Worcester...Boston, Samuel T.
Armstrong, [1819?] 652 p. CBB.   50164

[--] Mission to Sandwich Islands. [Boston, U. Crocker,
1819] MWA.   50165

-- Select hymns: the third part of Christian psalmody.
Ed. 3. Boston, Pr. by U. Crocker, for Samuel T.
Armstrong, 1819. 160 p. MB; MBC; MBev-F; MWA;
MWinchrHi; MeB; MeBat; OMC; RBr; VtMiS.   50166

[Worcester, Thomas] 1795-1878
    A discourse delivered before the New Jerusalem
church, in Boston, on Christmas day, December 25,
1818. Boston, Cummings and Hilliard, 1819. 23 p.
CSmH; DLC; ICMe; MBAt; MWA; PBa.   50167

-- The true God but one person...Boston, Pr. by Parmenter and Balch, 1819. 12 p. M; MH-AH; MWA.
                                                50168
Worcester Agricultural Society
    Worcester County Cattle show and exhibition of
manufactures. The Trustees of the Agricultural Society of the County of Worcester, desirous that the County should derive the earliest practicable advantages...
Announce to the publick their determination to have a
Cattle Show and Exhibition of Manufactures, at Worcester, on Thursday the seventh day of October next...
and they propose the following premiums to be awarded
for excellence on that occasion...Worcester, Mar. 24,
1819. Broadside. MH.   50169

Worcester north district medical association, Mass.
    Laws, rules, and regulations...Worcester, Mass.,
Pr. by William Manning, 1819. 15 p. CSt; MWA;
MWHi.   50170

The works of the British poets. Philadelphia, Mitchell,
Ames, and White, 1819-22. 50 v. (Vols. 26-33, 43-
50 have imprint: Boston, C. Ewer and T. Bedlington,
1822; v. 37 has imprint: Philadelphia, S. F. Bradford,
1822.) MWA; MWiW.   50171

Worlds displayed: for the benefit of young people, by a
familiar history of some of their inhabitants. Boston,
Lincoln & Edmands, Bible Warehouse, 1819. 52 p.
MHi.   50172

-- Philadelphia, Pr. by Lydia R. Bailey, for the
Philadelphia female tract society, 1819. 52 p. IU.
                                                      50173

[Worth, Gorham A.] d. 1856
    American bards: a modern poem, in three parts...
[Cincinnati, O.,] 1819. CSmH; DLC; N; O; OCHP;
RPB.   50174

Wright, Frances
    Altorf, a tragedy... Philadelphia, Carey, 1819.
83 p. MB.   50175

Wright, John S.
    Letters from the west, or, A caution to emigrants,
being facts and observations respecting the states of
Ohio, Indiana, Illinois... Salem, N. Y., 1819. 72 p. N.
                                                      50176

Wright, Nathaniel Hill
    Boston: or a touch at the times... Boston, Pr. by
Hews & Goss, 1819. DLC; MBAt; MWA; RPB. 50177

Wylie, Andrew
    An address, to the graduates in Washington college
... Sept. 30th, 1819... Washington, Pa., Pr. by Samuel
Workman, 1819. MWA.   50178

[Wynne, John Huddlestone]
    Choice emblems... Boston, Pr. by Lincoln & Ed-
mands, 1819. 24 p. MWA.   50179

[--] -- Boston, Pr. by Lincoln & Edmands, 1819. 24 p.
(Varied covers) MWA.   50180

X-Y-Z

Xenophon
Cyropaedia; or, the institution of Cyrus. Trans-
lated from the Greek by Maurice Ashley. Philadelphia,
Hopkins, 1819. MCon. 50181

Yale University
Catalogue of the faculty and students of Yale College, November, 1819. New Haven, S. Converse,
1819. 14 p. MeB. 50182

The Yankee or farmer's almanac containing a variety
of other matters. (By Thomas Spofford) Boston, Pr.
by J. H. A. Frost, for West, Richardson & Lord, proprietors of the copy right, 1819. 90 p. MTemNHi.
50183

Young, David
The perusal... Ed. 2. Elizabethtown, N. J., Pr.
by Peter Chatterton, 1819. MWA; RPB. 50184

Young, Edward
Night thoughts... New York, Stereotyped by C.
Starr, for R. & W. A. Bartow, 1819. 301 p. CtHT;
MWA; NN; ScAn; ViU. 50185

Young, Samuel B.
An oration, pronounced at Bennington, August 16,
1819: in commemoration of the Battle of Bennington,
fought August 16, 1777... Bennington, Vt., Pr. by
Darius Clark, 1819. 13 p. NHi. 50186

The young Christian's guide... Utica, N. Y., William
Williams, 1819. 111 p. DLC; MH; MWA; N; NBuG;
NUt; NUtHi; NbCrD; WHi. 50187

The young florists' companion... Hartford, Pr. by
Roberts & Burr, for S. G. Goodrich, 1819. 31 p.
CSmH. 50188

The young robber; or, Dishonesty punished, to which is
added, Mr. Goodman and his children, The way to be
good and happy, and the Ditch. New York, J. C. Totten, 1819. 24 leaves. NNC; PHi; PP. 50189

Youth's arithmetic.   Hartford, Lincoln & Stone, for S.
G. Goodrich, 1819. MWA.   50190

Zimmermann, Johann Georg
    Solitude... New York, Pr. by G. Long, for E.
Duyckinck, 1819.   392 p.   CSt; KyLoP; MB; MH-AH;
MWA.   50191

Zollickoffer, William
    A materia medica of the United States... Baltimore,
Pr. by Richard J. Matchett, 1819.   120 p.   DNLM;
MWA; MdBM; MdHi; NNNAM; NNC-P; OSW; PPAmP;
PPC; RPB.   50192